China's Media, Media's China

China's Media, Media's China

EDITED BY
Chin-Chuan Lee

Westview Press
BOULDER • SAN FRANCISCO • OXFORD

Copyright © 1994 by Westview Press, Inc.

Published in 1994 in the United States of America by Westview Press, Inc., 5500 Central Avenue, Boulder, Colorado 80301-2877, and in the United Kingdom by Westview Press, 36 Lonsdale Road, Summertown, Oxford, OX2 7EW

Library of Congress Cataloging-in-Publication Data
China's media, media's China / editor Chin-Chuan Lee.
    p.   cm.
  Includes bibliographical references and index.
  ISBN 0-8133-8800-7
  1. Mass media—Political aspects—China.   2. Mass media policy—
China.   3. Foreign correspondents—China.   4. Foreign
correspondents—United States.   I. Li, Chin-ch'üan, 1946–
P95.85.C6C45   1994
302.23'0951—dc20
                                                                                    94-949
                                                                                    CIP

Printed and bound in the United States of America

The paper used in this publication meets the requirements
of the American National Standard for Permanence of Paper
for Printed Library Materials Z39.48-1984.

10   9   8   7   6   5   4   3   2   1

CONTENTS

ACKNOWLEDGMENTS

A profound debt of gratitude is owed, first and foremost, to Mr. Yu Chi-chung for his continuing support to the China Times Center for Media and Social Studies at the University of Minnesota, which made this publication possible. Special thanks go to the Minnesota Journalism Center and the New Asia Cultural Foundation in Hong Kong for partial funding; to Dan Wackman, director of the School of Journalism and Mass Communication at the University of Minnesota, for his encouragement and support; and to the Institute of Ethnology at Academia Sinica for providing me with an intellectually stimulating and congenial environment to work on the project.

Contributors have graced the editor's constant requests for developing and revising their ideas; to them I am grateful. Also deserving my sincere appreciation are Laurie Dennis and, particularly, Karl Metzner for their excellent assistance in copyediting and coordinating manuscripts through many rounds of laborious revision to their present shape; Joseph Dennis, Karl Metzner, Laurie Dennis, and Yang Mei-rong for their valuable contribution in the translation of several chapters from Chinese into English; Alison Auch for pushing this project through at Westview Press; and the anonymous reviewer whose thorough and constructive comments have enhanced the overall quality of this volume.

I am indebted to the Association for Education in Journalism and Mass Communication and Kluwer Academic Publishers for their permission to reprint herein, with revision, the following copyrighted chapters: Chin-Chuan Lee, "Sparking a Fire: The Press and the Ferment of Democratic Change in Taiwan," *Journalism Monographs*, 138 (Apr. 1993); and Joseph Man Chan, Chin-Chuan Lee, and Paul Siu-nam Lee, "Fighting Against the Odds: Hong Kong Journalists in Transition," *Gazette*, 50 (1992): 1–20.

Finally, this volume is dedicated to Chia-Chih Lee, Chu-An Lee, and Chu-Min Lee for their patience and love.

Chin-Chuan Lee

NOTE ON ROMANIZATION

Throughout this volume, we use the pinyin system to romanize the names of people and places associated with the People's Republic of China. The Wade-Giles system is adopted for those tied to Taiwan, but for the sake of simplicity we drop the apostrophe. People and places associated with Hong Kong are romanized according to their Cantonese pronunciation. Chinese surnames precede given names, but we have followed the Western style for Chinese with Western given names and for other Chinese who are professionally known by names that follow the Western style.

PART ONE

OVERVIEW

1

AMBIGUITIES AND CONTRADICTIONS: ISSUES IN CHINA'S CHANGING POLITICAL COMMUNICATION

Chin-Chuan Lee

In a seminal article Tu Weiming articulates the heuristically useful albeit still somewhat ambiguous concept of a Cultural China made up of three distinct but interrelated symbolic universes.[1] The first universe consists of the People's Republic of China (PRC), Taiwan, Hong Kong, and Singapore, where ethnic Chinese constitute the majority. The second universe refers to the broad Chinese Diaspora scattered as an ethnic minority throughout North America and Southeast Asia. The third symbolic universe—intellectually united rather than ethnically demarcated by a community of scholars, journalists, writers, entrepreneurs, industrialists, and traders—has come to the forefront to shape discourse about Cultural China.[2]

This volume and its generously received predecessor, *Voices of China: The Interplay of Politics and Journalism*, represent a fusion of American and Chinese perspectives, as well as a dialogue between leading scholars and journalists in what Tu calls the third universe of Cultural China.[3] This volume expands on previous discourses about China's media and China as portrayed by the media. Hindsight has provided us with a finer vantage point to reflect on the media changes that have resurged after the Tiananmen crackdown in 1989. Commentators have paid inadequate attention to the media impact of global developments on China, just as their role in helping undo the Soviet empire and autocratic regimes in Eastern Europe as well as in easing democratic transitions elsewhere (including Taiwan) has largely been overlooked. Alongside a new world order evolves a new center-periphery relationship in the larger ecology of Cultural China, a relationship that may partially frustrate the last Communist giant's perpetual resistance to "peaceful evolution." This volume, by focusing once again on the interplay of journalism and political economy in China, attempts to offer a signpost to the process of change, with its analyses grounded in the past and visions geared toward the future.

Different cross-currents impinging on China's media politics have caused ambiguities and contained contradictions. Instead of attempting a comprehensive survey of the chapters herein, this introduction opts to string together several broad themes and sort out different levels of the discourses toward clarifying the ambiguities and contradictions which surround Chinese political communication.[4] These organizing themes consist of control, professionalism, political struggle, reform, opposition, and development models. Prominent are the following questions: has the PRC's economic reform unleashed a momentum sufficiently robust to loosen political and media controls? How has media control been averted, compromised, or resisted? What are the notable obstacles that Chinese journalists struggle to overcome? With the crumbling of Communist regimes elsewhere, will Taiwan, a peripheral influence, offer itself as a viable analytical model for understanding the PRC and its media? Will the PRC withstand the enduring pressure of advanced communication technologies? What conceptual framework will arise to inform post–Cold War media accounts of China?

MEDIA CONTROL: A COMPARATIVE VIEW

No media systems are totally free from control, but the causes and consequences of control vary significantly. An early, cogent statement of press control was expounded in the influential *Four Theories of the Press* by Fred Siebert, Theodore Peterson, and Wilbur Schramm. They attacked both authoritarian and Communist systems, while urging the libertarian press to adopt a "social responsibility" concept as espoused by the Hutchins Commission.[5] Since then, one of the major foci in radical media studies has been to debunk the vaunted independence, autonomy, and objectivity of the liberal press. Many critics have taken aim at the deficiencies—if not the total failure—of the liberal media and, in fact, liberal democracy itself. They have operated from the perspectives of either pragmatism or Marxist humanism under the influence of deconstructionists and anti-positivists.[6] They have served to sharply expose the ideological structure of American journalism, the imperatives of newswork, and the media's organizational affinity to officialism and corporate interests.[7]

In this process media professionalism—defined as a commitment to claims of objectivity, balance, and ideological neutrality—has also been severely assaulted. Epistemologically questioning media professionalism as the last bastion of raw empiricism, critics maintain that news is socially constructed and bears little correspondence to the external reality. The political import of this critique is that media professionalism represents what Gaye Tuchman calls a "strategic ritual" that shields journalists from public scrutiny and upholds legitimate institutions.[8] Objective reporting is said to "reproduce a vision of social reality which refuses to examine the basic structures of power and privilege" and "represent collusion with institutions whose legitimacy was in dispute."[9]

These critiques are unfailingly compelling and idealistic to the extent that, as James Carey notes, American journalism is deeply embedded in American culture, with its faults and triumphs characteristic of the culture as a whole.[10] Without a comparative framework, however, these criticisms tend to obfuscate the crucial boundaries between the liberal media and their authoritarian and totalitarian counterparts.[11] While attacked at home, American media and their professionalism are paradoxically admired and distrusted by Chinese and Third World journalists constantly under siege of state power.[12]

Institutionalized Censorship

The manufacture of consent is as central to the liberal media's ideological function as coercion is to the authoritarian and totalitarian media's propaganda. There is a qualitative difference, however, between these systems. Totalitarian regimes, according to Carl Friedrich, are characterized by a totalist ideology, a single party committed to this ideology, a fully developed secret police, and the monopoly of mass communications, operational weapons, and all (including economic) organizations.[13] The Leninist media, acting as loudspeakers of the revolutionary vanguard, allege to embody the mass will by upholding party creeds. But totalitarian regimes tend not to impose overt coercion on the media unless compliance cannot be otherwise secured.

Media censorship is institutionalized only when political leadership sees itself "as not totally penetrating and controlling its population and the journalism profession."[14] This was characteristic of media control in most bureaucratic–authoritarian regimes—ranging from Brazil and Spain to Taiwan and South Korea—before the onset of recent democratization. Lu Keng's apt comparison of the two rival Chinese regimes (Chapter 9) reveals that the authoritarian Nationalists have exercised more explicit media censorship than the totalitarian Communists. Lu argues that Chiang Kai-shek did not understand the press and would tolerate moderate criticism when his party was in firm control, whereas Mao Zedong used his absolute power to orchestrate a total control environment in which censorship was embedded and invisible.

But a crucial difference in control mechanisms can also be observed within the history of the PRC itself. Su Shaozhi shows in a painstaking analysis (Chapter 5) how the Chinese Communist Party (CCP) had imposed ideological control—through the interwoven webs of relentless mass campaigns, study groups, criticisms, and self-criticisms—so pervasive, totalistic, and penetrative as to render a specialized censorship agency redundant. It should be remembered that for 30 years (1949–1979) a nation of 1 billion people was governed without explicit civil, criminal, commerce, and press laws. Economic reform, as pragmatic as it seems, has also salvaged the CCP from the brink of losing its legitimacy after the Cultural Revolution, and has also weakened its media control. It is the reform of the 1980s, as Lowell Dittmer (Chapter 6) notes, that forced the regime to make attempts to secularize and rationalize the public sector.

China under Deng Xiaoping has consequently made tumultuous attempts to move from dependence on Mao's charismatic and absolute power (in Max Weber's term) to some sort of a legal-rational system. The primary goal is not to install a system of rule *of* law which subjects state power to judicial checks and balances, but instead to establish rule *by* law (*fazhi*) so that the legitimacy of the Party can be strengthened through the promulgation of more concrete guidelines. It is in this context that Judy Polumbaum (Chapter 7) has documented a series of administrative innovations developed to accommodate the vast sociopolitical change and thus bring the media increasingly under control by more explicit rules and bureaucratic procedures.

Professionalism

The relevance of media professionalism outside Western countries—as previously noted—is rather ambiguous, if not contradictory. In the case of China, its modern press, like the press in other Third World nations, was inaugurated at the end of the nineteenth century during the awakening of national consciousness as a result of coming into contact with the previously unknown European powers.[15] The primary function of the press was to advocate enlightenment, reform, and national independence. Some abstract goals of media professionalism have inspired Chinese journalists in their struggle against state censorship, while other elements (such as the professionally imposed code of ethics and responsibility) were weakened when they reached Chinese shores. These vaguely understood imported values have coexisted uneasily with a Confucian ethos that bestowed the moral high ground on intellectual advocacy on Taiwan, and has run counter to a Leninist ideology that assigns a vanguard role to the media in mainland China. How are we to evaluate critiques of media professionalism in the soil of Chinese culture where the very norm seems so underdeveloped?

Li Liangrong (Chapter 12) traces the history of battles fought over "objective reporting" in China that has oscillated with persistent and erratic gusts of the political winds. Marxist humanism and Western media models offer alternative interpretations to Communist ideological orthodoxy. Although Chinese journalists' understanding of Western objective reporting tends to be crude and distorted, and their own theoretical arguments unsophisticated, their yearning for professional autonomy seems nonetheless irrepressible.[16] They took Zhao Ziyang's calls for increased surveillance of government work through public opinion (*yulun jiandu*) to heart. But nothing of consequence came to fruition. Press freedom is not a gift of any leader's benevolence; a vibrant market, while producing new dilemmas, may best countervail arbitrary political infringement on press autonomy.

At the height of political liberalization in the late 1980s, the reformist Hu Jiwei, former director of the *People's Daily*, led the drive to formulate a press law that promised to enhance the transparency (*toumingdu*) of government policy process and legally ensure a certain degree of press autonomy. The effort was aborted by the Tiananmen crackdown. At present there seems to be a consensus that even a good law itself will not ensure its faithful implementation and may, in fact, provoke foes of reform to take advantage of a vigorous press to expose the excesses, corruption, and other negative side-effects of reform. Thus, many feel that the reformists should continue to promote the media's informational role in service of a "socialist market economy" as a way to weaken their traditional propaganda function. Once economic reform is irreversibly entrenched, however, greater demands for press autonomy will resume.[17]

The Tiananmen tragedy is a mighty reminder of possible vulnerabilities to press freedom in Hong Kong,[18] a colonial city whose economic power equals 19% of China's gross national product. It is a vibrant market that has bred "professional" media in coexistence with the traditional partisan media aligned along the CCP–KMT division. The survey conducted by Joseph Chan, Chin-Chuan Lee, and Paul Lee (Chapter 13) shows that journalists across the partisan spectrum have endorsed (if not fully practiced) the concept of media professionalism. Furthermore, all (including pro-Communist) journalists are *uniformly* apprehensive about the loss of press freedom after the colony's reversion to China in 1997.[19] It appears, however, that so long as the market remains vibrant, Hong Kong's liberal media order will survive China's political onslaughts. Equally important, the growth of media flow from Hong Kong is setting a formidable trend for popular culture and leisure in South China in spite of official attempts to clamp down. An indispensable financial beachhead for China, Hong Kong is also a fountain of ideas and information about China that gets fed back to the mainland.

The mainstream media in martial-law Taiwan, despite their close ties to the KMT, acted as essential fora for promoting abstract democratic values. While denigrating political opposition, these media also endorsed liberal intellectuals who derived their privilege to pontificate democratic values from a curious mixture of Confucian ethics (to establish a moral posture) and the ideology of Western professionalism (to voice their opposition to state media stricture). Similarly, oppositional politicians and media took on the KMT and pro-KMT media by appealing to these very values. Oppressed journalists thus treasured media professionalism as a symbolic shield against state control, even though it may have fallen short of the democratic ideals envisioned by Western critics. Media professionalism, however, cannot exist in social vacuum. As the market logic takes root in Taiwan, the imported norm of media professionalism has been selectively internalized as part of journalistic values. Now largely free of state intervention, the press is riddled by market concentration and an identity crisis over whether the island nation should seek *de jure* independence from or ultimate unification with China (see Chapter 10).

POLITICAL STRUGGLE AND MEDIA TECHNOLOGY

In a remarkably insightful analysis, Lowell Dittmer (Chapter 6) argues that information is hierarchically stratified in China: what purports to be *public* media available to the masses simply echoes official pronouncements, enforces mass conformity, and contains the *least* useful information, whereas the tiny power elite holds privileged access to the most useful internal information. Confucianism and Marxism-Leninism bestow the party-state a status as the sole repository of public interests which should maintain an appearance of unity and conformity. Even if political struggles or feuds over private interests are openly fought in the media, they are invariably cast in the moral claims of serving "public" ends. Deprived of information by formal media, the masses acquire "authentic" information through leaks, rumors, and mass campaigns, many of which have been orchestrated or manipulated by the elites. Because information means power in such a strictly controlled system, the authorities strictly control access to it. State secrets must be defined so all-encompassingly as to allow variable and arbitrary interpretations. Many dissidents, including Wei Jingsheng, have been punished ostensibly on account of disclosing state secrets.

The mass media in China, in sum, serve dual functions as an instrument of ideological control over the masses and a site of struggle among power elites. While Su Shaozhi addresses elite-mass control, Merle Goldman and Marlowe Hood account for intraelite struggle. Policy shifts in Communist China presuppose gaining ideological legitimacy. Because media control is essential to establish such legitimacy, Chinese leaders regularly manipulate the media to bolster their own positions, spearhead policy shifts, and sway the course of top-level factional warfare.

Goldman (Chapter 2) vividly describes how Hu Yaobang and his allies aptly blunted the ideological opposition of remnant Maoists in the early 1980s by launching a campaign to promote "practice as the sole criterion for testing truth." Interestingly, reformists had planted articles in minor in-house publications such as *Theoretical Trends* and *New Youth* to fine-tune a new ideological line and garner internal consensus before expounding them in chief Party organs as new theoretical orthodoxy. Toward the middle and end of the decade, semi-official journals such as the *World Economic Herald* and *New Observer* enthusiastically endorsed Zhao Ziyang's reforms. It appears that Zhao's allies might also have exploited them to manage the news and to pressure his critics. Unfortunately, unlike the ineffective Maoists Hu had faced, Zhao's foe this time was none other than the paramount leader, Deng Xiaoping, so the tragic consequences of the Tiananmen protest were, in retrospect, almost foretold.[20]

As Chinese leaders lash out at each other through analogy and historical allegories, factional warfare is openly unveiled in the media. During the 1980s, moreover, such journalists as Hu Jiwei, Liu Binyan, and Wang Ruoshui of the *People's Daily* became prominent victims of the seesaw warfare between conservative ideologues (Hu Qiaomu and Deng Liqun) and reformist leaders (Hu Yaobang and Zhao Ziyang) with both sides enlisting the press for political gain. According to Marlowe Hood's telling account, these leaders went beyond manipulating purely domestic media by exploiting international news and translated foreign reports on China to solidify their domestic policy positions and vilify their rivals (Chapter 3).

Another issue addresses the effects of the reform-driven internationalization of China; more precisely, how the increasing interdependence between domestic political needs and external media influences the course of Chinese politics. The outrage in the United States over the Tiananmen tragedy in 1989 was largely caused by live television coverage that brought images of peaceful Chinese students, brutal tanks, and bloodshed into American living rooms. Likewise, the student protest movement itself was partly fueled by the intense media interest and sympathy showered upon it. This point was highlighted when the Chinese authorities subsequently charged the foreign media with instigating the unrest, vowing never to let masses of foreign journalists congregate in China's capital again, as they did during Gorbachev's visit in 1989.

One of the most prominent targets of attack by China has been the Voice of America (VOA), whose organization, policies, and impact on China is described by David Hess (Chapter 16). As an informational and propaganda arm of the United States government forbidden to beam at domestic audiences, the VOA—and to a lesser extent the BBC—are accepted by many Chinese as credible windows on the outside world. Likewise, information that was originally leaked out to the foreign media via informal channels finds a ready market in China. Aside from VOA, China also vented its fury at the Hong Kong and Taiwan media and severely restricted their travel to the mainland in 1989. This ban was, however, dissolved by China's need to woo overseas Chinese capital, a need heightened by economic sanctions imposed by major industrial nations after the Tiananmen crackdown.

The foreign media have thus played an ambivalent role in China. They undoubtedly embody certain culturally incompatible values as well as Western propaganda interests. But the failure of China's media has forced many Chinese to depend on the foreign media for learning something (albeit with a particular angle) about China and other countries. Moreover, the "information revolution," including the use of facsimile and satellite technology, has quickened since 1989 and may sabotage the Party's monopoly on news and propaganda by importing banned images and ideas. It is even questionable if local governments—who make money by running cable television systems that depend on satellite broadcasts—would enforce the central government's crackdown orders.[21]

OPPOSITION

It is said that where there is control, there is always oppositional resistance. The popular saying in China that policy (*zhengce*) issued by the political center will be met with counter-measures (*duice*) in the local workplace suggests the possibility of deviations, compromise, subversion, and opposition. But knowledge of the extent, methods, and results of such activities can only be ascertained through empirical inquiries. In a fascinating account, Edward Friedman (Chapter 8) paints with numerous examples a daring picture of popular resistance in China. He argues that the dictators' attempts at message control have been oppositionally decoded by the populace in such a way as to discredit oppressors, to tell good guys from bad guys, to reinterpret official propaganda, and even to create their own oppositional symbols. Questioning the Gramscian concept of hegemony, Friedman further suggests that oppositional decoding offers a democratic alternative to dictatorship in China, while also addressing the nativistic and undemocratic tendencies reflected in this phenomenon.[22]

Friedman's lively account presents a stark contrast to the portrayal by Su Shaozhi of rigid and unchanging control (Chapter 5), and to Dittmer's analysis of a media control according to power stratification and dichotomization of the public versus private spheres (Chapter 6). Friedman's analytical lens seems to overlap somewhat with a current development in cultural studies (especially that with a post-modernist tinge) that shifts the primary locus of cultural significance from the text or message to text-context interaction or audience interpretations of the text.[23] This receiver-oriented approach is a welcome correction to the simple imputation of effect to message in traditional sender-oriented media studies.

Without specific field research on popular decoding in China, however, it is difficult to establish how far Friedman's insights can be generalized to different interpretative communities organized around geographical regions, social strata, or other criteria. Decoding can be enormously complex, contradictory, and confusing. Following Stuart Hall's influential conceptual categories, further study on this topic should concentrate on how much of the popular reaction to official propaganda represents "preferred readings" in accordance with the dominant messages, "negotiated readings" that claim exceptions to the rules implied in the acknowledged dominant meanings, and "oppositional readings" that retotalize the message within an alternative framework of reference.[24] Critics have charged that a romantic overemphasis on the audience's facility to deconstruct dominant ideology is a symptom of political impotence on the part of progressive intellectuals to organize change.[25] Public apathy instead of active deconstruction can also be one form of resistance.[26] Most reading between-the-lines in China appears to fall into the "negotiated" domain—which still accords the dominant ideology a privileged position—rather than the "preferred" or "oppositional" bipolars. Despite this deviation from previously accepted treatment of decoding, Friedman's analysis opens up a host of new issues to reinvigorate the debate about the nature of ideological control in China.

MEDIA REFORM

A useful comparison of China's media of today is Taiwan's media of yesterday. To elaborate, the KMT's continued imposition of formal media censorship on Taiwan was inspired by an acute legitimacy crisis arising from the external Communist threat, uncertain U.S. support, and potential internal rebellion. As Chin-Chuan Lee (Chapter 10) explains, the "limited openness" resulting from this legitimacy crisis has produced vigorous (if also incomplete) electoral politics, enabling the emergent oppositional forces to wage their little media guerrilla wars against official domination. Unlike the Communist media whose sole responsibility is to uphold official ideology, the capitalist media in Taiwan has another task: attending to *their own* legitimation. Put otherwise, the capitalist authoritarian media are both state ideological apparatuses and cultural commodities for which credibility is vital to success in market competition.

The inherent paradox between political control and economic liberalism has recently manifested itself in the mainland Chinese media. Carol Lee Hamrin (Chapter 4) argues that reform has fostered a technocratic infrastructure and an analogue of civil society, both of which depend heavily on a vast range and huge amounts of information, including Western scientific literature on development economics and modern technological advances, technical and managerial expertise, think-tank advice, and media reports. In the media realm, as documented in several chapters of *Voices of China*, journalists strove for greater autonomy through an ultimately unsuccessful press law. Growing diversity in overall media structure and content coverage is gradually stripping away the ideological straitjacket imposed by the CCP. Market mechanisms have also restructured the hierarchical order between the national media and their local counterparts.[27] Even some of the control mechanisms seem to have cracked at the seams during the heyday of reform between 1986 and 1989.

The Tiananmen crackdown dampened but did not terminate market momentum, which resumed its fiery pace by early 1992 and has sparked intense competition across and within media formats. As part of a concerted plan to dislodge inefficient state enterprises, all but such essential Party organs as the *People's Daily*, the *Economic Daily*, and *Qiushi* (*Seeking Truth*) will have their subsidies completely cut off by 1994. The state has acknowledged the economic significance of non-political coverage by no longer requiring afternoon and evening publications, news digests, culture and lifestyle papers, and trade journals to carry ideological propaganda. Editorial staff will be recruited on the basis of merit, not officially assigned. Advertising revenues have risen sharply, at the rate of 43% in 1992 over the previous year, to reach approximately U.S. $1 billion. Media outlets not only openly court commercial sponsors; they unashamedly try to profiteer from public relations services to industries and even by venturing into unrelated businesses, sometimes with ethically dubious approaches. The Party-run (especially national) media remain tightly controlled, while other types of media (such as evening and enterprise-owned papers) are given more leeway.[28]

The difficulty in resolving the tension between political control and economic openness has haunted the media with erratic oscillations and reversals. The cycle starts with the economic line taking command over the political line and emboldening the media (and others in the cultural circles) to assume a more critical posture toward the government. Whenever hardliners abruptly dump cold water on the economic fervor, however, the media tend to be caught unprepared and fail to withdraw in time to avoid a full-scale attack. This explains why several seemingly "happy beginnings" have sadly ended in destructive political campaigns: "anti-spiritual pollution" (1983), "anti-bourgeois liberalization" (1987), and the Tiananmen tragedy (1989). But each crackdown has engendered bolder action from successive waves of the reformist movement and has pushed China spiral-like toward greater openness in the process. The real challenge lies in consolidating quantitative changes to produce a qualitative change that breaks this vicious cycle of control, relative relaxation, and retrenched control.

CENTER AND PERIPHERY: CHINA'S MEDIA IN THE 1990s

China's pivotal market evolution in the 1980s has called into question many of the past studies intent upon drawing supposed parallels between the Communist media. China's media have also departed from the rigid, absolute, totalitarian control characteristic of the Cultural Revolution. Rather, their treatment is reminiscent of an authoritarian Taiwan under martial law, where the repressive KMT left civil and non-political sectors substantially alone and channeled creative public energy away into economic development. Even though none of the chapters in this volume directly draws this comparison, this relationship deserves some preliminary remarks.

Tu Weiming contends that the periphery (Taiwan and Hong Kong) will come to set the economic and cultural agenda for the center (China)—in selected geographical regions and to selected strata—thereby undermining political effectiveness of the center.[29] Edward Farmer (Chapter 14) indirectly affirms the likely "convergence" of Taiwan and mainland China due to their deep cultural bond. In fact, the examples of Taiwan, South Korea, and Singapore lurked in the minds of Chinese reformist leaders when they championed neoauthoritarianism and the coexistence of political dictatorship and economic freedom.[30]

The triumvirate in the first universe of Cultural China[31] is said (perhaps prematurely) to have formed an increasingly integrated Chinese economic power that promises to equal Japan's.[32] If the center has proven its capacity to absorb the periphery into its market system, the periphery seems to have set counter-agendas for the center in the spheres of popular culture, economic development, and technology. The PRC has avidly cultivated investment and expertise from Hong Kong and Taiwan, while trying to shut its door to the infusion of their "spiritual pollution." But many mainland publications and television programs have mimicked their overseas counterparts, and it is now impossible to shut the door without exacting a huge price. The absence of smoother channels of communication between authorities in China, Taiwan, and Hong Kong has increased the importance of "media watching" to the interpretation of each other's political events. Hundreds of overseas Chinese journalists have visited China, thereby facilitating the publication of articles written by disgruntled mainland writers and journalists. These articles published in "peripheral China," often only accompanied by a pseudonym, are written in violation of CCP policy and often travel back to the PRC and provoke official anger. Pressure is also being mounted on Beijing by Taiwan and Hong Kong—so far in vain—to open the mainland media market to overseas interests.

The periphery, especially Taiwan, seems to offer a point of *departure* for asking questions about how the contradiction of political control and economic reform will impinge on the PRC's media, if not a point of *return* that implies a convergence of outcomes. Peter Berger asserts that democracy presupposes capitalism, but not vice versa, and that East Asian capitalism is a "second case" of development worth comparing with the Western experiences.[33] What is pertinent to our concern here is whether economic development triggers political democracy and press freedom.

The answer, at first glance, is no. For at least two decades (1949–1970) the autocratic KMT regime had harshly trampled on civil liberties and press freedom in Taiwan amidst an "economic miracle." In fact, those days of despair appeared to validate the O'Donnell hypothesis that economic growth legitimized political, military, and press control by bureaucratic-authoritarian regimes, such as those in Latin America.[34] Upon reconsideration, however, economic prosperity did *eventually* spark the political insurgence in Taiwan that forced the state to progressively liberalize itself, enabling civil liberties, media freedom, and popular participation to take root (see Chapter 10). Many writers have viewed the O'Donnell hypothesis as an exception to the liberal expectancy, although these liberal proponents have not anticipated the complex causal mechanisms and the seemingly haphazard process that has marked the evolution of media in this paradigm.[35] Taiwan and other cases of democratic transition in the 1980s seem to support this conclusion.

What is the relevance of the Taiwan case to the PRC? Neither proponents of the media's pivotal role in national development nor their critics have offered much insight into the complex and often contradictory process of development.[36] They fail to provide a "thick description" of how the media contribute to national development in transnational and historical contexts. Despite differences in size and structure—Taiwan faced a structure of international political economy quite unlike the one presently confronting China—the behavior of the Communist regime strikes a uncanny resemblance to that of the martial-law Nationalist regime, and market reform has liberalized non-political sectors, including the media, in mainland China just as it did in Taiwan. Barring such "unknowns" as China's succession crisis, looking at Taiwan gives rise to two speculative observations regarding China in the 1990s.

Domestically, the decade-long marketization of political management has progressively depoliticized the state, economics and culture, thus creating considerable room for media liberalization. This impressive achievement—which has produced new winners and losers—does not belie its dark underside: social dislocation has manifested itself in rampant corruption and graft, rising regionalism, bureaucratic inefficiency, and chronic public outcry. Despite liberalization, there is also little indication of sustained democratic ferment. China appears to be decades away from the translation of liberalization into democratization—a process marked by the maturing of a civil society, a vigorous press, and stable political institutions in which the empowered subordinate classes can organize social movements to struggle for inclusion.[37] Future research should watch closely the interaction between the embryonic "civil society" and its use of fringe versus mainstream media, as well as the role played by the media in the service of social mobilization to counter official hegemony.

Severance of state subsidies to the media will, however, unleash their vital energy to meet intense market competition, causing them to cater to the growing needs and tastes of a diverse audience. It is therefore conceivable that economic information and human interest stories will gradually elbow out the staple of strident ideological extortion, while some semi-official and perhaps private media may rise to surpass official organs in credibility and popularity. The center will gradually loosen its control over local media despite intermittent attempts to crack down on blatant commercialization and sensationalism.

Internationally, little media (magazines, fax, and radio) may proliferate as big media (such as satellite broadcasting) come of age and the pace of interaction between the domestic and non-domestic media quickens. These trends will function to enfeeble the monopolistic hegemony of the Party organs. But the process may be marked by the tortuous repetition of the cycle of official crackdowns, the revival of media activism, and the central authorities' struggles over critical dilemmas. In addition, astounded by the high international cost of the Tiananmen crackdown, Chinese leaders will have to treat political and media dissidents with more sensitivity by greater reliance on cooptation rather than overt coercion. This softened approach may be a partial response to avert or preempt international pressure brought on China to observe human rights, but this same pressure will also embolden dissidents to request support from the international community. As happened in Taiwan, greater international interdependence demanded by the imperative of vigorous economic reform may thus blur the original boundary between domestic politics and global agenda.

NEW FRAMEWORKS OF UNDERSTANDING

U.S. scholars, journalists, and policymakers have only recently begun to treat the PRC outside the confines of the superpower contest between the United States and the former Soviet Union—an ideological framework dramatized by Henry Kissinger's perversely amoral display of power politics. Taiwan has only commanded trivial attention. As China assumes a more complex position in the United States' post-Cold War foreign policy, thorny issues of China's trade practices, human rights violations, and arms proliferation loom large on the horizon. Although these issues were raised soon after the ascendancy of Deng Xiaoping, the media and government officials in the United States have avoided serious treatment of these concerns until very recently.

In a personal account Edward Farmer (Chapter 14) elucidates how the Cold War has served as an overarching framework for his understanding of China; this outlook has, in fact, indelibly informed several generations of U.S. scholarship on China and Sino-American relations. The U.S. media's vacillating coverage of China between cycles of romanticism and those of cynicism parallels Farmer's personal experiences. This prompts Farmer to lament at one point: "The rise and fall of American enthusiasm for China has more to do with what is happening in the United States than it does with what is happening in China."[38] The outdated Cold War perspective should not be replaced by another set of abstract and grossly reductive generalities; needed are richly contextualized and concretized modes of understanding.

Hsiao Ching-chang and Yang Mei-rong (Chapter 17) describe how the presumption of "seeing as believing"—a mark of raw empiricism—deceived American reporters in their perception of China in the early 1970s, as opposed to more expertly reasoned analyses of the Cultural Revolution done at a distance prior to President Richard Nixon's China visit. The art of China reporting has matured considerably since then; the performance of some correspondents operating under trying circumstances can even be described as outstanding. On the other hand, Wendy Tai (Chapter 15) presents the dilemma of a Chinese-American reporter caught between an emotional attachment to Chinese friends and relatives and the professional detachment demanded by her status as a U.S. journalist.

Noting China's unique size, diversity, language, culture, and history, Michel Oksenberg (Chapter 11) provides a sober analysis of the choices confronting U.S. journalists. These choices point, in particular, to the relationship between U.S. journalists and Chinese sources within and outside the government, the home audience's appetite for China news, the journalists' work routines and role constraints, as well as pressure from their professional peers and organizational superiors. In the last analysis, media perception of China remains deeply embedded in U.S. mainstream values.[39] Research on the sociology of media organizations, including comparative case studies which include China correspondents, could further illuminate these problems.[40] Oksenberg argues that the U.S. media should try to penetrate top-level politics in China, lay out the diverse developments in the Chinese interior, local regions, "peripheral China," and their subsequent impact on the "core." The U.S. media should also chart the increasingly close linkage between China's domestic agenda and its global concerns.

It appears that the end of the Cold War will make China more accountable to certain international norms of conduct in the common interests of human rights, trade, environmentalism, and security. This is antithetical to an earlier position that China should be examined *ipso facto* without the superimposition of external precepts.[41] China's rising aspirations for world trade and recognition, as seen in its application for GATT membership and bid for the Olympics in 2000, make it more difficult to extricate the once isolated country from global constraints and to insulate it from the infusion of foreign thought. One hopes that U.S. journalists will approach their coverage of China with more balance and detachment, and not fall prey to the various spikes of romanticism and cynicism which marked earlier times. But let us be reminded that their journalistic canons have been—and always will be—embedded in the mainstream values of the home country and its shifting foreign policy concerns.

NOTES

1. Tu Weiming, "Cultural China: The Periphery as the Center," *Dædalus* 120, no. 2 (1991): 1–32.

2. Asked why U.S. scholars specializing in China would be perceived as members of Cultural China whereas U.S. experts on France may be not accorded a similar status in Cultural France, Professor Tu responded that France could be considered the center of legitimate authority and insight for the discourse about France, but that the first and second universes in Cultural China have failed in their equivalent intellectual and moral responsibilities.

3. The present volume has evolved from the second conference on "Voices of China: Ambiguities and Contradictions in China Reporting and Scholarship," held at the University of Minnesota from 4–6 October 1991 under the auspices of the China Times Center for Media and Social Studies. This volume's predecessor is Chin-Chuan Lee (ed.), *Voices of China: The Interplay of Politics and Journalism* (New York: Guilford Press, 1990.

4. I would like to acknowledge Tsan-kuo Chang, Chi-hsien Chen, and Karl Metzner for providing helpful comments on the draft of this chapter.

5. Fred S. Siebert, Theodore Peterson, and Wilbur Schramm, *Four Theories of the Press* (Urbana: University of Illinois Press, 1963); Margaret A. Blanchard, "The

Hutchins Commission, the Press, and the Responsibility Concept," *Journalism Monographs*, no. 49 (May 1977).

6. For a sophisticated synthesis and critique, see Hanno Hardt, *Critical Communication Studies: Communication, History and Theory in America* (New York: Routledge, 1992).

7. See John Keane, *The Media and Democracy* (Cambridge, England: Polity, 1991); Sue Curry Jansen, *Censorship* (New York: Oxford University Press, 1991).

8. Gaye Tuchman, *Making News* (New York: Free Press, 1978).

9. Michael Schudson, *Discovering the News: A Social History of American Newspapers* (New York: Basic, 1978), p. 160.

10. James W. Carey, "The Dark Continent of American Journalism," in Robert Karl Manoff and Michael Schudson (eds.), *Reading the News* (New York: Pantheon, 1986), p. 194.

11. For a conceptual analysis, see Juan J. Linz, "Totalitarian and Authoritarian Regimes," in Fred Greenstein and Nelson Polsby (eds.), *Handbook of Political Science* (Reading, MA: Addison-Wesley, 1975).

In *Manufacturing Consent* (New York: Pantheon, 1988), Edward Herman and Noam Chomsky provide powerful case studies to illustrate how U.S. media serve as an instrument of American foreign policy, but their theoretical model may be too mechanistic to allow for the media's "relative autonomy" and to account, in detail, for the more subtle production and reproduction of ideological consensus, such as explained by Daniel Hallin in *The "Uncensored War": The Media and Vietnam* (New York: Oxford University Press, 1986) and Edward Said in *Covering Islam* (New York: Pantheon, 1981). Michael Schudson also takes the Herman-Chomsky "propaganda model" to task for being "a blunt instrument for examining a subtle system, a system with more heterogeneity and more capacity for change than they allow." Michael Schudson, "The Sociology of News Production Revisited," in James Curran and Michael Gurevitch (eds.), *Mass Media and Society* (London: Edward Arnold, 1991), p. 146.

12. See e.g., Jane Leftwich Curry, *Poland's Journalists: Professionalism and Politics* (New York: Cambridge University Press, 1990); Jane Leftwich Curry and Joan R. Dassin (eds.), *Press Control Around the World* (New York: Praeger, 1982).

13. Carl J. Friedrich, "The Evolving Theory and Practice of Totalitarian Regimes," in Carl J. Friedrich, Michael Curtis, and Benjamin R. Barber, *Totalitarianism in Perspective: Three Views* (New York: Praeger, 1969).

14. Curry and Dassin, *Press Control Around the World*, p. 256.

15. Herbert Passin, "Writer and Journalist in the Transitional Society," in Lucian W. Pye (ed.), *Communications and Political Development* (Princeton: Princeton University Press, 1963), pp. 128–48.

16. Chin-Chuan Lee, "Mass Media: Of China, About China," in Lee, *Voices of China*, pp. 11–14.

17. Based on my interviews in late 1992 with several major media scholars in Beijing, who requested anonymity.

18. Chin-Chuan Lee and Joseph Man Chan, "The Hong Kong Press in China's Orbit: Thunder of Tiananmen," in Lee, *Voices of China*; Joseph Man Chan and Chin-Chuan Lee, *Mass Media and Political Transition: The Hong Kong Press in China's Orbit* (New York: Guilford Press, 1991).

19. This study was cited by Congressman John Porter (R–Illinois), a member of the Subcommittee on Human Rights in the U.S. House of Representatives, when he introduced a bill in 1993 aimed at protecting Hong Kong journalists after 1997.

20. See Lee, *Voices of China*, especially chapters by Ruan Ming, Liu Binyan, and Hsiao Ching-chang and Yang Mei-rong.

21. Nicholas D. Kristof, "Via Satellite, Information Revolution Stirs China," *New York Times*, 11 Apr. 1993. The widespread use of fax machines around 1984 hastened the collapse of press control mechanisms in Taiwan, and satellite spill-over from Hong Kong and Japan coupled with illegal cable systems have served to subvert state control of television in Taiwan.

22. Many people, however, would take exception to Friedman's interpretation of Antonio Gramsci's project as upholding Leninist dictatorship. Gramsci developed his theory in a fascist prison, arguing that revolution did not take place in Western bourgeois regimes, as Marx had anticipated, because of their ability to reproduce social consent while simultaneously imposing coercion. Like most Western Marxists, Gramsci rebelled against capitalism on the one hand and Leninist rigidity on the other in his pursuit of Marxist humanism. See Alvin Gouldner, *Two Marxisms* (New York: Seabury Press, 1980). In the last 15 years "hegemony" has been developed as a central concept in critical media scholarship, especially that informed by British cultural studies. See Stuart Hall, "The Discovery of 'Ideology': Return of the Repressed in Media Studies," in Michael Gurevitch et al. (eds.), *Culture, Society, and the Media* (New York: Methuen, 1982).

23. The voluminous literature includes John Fiske, *Television Culture* (New York: Routledge, 1987), pp. 62–83. Other sociologists who combine in-depth focus-group interviews with textual analysis include William A. Gamson, *Talking Politics* (New York: Cambridge University Press, 1992) and Tamar Liebes and Elihu Katz, *The Export of Meaning: Cross-Cultural Readings of "Dallas"* (New York: Oxford University Press, 1990).

24. Stuart Hall, "Encoding/Decoding," in Stuart Hall, D. Hobson, A. Lowe, and P. Willis (eds.), *Culture, Media, Language* (London: Hutchinson, 1980), pp. 128–39.

25. Todd Gitlin, "The Politics of Communication and the Communication of Politics," in Curran and Gurevitch, *Mass Media and Society*, pp. 329–41.

26. Nicholas D. Kristof, for example, writes: "A few years ago, when the hard-liners were at the apex of their power, most ordinary workers and young people in towns around the country did not feel so much repressed by Communism as bored by it. ... When pressed about the reasons for their alienation, they did not mention the lack of a vote so much as the lack of decent entertainment. The problems with the newspapers and television, in the minds of many people, was not so much that they lied but that they were so excruciatingly dull." "China Warms to Sex, Art and Other Entertainment," *New York Times*, 24 Feb. 1993, sec. B1.

27. See Lee, *Voices of China*, pp. 14–18, and chapters by Judy Polumbaum, Jinglu Yu, and Lynn White III.

28. Joseph Man Chan, "Mass Media: Commercialization without Independence," in Joseph Cheng and Maurice Brosseau (eds.), *China Review 1993* (Hong Kong: Chinese University Press, 1993). The *People's Daily*, for example, is trying to enter into real estate and data services businesses.

29. Tu, "Cultural China."

30. Ruan Ming, "Press Freedom and Neoauthoritarianism: A Reflection on China's Democracy Movement," in Lee, *Voices of China*.

31. Tu, "Cultural China."

32. Steven Greenhouse, "New Tally of World's Economies Catapults China into Third Place," *New York Times*, 20 May 1993, sec. A1, A6.

33. Peter Berger, *The Capitalist Revolution* (New York: Basic Books, 1991), pp. xv, 140–71.

34. Guillermo A. O'Donnell, *Modernization and Bureaucratic-Authoritarianism* (Berkeley: Institute of International Studies, University of California, 1973); Guillermo A. O'Donnell, "Reflections on the Pattern of Changes in the Bureaucratic-Authoritarian State," *Latin American Studies* 8 (1978): 3–38.

35. Larry Diamond, "Economic Development and Democracy Reconsidered," *American Behavioral Scientist* 355 (1992): 450–99; Dietrich Rueschemeyer, Evelyne Huber Stephens, and John D. Stephens, *Capitalist Development and Democracy* (Chicago: University of Chicago Press, 1992).

36. For the liberal exposition, see Daniel Lerner, *The Passing of Traditional Society* (New York: Free Press, 1958); Wilbur Schramm, *Mass Media and National Development* (Stanford: Stanford University Press, 1964); Everett M. Rogers, *The Diffusion of Innovations*, 3rd ed. (New York: Free Press, 1983); and Ithiel de Sola Pool's posthumous publication, *Technologies Without Boundaries* (Cambridge: Harvard University Press, 1990). The most prominent radical critic of this perspective has been Herbert I. Schiller, whose works include *Mass Communication and American Empire*, 2nd ed. (Boulder, CO: Westview, 1992); *Communication and Cultural Domination* (White Plains, NY: M.E. Sharpe, 1976); *Who Knows?* (Norwood, NJ: Ablex, 1981); and *Information and the Crisis Economy* (Norwood, NJ: Ablex, 1984).

37. This statement follows the line of argument taken by Rueschemeyer, Stephens, and Stephens, *Capitalist Development and Democracy*.

38. Edward L. Farmer, "Sifting Truth from Facts: The Reporter as Interpreter of China," in Lee, *Voices of China*. Other chapters by Brantly Womack and Amanda Bennett in the same volume are also highly illuminating.

39. Lee, "Mass Media: Of China, About China," pp. 19–27.

40. For a concise summary, see Denis McQuail, *Mass Communication Theory*, 2nd ed. (Newbury Park, CA: Sage, 1987), pp. 135–87.

41. For a critique, see Harry Harding, "From China, With Disdain: New Trends in the Study of China," *Asian Survey* 22 (1982): 934–58.

PART TWO

CONTROL, CHANGE, AND OPPOSITION

2

THE ROLE OF THE PRESS IN POST-MAO POLITICAL STRUGGLES

Merle Goldman

Freedom of expression has not been guaranteed by law in the People's Republic of China under either Mao Zedong or Deng Xiaoping. With the exception of the Hundred Flowers movement in the first half of 1957, the media were tightly controlled by the Chinese Communist Party (CCP), specifically by its Propaganda Department, throughout the Mao era (1949–1976). The media usually spoke with one voice, albeit in subtly different tones, until factional struggles within the leadership could no longer be contained behind closed doors. This occurred in the mid-1960s when Mao believed that he could no longer get his views published in the Party newspapers in Beijing, including the *People's Daily*, the official organ of the Party's Central Committee. Mao went to Shanghai and launched the Cultural Revolution in the media there with the help of Ke Qingshi, the city's Party Secretary. One of Mao's and his allies' first moves in the Cultural Revolution in the spring of 1966 was gaining control over the propaganda apparatus, particularly the *People's Daily.*

Because control over the media was somewhat looser and factions more open in the Deng Xiaoping era, beginning in 1978, different newspapers and journals tended to represent different political factions. Through most of the Deng era until the 4 June 1989 crackdown, the *People's Daily* tended to represent the views of the reformist leadership of Hu Yaobang, Zhao Ziyang, and, most of the time, Deng Xiaoping. *Red Flag*, the Party's ideological journal, tended to represent the views of Deng's Long March companions, the revolutionary elders, until it was closed down by Zhao Ziyang in 1988. Its replacement, *Seeking Truth (Qiushi)*, then became the mouthpiece of the elders and their younger associates. At critical moments in their power struggles, however, political factions sought to dominate all the national media. Thus, when remaining Maoists clashed with the returning Party hierarchy after the Cultural Revolution in the late 1970s and when reformers went up against the revolutionary elders during the Tiananmen Square demonstrations of 1989, the media played a pivotal role in shaping Chinese politics.

REFORMERS USE THE PRESS AGAINST MAOISTS

In an effort to hold on to power after the Cultural Revolution, Maoists still in control of the Party Propaganda Department published a joint editorial on 7 February 1977 in the *People's Daily*, the *Liberation Army Daily*, and *Red Flag* to assert their authority.[1] The editorial, "Study Documents Well and Keep Hold of the Key Link," declared that "[w]hatever policy decisions were made by Chairman Mao must be resolutely upheld by us. Whatever instructions were given by Chairman Mao must be firmly and unwaveringly followed by us at all times."[2] On the basis of this outlook, the "two whatevers" faction label was attached to the remaining Maoists. In fact, even before Deng made his formal return to power at the Third Plenum of the Eleventh Central Committee in December 1978, Deng had written a letter to the Central Committee on 14 April 1977 criticizing the "two whatevers" for distorting Mao's thought.

In an effort to counter the "two whatevers," Deng's protégé Hu Yaobang, who had already returned to power as a vice president of the Central Party School, launched a campaign-like discussion using the slogan, "Practice is the sole criterion of truth." With the guidance and help of members of the Central Party School, Hu used pragmatic criteria to evaluate Mao's ideas and policies. Accordingly, Hu and his associates criticized Mao's personality cult, his emphasis on the power of the will, his use of class struggle in Party campaigns, and charged that his communal agricultural policies were unproductive and, in fact, destructive. This was the first time since 1949 that Mao, his ideology, and his policies had been directly challenged from within the political establishment.[3]

Hu and his associates used the press to launch this discussion on the "practice criterion" not only to reverse Maoist policies and revise ideology, but also to push the remaining Maoists out of the leadership. Hu established the Theory Research Office in the Central Party School and the journal *Theoretical Trends (Lilun Dongtai)* to do this. Soon after the first issue of *Theoretical Trends* appeared on 15 July 1977, the three national newspapers—the *People's Daily*, the *Guangming Daily*, and the *Liberation Army Daily*—and others reprinted a number of its articles under the byline "special commentator." Ordinarily, a commentator article in the *People's Daily* would have required the approval of Wang Dongxing, Mao's former bodyguard and a Party vice chairman in charge of propaganda who still oversaw the *People's Daily*. Because these articles were from *Theoretical*

Trends, however, it was not necessary to secure his permission. In this way, Hu and his network were able to evade the censorship of the Propaganda Department and reprint many influential articles from *Theoretical Trends* in the mainstream media.

The article "Actual Practice is the Only Criterion for the Examination of Truth," which appeared in *Theoretical Trends* on 10 May 1978, was their initial volley in the attack on the "two whatevers." It was originally written by Hu Fuming, a teacher at Nanjing University, but was greatly revised by members of the Theory Research Office. Hu Fuming had first submitted the article to the *Guangming Daily* where Yang Xiguang, a former member of the Central Party School, was editor-in-chief, and Ma Peiwen served as head of the newspaper's Party group. Both men were members of Hu Yaobang's intellectual network. At the same time, Sun Changjiang in the Theory Research Office had written his own article on the practice criterion. Although previously an activist in the Cultural Revolution, Sun had become thoroughly disillusioned with Mao's thought and practice. With the help of Wu Jiang, the veteran theorist and Director of the Theory Research Office, Sun persuaded Hu Yaobang that practice should be the main criterion for judging events, including Mao's ideology and policies. On 13 April 1978 Yang Xiguang introduced Sun to Hu Fuming. With the advice of Wu Jiang, Sun produced a single article out of the two drafts on the practice criterion. After this article was published in *Theoretical Trends* on 3 May 1978, it was reprinted as a "special commentator" article in the *Guangming Daily* on 11 May and in the *People's Daily*, the *Liberation Army Daily*, and by the New China News Agency (Xinhua) on 12 May.

Thus, in response to the "two whatevers" editorial in the two newspapers and a journal, the Hu Yaobang group published their counterattack in the three newspapers and the Party's major news agency. Hu made the decision to reprint the article in the national newspapers to give it the Party's imprimatur. Except for Hu Yaobang's associates at the Central Party School and the *Guangming Daily*, the only other people who knew about the article's origins were Hu Jiwei, the editor-in-chief of the *People's Daily*, and Wang Ruoshui, his deputy editor in charge of the Theory Department at the paper. All of these people had been associated with Hu Yaobang in the China Youth League or other Party organizations in the 1950s.

Although Hu Yaobang had made the decision to publish the article in the major national media, it was in accordance with Deng Xiaoping's views. When Deng made his first informal reappearance after the Cultural Revolution in July 1977, he had used a slogan both Maoist and traditional—"seek truth from facts"—as the first salvo against Maoists and Maoist policies. Even before that, on 24 May 1977, Deng related that he had told some remaining Maoists that "[i]f you stick to the 'two whatev-

ers,' then to overturn the verdict on me (*wei wo fan an*) makes no sense. ...
It just won't do to take words spoken by the Chairman at one point, under
one set of conditions, and apply them to a different issue, a different
event, or a different situation."[4]

Despite Deng's apparent support for the shift away from Maoist policies, Wu Lengxi—a long-time Party official, member of the Central Committee, and editor-in-chief of the *People's Daily* between 1958 and 1966—
angrily criticized Hu Jiwei, one of his former deputies, on the day the *People's Daily* published the "practice criterion" article. Wu's arguments
against the article expressed views that elders such as Chen Yun, Li
Xiannian, Wang Zhen, and Peng Zhen later used in the 1980s in their
struggle with reformers and Hu's intellectual network. Wu attacked the
article's argument that the truth is unknowable until proven in practice,
charging that the article "supported the notion of doubting everything"
and went so far to "argue that some of Mao's instructions are incorrect
and that we must not deal with Mao's instructions as if they were dead
dogma or worship them as if they were the Bible." If Mao's ideology were
questioned and revised as suggested in this article, Wu asked how Chinese could "still be able to remain united as one? Will there still be stability and unity in our country?"[5] Wu articulated the fear that was later to
obsess the elders—that any change in Marxism-Leninism or the Leninist
Party-state would destabilize and disunite the country. At the same time,
because the article had been reprinted in the *People's Daily* without his approval, Wang Dongxing regarded it as a threat to his and the Maoists' authority. On 17 May 1978 he called for an investigation to find out who was
behind the article's publication. Moreover, Zhang Pinghua, the Maoist
head of the Propaganda Department, told his associates in the Department they could criticize the article.

Although Deng appeared to have been unaware of the prior
preparations for the article, the controversy it provoked aroused his curiosity by late May or early June 1978. On 2 June 1978, at a conference on the
political work of the army, he publicly took sides in the debate by criticizing those comrades "who think that it is enough just to copy or borrow
what was originally said by Marx, Lenin, and Mao in its entirety."[6] Deng's
clear-cut stand swung wavering Party leaders to Hu Yaobang's side. Hu
Jiwei then gave Deng's 2 June speech front-page coverage in the *People's
Daily*, further giving it the imprimatur of official policy.

Nevertheless, as Wu Lengxi's phone call revealed, the efforts of Hu
Yaobang and his network to dispense with the Maoist legacy encountered
opposition from Party elders at the very beginning of the Deng era. These
elders agreed to get rid of the Maoist faction, but not necessarily to reject
Mao's views and pre-Cultural Revolution policies. Hu Qiaomu, a spokesman for the elders, visited Hu Yaobang on 20 June 1978 and urged him to

stop immediately the public debate on the practice criterion and order *Theoretical Trends* to avoid the subject. At that point, Hu Yaobang advised Wu Jiang and Ruan Ming, the editor of *Theoretical Trends*, to suspend the discussion for the time being.

Hu, however, could not control his intellectual associates. Wu Jiang, with the assistance of Sun Changjiang, had written a new article to rebut Wu Lengxi's criticism and brought it to the attention of Luo Ruiqing, General Secretary of the Central Military Commission. Like his fellow elders, Luo had suffered greatly in the Cultural Revolution but, unlike them, he was not as fearful about revising previous practices. He agreed to publish the rebuttal in the *Liberation Army Daily* and assumed responsibility for the article after his suggested revisions had been made. This article, "A Most Fundamental Principle of Marxism," was published on 24 June 1978 under the "special commentator" byline. It reemphasized the need to revise ideology in light of changing times. Luo died shortly after the article appeared.

Hu Yaobang then called for the publication of a third article, "All the Subjective World Must be Examined by Practice," which expressed similar ideas. It was first published in *Theoretical Trends* on 10 September 1978 and later in the *People's Daily* as a "special commentator" article. While these continuing volleys against Mao's legacy infuriated Maoists and some of the elders, they attracted widespread attention and helped prepare the ideological grounds for the approval of Deng's pragmatic reform program at the Third Plenum in December 1978. Despite the traumas that Chinese had suffered during the Mao era, it was not until this media campaign advocating the practice criterion that others began to question and criticize Mao's ideas and policies openly.

Another media conflict between the Maoists and reform officials erupted over the publication of *China Youth*, China Youth League journal which was under the influence of Hu Yaobang. It was to reappear after a 12-year suspension on 11 September 1978 until Wang Dongxing ordered it withdrawn as a way to counterattack Hu. The inaugural issue carried several articles positively evaluating the 5 April 1976 Tiananmen Square protest directed against Mao, the Gang of Four, and the Cultural Revolution, and in support of Deng and his pragmatic policies. *China Youth* relabeled this "counterrevolutionary" protest "revolutionary" and denounced the security police who had suppressed the demonstrators. Furthermore, a contributing commentator article, "Eliminate Blind Faith, Get a Good Grasp of Science," once more criticized Mao's legacy by comparing the cult of Mao with blind religious faith and superstition.

Hu directed Hua Guofeng, Mao's putative successor, to rescind Wang's order banning the issue. The issue finally appeared in bookstores around 20 September 1978. Wu De, the mayor of Beijing who had led the crackdown on the 5 April 1976 demonstrators, was dismissed on 11 October 1978, and hundreds of jailed 5 April demonstrators were released. A collection of poems recited on Tiananmen Square at that time, including works which compared Mao with China's ancient emperor, the despotic Shi Huangdi of the Qin dynasty (221–202 B.C.), was published with a title page in Hua Guofeng's own calligraphy as a sign of official approval. On 14 November 1978 the designation of the 5 April 1976 protest as a counter-revolutionary movement was officially withdrawn.

China Youth not only became another major media forum which criticized Maoist policies, it began to focus the blame for Mao's policies on another issue Hu Yaobang and his associates had discussed, the Leninist political system that had given Mao unlimited power. In a November 1978 article, "It is Necessary to Bring Democracy into Full Play," for example, two young writers asked, "how could the Gang of Four have run amuck in such a way over the past several years? Why did the Chinese people tolerate them? ... Why couldn't the hundreds of millions of people have exposed them in time to prevent such a disaster?"[7] The authors charged that such a disaster could not be blamed solely on one individual or a small group, but was the product of China's political structure and history. But instead of emphasizing China's "feudal" past and blaming the Gang of Four, the standard explanation for the Cultural Revolution, they pointed to "the absence of reliable organizations and systems to safeguard socialist democracy."[8] In addition, they demanded freedom of the press in order to expose the defects and mistakes of officials.

By the fall of 1978 the press was not only attacking the Maoists and the Maoist ideology, it was also beginning to question the Leninist political system and helped mobilize others in the attack. The official press under the jurisdiction of Hu Yaobang discussed democracy as a prerequisite to economic reform before the Democracy Wall movement of ex-Red Guards turned to posters and self-printed pamphlets to express similar views in late 1978 and early 1979, and before ex-Red Guard Wei Jingsheng coined it the "Fifth Modernization." Thus, the official media's advocacy of the practice criterion, the reversal of Maoist policies, democratic reform, and the Democracy Wall movement provided the intellectual and political environment that helped Deng launch his decade of reform at the Third Plenum in late December 1978.

THE PIVOTAL ROLE OF THE PRESS IN THE 1989 TIANANMEN SQUARE DEMONSTRATION

The press once again played a pivotal role at a critical turning point during the 1989 Tiananmen Square demonstration and the power struggle between the elders and Zhao Ziyang, the latter supported by allies of Hu

Yaobang. Hu Yaobang died on 15 April 1989. On 22 April 1989, as the Party hierarchy attended his official funeral in the Great Hall of the People, student demonstrators held an unofficial ceremony on the Square outside the Great Hall, in which around 100,000 people participated. Editors and journalists from three media outlets which had consistently supported the reform policies of Hu and Zhao took part in the unofficial ceremony. Among them were some 20 editors and journalists from the *Science and Technology Daily*, whose deputy editor, Sun Changjiang, had been a speech writer for Hu Yaobang until 1982. The reformist journal *New Observer* and the semi-official *World Economic Herald*, published in Shanghai, presented their own wreathes at the unofficial funeral.

The editors of these three papers had also participated in the memorial services held by Hu's network on 19 April. *New Observer* and the Beijing office of the *World Economic Herald*, headed by the young Zhang Weiguo, convened the ceremony. It took the form of a seminar presided over by *New Observer* editor Ge Yang in the conference room of the Ministry of Culture, headed by Wang Meng, a Hu appointee. These two publications had been major forums for Hu's intellectual network over the decade and had published interviews in which Hu's allies continued to press for political reform even after Deng Xiaoping abandoned the effort in 1987. Editors and journalists from official and semi-official publications as well as scores of Hu's associates presented a positive evaluation of Hu in direct opposition to the Party's more reserved official view.

Recalling their contacts with Hu over the years, many of his colleagues carried out the reappraisal of Hu that the Party had avoided after dismissing him in January 1987. Chen Zeming, a representative of the non-official journals that began to mushroom all over the country in the mid-1980s, also participated. Chen had edited *Beijing Spring* during the Democracy Wall movement and had founded the first independent social science think-tank—the Beijing Social and Economic Research Institute—in 1986. He also published *Economic Weekly*, a journal edited by his Democracy Wall movement colleague, Wang Juntao. *Economic Weekly*, a periodical Chen financed with money from private correspondence schools he had established in the mid-1980s, had become a major media voice for political reform.

At the conclusion of the seminar, the editor-in-chief of the *World Economic Herald*, Qin Benli, instructed Zhang Weiguo to devote as many pages as needed to the seminar speeches. That Qin decided to publish the positive appraisals of Hu was not surprising, considering that his paper had been closely associated with Hu's network and Zhao's think-tanks. Qin and Ge Yang had been early participants in the Party underground before 1949. Like Ge, Qin also had spent most of his career during the Mao era in disgrace. Qin was purged in 1957 because his paper, Shanghai's

Wenhui Daily, had been specifically singled out by Mao for having a "bourgeois orientation." Qin was then excluded from newspaper work, persecuted, and subjected to two years of solitary confinement during the Cultural Revolution.

When the Party rehabilitated Qin at the beginning of the Deng era, the China World Economic Association and the World Economic Research Institute of the Shanghai Academy of Social Sciences asked him to launch a newspaper. Despite his official affiliation with the Shanghai Academy, Qin began the *World Economic Herald* in 1980 virtually from scratch. Some prepaid advertising money, a private contribution from the reformist economist Qian Junrui, and the sale of some of his belongings supplied enough money to hire seven veteran newspaper people, most of whom were, like himself, at some stage of retirement. Although his editorial board included the foreign affairs official Huan Xiang and Hu Yaobang confidant Yu Guangyuan, Qin conceived of the *Herald* as an unofficial voice controlled by its editors and jounalists. Able to hire and fire personnel without official approval, the *Herald* started to recruit aspiring young reporters in 1981, and had a staff of about 100 and a circulation of around 300,000 by 1989.

Although the *Herald* was housed in a former French missionary school that belonged to the Shanghai Academy and was printed under the Academy's auspices by Shanghai's *Liberation Daily* for a fee, it was run as a quasi-private paper. It published articles without getting approval from Shanghai officials and the city's Propaganda Department. Nevertheless, as it increasingly focused on political issues in the second half of the 1980s, it came into conflict with the elders. They criticized the *Herald* for defending and reprinting a controversial article published in 1985 by the scholar Ma Ding which had asserted that China could benefit more from studying Western economic techniques than Marxist economic theories. It also published excerpts of Fang Lizhi's speeches in fall 1986, in which he urged university audiences to take power into their own hands, and the theorist Su Shaozhi's controversial speech at the tenth anniversary of the Third Plenum in 1988, which criticized the elders' spokesmen and defended members of Hu's network. The *Herald* was only able to survive because of Zhao's protection.[9]

Qin decided to publish the proceedings of the seminar on Hu a day earlier than normal so that they would appear on 22 April, the day of Hu's official funeral. When Shanghai Propaganda Department officials learned about Qin's plan, they ordered him to show them the final article proofs and recommended the deletion of several hundred characters. Qin refused. Jiang Zemin, then mayor of Shanghai, criticized Qin personally for ignoring Party discipline. Qin finally agreed to delete some words, but some 160,000 copies of the issue had already been printed in their unaltered form and sent to Beijing before his orders were received.[10] On 26 April the Shanghai Party Committee suspended Qin from the Party and as editor and sent in a task force to rectify the *Herald*.

The following issue, appearing on 8 May 1989, contained the staff's denunciation of Qin's firing and the assertion of the China World Economic Association, a *Herald* sponsor, that only the Association, not the Shanghai Party Committee, had the power to dismiss Qin and replace the staff.[11] In response, the Party suspended the paper. Qin convened the editorial board at his home to discuss a protest statement, and several hundred copies of the statement were soon issued. Qin's associates called foreign correspondents asking for their support. Qin refused to make a self-criticism as demanded by the Shanghai Party Committee. The *Herald*'s Beijing editor, Zhang Weiguo, also refused, explaining that the Party had no jurisdiction over the *Herald* because it was run without state money.[12] Zhang further pointed out that there were about 47 other newspapers like the *Herald* which were run by its members, rather than the Party or government, and that they also should be allowed to control their own activities.

Similarly unprecedented was the civil suit that the *Herald* staff brought against the Jiang Zemin for "harming the reputation of the *World Economic Herald*."[13] Two civil litigation experts from People's University volunteered their services and the civil law department at the University of Politics and Law in Beijing volunteered to help file the writ. This was the first time a Chinese newspaper had sued a Party leader. The *Herald*'s suit sparked other papers and writers to bring suit against the authorities for defamation and interference.

The Party's moves against the *Herald* galvanized China's journalists into concerted action for the first time in the People's Republic. Journalists protesting the treatment of Qin and the *Herald* were the first professional group to join the students in the 1989 Tiananmen Square demonstration. On 4 May about 500 journalists took to the streets with banners calling for "Support of the *World Economic Herald*" and "Freedom of the Press." Shortly thereafter, other professionals, academics, and bureaucrats joined the demonstration. The journalists helped to enlarge the demonstration far beyond a student movement.

Dai Qing—the *Guangming Daily* journalist who had written an exposé of the Party's repressive treatment of the former editor-in-chief of the *Guangming Daily*, Chu Anping, during the Anti-Rightist Campaign in 1957—played an important role in mobilizing jounalists to support Qin and the *Herald*. She contacted *China Youth*, the *Guangming Daily*, and Chen Ziming of the *Economic Weekly* to support Qin in his struggle with the Shanghai Party authorities. Several hundred journalists from papers such as the *People's Daily*, the *Worker's Daily*, the *Farmer's Daily*, and the Chinese Women's Federation paper also sent a petition to the Shanghai Party

Committee protesting Qin's treatment. *Asia-Pacific Economic Forum*, a semi-official weekly connected with the Guangzhou Academy of Social Science, held a press conference in Beijing to express public support for the *Herald*.

Members of Hu's network drafted an "open" letter to the Shanghai Party Committee entitled, "Defend Freedom of the Press," signed by 50 prominent intellectuals, among them Yan Jiaqi, Xu Liangying, Su Shaozhi, Yu Haocheng, Zhang Xianyang, Bao Zunxin, and Su Xiaokang, a principal writer and editor of the controversial television series "River Elegy." Many of these intellectuals, who had themselves used the *Herald* as a forum, pointed out in their "open" letter that the Party's actions were contrary to Article 35 of the Chinese Constitution, which guarantees freedom of the press.

An organized protest of journalists and intellectuals in support of a newspaper under attack by the Party was unprecedented. Equally significant, the journalists used the demonstration to press their own particular demands. On 9 May a petition signed by more than 1,000 journalists was delivered to the Chinese Journalists' Association asking for a "dialogue on press reform." Since the mid-1980s journalists had been calling unsuccessfully for a detailed press law. With their efforts to establish a press law by working within the system thwarted, they turned to public protest.

Despite constraints, a few of China's official newspapers also played a crucial role in expanding the social base for the 1989 demonstration. At the forefront was the *Science and Technology Daily* with Lin Zexin, an old revolutionary journalist, as editor-in-chief and Sun Changjiang as deputy editor. In commemoration of Hu, the *Science and Technology Daily* published the first factual account of the student demonstrations accompanied by a large photo on 19 April 1989. Copies were quickly posted on the walls of Beijing University, drawing huge crowds. Lin published the first reports about the demonstrations because the editors of the *Science and Technology Daily* had been overlooked when Hu Qili, the Politbureau Standing Committee member in charge of the media, called senior editors to a meeting and ordered them not to report on the demonstration. In fact, the *Science and Technology Daily* ran its first report on the very day of that meeting. Notwithstanding Hu Qili's order, Lin and Sun continued to publish relatively objective accounts of the demonstrations.[14]

By the time the *Science and Technology Daily* journalists returned to their offices after Hu's official funeral on 22 April, they had decided to report on the students' unofficial ceremony. At a meeting that lasted into the night of 23 April, the younger journalists were so committed to presenting full coverage of the ceremony that they persuaded a majority of the staff to threaten resignation if that were not done. Urged by Sun Changjiang, Lin finally agreed. On 24 April an article entitled, "Under Wind and Rain, Sing a Song to Say Goodbye to You," reported on the unofficial funeral and the participants' demand to quicken the pace of political reform. It also carried five photos of the unofficial funeral and other related stories. By contrast, the other official media covered only the official funeral without even mentioning the unofficial one. When the authorities attempted to stop the distribution of this issue through the mails, the staff personally carried stacks of the paper to post offices around Beijing.

In the face of the expanding demonstration, the elders also tried to regain control of the situation by using the press. They counterattacked with the publication of a *People's Daily* editorial on 26 April. The editorial was based on a speech that Deng Xiaoping had made the day before. The speech, in turn, was based principally on information Deng received from Li Peng and the leaders of the Beijing Party Committee, not information presented in the *Science and Technology Daily*. Rather than depicting the demonstration as a movement for reform within the prevailing political system, the speech presented it as a threat to the regime, the Party, and the leadership itself. Xu Weicheng, head of the Beijing Party Committee's Propaganda Department, had written the editorial, which was then revised by a committee under the direction of Hu Qili. It characterized the demonstration as "a premeditated conspiracy to bring about political disorder" and blamed "a small minority of people with ulterior motives" who intended to "create national turmoil and sabotage political stability."[15] Deng's comment that "[t]he disturbance must not be allowed to spread to society and secondary schools"—reflecting the leaders' fear that the demonstration might be part of another Cultural Revolution—did not surface in the editorial.[16]

Instead of quelling the demonstrators, however, this editorial provoked more people in Beijing to join the demonstration in support of the students. The press again played a pivotal role in expanding support for the demonstration, sparking a reaction among people in Beijing. After the number and volatility of the demonstrators increased in response to the 26 April *People's Daily* editorial, Ge Yang's *New Observer* began publishing objective accounts of this spontaneous mass protest on 27 April. Although a few other official newspapers such as the *Worker's Daily*, the *Farmer's Daily*, and the *Beijing Youth News* began to write a bit about the demonstration, none of them gave as full an account as the *Science and Technology Daily*.

It was not until 6 May that the official media began full and balanced reporting on the Tiananmen Square happenings. This was initiated when Zhao Ziyang told Hu Qili—in an effort to bolster his position in his struggle with the elders—that there was "no big risk to opening up a bit by reporting on the demonstration and increasing the openness of the news."[17] With Zhao's encouragement of fuller coverage in the media, especially in the *People's Daily*, the public gained the impression that the demonstration had received the Party's approval. Believing that this lessened the risk of punishment for participation, more segments of China's urban population were emboldened to join the demonstration.

People's Daily director and editor-in-chief Qian Liren and Tan Wenrui, veteran Party officials as well as veteran editors, went along with Zhao's orders. But the two younger deputy editors, Lu Chaoqin and Yu Huanchun, were responsible for the two-week front-page coverage of the demonstration. Thus, the offical media's coverage—especially that of the *People's Daily*—and their participation in the demonstration were instrumental in transforming it from a student protest into an urban protest which encompassed virtually all segments of Chinese urban society in the last week of April and the first two weeks of May. Thus, while a stalemated power struggle, accelerating inflation, and blatant corruption formed the backdrop of the largest and longest spontaneous demonstration in the People's Republic, the role of the press in enlarging the demonstration was equally important.

Therefore, it was not surprising that those press units which had objectively covered the demonstrations were thoroughly purged immediately after the 4 June crackdown. In addition, the *World Economic Herald*, *New Observer*, and *Economic Weekly* were closed down altogether. Sun Changjiang was retired from the *Science and Technology Daily*, and staff at the *People's Daily* were replaced by editors and journalists from the provinces and the military.

CONCLUSION

The pivotal role of the press in bringing reformers and reform policies to power in the late 1970s and mobilizing a massive, unprecedented demonstration for political reform in the late 1980s suggests that the press played a crucial role in China's ideological and power struggles during the Deng Xiaoping era, especially when normally authoritarian controls weakened. If and when China truly achieves freedom of the press guaranteed by law, making possible the expression of a broad range of political views in the media, the press may ironically no longer play as influential a role in political struggles as it has in the past. Because the press will carry a variety of views—even within the same newspaper—and will be owned by a variety of groups, it is unlikely that political leaders will be able to use it as directly as before in conflicts over policy and power.

NOTES

1. This joint publication in the two national newspapers and premier theoretical journal was the same technique that the Maoists used in the Cultural Revolution to oppose the Party hierarchy.

2. *People's Daily*, 7 Feb. 1977, p. 1.

3. For an excellent analysis of this discussion, see Michael Schoenhals, "The 1978 Truth Criterion Controversy," *China Quarterly*, Sept. 1991, pp. 243–68; Ruan Ming, "Press Freedom and Neoauthoritarianism: A Reflection on China's Democracy Movement," in Chin-Chuan Lee (ed.), *Voices of China: The Interplay of Politics and Journalism* (New York: Guilford Press, 1990).

4. Schoenhals, "Truth Criterion Controversy," (from "Deng Xiaoping's Speech on a Meeting with Deng Liqun"), p. 251.

5. Ibid., p. 261.

6. Sun Changjiang, "From the Criterion of Practice to the Criterion of Productive Forces," *People's Daily*, 9 May 1988, p. 5, translated in FBIS, 18 May 1988, p. 27.

7. Li Chun and Li Yinho, "It is Necessary to Bring Democracy into Full Play," *China Youth*, no. 3 (1978), reprinted in *People's Daily*, 13 Nov. 1978, translated in FBIS 15 Nov. 1978, p. E2.

8. Li, "Bring Democracy into Full Play," FBIS, 15 Nov. 1978, p. E3.

9. Hsiao Ching-chang and Yang Mei-rong, "'Don't Force Us to Lie': The Case of the *World Economic Herald*," in Lee (ed.), *Voices of China*, pp. 111–21.

10. Xinhua, 18 Aug. 1989, translated in FBIS, 21 Aug. 1989, p. 23.

11. FBIS, 21 Aug. 1989, p. 24.

12. *Ming Bao*, 7 May 1989, p. 2, translated in FBIS, 8 May 1989, pp. 29–30.

13. FBIS, 8 May 1989, p. K30.

14. Seth Faison, "The Changing Role of the Chinese Media," in Tony Saich (ed.), *The Chinese People's Movement* (Armonk, NY: M.E. Sharpe, 1990), p. 148.

15. *People's Daily*, 26 Apr. 1989, p. 1.

16. *Huaqiao Ribao* (New York), 7 June 1989.

17. Chen Xitong Speech. Xinhua, 6 July 1989, translated in FBIS, 6 July 1989, p. 28.

3

THE USE AND ABUSE OF MASS MEDIA BY CHINESE LEADERS DURING THE 1980S

Marlowe Hood

The search for truth is often thoughtlessly praised; but it has something great in it only if the seeker has the sincere, unconditional will for justice.

Objectivity and justice have nothing to do with each other.
—Friedrich Nietzsche, "The Use and Abuse of History,"
Thoughts Out of Season (1873)

Friedrich Nietzsche's impassioned manual on how to manipulate the writing of history to serve contemporary ends is an insult to anyone who cherishes the integrity of the past. This notorious essay, from whose title I borrow for my own, however, offends not because of the author's judgment that it is impossible to render an objective historical account—surely we agree, by now, that such claims to objectivity are pure conceit—but because he insists that it wouldn't be worth the effort even if we could. Truth, suggests Nietzsche, is the hobgoblin of small minds.

This is a very dangerous way of thinking. But it serves as an excellent starting point in looking at the instrumentalist approach of China's Communist leaders toward what we sometimes flatteringly call "instant history": the daily torrent of words and images in newspapers, magazines, and television that comprises "the news."[1] The particularly Western notion of neutrality enshrined in both our scholastic and journalistic credos has never even been entertained among the handful of men and women who govern China nor, for that matter, among most of the media professionals who chafe under their rule. Sporadic public debate flared during the 1980s as to whose mouthpiece the media were—the people's or the Communist Party's (CCP)—but that it was a mouthpiece was never seriously called into question.

Looking at open and clandestine media manipulation by China's central leaders in terms of use and abuse has at least two advantages. First, it allows us to focus on what actually happened instead of what should have happened as measured against an alien concept of the proper function of the media in relation to political power.[2] We may abhor the cynical or even the well-intentioned manipulation of news, but we must at the same time suspend judgment long enough to decipher the internal logic of the Chinese media system and the motivation of the manipulators. Second, the categories of use and abuse help us to make distinctions between good and bad policy or, if one insists that *all* manipulation is offensive, between bad and worse. Hu Qiaomu anonymously wielding his poison pen to destroy personal and political enemies is surely more odious than Zhao Ziyang trying to weed out corrupt bureaucrats by orchestrating investigative reportage. But the press is no less an instrument in one case than the other. No CCP leader has ever expressed embarrassment in describing the media as a propaganda tool.

It is a commonplace, of course, that the Chinese press has served mainly as the "throat and tongue"—to use the official metaphor—of the CCP and its political whims. To the media's credit, in April and May 1989 the lap dog began to bite, breaking old taboos and expanding the parameters of acceptable public discourse. But even during this extraordinary moment, the press was operating roughly within the perceived guidelines of a particular faction, albeit a losing one, within the central leadership.

My aim in this chapter is to draw from my research and my experience as a journalist working in China for foreign newspapers from 1985 through the sad events of June 1989 to illustrate some of the means by which the print media—sometimes including the foreign press—were manipulated by political authority during the decade of reform, primarily the latter half. I assign my examples to three different categories of use and abuse: information gathering, factional struggle, and maintaining social order. Except where it overlaps with these groupings, I have omitted the most obvious function of the media—as a tool for national integration and mass indoctrination—precisely because it is so obvious and has been discussed in detail by others.[3]

KEEPING TABS ON THE MASSES

It is sometimes said that totalitarian (or would-be totalitarian) regimes are indifferent to public opinion. If the state has the means to control its citizens, dissatisfaction among the populace does not matter. If Pol Pot, at one extreme, can transform an entire country into "one big work camp" (his own boast), then surely a well-run or more benign police state in which people have enough to eat and a reasonable degree of mobility has no particular need to heed the masses.

Logical, but false. Any leadership needs to determine if policies work and are popular and, if not, why. Leaders of a Leninist regime are especially sensitive to the extent and nature of grassroots grumbling precisely because such disaffection finds no stable institutional outlet. Mao's "mass line" proved treacherously flexible: all too often those who dared speak critically suddenly found themselves beyond the pale, classified as "enemies of the people" and, therefore, unqualified to express themselves at all. One learns to keep quiet.

But how, then, does a Communist party in power determine the will of the masses, whether with the aim of fulfilling or thwarting it? In an atmosphere of intimidation, and in the absence of democratic institutions, how can it gather reliable information? When the people cannot choose between candidates or policy options, and when there are no public opinion polls to monitor their aspirations and frustrations, how does a notoriously isolated leadership feel the pulse of the nation?

Intraparty reports and investigative tours by senior officials are two crucial conduits for such information. But they are flawed. Mao Zedong and his colleagues basked in the illusion that the Great Leap Forward was a stunning success based on false reports from the field. In 1985 General Secretary Hu Yaobang publicly criticized a local official for creating a facade of prosperity in preparation for his visit, a form of deception foreign journalists sometimes think is reserved for them.

But the single most important source and channel of information from below is arguably the Chinese press. The media are not only the "mouth and tongue" of the Party, but also its eyes and ears. The reams of official pronouncements since the trauma of June 1989 on the politically correct role of the press have focused almost exclusively on the need for positive propaganda and enhanced party supervision. The stakes are high, as CCP General Secretary Jiang Zemin observed in a speech at a journalism "seminar" in November 1989: "The turmoil and rebellion ... shows how much harm and what tremendous losses will be caused if something goes wrong with media and propaganda work, if the propaganda machine is not in the hands of genuine Marxists."[4] But in another speech at the same event, then Propaganda Chief Li Ruihuan emphasized a different, seldom publicized function of the media. "News units should reflect problems to the higher authorities," he told the assembled editors and journalists, "by means of reference materials and briefings for internal use. *They should make every effort to ensure the accuracy of the materials and not adulterate them, lest they should provide erroneous information.*"[5] (emphasis added)

Comrade Ruihuan's exhortation is richly suggestive. It hints at the massive apparatus of China's internal media, an enormously influential parallel press operating within the same skin as open publications. And his unfamiliar admonishment to be accurate and avoid adulteration also reveals a different set of operating principles. But these separate requirements for the hidden press indicate not so much a cynical double standard as the conviction that the two kinds of media serve distinct purposes.

Li's speech raises another point, both intriguing and frustrating. If we are to judge the professionalism of Chinese journalists, it cannot be on the basis of their openly published work—written and edited under constraints that almost guarantee ideological distortions, vagueness, and inaccuracy—but on the basis of these internal publications. The problem, of course, is that we are not supposed to see them.

New China News Agency (Xinhua) has the largest and most articulated internal news system of any organization in China. Interviews with former and current Xinhua reporters and editors yield a complex map of these restricted-access publications, indicating both the intricacy of the network and the extreme secrecy of some of its parts.[6]

With a circulation of approximately seven to eight million and simultaneous printing in 25 cities, *Reference News* (*Cankao Xiaoxi*) is probably the most read newspaper in China.[7] To the attentive reader, it may serve as a guide to behind-the-scenes domestic policy debates and factional struggle. *Reference Information* (*Cankao Ziliao*) also publishes translated articles from abroad, but is far more comprehensive and restricted in circulation. Whereas *Cankao Xiaoxi* is distributed through the mail, *Cankao Ziliao* is delivered by Xinhua personnel.[8] Distributed at the section (*si*) level and above, *Cankao Ziliao* is marked "internal reference material" (*neibu cailiao*) and "handle carefully" (*juyi baocun*). A "secret" (*jimi*) designation was dropped in the early 1980s. Higher up on the totem pole is a three-ten page daily report called *Internal Reference* (*Neibu Cankao*). Marked "secret," printed in numbered editions, and distributed at the ministerial (*bu*) level, it contains sensitive reports, some translated from the foreign press and others written expressly for internal publication by domestic and international Xinhua journalists. We can be certain, for example, that *Neibu Cankao* has been chock full of information and analysis on the disintegration of the Soviet Union.[9] Finally, we reach the rumor-enshrouded strata in which documents circulate among virtually a handful of senior leaders. The most classified Xinhua reports are informally called "red head reference" (*"hong tou cankao"*). Sometimes handwritten to verify authenticity, these reports are issued on an occasional basis to as few as a dozen people. Excerpts from Roxanne Witke's book on Jiang Qing and a report on its publication, for example, were apparently the focus of one of the more sensational *"hong tou cankao"* of the mid-1970s.

Though Xinhua is the main source of classified information produced by a news organ, virtually every major newspaper puts out several internal reference publications as well. Among the most important—and least appreciated among China watchers—are compendia of letters to the editor circulated at a surprisingly high level of authority. The *People's Daily's* Masses Letters Department, for example, sifts through anywhere from 30,000 to 50,000 letters a month to compile a daily, eight-page digest. Based on my reading of several dozen issues from 1978 to 1988, it seems that the selection criteria are very nearly opposite to the ones used for letters actually printed in the newspaper: whereas published letters are usually vague, trivial, and polished, those chosen for internal reference are highly detailed, address specific cases of policy failure or criminal conduct, and, in keeping with Li Ruihuan's guidelines, are unadulterated.

It would be hard to exaggerate the importance of letters to the editor as a source of hard, albeit impressionistic, information for a leadership that cannot trust reports filtered through multiple layers of self-interested functionaries. (They also serve as a "court of last appeal" for otherwise powerless individuals unable to solve problems at the grassroots level, especially problems caused by local officials normally charged with handling such complaints.) The large staffs at major newspapers who process these letters have quasi-police authority and regularly send investigative teams into the field. One would hope that the system takes these often spine-chilling pleas seriously in order to serve justice, certainly a motivation for many rank-and-file journalists I have met. To the extent, however, that the leadership maintains the integrity of the letters to the editor forum, it is to keep an institutional window open to a reality desperately unfamiliar to them.

Some universities and research institutes working mainly under the aegis of Zhao Ziyang and his lieutenants began experimenting with opinion polls in the mid- and late-1980s. Pioneering efforts by a survey team in the China Research Institute for the Reform of the Economic System (CRIRES), for example, probed behavior and opinion in face-to-face questioning and anonymous questionnaires.[10] Such efforts, alas, were for the most part flawed. The polls were designed and used primarily to justify past and present policies, not to serve as sources of unbiased information. Thus, even if researchers were rapidly refining their techniques, a changeable political climate discouraged honest replies and, finally, scuttled such operations altogether.

At least one notorious survey widely publicized at the time, however, was right on the money. In 1988 a group from People's University asked 1,800 journalists whether they thought Chinese newspaper readers believed the domestic press. Only 1.1% of the journalists replied in the affirmative. This discouraging self-appraisal was echoed again during the demonstrations in April and May 1989 when marching journalists carried a banner reading, "Don't believe us—we tell lies."

THE MEDIA AS A WEAPON IN FACTIONAL WARFARE

Even as the media gather and cull information for leaders, they serve another—and often contradictory—function: as a battleground. The history of the CCP is a 70-year chronicle of factionalism, purges, counter-purges, and attempted coups. Survivors are, by definition, masters in the art of infighting. Official ideology, however, has never openly admitted the legitimate existence of competing factions within the Party. Described euphemistically as "different points of view," fundamental disagreements on questions of policy, ideology, or distribution of power have themselves been purged from political discourse as theoretically impossible. When conflicts become irreconcilable, they can be resolved only by vanquishing one of the competing groups, which is then inevitably revealed as having been an enemy of socialism from the outset.

Where does that leave the media? In the context of a raging, behind-the-scenes battle between political heavyweights, each with influence over segments of the press, how do editors and reporters manage to serve their patrons and hang on to their jobs while maintaining the illusion of unity?

Reading Between the Lines

About a year after I started reading the Chinese press on a daily basis in connection with my work as a journalist, I began to see the vague contours of an answer hovering somewhere between the lines on the printed page and did what any alert Chinese reader does: look for the subtext. I recall, for example, some of the portentous messages that jumped out at me from between the lines of the open press in the crucial months of February and March 1989.

George Bush met with Zhao Ziyang and other senior Chinese leaders during his visit to China in February 1989. The general atmosphere at the time of the meeting was tense for several reasons, at least two of which were readily apparent. A group of 31 Chinese intellectuals—some of them prominent establishment figures such as Xie Binxin and Su Shaozhi—had only a week earlier confounded the leadership by signing an unprecedented petition to Deng Xiaoping calling for the release of political prisoners, including Wei Jingsheng. By coincidence, I had a previously scheduled meeting with *People's Daily* editor Tan Wenrui the day after the petition was revealed in an impromptu press conference by two of the signatories. Tan, with whom I had spoken on several previous occasions, was unnaturally pale. His hands trembled slightly. "We don't know what to do," he muttered several times when I asked about the petition. "The situation is very serious."

The other source of tension was an extraordinarily clumsy attempt by President Bush to demonstrate his commitment to human rights. Under pressure from Congress to close the gap in his administration's double standard on the issue—tough on the Soviet Union, soft on China—someone advised the president to invite Fang Lizhi to dinner, a gesture inspired, perhaps, by Ronald Reagan's successful dissident banquet in Moscow. The problem, of course, was that Yang Shangkun and other very senior and very conservative leaders were among the invited guests. We all know what happened.[11]

The Bush-Zhao meeting took place hours before the soon-to-be infamous Texas barbecue got underway. When Xinhua released excerpts from Zhao's comments over the wire, I was dumbfounded. The General Secretary had told President Bush—and, in the process, attentive Chinese readers—that reformist policies and the political faction upholding them were in imminent danger. He suggested that the budding dissident movement, which he gently characterized as "impatient," was a threat to reform mainly because it gave Zhao's *real* political enemies an excuse to engineer his ouster. "Please don't undercut my tenuous position," he seemed to tell Bush, "with inflammatory and ill-conceived gestures toward human rights." So elliptical was Zhao's warning, however, that the message probably did not get through. And even if it did, by then the die was cast. Although rumors of Zhao's impending demise were rampant by the beginning of 1989, this episode was the first clarion signal from the source himself that he and his entourage were, to borrow one of Bush's less felicitous metaphors, in deep doodoo.

Soon after this incident I found another bit of Aesopian evidence pointing to a major rift within the leadership. In a long and eerily cryptic article in the February issue of *Qiushi*, the Party's leading theoretical journal, Li Keyin described what he called "the schemer." This is the type of person, he wrote, "who comes out of nowhere and at any time, brandishing swords and axes, and is by nature good at biding his time and sizing up the situation." Using Gang of Four member Yao Wenyuan as the sole example, the essay explained the schemer's *modus operandi*: "He knows only too well that, if he wants to advance by scheming against others, he cannot do so single-handedly, but must have 'patrons' and 'behind-the-scene-backers.' This requires 'calculation', too. Who is stronger? Who is weaker? Who can truly protect him and help him advance?"

Patron-client relationships give rise to factionalism, which is why the key words in the passage above are within inverted commas in the original. Factions, remember, officially do not exist within the CCP. Li's observations might seem elementary to any student of political science, but to find them expressed, however vaguely, in China's most important Party journal was startling indeed. Li reinforced his point by saying,

[w]e must not underestimate the presence of these people and their power. No one can guarantee that today we do not have people sharpening their swords and biding their time in the dark. When they calculate the time is ripe, they will come out, brandishing their swords and axes and working in concert with their allies. ... Their action will lead to large or small 'bloody incidents,' throwing people into bewilderment.

This analysis proved rather prophetic, even if in the manner of an astrologer's prediction.

When I read this for the first time, Zhao's words to Bush echoed in my ears. A few weeks later, just before the opening of the National People's Congress in March, a third alarm sounded in my head. Days before Premier Li Peng was to deliver his "Government Work Report," an annual state-of-the-union address, Zhao delivered a closed-door speech of his own that was widely excerpted in the Chinese press. When I got hold of a draft copy of Premier Li's Work Report, I understood the timing of Zhao's comments. The two speeches differed dramatically (by Chinese standards) in their assessment of achievements during the previous four years. In what became a code phrase for Zhao supporters, the Party General Secretary insisted in his wide-ranging evaluation that there had been "no major mistakes" during the first decade of reform. Li's speech was highly critical by comparison. Given the importance attached to official verdicts, this divergence was clearly significant, and Zhao's comments clearly infringed upon Li's authority.

The ever-present subtext, deliberately hidden or obscured in messages that could not be spelled out in so many characters, revealed itself in the Chinese press. The various subgenres of elliptical messaging is one of the ways media are used, like the puppets in a Javanese shadow play, to wage political warfare. Four such techniques of waging political warfare are: the use of historical analogies; the manipulation of foreign news; the manipulation of foreign news about China; and competing attempts to reorient and restructure the media itself.

Attack Through Analogy

During the Cultural Revolution, the press was a minefield of literary tropes and historical allusions, veiled and not-so-veiled vilifications of prominent leaders who could not be openly identified until, like Lin Biao, they had been defeated or banished.[12] The references to the Duke of Zhou (*Zhou Gong*) during the 1973–1974 campaign against Confucius were unmistakable broadsides against Premier Zhou Enlai. A year later the same device was used in denouncing the "capitulationist" Song Jiang in the novel *The Water Margin*, a clear jab at Vice Premier Deng Xiaoping. Many writers and leaders, from Lin Biao to "Li Yizhe,"[13] have invoked Qin

Shihuang to obliquely criticize Mao, a comparison the Great Helmsman apparently found flattering only when he made it himself. These are all examples of the ancient art of "attacking by innuendo" (*hansha sheying*), literally "holding sand and throwing shadows."

Character assassination by historical analogy was less frequently used during the 1980s, though it certainly remains in the general repertoire. Deng Xiaoping is often lampooned in the overseas Chinese press as a latter-day Empress Dowager, and one probably would not have to search far in the mainland press to find a suspicious reference to the failed monarch of the Qing Dynasty.

Manipulation of Foreign News

Factional sniping that appeared during the tumult of 1989 strongly manifested itself in the Chinese media's treatment of foreign news. On 21 May, the day after martial law was declared in Beijing and army personnel moved into the editorial offices of the *People's Daily*, the paper ran a page-one story on the resignation of the Italian Prime Minister. It did not take too much imagination to realize that Li Peng was the target. After all, since when was a change of government in Italy a front-page story? The very next day, a pro-Zhao *People's Daily* editor pointed out to me with obvious satisfaction a subheadline for a story about Hungary which read: "It is forbidden to use the army to resolve political problems."

These parting gestures were more of an embarrassment to Li Peng and his patrons than a serious challenge. But foreign news reports have also been used to bolster policy positions on domestic issues through the use of positive and negative example. The *World Economic Herald* excelled in this device, publishing articles on Jimmy Carter's 1978 civil service reform, the function of Japan's bureaucracy, and changes in the Hungarian government for promoting administrative reform at home.[14] Even more common was the strategic selection and editing of foreign news stories—which often carry more authority than Chinese reports—in *Reference News* and especially *Reference Information*.[15]

Manipulation of Foreign News About China

Some of the most carefully manipulated foreign reports, however, were those about China itself. They includes reports on the contract (*chengbao*) system—a centerpiece of reformist economic policy formally enshrined in documents and the media during the 13th Party Congress in October 1987. The catch-all term referred to a decentralization of authority that was designed to do for the urban sector what the return to family farming had done for rural China in the early 1980s. But by the beginning of the 1988, it was becoming all too clear—as least to me—that the urban contract system was not living up to expectations. Indeed, it was in disarray. Not only was it failing to invigorate state-run enterprises deeply mired in red ink, but it was being extended in ludicrous and irresponsible directions.

Trying to convince factory managers to shoulder greater responsibility for profit and production was one thing, but implementing a quota system in schools, hospitals, police stations, news rooms, art troupes, and even family planning offices was quite another. Teachers were being fined or awarded bonuses depending on how many of their students passed regional and national exams; journalists were paid by the column inch, and artists by the yard; sports schools were signing contracts guaranteeing bronze-, silver-, and gold-medal winners; and hospitals, suddenly responsible for profitability, instituted patient quotas and minimum-sale contracts with state-run pharmaceutical manufacturers.

An example that prompted me to devote one of my weekly columns in the *South China Morning Post* to this subject encapsulated the absurdity. A worker in a small Henan city, Li Xinwen, found himself in possession of a stolen bicycle after thwarting an attempted robbery. But when he went to the local constable to complete his good deed, he was turned away. "We don't handle that sort of thing," he was told. Incredulous, Mr. Li tried two other neighborhood police stations, meeting each time with the same result. Finally he managed to coax an explanation from a sympathetic cop for such irrational behavior. "We have signed contracts to maintain the number of criminal incidents in our area below a certain threshold," came the reply. "If we take the stolen bike, we might exceed our quota for the month and lose part of our bonus."

Privately, several Chinese policy analysts expressed concern about the social and economic consequences of this policy. Moreover, although the press had become more adventuresome in airing debate on crucial issues of the day, nary a critical word on the contract system found its way into print. A disgusted senior policy adviser told me, "We have a saying now, 'Like the tiger's ass, there are two things we dare not touch these days: Deng Xiaoping's *mao* and Zhao Ziyang's *bao*.'"[16]

About a week after my extremely mocking column appeared in print, *Reference News* picked it up.[17] Although this was not the first time one of my stories had been translated—many foreign correspondents in Beijing are thus honored at one time or another—it led the page and was largely intact, except for the crack about the tiger's ass.

Months went by, and the Chinese press continued to gush enthusiastically about the contract system's curative powers. I was not the only one annoyed. Indeed, the well-placed policy adviser who had expressed such strong misgivings in our earlier conversations got back in touch. A critic of Zhao's economic policies, he had become frustrated trying to air his views, even behind closed doors. He had a proposition for me. "Let's talk about this," he said. "My point of view has been silenced. But if you write a well-reasoned article on the problems with the contract system, it will be translated and published internally." I shared his assessment on the issues, but felt uneasy. I told him I could not make any promises. Then we had a long chat.

The result was a second column in August. Sure enough, an abridged version quickly showed up in *Reference News*.[18] But it also later appeared in the more influential *Reference Information* precisely at the time that Zhao was being stripped of his economic decision-making authority at the annual policy summit-by-the-seaside at Beidaihe. My translated and—thanks to the Chinese policy analyst—well-informed column was no doubt good ammunition for conservative snipers. It is strange and not a little unsettling to think that I contributed, even if in an infinitesimally small way, to some larger scheme to undo Zhao Ziyang's power.

STRUGGLE TO RESTRUCTURE THE MEDIA

The three ways outlined thus far in which the media are used in factional warfare—attack through analogy, manipulation of foreign news, and manipulation of translated reports on China—are all peripheral to the main event: the struggle to define and reorganize the media themselves in the service of political ends. One of the best barometers of factional struggle during the 1980s was the ten-year tussle over the drafting of China's ill-fated press law.[19] Not only did this unusually open policy debate mirror deep rifts within the leadership, it revealed that control of the media itself had become crucial in the competition for political power.

The top tier of the CCP has always been rife with divisions and rivalries, some more divisive than others. If infighting has been the constant, however, its relation to the media has taken several distinct forms since 1949. Before the Cultural Revolution most internal leadership conflicts were resolved—whether through consensus, intimidation or purges—before the results were presented to the public. The media fulfilled their function as a mouthpiece by broadcasting the information precisely as dictated by the Party's Propaganda Department. If the press contradicted itself from one month to the next, it was generally not because competing factions within the media represented competing patrons, but because the center had collectively changed its mind.[20]

During the Cultural Revolution, factionalism became so intense that it shattered the pretense of unity. Mao Zedong short-circuited the Party hierarchy and reached out directly through the *People's Daily* to unleash a torrent of violence against his one-time colleagues. "Bomb the Headquarters!," he exhorted, and 40 million teenage revolutionaries followed his command. After Mao and his wife, Jiang Qing, consolidated their hold over the national press, virtually all of the senior leaders who are still in power today, including Deng, lost access to the media. Being locked out was a powerful lesson. The press, they learned, could be used as a weapon in political warfare, not just as a loudspeaker to announce the outcome of hidden conflicts. But one consistency remained: even in the chaos of near civil war, the media reliably presented the views of whichever faction controlled their resources at the moment. While now a bludgeon as well as a vessel, it had no real independence.

When China emerged in the late 1970s from the maelstrom of Mao's errant experiment, Deng tried to restore the press and the newly important medium of television to their original function. The CCP was reunified, and so too, he thought, should be the media. For a while it worked. But then a strange thing began to happen: slowly, fitfully, the media began to develop a voice of its own.

Several forces conspired to make that happen. A new generation of ex-Red Guards—steeped in a tradition of rebellion and disdain for authority—were no longer willing to emulate model-hero Lei Feng and become "rustless screws in the wheel of socialism." This was also the attitude among the older generation of intellectuals whom Deng recalled from 20 years of exile to assume key positions within the media and academe. While many of these former "rightists" rejoined the Party eagerly, it was on the assumption that real political change was finally on the agenda. It did not take long for them to be disappointed. The "open door" soon released a flood of strange and intoxicating information about the power of the media in open societies, the right to free speech, and the precepts of democracy. These seemed, moreover, to resonate with Deng's new insistence of rule by law rather than by fiat. China's Constitution, he insisted, should have more weight that the paper it was written on.

And so began the discussion—and then the debate—on a press law; a statute that would define the rights and duties of journalists, permissible forms of ownership and, most crucially, the role of the CCP. Somehow it was acknowledged that there should be such a law, but agreement as to its contents remained elusive.

Indeed, Deng and his even more ideologically conservative cohorts kept jerking the press back toward the standards of what they saw as the "golden age" of Chinese socialism, the 1950s. Both major spasms of Marxist orthodoxy during the 1980s—the campaigns against "spiritual pollution" and "bourgeois liberalization"—targeted people in the media. *People's Daily* editor Wang Ruoshui was targeted in the former and folk-hero journalist Liu Binyan in the latter. But the most chilling reminder of the media's continuing subservience, made all the more so by its timing and its messenger, came during the high-water mark of the entire reform effort. Hu Yaobang, whose fatal heart-attack during a Politburo meeting sparked the crescendo of demonstrations leading to 4 June, is remembered by Chinese intellectuals—rightly or wrongly—as a champion of openness. When Hu, therefore, as General Secretary delivered a key speech in February 1985 (two years before he was sacked) unambiguously affirming the media's role as the "throat and tongue" of the CCP, it was doubly disheartening.[21]

But if Hu spoke the part, the script was unmistakably written by Deng. It revealed both his shrewdness and the fault line in his reformist vision. For many Chinese, *glasnost* in the Soviet Union was an inspiration; for Deng, it was a caution and a vindication of his long-standing reform strategy: Free the economy, but keep a tight rein on political power. Gorbachev's undoing suggests that Deng's survival instincts were correct. Deng did not anticipate, however, that the media and other institutions in society would develop their own institutional momentum. Even after the press revolt in spring 1989, Deng spoke of the "black hands" of enemy factions manipulating behind the scene. To a certain extent, as I will illustrate, Zhao Ziyang did use the media to exercise and expand his political power. But by the time Zhao fell from grace, the press had also—for the first time—developed interests of its own.

Despite these constant reminders that the press was on a short leash, however, open debate about the press law remained revealingly pointed until 1989. True, compared with the Soviet Union, where former political prisoners were selling anti-Party gazettes on street corners, the parameters of discussion were rather narrow. But compared with what came before and after, the in-print demands for a free press, private ownership of newspapers, and even a Chinese freedom of information act were pretty heady stuff.

The center continued to emit decidedly mixed signals as to the media's proper role in politics and society. The behind-the-scenes conflicts producing this dissonance came into sharper focus immediately before and after the 13th CCP Congress in October 1987, when Zhao Ziyang, who had replaced Hu as Party head, unveiled arguably the first significant change in media policy since the 1950s. The press, announced Zhao, was henceforth to perform three main functions: to oversee public officials, to report on important events, and to reflect debate on key policy issues. While certainly modest goals by Western standards, his guidelines were a radical departure from the traditional "mouthpiece" function. This was China's answer to glasnost, and Zhao called it *toumingdu*, or transparency. For reform-minded journalists and editors, Zhao's speech was a call to arms. For the entrenched Party bureaucrats and ideologues they were trying to unseat, it was a declaration of war.

Holding that the expansion of the Chinese media's powers was an end as well as a means, a benchmark of political reform as well as a tool of political struggle, simply acknowledges that when politics and power overlap, so too do principle and self-interest. Zhao's revised press guidelines advanced the democratic ideals of open and accountable government even as they served—at least in the short term—his factional agenda. Trying to tease these two impulses apart will not tell us whether Zhao was a failed hero or a failed schemer (we can never know his particular mix of motives), but it may help us assess the impact of the changes he set in motion.

Partly orchestrated from above and partly springing from spontaneous editorial enthusiasm, the 1987 reforms broadened and deepened the acceptable range of reportable topics, encouraged a far more active and critical role than had ever been openly sanctioned, and set in motion a self-reinforcing momentum against entrenched bureaucratic interests. Even otherwise trivial "news," when carefully calibrated, could pack a symbolic wallop. A May 1988 photograph of a powerful provincial party boss being led away in handcuffs because he had roughed up a highway toll collector trying to do her job, for example, created a minor sensation throughout the country.[22] Seldom had a senior cadre been arrested for the kind of belligerent arrogance that had virtually become the prerogative of officialdom, and never had one been thus humiliated on television and the front page. Equally unprecedented was another incident widely reported that month in which the general manager of a state-run factory in Henan "fired" his plant's Communist Party secretary.[23] The first story was designed to encourage whistle-blowers and intimidate abusive cadres, the second to both signal and accelerate the Party's diminishing role in economic affairs. Each had a friendly and a hostile audience. So clear was the message in the stories, they might as well have been signed editorials.

Zhao and his supporters also pursued their political aims indirectly through investigative reporting and the strategic placement of reform-minded personnel in key national and provincial media, men and women such as Zhang Shanju, a 32-year-old journalist parachuted behind "enemy lines" into the conservative stronghold of Guiyang to assume the page-one editorship of the *Guizhou Daily*. During his brief tenure from mid-1987 to June 1989, Zhang engineered anti-corruption reporting and instituted a telephone "complaint hotline" in his battle against local potentates and crooked cadres.

Not only were provincial Party dailies and national papers such as the *Legal Daily*, the *China Youth Daily* and the *People's Daily* suddenly chock-full of revealing examples of official malfeasance, many of these cases—in a sharp departure from established practice—were "unresolved" at the time of publication. Prior to 1987 the few significant exposés of cadre misconduct that found their way into print were invariably vetted internally beforehand, and then creatively tailored and sanitized to present the Party in a positive light. This "traditional" way of disciplining errant officials conformed to the separate functions of open and internal media reaffirmed by Li Ruihuan in the wake of June 1989: Wash dirty linen behind closed doors before hanging it up to dry.

Even during the short-lived period of relative press freedom, elements within the leadership sought to exert a restraining influence. The Press and Publications Administration was born out of the conservative backlash in January 1987 that ousted Hu Yaobang and pilloried Fang Lizhi and Liu Binyan. The Administration's director, Du Daozheng, was charged with the ideological housecleaning of every one of the thousands of newspapers and magazines in China. He was also given a leading role in the drafting of the press law, ensuring a gridlock with more liberal drafters such as former *People's Daily* editor Hu Jiwei. In April 1988 Du explained to a roomful of domestic and Hong Kong journalists the dangers of dealing with Party matters in the press. Serious "mistakes" committed by Party members are best reported in internal, closed circulation journals, he said, "just in case there are errors in the investigation."

But by the mid-1980s the old formula no longer worked.[24] China's legions of venal functionaries had long since become adept in the art of blunting or derailing closed-door investigations. "Quite a large number of bureaucrats are not afraid of internal criticism," wrote freedom of the press advocate Hu Jiwei in May 1989. "They are only afraid of criticism in the press. They are not afraid of going to court, but afraid of appearing on television."[25] Once their names were in print, Hu argued, it was much harder for corrupt officials to manipulate the *guanxi wang*, or "relations net(work)," that might otherwise shield them from censure or prosecution.

Old guard ideologues and infixed functionaries thus joined forces in resisting Zhao's reforms. The former feared a press independent of Party control, the latter a press with investigative teeth. The vehemence of their counterattack suggests both that reform-oriented salvos hit their mark and that Zhao's policies were politically directed. Even before conservatives regained control of the national media with the declaration of martial law on 20 May 1989, those threatened by a more aggressive press fought back.

Sometimes the results of the struggle were ludicrous, as in the case of Wu Wei city in Gansu Province. When Wu Wei delegates to the District People's Congress met in March 1988, the local leadership—no doubt mindful of shifting political winds in Beijing—asked the 14 representatives to speak their minds. "Talk from the heart, tell us the truth," encouraged District Vice-head Liu Shengrong. "We don't want to hear how great everything is—if you have any complaints … don't be afraid to speak frankly." And so they did. The next morning the local Party Secretary read a summary of the unusually critical meeting on the front page of the *Wu Wei Daily*. Within an hour, eight journalists were on the street with a mission: repossess each and every one of the 10,000 issues of the 16 March edition of the *Wu Wei Daily*. (They only recovered about 110.)

Back in Guiyang, Zhang Shanju faced opposition from entrenched cadres who had, he said, adopted the "three not afraids" motto: Don't be afraid if your thinking differs from the (reform-minded) Central Committee, don't be afraid to condemn what the central government calls "socialism" and "capitalism," and don't be afraid of investigations launched from Beijing. Elsewhere, Zhao's enemies overcame their distrust of an increasingly vocal judiciary and filed lawsuits against newspapers and individual journalists who had offended their Leninist sensibilities.[26]

While conservative opposition was muted before June 1989, the post-massacre press provides a convenient index of the articles and television programs that had most raised conservative hackles. Even three years later Party hacks continued to churn out a steady stream of turgid, vituperative attacks against targets as varied as the pro-Zhao television documentary *River Elegy*, the journalistic writings of the key proponents of profound political reform, and even a *People's Daily* article from August 1988 describing how Marxist educators were upbraided in a meeting with young entrepreneurs in Shekou, a special economic zone. Once again, the weed-killers have set to work.

MANIPULATING "PRESS FREEDOM"—1989

The spring of 1989 was in many ways an exception to the rule, when editors and journalists not only exerted a new-found independence in reporting on events around them, but also joined in the public outcry for democracy and against official corruption. Although impugning the motives or courage of most of the Chinese media workers who took a stand during that time, we must recognize the extent to which the explosion of "press freedom" was politically guided and manipulated by Zhao Ziyang and his allies. Three incidents from the crucial ten days prior to the declaration of martial law highlight the partisan role of the media in the political struggle that was tearing the leadership apart.

The effect of a special *People's Daily* supplement (*Renmin Ribao (haowai)*) on 19 May in drumming up public sympathy for a politically-doomed Zhao has been described elsewhere.[27] Whereas the General Secretary had been attacked along with Li Peng and Deng Xiaoping in public demonstrations earlier that month, the supplement—which claimed that Zhao had lobbied for political reform against his colleagues in a series of Communist Party Standing Committee meetings—was instrumental in orchestrating a groundswell of popular support. Astute Chinese had already inferred from media coverage that Zhao was engaged in a political showdown with Deng, as revealed by Zhao's extraordinary televised 16 May meeting with Mikhail Gorbachev in which Zhao turned abruptly toward the camera and, in effect, blamed China's problems on the aging patriarch.[28]

Equally revealing of the media's role in helping Zhao's cause was a scantly publicized meeting on 11 May between Hu Qili—Zhao's only political ally on the five-man Standing Committee, and a reluctant one at that—and the staff of the *China Youth News*. A terse Xinhua bulletin reported the next day that the meeting had taken place, but provided no details. It noted only that Hu, in charge of propaganda work, "listened to opinions raised by the participants," and that Beijing journalists had signed a petition a few days earlier calling for a dialogue with Party and government officials.

Hu, it turns out, did more than listen. Apparently unaware that his words were being recorded, saying, "I would not dare come if I thought this would be reported," Hu made a speech. In sharp contrast to his public pronouncements on the media, which toed the conservative line laid down in the fall of 1988, Hu urged the assembled journalists to be bold. "Press reform is an important part of our political reform," he said. "We have reached the stage where press reform can no longer wait." Changes since the watershed 13th Party Congress, he continued, were "far from enough."

In light of the ongoing demonstrations and the continuing occupation of Tiananmen Square by tens of thousands of students, these were incendiary remarks. His assignment was no doubt to throw water on editors and journalists who day by day were growing more outspoken in their coverage of events, but he added fuel to the fire instead. "We reported the demonstrations, didn't we? And nothing bad happened," he said at one point, putting himself on the side of the journalists. "Therefore more openness is good. ... Some say that since we have the [April 26] editorial [in which Deng condemned protesting students], then we should crack down. How could we? ... The students actions are not beyond the pale."

One could argue, of course, that Hu Qili was simply trying to disarm the editors and journalists by bringing them within the fold. But which fold? Any ambiguity as to whose interests Hu represented was dispelled when he put his comments in the context of the sharpening power struggle that had already split the leadership. "The situation is still developing and there are always two possible results: good or bad," he said with calculated vagueness. "With so momentous an event as this, it would be very strange if no one tried to make use of it, *and not all who want to make use of it are bad people.''* (emphasis added) Hu could not have made his appeal any clearer if he had been a recruiting agent for Zhao's personal army. It was a daring political gamble, and it failed.

ABUSING THE MEDIA TO MAINTAIN SOCIAL ORDER

If all of the means by which Chinese leaders manipulate the media illustrated thus far have hovered somewhere between use and abuse, there is another that is unequivocally heinous. Like most societies lacking an independent judiciary and enforceable laws guaranteeing basic rights, China often uses the media to broadcast the execution of alleged criminals in order to enforce social order. Deterrence of would-be offenders is an acceptable consideration in the sentencing of criminals even in nations with strong legal systems. But in China, "killing the chickens to scare the monkeys"—or, more often, to scare other chickens—is often carried out with little regard to guilt or innocence and even less regard as to whether the punishment fits the crime. Indeed, in some cases the sole purpose of taking human life is to make an editorial point.

One particularly egregious example says it all, though there are thousands more to choose from. Nineteen ninety was a nerve-wracking year for Chinese leaders as they attempted to repair the political damage caused at home and abroad by their brutal suppression of the previous year's anti-government protests. Much of their energy was focused on preparing for the high-profile Asian Games, which China was to host for the first time in the fall. Under the direction of the central government, Beijing authorities completed several large-scale construction projects, launched a major urban "beautification" campaign, and imposed strict order on the capital.

As part of this last objective local officials decided to make an example of three hapless delinquents who had the great misfortune to be in the wrong place at the wrong time. "Lately, in order to create a stable and harmonious social climate in the run-up to the Asian Games, severe punishments have been inflicted on those who upset the stability of the capital," explained the *Beijing Evening News* in announcing the execution of the three men. Their crimes? They were convicted on one count each of robbery and petty larceny during the turbulent spring of 1989, offenses which, in other circumstances, would have netted them a year or two in a labor-reform camp.

At least 45 workers are known to have been executed because of their role in the demonstrations and riots, all of them very publicly. One wonders, though, whether these cautionary killings will come back to haunt the executioners. Can anyone who saw it ever forget the expression of contemptuous defiance on the face of Yan Xuerong as he was sentenced, on national television, by a Shanghai court to be shot the following day? It is a look that will not die.

NOTES

1. Interestingly, both "news" and "history" carry the same dual meaning: an actual sequence or collection of events, on the one hand, and the written record of those events, on the other.

2. This does not suggest that the Western ideal of impartiality—rejected *ipso facto* by the ideology of state socialism as either self-deception or a bourgeois ruse—is matched in reality. As China's official ideologists gleefully point out, the collection, compilation, and distribution of news in open societies is subject to many potentially distorting pressures, including the bottom line, advertisers, corporate sponsors, government, and editorial bias. Still, the advantages over other media environments remain huge: for the resourceful reader, diversity; for the reporter or editor, varied employment options.

3. A small but woolly literature in American political science on communication in totalitarian societies—mainly the Soviet Union and China—is largely concerned with top-down questions of mass mobilization, political indoctrination, and national integration. For a summary, see Ithiel de Sola Pool, "Communication in Totalitarian Societies," in Ithiel De Sola Pool and Wilbur Schramm (eds.), *Handbook of Communication* (Chicago: Rand McNally, 1973).

4. "Jiang Zemin Gives Speech on Mass Media Work," Xinhua (Chinese), 29 Nov. 1989. An abridged version of the speech was published as "Several Questions Concerning Journalistic Work—An Outline of a Speech at the Study Class of Journalistic Work," *Qiushi (Seeking Truth)*, no. 3 (Mar. 1990).

5. "'Uphold the Principle of Giving Prominence to Positive Propaganda' Speech by Li Ruihuan at the 25 November 1989 Seminar on Journalism," Xinhua (Chinese), 2 Mar. 1990.

6. My outline of internal publications is based primarily on interviews with former Xinhua reporters and editors currently residing in the United States. The Hong Kong monthly *Kaifang (Openness)* offers a somewhat different taxonomy: (1) *Internal Reference (Nei Cankao*, also called *Da Cankao*)—published twice weekly, distributed at county/section (*xian/ke*) level and above; (2) *Selection of Internal Reference (Neican Xuanbian)*—a policy oriented weekly, distributed at section level and above; (3) *Final Proofs of Domestic Trends (Guonei Dongtai Qingyang)*—a loose-leaf, 40-100 pages per day, with a highly restricted circulation; (4) *Supplemental Final Proofs (Qingyang Fuyue)*—occasional reports, mainly for the State Council, Politburo, and Ministries; (5) *Final Proofs of Trends (Dongtai Qingyang)*—compiled from reports by Xinhua's 90-plus foreign bureaus covering foreign news and foreign reports on China and distributed at ministerial and provincial leadership levels; (6) *International Internal News (Guoji Neican)*—a digest of international news with a wider circulation than *Dongtai Qingyang*; (7) *Internal Reference Information (Cankao Ziliao)*—a twice daily compilation of foreign and international news which is more comprehensive than *Cankao Xiaoxi*; (8) *Internal Reference Reports (Baodao Cankao)*—a compilation of internal speeches and informal statements by senior leaders which

provides guidelines for journalists. See also Jennifer Grant, "Internal Reporting by Investigative Journalists in China and its Influence on Government Policy," *Gazette* 41, no. 1 (1988).

7. Officially, it is for the eyes of Party members and cadres only, but it has been easily available in most major cities since the 1980s. As early as 1982, for example, a copy was routinely posted on the bulletin board of the foreign students' dormitory at Beijing University. A four-page daily in tabloid format, it is a digest of translated news items from around the world which devotes a half-page in every issue to foreign reports about China. Jorg-Meinhard Rudolf, "*Cankao-Xiaoxi*—Foreign News in the Propaganda System of the People's Republic of China," *Occasional Papers/Reprints Series in Contemporary Asian Studies*, no. 6 (1984).

8. On each of my occasional visits to the editorial offices of the *People's Daily* in 1988, several copies were always visible on the desks of senior staff. Until recently, it was published twice daily in a notebook format of 40–70 pages, but in 1990 publication was cut back to one edition per day.

9. Xinhua's *International Internal Reference*, for example, published a book length digest of reports by Xinhua reporters on Hungary and Poland in October 1989, and one entitled "The Current Situation in the Soviet Union" in June 1991.

10. It is no coincidence that the former head of CRIRES's survey unit, Meng Fanhua, had logged nearly 20 years in the Masses Letters Department at the *People's Daily*.

11. The U.S. Embassy staff seemed oblivious to an inevitable public relations disaster. "I guess the Chinese aren't too happy that Fang is coming to dinner," quipped one press attaché gleefully on the day on the banquet, as if the Bush administration had handled a delicate situation masterfully.

12. I am grateful to Geremie Barmé of Australian National University for pointing out many of the following examples.

13. Li Yizhi is the collective pen name of three former red guards who wrote a 20,000-character "big character poster" (*dazibao*) in 1974 attacking what had not yet been dubbed the Gang of Four and calling for democratic reforms. Posted in public, the fact that it was allowed to stay up for several days showed that the authors enjoyed the backing of an opposition faction.

14. Several of these examples were noted in Li Cheng and Lynn T. White III, "China's Technocratic Movement and the *World Economic Herald*," (Draft manuscript, Princeton University, 1990).

15. Tu Weiming, "Cultural China: The Periphery as the Center," *Dædalus* 120, no. 2 (Spring 1991).

16. *Mao* means "cat", and refers to Deng's dictum: "It doesn't matter whether the cat is black or white, as long as it catches mice." *Bao*, a shortened form of *baocheng*, refers to the contract system.

17. Marlowe Hood, "Beijing's Contract System Keeps the Competitive Spirit Flowing," *South China Morning Post*, 27 Mar. 1988; "Xianggang *Nan Hua Zao Bao* Ping Zhongguo Tuichang Chengbaozhi: Fei Shengchan Bumen Gao Chengbao 'Yi Hong Er Qi' Houguo Kanyu" ("Hong Kong's *South China Morning Post* Criticizes China's Popularization of the Contract System: Non-Productive Sectors Rushing Headlong Toward Implementation of the Contract System is a Cause for Concern,") *Reference News*, 3 Apr. 1988.

18. Marlowe Hood, "The Contract System Fails to Live Up to Expectations," *South China Morning Post*, 21 Aug. 1988; "Xianggang *Nan Hua Zao Bao* Shuo: Chengbaozhi Wei Neng Shoudao Yuqi Xiaoguo You Si De Yuanyin" ("Hong Kong's *South China Morning Post Says*: 'Four Major Reasons the Contract System Has Failed to Live Up to Expectations',") *Reference News*, 1 September 1988.

19. Never passed, the draft law was shelved after ideological conservatives consolidated control of the propaganda bureaucracy in June 1989. For a discussion of the complicated policy debates centered on the press law, see Judy Polumbaum, "The Tribulations of China's Journalists After a Decade of Reform," in Chin-Chuan Lee (ed.), *Voices of China: The Interplay of Politics and Journalism* (New York: Guilford Press, 1990). See also Marlowe Hood, "Fight for a Free Press," *South China Morning Post*, 24 Apr. 1988, p. 4; Hu Jiwei, "On the Freedom to Discuss 'Freedom of the Press'," in China Journalism Study Association (ed.), *Collected Essays on Freedom on the Press* (*Xinwen Ziyou Lunyi*) (Shanghai: Wenhui Press, 1988).

20. Abrupt changes in agricultural policy from 1955 through the beginning of the Great Leap Forward in 1958, for example, were chronicled in the media with little variation at any given time and without reference to policy debates at the top. One inferred internal conflicts by hermeneutic analysis of important speeches rather than uncovering differences within a nearly uniform press. See Parris H. Chang, *Power and Policy in China* (College Park, PA: Pennsylvania State University Press, 1978).

21. Hu Yaobang, "On the Party's Journalism Work" (Speech delivered to the CCP Central Committee Secretariat, 8 February 1985). The speech was published in the *People's Daily* on 14 Apr. 1985.

22. Marlowe Hood, "Passions Roused at Sight of Official in Handcuffs," *South China Morning Post*, 25 May 1988.

23. Marlowe Hood, "Factory Manager Fires Party Leader," *South China Morning Post*, 27 May 1988.

24. Intraparty discipline had always been a problem precisely because inspection mechanisms were so susceptible to corruption in the absence of independent and publicly accountable monitors. But by the mid-1980s institutional checks against malfeasance had broken down almost entirely.

25. Hu Jiwei, "There Will Be No Genuine Stability Without Press Freedom," *World Economic Herald*, 8 May 1989, p. 3.

26. See, for example, a two part article in the *Legal Daily* detailing a lawsuit brought against the newspaper by an allegedly corrupt county court that had been the target of an earlier investigation. "Guanyu 'Waiqu Shishi, Cuogai Zonghe Cailiao' Wenti ("On the Problem of 'Distorting Facts and Tampering with Summation Materials',") *Legal Daily*, 10 Aug. 1988. Investigative journalist Liu Binyan was also the object of several unsuccessful libel suits.

27. Marlowe Hood, "Zhao Hero of Hour as Crisis Near Flashpoint," *South China Morning Post*, 21 May 1989.

28. In the meeting, Zhao suddenly turned to the camera and "revealed for the first time that a decision was made at the first plenum of the 13th Party Central Committee to the effect that Deng's guidance is still needed in dealing with most important issues." "Zhao Ziyang Meets Gorbachev," Xinhua, 16 May 1989.

4

CHINA'S LEGITIMACY CRISIS:
THE CENTRAL ROLE OF INFORMATION

Carol Lee Hamrin

The relationship between state and society in the People's Republic of China was substantially altered in the 1980s. Domestic reform and openness to the outside world marked this development. Chinese leaders under Deng Xiaoping entered the 1980s determined to regain the cooperation of the educated elite, "open up" the economy and society, and obtain foreign economic resources. They used reform measures in an attempt to reinforce the symbolic legitimacy and operational authority of the party-state. Despite having accomplished an economic miracle through these well-chosen means, the Communist regime exited the decade with a mega-crisis of legitimacy and much weakened authority. The following analysis of the dynamics involved in this irony of historical proportions, and what it portends for China's future, points to the central importance of information.[1]

Bitterness resulting from Maoist political campaigns and an alienation arising from revelations of economic advances outside China made ideological promises of a Communist utopia through infallible Party leadership untenable even before the death of Mao Zedong. With Mao gone and only a few aging revolutionary founders left, the Chinese Communist Party (CCP) had to replace its charismatic claim to legitimacy as the leader of national revolution by performance criteria better suited to the modern age—economic development and international status.

Beginning in 1978, post-Mao leaders felt compelled by an overwhelming sense of crisis to repudiate major tenets of the Mao era and set off in new policy directions in order to stem the hemorrhaging of Party legitimacy. They sought to modify the basic system just enough to preserve it. There was some recognition of the importance of justice; thousands who had been imprisoned or discriminated against since the late 1950s obtained redress and greater freedom of lifestyle was allowed. But the Party focused on decentralization and marketization measures needed to promote rapid economic growth and raise the standard of living. Over time, these modifications of the Maoist system led to other changes and began to take on a life of their own, creating unintended and escalating demands for greater prosperity and more freedom, including freedom of information.

The CCP hoped rapid economic growth would strengthen its legitimacy in a "vertical" comparison with the historical past. But by late in the 1980s, the speed and direction of political change in China's two major "horizontal" comparative referents for legitimacy—other socialist countries and other Chinese societies in Asia—fueled new expectations and demands within the urban elite for freedom and social justice. The hurricane of the post-industrial revolution, fed by creative use of intellectual resources (information and skills in processing information), hit the cities of the Chinese coast with full-gale force, introducing new universal and nonmaterialistic values.

The domestic and international media and communication conveyed through modern means by those involved in cultural and educational exchange programs, tourism, and business played a central role in bringing about this dramatic revolution of urban elite expectations. The powerful but unplanned and unexpected corrosive effect of information on regime legitimacy was the natural consequence of the necessary means forced on the CCP to accomplish its economic performance goals—exposure of the elite to new ideas and skills and their inclusion in decision-making. These steps amounted to an undeclared but profound political reform in the relationship between state and society.

ECONOMIC REFORM FOSTERS
A DEPENDENCE ON INFORMATION

Deng Xiaoping's reform program began in mid-1978 with an assault on ideological strictures on thought and information. The old-style propaganda system, which functioned as a self-legitimation process, was dependent on limiting sources of information and modes of thinking to those endorsed by the state. The resulting intellectual stagnation denied the regime itself key resources for economic development—ideas and skills for economic planning and implementation. By the time of Mao's death, the leadership was totally dependent on a rigid public propaganda system of official elites and a conspiratorial internal informant system.[2] Neither system could effectively assess the regime's policy problems and options.

Deng Xiaoping's campaign to "emancipate the mind" and "seek truth from facts" was intended to harness intellectual resources on behalf of the regime. It created the foundation for all the other reforms, economic and political. The PRC stopped jamming foreign broadcasts (both governmental, such as VOA and BBC, and private, such as religious broadcasts); allowed the import and circulation of foreign publications; sent Chinese students, scholars, and officials abroad in search of new ideas to assist in China's economic development; and began to widen the circle of policy research and decision-making to include the educated elite and foreign actors.

This change was first evident in the economic and science spheres; the urgent imperative of economic development forced leaders to allow the absorption and application of vast bodies of information on developmental economics and modern technological advances. This openness, however, was gradually extended to other areas as the social sciences were reconstituted and professional organizations and exchanges were set up in a wide range of fields during the 1980s. While there always remained some "taboo" areas of exploration, the parameters for research and publication kept expanding and the criteria for acceptance became increasingly scientific rather than ideological.

This process began in early 1979 when four high-level policy research groups were set up with a mandate to identify the reasons for China's past economic failures and devise new economic plans. These groups covered technology transfer, structural readjustment, economic theory, and economic system reform. A number of task forces subordinate to the four groups addressed special problems, including price reform, urban collective enterprises, population projections to the year 2000, and alternative economic models.[3] In late 1980 an important step toward political reform was accomplished when this research effort was moved from the Party's propaganda system to its economic system under the control of newly-appointed Premier Zhao Ziyang. From this point the government began to gain power and influence relative to the Party for the first time since the mid-1950s.

The prestigious members of these groups were long-time economic officials and researchers well known to each other, each with multiple personal and official ties in the main economic bureaucracy. Many had been part of an informal, small-scale economic policy discussion group which had met biweekly from 1956 to 1966. One might view them as China's own "thaw generation," which included a number of prominent victims of the 1957 Anti-Rightist Movement.[4]

Hu Yaobang and Zhao Ziyang, representing a new generation of leaders who had joined the CCP out of nationalist rather than ideological commitment during World War II, proved willing and able to use these offi-

cials and specialists to promote their reform agenda. Zhao's high evaluation of the policy role of specialists was first reflected during his tenure in
Sichuan, when he personally directed the work of the provincial academy
of social sciences, headed its economic research institute, and insisted on
sitting in the audience rather than on the podium to learn from visiting
economist Sun Yefang. Zhao's encouragement of bold research and experimentation by specialists became a hallmark of his leadership style.[5]

As Chinese researchers scrambled to catch up with changes in international thought they had missed during their 15-year isolation, they not
only read voraciously, but also traveled abroad and invited foreign scholars to visit and lecture in China. Very quickly, specialists began to look beyond the experiences of Eastern Europe. Political economists like Yu
Guangyuan, Liu Guoguang, and Su Shaozhi visited Hungary in 1979; in
1980 Zhu Rongji and other officials from the Import-Export Commission
traveled to foreign economic development zones in Southeast Asia, Ire-
land, and Sri Lanka.[6]

Orthodox Marxist concepts and language gave way to the more scientific language of Western literature on alternative development strategies.
This, too, led to an important step in political reform—approval of a new
institute and related activities to refurbish Marxism-Leninism by "updating" its categories of thought and its methodology. This shift removed the
protective status of official dogma and exposed the ideology to more
equal competition. From the beginning, specialists pressed for the right to
publish their internal work in the proliferating professional media outlets
to establish their reputations at home and abroad. Reform leaders saw the
value in this for building support for reforms with the political elite and
educated populace.

By 1981 three projects were launched in response to a directive by Hu
Yaobang to sketch a vision and a set of goals for China to achieve in 20 to
30 years.[7] These projects included an ongoing seminar on alternative development strategies, a study of alternative target models—including reviews of China's past development and the experiences of other developed and developing countries—and an experiment in Western
forecasting along the lines of the *Global 2000* study. Meanwhile, Zhao
Ziyang encouraged the State Economic System Reform Commission and
its lower-level counterparts to conduct experiments in organizing rational
regional economies centered on China's large and medium cities.[8] These
projects together transformed the mental landscape of the Chinese political elite.

For example, the *China 2000* study, carried out in two stages from 1981–
1985, produced a pioneering report based on the principles of system science and the techniques of computer modeling.[9] Most elements of this approach—its integration of the concerns of natural and social sciences, its
combination of qualitative and quantitative methods, its comprehensive

analysis of the whole socioeconomic/scientific/technological system, and its exploration of both short-term and long-term prospects—were completely new to China.

New avenues were opened up for policy research and implementation. For the first time, hundreds of China's leading social scientists—many of them retooled engineers—became familiar with system thinking, cybernetics, forecasting models, applied mathematics, and computer techniques. A new generation of social scientists was recruited and trained in new skills, absorbing a new epistemology involving theoretical, comparative, and futurist perspectives.

The primary intent and one result of the study was to force China's traditional central planners to set more realistic and coordinated output targets for the Seventh Five-Year Plan (1986–1990). But the process also improved collection and sharing of statistics throughout the bureaucracy, strengthened coordination in the State Council, and promoted better training, research, and policy implementation at local levels. The shift of the project from Party to government supervision, for its second stage, added to the growing expansion of government influence in the system. This shift contributed, moreover, to the change in criterion for legitimacy from the "vertical" to the "horizontal." The broadly comparative perspective of the report put pressure on the regime to perform as well as other rapidly developing economies in Asia, not merely to do better than previous Chinese leaders.

The *China 2000* study revealed the growing use of public media in the decision-making process. The results of the first stage were restricted to papers circulated at working meetings or conferences in the early 1980s. The Chinese, however, published key findings of the study in the United States at the insistence of the American author of the *Global 2000* report, who had suggested China do its own study, trained researchers, and introduced the Chinese to other resources. During the second stage of the study, however, the Chinese administrators of the project themselves saw the value of publicizing various stages of results in both Chinese and English. They were published in Chinese to enhance the reputation and influence of the Institute and its Director, Ma Hong, and thereby build public support for the Seventh Five-Year Plan and its architect, Zhao Ziyang. Publication in English increased the opportunity for scholars to travel abroad and acquire foreign support from organizations such as the World Bank.

INTELLECTUALS GAIN POLITICAL INFLUENCE

In the last half of the 1980s the participation of the broader intellectual elite in politics began to be institutionalized in a number of ways. First, recruitment and promotion procedures for important positions in the system were revised to emphasize technical expertise in addition to Party loyalty. Specialists began to play key decision-making roles in factories, hospitals, and schools, as well as in key Party and military organs and government ministries.

Second, the Party sought to create a regularized system of broad consultation and advice. Policy researchers who had taken temporary leave from government and academic bodies to serve on ad hoc study groups under the Party Secretariat in the early 1980s became full-time professional employees of think tanks in the central and local governments. Professional associations and activities proliferated. Centered on publication of findings, they crossed the compartmentalized boundaries of functional systems and created new group identities.

Under Zhao Ziyang in the State Council, five "brain trusts" gained unprecedented prestige and influence: the Rural Policy Research Center; the Science Commission's Research Center for Science and Technology Development; the Economic System Reform Institute; the Development Research Center; and the Center for International Studies. The Chinese Academy of Social Sciences (CASS) and its graduate school provided these organs with newly-trained and creative young minds. Shanghai's Academy of Social Sciences, Institute of International Studies, and *World Economic Herald* comprised adjunct think tanks, connected to Zhao Ziyang through international affairs adviser Huan Xiang and former Mayor Wang Daohan.[10]

Both the National People's Congress (NPC) and the Chinese People's Consultative Conference (CPCC), home to China's eight non-Communist parties, were allowed to establish functional working committees and recruit and organize experts from the intellectual community. They conducted inspection tours and research in order to advise on development issues and proposed state projects such as the mammoth Three Gorges dam on the Yangtze (Changjiang) River.[11]

As intellectuals alone were given more access to decision-making, they at first adopted a comfortable, traditional role as an elite social "bridge" between political leaders and the citizenry. In this capacity they both instructed the citizenry to obey Party policy and conveyed popular desires to the leadership. They did not press for greater freedoms for other social groups such as private entrepreneurs, labor unions, or religious institutions, and they avoided an oppositionist stance. As intellectuals became an important part of the constituency of the Party's reform wing, a trend toward mutual dependence between politicians and intellectuals developed and their newfound influence in political decision-making allowed them to press their own interest as a professional elite.

Even more striking was the growing influence of foreign actors on policymaking. By the mid-1980s China had moved well beyond accepting advice from individuals such as Japan's famous economist, Saburo Okita, or the architect of Singapore's economic development program, First Deputy Prime Minister Goh Keng Swee. Important international economic organizations, most notably the World Bank, increasingly influenced the internal decision-making process.

The World Bank's training program, its stable of consultants familiar with different development experiences around the world, and its capable staff impressed Chinese leaders. In the summer of 1983 Deng Xiaoping invited the Bank president, A.W. Clausen, to involve the Bank in China's macroeconomic planning process during the creation of the Seventh Five-Year Plan.[12] The resulting project consisted of nine studies of foreign experiences with application to China, a quantitative model of the Chinese economy, and an analysis of three major alternative projections to the year 2000. It represented an unprecedented degree of Chinese-foreign collaboration and foreign influence on Chinese decision-making. Over time, the whole range of such foreign involvement in China—from the International Monetary Fund (IMF) to a NATO committee which devised sensitive technology transfer policies—became an informal, indirect political constituency for the reform program.[13] Intellectuals with foreign language and professional skills played a central "bridge" role in this process. Their participation accompanied foreign requests to open the system, such as the World Bank's condition that data be made public before they could be exchanged, and forced the exchange of ideas into the public sphere.

Zhao Ziyang proved especially astute in taking advantage of these new informational, management, and financial resources for his political purposes. In the process, he increased the influence of the State Council at the highest levels of decision-making. Competing ideological campaigns in 1983 revealed the striking impact of these new domestic and foreign resources on Chinese politics. Early in that year reformers in the leadership sought to gain greater support within the central elite by exposing it to futurist writings from the West, such as Alvin Toffler's *The Third Wave*, as well as the results of the first stage of the *China 2000* study.[14] Official commentary on these writings strongly suggested that China should press for more radical socioeconomic reform if it wanted to become an international competitor by the end of the century.

On National Day, 1 October 1983, Deng Xiaoping endorsed an effort to reform education, implicitly including political education, to meet the needs of "modernization, the world, and the future." On 9 October, Zhao instructed a small group of government specialists to do a concentrated study of the revolution in information technology and to recommend appropriate policy responses for China. But a conservative counter-campaign to "eradicate spiritual pollution" specifically targeted those who were introducing futurist themes and put reformers on the defensive.[15]

Zhao, Hu Yaobang, and other Deng allies quickly mobilized the think tanks to counterattack in the name of science.[16] A series of special policy research meetings were convened from late 1983 to early 1984, bracketing Hu's visit to Japan and Zhao's to the United States. By the end of 1984 over 2,000 Party and government officials, including members of the Politburo, the Secretariat, and the military, had attended a series of workshops on the technological revolution. Speakers from government think tanks described trends in fields such as microelectronics and explained modern management principles based on systems engineering. The Chinese media extensively publicized these presentations as part of a campaign to build political support for the reform program.

The results of this initiative included a greatly expanded annual plan for the importation of advanced technology, a plan to computerize banking, computer familiarization courses for managers of China's 3,000 largest state enterprises, and a last-minute reformulation of the Seventh Five-Year Plan. The latest draft of the Plan, formulated under Zhao's personal purview, required the marshalling of immense domestic and foreign resources and intended to create a new spurt of development and reform by 1990.

This political campaign cleared the way for the economic reform blueprint of October 1984, the expansion of the Special Economic Zones (SEZs), the opening of 14 coastal cities to foreign investment, and bold efforts to reform all fields of work to mesh with and support the imperatives of rapid technological development.[17] Both domestic and foreign reform constituencies benefited greatly from this new policy thrust. Intellectuals gained influence and promotions—although not necessarily commensurate material benefits—while foreign partners gained wider access to China. The new coastal strategy went hand in hand with a peaceful reunification approach to Hong Kong and Taiwan.

A new foreign policy promoting peace and development was marked by flexibility and expanded cooperation with the West and Japan for the sake of technological development. This approach superseded a more rigid and ideological policy of "equidistance" advocated by foreign ministry conservatives who wanted to concentrate on expanding Sino-Soviet détente for the sake of ideological legitimacy. The new foreign policy was most notable for its willingness to import foreign ideas and management skills, regardless of ideological origin.[18]

National security adviser Huan Xiang played a unique role in translating the new thinking about global economic and technological trends among economic specialists into an international relations theory that prodded more creative thinking within the foreign affairs community. Huan took the lead in reconceptualizing national strength and reformed traditional views predicated on balancing geopolitical and military power by giving greater weight to economic influence and technological strength. Younger analysts boldly predicted a global trend toward economic specialization, interdependence, and cultural cosmopolitanism, and recommended China's wholehearted participation.[19]

By the late 1980s China was on the verge of important breakthroughs in the freedom of thought and information, the conceptualization of policies, and state–intellectual relations. As the economic reforms began to founder on the hard shoals of price inefficiencies, reform politicians sought to grant a voice to previously disenfranchised sub-elite constituencies who would support reform. As reformers became worried about faltering public support, they encouraged public opinion polling by the government and independent groups and tolerated the emergence of such semi-autonomous media as the *World Economic Herald*. Intellectuals, in turn, used these new vehicles to press the reform leadership farther than they themselves had planned to move in changing the political system. The *World Economic Herald*, for example, developed the ping-pong tactic of "hitting line balls" (*cha bian qiu*), whereby one aimed for the edge of discourse on the political table. This tactic pushed the boundaries of the permissible and broke many taboos. Featuring essays, reports, and letters written by prominent intellectuals, the *Herald* argued that economic reform would make progress only if political reform were carried out.[20]

Meanwhile, China's policy process was increasingly subject to pressure from regional and international interests. Reform efforts to spur economic takeoff in Guangdong and Hainan through massive investment from Hong Kong and Taiwan meant that elite and public opinion in those areas had to be factored into decision-making. Many younger urban reform officials and advisers became convinced that China needed a new socioeconomic paradigm that encompassed a mixed planned-market economy, a scientific culture, and an ideology based on democracy and humanism to meet the challenge of regional and global competition. Such a program implied the need for a generational change in personnel and a major revamping of the closed Leninist political system, sparking discussions which filled the pages of reformist publications. As the yearning among journalists for media reform grew—including greater freedom to report on and criticize government policies—economic reform and the growth of market forces reduced the ideological rigidity of the media while expanding the scope of their genre and content.[21]

CREEPING POLITICAL REFORM

The opening up of the Chinese system—fueled by the information revolution—interacted in complex ways with a simultaneous decade-long process of generational succession to produce *de facto* political reform. From the beginning, most reform politicians and advisers had hoped that modifications in the Party leadership system would be sufficient for economic development and the relegitimation of the regime. The problem was viewed as abuse of the basic socialist structures, rather than a fundamental systemic failure. The carefully limited attacks on Mao's ideology and personality cult, and the reorganization of the Party Secretariat and the State Council from 1980–1982, were meant to legitimize more efficient leadership mechanisms and a set of younger leaders, not to undermine Party legitimacy or to open up the system to broad participation.

Through the 1980s the Deng-Hu-Zhao triumvirate was remarkably successful in appointing capable administrators, creating realistic policies, and building consensus and support through broad consultation within the political elite. The system of Party and government communication and decision-making became more regular, more democratic, and more transparent to the public through the media.

Beginning in 1985, however, the imperatives of economic reform were driving ever more fundamental changes in Chinese politics. As reforms in management of the economy, science and technology, and education were implemented throughout the system, the office of Premier Zhao Ziyang and its auxiliary offices and State Council think tanks became more influential. Hu Yaobang began to revamp the propaganda, personnel, and internal security systems to meet the needs of reform and openness. This liberalization was evident in domestic and foreign interaction at all levels from 1986 to 1988, including the mass media, scientific research, and popular lifestyles. Reformers even experimented with provincial Party and state elections involving multiple candidates.[22]

The national security sector—comprising foreign affairs, military affairs, and intelligence organs—also began to feel the pressure. A major streamlining and restructuring of the military—intended to make its considerable resources available to the civilian economy—was underway after 1985, justified by new predictions of regional and international détente.[23] An example of the new winds blowing were unprecedented conferences of international affairs specialists held in 1985 to explore foreign policy options. One gathering convened by the Institute of Contemporary International Relations under Huan Xiang's sponsorship was the first to allow nongovernmental experts to critique errors and recommend changes in foreign policy.[24] Papers on foreign policy options were published for the first time since 1949. These conferences were used to widen consensus on Deng's new strategic perspectives, elicit views on regional policies, and emphasize economic diplomacy and development in the foreign affairs apparatus.

The loosening of internal Party discipline and social control without the institution of a new constitutional-legal framework, however, undermined regime legitimacy and authority in a number of complex ways. Official and unofficial economic actors used their access to new resources to further their own interests at the expense of the regime's. These problems highlighted an urgent need for experimentation with more fundamental political reform to shore up central authority in making and implementing policy as well as to ensure continued elite and popular support.

At the 13th Party Congress in late 1987 a new batch of elders was retired from office and, for the first time, a younger generation of leaders dominated both the Politburo and its Standing Committee. The 13th Party Congress platform reflected plans for historic breakthroughs in a number of sensitive political areas, including legal protection for private ownership and the launching of civil service reforms that would remove Party leading groups from government organs.[25]

Reformers apparently hoped that modernization goals could be achieved by a stronger and more accountable government rather than a genuine separation of powers and external democratic checks. More freedom of information was to play a central role in this approach. In 1988 Zhao Ziyang called for greater "transparency" in both the Party and the government to be implemented through internal regulations, public opinion polling, and greater press freedom.[26] Zhao's backing of the nationwide airing of the controversial television documentary "He Shang" ("River Elegy") was the most striking example of his attempt to build personal public support. Some of China's foremost intellectuals implicitly supported Zhao's solutions by discussing their country's socioeconomic, environmental, and political problems in this documentary.

Zhao also attempted to assert government control over the Party's Military Commission and Political and Legal Affairs Commission, which oversees internal security. Legislation was being drafted to expand the political roles of the NPC and the Consultative Conference, and to provide stronger protection for civil liberties, including freedom of the press and freedom of religion.[27]

The Party itself was to become more democratic by taking away decision-making power from a handful of senior leaders and elders. The Central Committee began to hold two plenary sessions per year instead of one, and the Politburo, which now had representatives from key provinces, met more regularly without the involvement of the elders and with some publicity on the issues under decision. Zhao attempted to streamline and professionalize the Party's leadership groups responsible for coordinating functional policy arenas, such as foreign or economic affairs. Throughout the bureaucracy, Zhao emphasized the importance of delegating power, clarifying responsibility, and introducing work evaluations and internal supervision systems.[28]

Hidden behind the facade of democratization, however, lurked some mechanisms that would have strengthened the personal hold on policy-making of the senior executive, backed by a powerful "brain trust." Articles written by Party staffers and reform intellectuals in early 1988 called for adoption of "neoauthoritarianism," whereby a powerful but enlightened leader would force through rapid marketizing economic reforms and set the stage for later democratic political reforms.[29] Some pointed to the so-called East Asian Model as the precedent for this; others highlighted President Gorbachev's example.

Conservatives feared a power grab by Zhao, while many intellectuals committed to democratic ideals were outraged by this further rationale for delaying liberal reforms. Zhao's resulting loss of personal popularity contributed greatly to his middle-of-the-road tactics in early 1989 and his hesitancy in supporting the democracy movement. As always, when the power politics of political succession intervened, top leaders used the existing levers of power to place supporters in power and weaken rivals, thereby undermining reform efforts.

A combination of halfway measures, greater information, and heightened expectations undermined political stability and regime legitimacy. The growing evidence that the benefits of reform were not equitably distributed and that the naked succession struggle at the top was endangering the reform program itself led to a serious decline of public confidence in the regime by 1988–1989. This combined with the specter of Deng Xiaoping's demise and subsequent policy reversals to fuel a crisis mentality. People began to act in their own short-term economic and political interests. The impatience of the urban elite was further fueled by the knowledge of radical political reforms introduced in the Soviet Union and Eastern Europe with Gorbachev's encouragement. In contrast, China's leaders appeared reluctant and unimaginative.

As many in the elite lost confidence in Party-led top-down reform, they became open to adopting Western-style democratic institutions and traditions to create external checks on Party power. From this emerged China's first post-1949 civil rights movement, beginning with petitions to the government in early 1989 requesting the release of political prisoners and protection of civil rights and culminating in the hunger strike on Tiananmen Square in the following May and June.

The spring 1989 confrontation in Beijing resulted from paralysis at the top of the Party, but it also reflected a clash between newly-polarized sociopolitical groups. China's most educated and cosmopolitan officials, scholars, and students, who viewed themselves as part of a global process of citizen political activism, opposed the insular revolutionary elders who founded the PRC and claimed the unfettered right to direct the future of the nation. When intellectuals called on the legislature to convene an extraordinary session to mediate the crisis, Deng Xiaoping and the other elders bypassed all regular Party and state institutions and called upon personal loyalists in the army to force through their preferred solution to the crisis. The main casualty at Tiananmen would have been the effectiveness and legitimacy of the CCP regardless of the outcome.

CHINA IN THE THROES OF GLOBAL TURBULENCE

Since 1989 the CCP has not been able to fundamentally redress its legitimacy crisis. Temporizing measures, such as higher salaries and subsidies for urban consumers, have not dealt with the challenges the regime must face. Leaders tainted by complicity in the Tiananmen massacre and the subsequent coverup and repression cannot regain the loyalty of younger generations of urban officials, specialists, and students now accustomed to greater freedom and willing to press for its expansion directly and indirectly.

But international trends make addressing China's crisis by resuming gradual and moderate political reform under a new group of Party leaders unlikely. Any leadership without the elders will be weak and, therefore, bound to maintain relatively open information and economic policies; the new social forces at home will continue to have access to informational and economic resources sufficient to sustain hope and the basis for change. The awareness that Party rule has collapsed in its homeland, moreover, has had an irreversible negative impact on Party legitimacy in China.

New levels of awareness and new skills in critical thinking and social organizing have permeated three-fourths of the populace, including illiterate peasants and others in the rural interior, through television. This was evident in the occurrence of anti-regime demonstrations even in small towns throughout China in late May and early June 1989, following the unprecedented showing of Tiananmen events on nationwide television for a few brief days.

Failed Leninist reform in China in the 1980s was symptomatic of a global shift from the industrial era to a new socioeconomic era shaped by the forces of new technology in information processing and communication.[30] Societies everywhere are experiencing crises of state authority, as loyalties shift to subnational and supranational groups. New political systems are required. Events in Eastern Europe and the former Soviet Union since 1989 strongly suggest that Leninist systems are too rigid to evolve smoothly into new systemic formations more suited to a new era. The reimposition of Leninist controls in China is likely to prove a temporary aberration due more to a combination the residual power of the elders, chance, and the weakness and vacillation of younger leaders than to systemic or cultural uniqueness. It is hard to imagine that China will not produce younger political leaders who will use new political institutions to better understand and mobilize the greatly expanded skills of the intellectual and technological elite and the new value orientations of the urban populace in pursuit of power in the postindustrial era.

NOTES

1. This chapter represents the personal views of the author, not the official views of the U.S. government.

2. See Merle Goldman, "The Role of the Press in Post-Mao Political Struggles"; Marlowe Hood, "The Use and Abuse of Mass Media by Chinese Leaders During the 1980s"; Su Shaozhi, "Chinese Communist Ideology and Media Control"; and Lu Keng, "Press Control in 'New China' and 'Old China'," in this volume.

3. Carol Lee Hamrin, *China and the Challenge of the Future: Changing Political Patterns* (Boulder, CO: Westview, 1990) pp. 34–35, 55 (note 12).

4. Interview with Yu Guangyuan, Beijing, May 1986.

5. Interview with officials at the Liaoning Academy of Social Sciences, which had special ties with its counterpart in Sichuan, in Shenyang, May 1986. Zhao Ziyang's respect for Sun was also reflected in the premier's visit to his deathbed in 1983, as mentioned in Barry J. Naughton, "Sun Yefang: Toward a Reconstruction of Socialist Economics," in Carol Lee Hamrin and Timothy Cheek (eds.), *China's Establishment Intellectuals* (Armonk, NY: M.E. Sharpe, 1986), p. 151.

6. Yu Guangyuan, *Lun Woguo de Jingji Tizhi Gaige, 1978-85 (On Our Country's Economic System Reform)* (Changsha, China: Hunan People's Press, 1985), pp. 1–5 discuss the impact of the visits by scholars. I was told about the Economic Development Zones (EDZs) study tours by Zheng Ge, deputy director of the State Council Special Economic Zone (SEZ) Office in Beijing in May 1986.

7. Hu Yaobang's directive was cited in Ma Hong, "Toward an Overall Development Strategy for the Economy, Society, Science, and Technology," *Jingji Wenti (Economic Issues)* (Taiwan) 1 (25 Jan. 1984): 2–9, translated in Joint Publications Research Service China Report [hereafter JPRS] 84-059, 19 July 1984, pp. 13–26, and was confirmed in personal interviews with officials at the State Council Development Research Center in Beijing in November 1985.

8. Interview with officials and staff of the Liaoning Economic Research Center, May 1986; Zhao Ziyang, *Work Report to the National People's Congress, December 1981.* FBIS China Daily Report [hereafter FBIS], 16 Dec. 1981, pp. K1–35.

9. For details on the origin of the *China 2000* study and the development of its first stage, see Hamrin, *China and the Challenge*, pp. 46–50, 61–62, notes 54–58. For the second stage and its impact, see ibid., pp. 123–27.

10. Nina Halpern, "Scientific Decision-Making: the Organization of Expert Advice in Post-Mao China," in Denis Fred Simon and Merle Goldman (eds.), *Science and Technology in Post-Mao China* (Cambridge, MA: Harvard University Council on East Asian Studies, 1989), pp. 157–74.

11. For a study of reform in the NPC–CPPCC system, see Kevin J. O'Brien, *Reform Without Liberalization: China's National People's Congress and the Politics of Institutional Change* (New York: Cambridge University Press, 1990).

12. The following background on the World Bank study is from Hamrin, *China and the Challenge*, pp. 129–33.

13. See Hamrin, *China and the Challenge*, pp. 129–30; Harold K. Jacobson and Michel Oksenberg, *China's Participation in the IMF, the World Bank, and the GATT: Toward a Global Economic Order* (Ann Arbor, MI: University of Michigan Press, 1990).

14. For more on the competing political campaigns of 1983, see Hamrin, *China and the Challenge*, p. 77 and accompanying notes. Toffler visited China on a lecture tour in January 1983, and translations from his books and a documentary video about him began circulating internally.

15. See Thomas B. Gold, "Just in Time! China Battles Spiritual Pollution on the Eve of 1984," *Asian Survey* 24, no. 9 (Sept. 1984): 947–74, for an accurate and detailed analysis of the campaign.

16. The workshops are described in Chen Tuguang, "A Big Event in Science in China 1984," in *Kexuexue yu Kexuejishu Guanli* (*The Study of Sciences and the Management of Science and Technology*) (Tianjin), no. 12 (12 Dec. 1984), pp. 13–15, in JPRS CST-85-021 (8 July 1985), pp. 8–12. See Hamrin, *China and the Challenge*, pp. 78–79 and accompanying notes for details of the counter-campaign.

17. For details on the new economic and coastal policy guidelines of 1984, see Hamrin, *China and the Challenge*, pp. 81–84 and accompanying notes.

18. Hamrin, *China and the Challenge*, pp. 85–94, details the development of a new foreign policy and policy toward reunification.

19. Huan Xiang had been involved in Zhou Enlai's visit to Bandung in 1954 and was one of China's most prominent ambassadors to the West. He was an especially influential adviser to Deng and Zhao after 1980, when Zhao attempted to develop the State Council Center for International Studies—under Huan's direction—into a powerful counterpart to the U.S. National Security Council. Although sources disclosed to me that the Chinese Foreign Ministry successfully fought to keep this emergent competition weak institutionally, Huan became a one-man think tank and policy coordinator for the leadership.

20. Hsiao Ching-chang and Yang Mei-rong, "'Don't Force Us to Lie': The Case of the *World Economic Herald*," in Chin-Chuan Lee (ed.), *Voices of China: The Interplay of Politics and Journalism* (New York: Guilford Press, 1990).

21. See Lee, *Voices of China*, parts I–II.

22. See O'Brien, *Reform Without Liberalization* for more on the several experiments with elections of representatives to the NPC. Elections of local Party and government officials were few and not well publicized. I have been told, for example, of one 1988 election in Xiamen where the son of a senior retired Party leader unexpectedly was elected mayor and prudently declined. In preparation for the 1987 13th Party Congress, reformers used the "democratic" mechanism of multiple candidates for Central Committee membership slots to ensure the nonelection of hardliner Deng Liqun, thereby barring him from the Politburo and arousing the wrath of his patrons.

23. Hamrin, *China and the Challenge*, pp. 130–42.

24. This information is based on interviews held in Beijing with participating foreign affairs specialists in November 1985 and May 1986. Around this time, the staff offices of the Party's foreign affairs leading group were strengthened to better coordinate policy and represent economic concerns.

25. See Hamrin, *China and the Challenge*, pp. 192–95. See Zhao Ziyang's work report to the Congress, Xinhua, 25 Oct. 1987, in FBIS-CHI-87-206S (Supplement), 26 Oct. 1987, pp. 10–33; and Hamrin, *China and the Challenge*, p. 208, note 70, for references to reports on the process of drafting the work report. For details on the political reform process, see Chen Yizi, *Zhongguo: Shinian Gaige yu Bajiu Minyun* (*China: The Decade of Reform and the 1989 Democracy Movement*) (Taipei: Economic Review Press, 1990), esp. Chapter 5.

26. See Judy Polumbaum, "The Tribulations of China's Journalists After a Decade of Reform," in Lee, *Voices of China*, pp. 39–43.

27. In 1985 organizations in the appropriate functional systems were told to begin drafting legislation to protect these various rights. Heated debate accompanied each round of drafting and delayed enactment of such laws well into the post-Tiananmen period.

28. See Carol Lee Hamrin, "The Party Leadership System," in Kenneth G. Lieberthal and M. David Lampton (eds.), *Bureaucracy, Politics, and Decision Making in Post-Mao China* (Berkeley, CA: University of California Press, 1992), esp. pp. 109–11.

29. See Stanley Rosen and Gary Zou (eds.), "The Chinese Debate on the New Authoritarianism (I)–(III)," *Chinese Law and Government* (Winter 1990–Summer 1991); Ruan Ming, "Press Freedom and Neoauthoritarianism: A Reflection on China's Democracy Movement," in Lee, *Voices of China*.

30. For an outstanding explication of these international trends and their impact on state authority, see James Rosenau, *Turbulence in World Politics: A Theory of Courage and Continuity* (Princeton, NJ: Princeton University Press, 1989). Rosenau identifies "micro-level" changes in the skills and orientations of individuals associated with the microelectronic revolution and posits shifts in individual skills toward the following: adaptive rather than habitual modes of learning, more highly developed analytic abilities, more complex cognitive maps, more elaborate role scenarios, and more active and refined capacities for goal-oriented, psychic energy. He identifies new orientations that question compliance with authority, adopt performance criteria for evaluating legitimacy, focus loyalties away from the nation-state toward subnationalist and supranationalist groups, and concentrate on local rather than distant points of social action.

These changes at the micro-level, according to Rosenau, are accompanied by a host of emerging macro-problems that transcend national boundaries, such as currency crises, pollution disasters, terrorist attacks, and ozone depletion. These micro and macro changes provide recurrent reminders of the limits of effective action available to national governments, and this in turn fuels questioning of the nature and scope of political authority among citizens. He posits these trends as the sources of persisting "turbulence" as societies everywhere undergo a mushrooming of social pluralism, a declining effectiveness of governments, the fragmentation of the state system, and accompanying crises in authority structures, pp. 335–36.

5

CHINESE COMMUNIST IDEOLOGY AND MEDIA CONTROL

Su Shaozhi[1]

In a Leninist state, the Communist party holds a monopoly on state power and defines "ideology"[2] as what Karl Marx called the "second side" of the superstructure,[3] namely, the ideas and convictions that support the existence of the system. This economically based ideology broadly encompasses such elements as public opinion, morality, theoretical thought, political ideas, philosophy, religion, art, and literature. Communist parties have been committed to a totalist ideology. As Stuart Schram has observed, "In China, as well as in the Soviet Union, ideology means the idea, theory or hypothesis recognized by the leaders."[4] This forms what Moshe Lewin calls the triad of "power[party-state]-ideology-culture," whereby dissent is suppressed.[5] Chinese academics called this phenomenon "cultural despotism," which was known in the Soviet Union as Zhdanovism.

A key feature of totalitarianism is the combination of a totalist ideology, a single party committed to this ideology, and the monopolistic control of mass communications.[6] China is such a state, and more. Unique historical conditions have established a totalitarian political system more thoroughly in China than elsewhere. In China, ideological spheres—whether on a theoretical plane or in the context of cultural activities—are not only controlled but downright monopolized.[7] During the Cultural Revolution (1966–1976), this control reached an absurd level; anyone who dared to express ideas even minimally different from Mao Zedong's was condemned as a "class enemy." But while coercive power may shut people's mouths, it rarely wins their hearts. Thus, the Chinese public spontaneously erupted against the Gang of Four—symbols of the coercive power of the State—and in fact against Mao himself during a demonstration on 5 April 1976 in Tiananmen Square. This demonstration was summarily put down, but the demonstrators were exonerated soon after Mao died a few months later. Notwithstanding this and other occasional public outcries, ideological control has remained firmly in the hands of the Chinese Communist Party (CCP) and has brought tremendous catastrophe to China.

The reform decade of the 1980s, despite occasional ideological crackdowns, was a period of active growth in China's academic, theoretical, and cultural realms. This progress was interrupted by a crackdown which used unsubtle military force to bring the democracy movement to an abrupt end in 1989. Since then the CCP has once again intensified its ideological control in order to bolster a regime that has lost its legitimacy.

LENINIST IDEOLOGY

Ideological control in a Leninist state has several theoretical origins. First, Marx conceptualized that the economic base determined the legal, political, and ideological superstructure *and* that this superstructure, in turn, consolidated the economic base. Lenin, however, claimed that the primary function of the second side of the superstructure—ideology—was nothing but the legitimization of the economic and political system of Soviet Communism.

Second, both Marx and Engels held that the working class could emancipate itself through practical struggle, and that socialist theory was a product of the workers' movement.[8] Lenin, however, claimed that socialist consciousness could not emerge *sua sponte* from the working class, but had to be instilled by a Communist party led by professional revolutionaries.[9] Stalin further idealized the Communist Party in the Soviet Union as an educator, leader, and commander of the working class which could use coercion to fulfill its roles.[10]

Third, Lenin argued that the public will had to be strictly brought under the unified command of a single leader to achieve large-scale production under a socialist system. In other words, only a dictatorship could unify those who lack the correct class consciousness.[11] Lenin's arguments were not limited to the economic sphere, but could also legitimize hierarchical "thought education," policy direction, and ideological control. Stalin embellished Lenin by proclaiming that the Party should simply decide everything.

Fourth, the Soviet Communist Party under Lenin and Stalin envisioned the cultivation of "new people" uniquely imbued with "socialist morality" who acted spontaneously and habitually in accordance with socialist values.[12] These "new people" should possess an unlimited capacity for work without concern for reward, a boundless love for their country, and an unselfish subordination of personal to national interests. Inasmuch as there was not enough time to await spontaneous formation of "new people" at a natural pace commensurate with the appropriate stage of social development, they held that the Communist Party had to take the forming of "new people" as a central ideological task.

Fifth, Mao Zedong was deeply rooted in a romantic belief that in order to seize power, a leader must mold public opinion. At the Tenth Plenum of the Eighth Central Committee in 1962, Kang Sheng submitted a note to Mao which read, "It is a great invention to use novels to engage in anti-Party activities." Reading the note aloud, Mao said, "Those who seek to overthrow a regime have to develop a theory and do some ideological work. This is true both for the revolutionary class and for the counter-revolutionary class."[13] Later he expanded this proposition in his *Notes on Political Economy*, where he reiterated the pivotal role of molding public opinion in seizing a regime and within a regime. In a Leninist state, public opinion is thus an essential instrument of political struggle. Its rigid control is indispensable.

AIMS OF IDEOLOGICAL CONTROL

The CCP pays utmost attention to ideology, genuinely convinced that ideology forms an atmosphere favorable to political development. Furthermore, ideology is viewed as an instrument for building a new society and carrying out political struggle. "The gun and the pen," according to Lin Biao, "we depend on them to seize a regime."[14] This is a graphic illustration of Mao's ideas that "political power grows out of the barrel of a gun" and "public opinion should be molded to seize power."

Before the CCP attained power, it used ideological control to mobilize public support for the goals of socialism. Despite reasonable initial intentions, the unrealistic nature of this control eventually depleted public confidence in the CCP's ideology. Later, once the CCP gained power, power corrupted the CCP. The absence of democratic mechanisms in China to check this abuse of power led to economic disasters and political tragedies. As a result, the gulf between socialist reality and Marxist myths grew wider. Anxiety replaced idealism among CCP leaders who felt their power ebbing.

Marx argued that the vast division between mental and physical labor under capitalism detached ideas from material existence. Instead of depicting the real world, he argued, capitalists legitimized the dominance of their class by making capitalism appear desirable and inevitable to workers. This "distorted" picture of reality—what Marx called "false consciousness"—may prevail upon presocialist societies, but a socialist revolution should cause perception to conform with material existence.[15] Ideology, according to Marx, should be an accurate and scientific representation of material existence validated by practice.

Ironically, in the now-declining Leninist states, ideology has itself become "false consciousness," displaying an ever-widening discrepancy between reality and socialist ideals. To bridge this chasm, the CCP has had to unashamedly hide such facts as the tens of millions who starved during the Great Leap Forward, fabricate such testimony as the denunciation of top leader Liu Shaoqi as a "traitor, renegade, and scab" during the Cultural Revolution, and produce such elaborate lies as the official explanation of the 1989 Tiananmen crackdown as a response to a riot. The authorities—fabricators of "false consciousness"—are so apprehensive about revealing the truth that they have no alternative but to resort to harsh control of public opinion. As Schram aptly observes, "Marxist-Leninist theory is merely a facade, and the key to the actions of the leadership is in fact some occult 'operational code of the Politburo'."[16] The CCP leadership does everything in its power—including defying its own dialectical logic—to protect its vested interests and, in the process, avoids new, challenging thoughts. Thus, in order to justify the CCP's political and economic policies, keep socialism alive despite mounting problems, instill a common language and values, maintain the sole legitimacy of the existing system, and curb dissent and instability, the authorities must continuously fabricate public opinion and control ideology.

Ideological control is not uniformly strict in China. The Central Propaganda Department, for example, relaxed control when it implemented a policy marked by tolerance, generosity, and lenience in early 1988. On the other hand, ideological control turns relentless and ruthless when political and economic crises emerge, complaints soar, and regime legitimacy wanes. This general tendency explains the CCP's reversion to tight ideological control after the Tiananmen crackdown.

MECHANISMS OF IDEOLOGICAL CONTROL

The political organization of China is composed of the following overlapping entities:

I.   Party System
     (a) CCP Committees
     (b) CCP Advisory Committee
     (c) Commission for Inspecting Discipline
II. Government System
     (a) People's Government
     (b) People's Congress
     (c) Political Consultative Committee

III. Military System
The Central Military Affairs Commission (MAC), which controls seven military areas through three headquarters (the Headquarters of the General Staff, the General Political Department, and the General Logistics Department).[17]

These structures, in turn, may be subdivided into *five geographical government levels*: central, provincial, municipal, county, and township. The CCP further divides the political structure of the whole Chinese society into *six systems* or *spheres* (*xitong*): military, political/legal, administrative, "united front," mass organization, and propaganda.[18]

The CCP's Central Propaganda Department commands the propaganda departments of CCP committees at different levels and thereby controls China's print and broadcast media, journals, books, television, movies, literature, arts, and cultural establishments.[19]

This system is based on the Chinese constitution and CCP regulations, but the network of ideological control is far more sophisticated and penetrating than it appears on paper. It touches every social cell. This network comprises seven components:

1. The professional propaganda system of the CCP, including the Central Propaganda Department, propaganda departments of CCP committees at the five government levels and in the six systems (*xitong*) set forth above, and CCP propaganda departments in enterprises and institutions.
2. The military system, which controls propaganda units at all levels—ranging from military districts to subareas and departments down to the company level—through the General Political Department of the three headquarters.[20]
3. The CCP school system, which covers institutions ranging from the Central Senior Party Academy to CCP schools at provincial, municipal, and county levels. The Central Senior Party Academy is on the same governmental level as the Central Propaganda Department and is generally under the direct leadership of the Standing Committee of the CCP Political Bureau.
4. The educational system, including propaganda departments of the State Education Committee, universities, colleges, middle schools, and primary schools. This system is led by the Central Propaganda Department, propaganda departments of all of the CCP committees, and the education and health work department (*jiaoyu weisheng gongzuo bu*) of provincial and municipal CCP committees.

5. The scientific research system, overseeing the Chinese Academy of Science and its branches, the Chinese Academy of Social Science (CASS), and the various provincial and municipal academies of social science. Like the educational system, this system is also under the leadership of the Central Propaganda Department.
6. Democratic parties and mass organizations, which are also under the ideological supervision of the Central Propaganda Department.
7. The mass media and publication systems.

This all-pervasive network of ideological control falls formally within the jurisdiction of the CCP's Central Propaganda Department. In practice, however, the Standing Committee of the Politburo has always named a member of its own to supervise propaganda work. In the context of factional fighting, an inordinate amount of the real power in the ideological area resided until recently in the hands of Hu Qiaomu and Deng Liqun, even though both had lost their membership in the CCP Central Committee and its Standing Committee. These two men exercised vast power—even in the absence of commensurate official titles and responsibilities—because top-level hardline leaders supported them.[21]

Ideological control in the wake of the Tiananmen crackdown was different from that in the past—people simply lied to pass official investigations and the authorities were satisfied as long as they could report something to their superiors. Ironically, Deng Xiaoping once tried to encourage people to speak out when he said, "What we are afraid of is that not even a crow or sparrow can be heard" (*ya que wu sheng*). The calm veneer of silence, however, conceals an active undercurrent of opposition and cynicism. As the drastic changes that have befallen Lenin's homeland are taken into consideration by Chinese, they will have a profound impact on China. The reforms of the 1980s have helped foster a plurality of interests, making it impossible for even the CCP to strangle dissent. When the time comes for the dam to break, different ideologies will surely breach the floodgates.

MEASURES OF IDEOLOGICAL CONTROL

Positive Education

The CCP's ideological control incorporates sophisticated "hard" and "soft" tactics employed during political struggles. On the eve of the Communist triumph over the Kuomintang (KMT), the CCP organized numerous study groups and cadre schools in major cities to "indoctrinate" the people. My first contact with the basic tenets of Marxism-Leninism—then hailed as a new philosophy of life—was in 1949 through attendance at a two-month summer study group organized by the CCP on behalf of graduate students at universities in northern China. CCP cadres, at that time, set good personal examples. They were admirably amiable, approachable, and open-minded about criticism. We were drawn to support the CCP, which was far more popular than the corrupt KMT.

Since 1949 positive education has become a routine of life, pervading the different levels of CCP schools, the Socialist College of Democratic Parties, the Communist Youth League schools, and the trade unions' cadre schools. Students receive a heavy dose of Marxism-Leninism, Mao Zedong Thought, and CCP history and policy. They undergo political study at the time of formal entrance and attend a rotating training program. Workers are also released from their regular work schedule for attending temporary classes or for obtaining instructions on such special topics as the CCP Constitution. Cadres immerse themselves in extended theoretical sessions and briefer policy studies once or twice a week. Political study sessions must "not be altered under any circumstances" and are deemed crucial enough to occupy a significant part of the working day.

Positive education is aimed at what has been graphically referred to as "inoculation" and "sterilization." To abort possible spillover influences inspired by perilous changes in the Soviet Union and Eastern Europe, for example, the Chinese masses were preemptively inoculated through organized study sessions which denounced the road of "peaceful evolution." If inoculation is preventive and anticipatory, sterilization is *ex post facto* and remedial. When Zhou Yang, a major literary figure, attempted to counter growing alienation by expounding the ideals of socialist humanism, the CCP subjected university students throughout the country to a sterilization program that castigated Zhou on the basis of an article written by CCP ideologue Hu Qiaomu—"On the Problems of Humanism and Alienation." The widening gulf between socialist reality and Marxist myth, however, has caused an increasingly resentful and ritualistic reaction to such positive educational policies and sessions.

Campaigns in the Intellectual Sphere

Alongside positive education, the CCP has depended on campaigns and forms of criticism which combine academic and political elements to enforce its ideological control. After the founding of the People's Republic in 1949, the earliest and largest "thought-remolding" campaign was launched in the autumn of 1951 and lasted into the following autumn. This campaign, which originated in universities and colleges, quickly embraced intellectuals and people from all walks of life. Intellectuals were asked to "self-examine" the harmful effects of bourgeois education, also taking into consideration their behavior in the "old society." The CCP's harsh treatment caused a loss of dignity and self-worth among intellectuals, especially when their contribution to "building New China" was unfavorably compared to the efforts of highly-touted manual laborers.

Speaking to a meeting of graduate students in Beijing on 10 August 1961, Marshall Chen Yi warned that "Remolding one's ideology should mainly depend on self-consciousness. We cannot solve ideological problems by coercion or by mass pressure. We cannot hurt one's emotions and attack one's soul."[22] This caveat, however, was downplayed as the CCP made thought-remolding a long-term task through successive campaigns. Demeaning tactics were never eradicated.

While in theory more lenient than political criticism, academic criticism has invariably been transformed into political criticism. One of the first precedents was set by a campaign criticizing the film Wu Xun[23] in the spring of 1951, which was intended to be academic but resulted in political repercussions. During this campaign, Mao himself wrote a People's Daily commentary which assailed its producer, Sun Yu; a lead actor, Zhao Dan; and writers who had mistakenly praised the film.

Premier Zhou Enlai disapproved of the excesses of such criticism. In 1961, a time of relative relaxation, he sharply caricatured the practice of great criticism (da pipan) this way: "[We] seize someone's mistake (zhua bianzi), then put ideological and political caps on it (dai maozi), and finally whip around a big organizational stick (da gunzi). ... [We] dig one's problems up by the roots (wa genzi), link them to one's history and implicate one's family."[24] This is a vivid description of the excesses that were typical in academic-turned-political criticisms. The campaign to criticize Wu Xun set a cataclysmic precedent for CCP interference in matters of literary and artistic creation, which were increasingly judged by a few dubiously qualified people or mobilized mass movements. A catalogue of academic criticism during the mid-1950s, though incomplete, may demonstrate the magnitude of their politicization. It would include criticism of Yu Pingbo's studies on the novel Dream of the Red Chamber (October 1954), Liang Sicheng's architectural thought, Shang Yue's historical thought, Liang Shuming's philosophical thought (1955), Hu Shih's liberalism, and Hu Feng for allegedly scheming "a counterrevolutionary clique" (February–May 1955).[25]

During the Anti-Rightist Movement of 1957 criticism was directed at the "Anti-Party Group of Ding Ling and Chen Qixia" in the literary and artistic sphere, the "Anti-Socialist Scientific Program," "bourgeois sociology," and "bourgeois journalism" in the social sciences, and the novel Liu Zhidan (September 1962). The movement to "Remove the White Flag" (ba bai qi) (1958) criticized "white specialists" who devoted themselves to professional work but not to ("red") political activities. A series of criticisms followed the Eighth Plenary Session of the Eighth Central Committee of the CCP—at which Mao Zedong reemphasized class struggle—which attacked the ghost drama *Li Huiniang* (May 1963), films and dramas (August 1963), and people such as Qu Baiyin (musician), Shao Quanlin (writer), Zhou Gucheng (historian and philosopher), Yan Xianzhen and Feng Ding (philosophers), Sun Yefang (economist), and Jian Bozan (historian).

The Cultural Revolution was launched with a campaign to criticize Wu Han's historical drama, *The Dismissal From Office of Hai Rui* (*Hai Rui Ba Guan*). Academic and political casualties of Communist efforts to "sweep away all monsters and demons" (*niu gui she shen*) were too numerous to index here.

As mentioned above, academic criticism often ultimately escalated into political criticism. The criticism of Hu Feng alone implicated hundreds of people. In the area of science, an estimated 34 criticisms have been conducted since 1949, none of which have proven justified, and many quite ridiculous. Yao Wenyuan, a member of the Gang of Four, wrote a paper criticizing Albert Einstein—despite his total ignorance of fundamental physics. The post-Cultural Revolution rehabilitation of the victims of these movements and campaigns, moreover, amounts to an open admission of the policy blunders and tremendous failures of the CCP.

Political Criticism

Instances of academic-turned-political criticism organized by the CCP often grew to proportions which belied their modest beginnings. For example, criticism of Hu Feng's literary thought was radically transformed into an accusation that he was trying to form a counterrevolutionary clique. Building on this scenario, a movement was then mobilized to eliminate alleged counter-revolutionaries who were "hiding" in the CCP, government and revolutionary organizations, and other parties sanctioned by the CCP.[26]

Some of the movements masterminded by the CCP include the "Rooting Out Counter-revolutionaries Campaign," the "Anti-Three and Anti-Five Campaign," the "Anti-Rightist Movement" that implicated half a million people, and political criticism of the "Ten Intraparty Struggles Over Correct Political Lines." Also worth mentioning are the movement against rightist tendencies within the CCP and the "Four Cleanups" socialist education movement. And there was the Cultural Revolution itself.

The post-Mao leadership vowed to concentrate on economic construction rather than political movement. Nevertheless, the CCP more recently launched the "Anti-Spiritual Pollution Struggle" (1983) and the "Anti-Bourgeoisie Liberalization Struggle" (1987), both of which had the substantive impact, if not the labels, of movements. Also, in the wake of the Tiananmen crackdown, the CCP instigated an "Anti-Peaceful Evolution

Movement." In sum, movements or campaigns have succeeded one another since 1949 to become the most crucial instrument of control for the
CCP, victimizing the majority of China's intellectuals and wasting countless work days.

Molding Public Opinion and Theories

The Chinese media habitually conceal facts and consciously promote
falsehoods, reporting nothing but happy news about the Communist system in China. This is no secret. The media must receive permission from
the leadership before it divulges information about them. This practice
has led Hu Jiwei, former director of the People's Daily, to lament that journalists must pay obedience to the CCP,[27] and has caused journalists who
participated in the ill-fated democracy demonstrations in 1989 to cry out,
"Don't force us to lie!" Under the reign of the personality cult, the remarks
of the supreme commander—Mao's in the past and Deng's at present—
assume a place of central theoretical importance and serve as guiding
principles for practical behavior. For example, Mao's praise of the egalitarian leader of an ancient peasant uprising, Zhang Lu, became a point of
orientation for the People's Commune movement.[28]

The CCP subjects the press, including journals, publishing houses, and
official literary associations to stringent registration requirements. Books,
for example, must be inspected and assigned an official publication number before going to press. Censorship is imposed prior to and after the
publication; academic taboos are prevalent and formidable. Appointment
of senior ideological officials must be approved by a CCP committee and
even the Central Organizational Department. Discipline within this group
is stringent; negligent senior officials are punished.

Consequences of Ideological Control

In the Leninist state the truth of authority replaces the authority of truth.
Specifically, the consequences of Communist ideological control are fourfold:

First, cultural despotism prevails. The supreme Party leader is the penultimate interpreter of Marxism-Leninism. This authoritarian attitude had
a chilling effect on intellectual and material development in the Soviet
Union and has done the same in China. Despite the huge amount of
money poured into establishing some of the world's most gigantic research institutes in the Soviet Union, their scholarship contributed little to
the understanding of Marxism-Leninism outside the area of textual analysis. This is also true in China.

Addressing economic development, Stalin's endorsement of Lysenko
and censure of Mendel's genetic research as a bourgeois pseudo-science
irreparably impeded Soviet biological and agricultural advancement.

Likewise, Mao's dismissal of the Malthusian theory and condemnation of Ma Yinchu's proposal for birth control are the direct causes of China's population explosion, which has created an extraordinarily heavy burden on the Chinese economy. Cultural despotism breeds ideological tzars throughout society who disguise themselves as Marxist embodiments of the Party to monopolize thought and silence dissent. In China, dissenters have been ostracized as members of the three anti-elements: anti-Party, anti-socialism, and anti-Mao Zedong thought. Academic inquiry and literary and artistic expression have been the tragic victims.

Second, the CCP blatantly interferes with free discourse and imposes a myriad of taboos on academic development. The politically sensitive nature of academic criticism has caused the CCP to discontinue prematurely studies of vital importance. For example, Sun Yefang's bold explorations in the early 1960s into questions governing the economic laws of commodity production and value in socialist systems were not only brutally attacked, but even earned him imprisonment during the Cultural Revolution. The questions he raised were off-limits to economists for the two decades that followed, much to the detriment of China's economic development.

Third, ideological control has ossified thought. The pace of China's reform has been critically retarded by dogmatic views held about science and technology, and by an equally stifling interpretation of economic and political modernization. Ideologues disdain the significance of education and intellectuals by praising manual labor without recognizing the valuable role of mental labor as a mode of production. People dare not speak out for fear of criticism, persecution, or imprisonment. Savage class struggles have induced mutual suspicion and provoked strife—even within the family. Human nature is grossly distorted while China finds itself in an ideological vacuum and moral morass.

Fourth, while the media are reduced to mere apologists of the rulers, public opinion fails to act as a force of social surveillance. The monopolistic CCP-controlled media retain little public confidence while hearsay flourishes and foreign broadcasts serve as the most trusted source of information. China's crisis today stems in large measure from the moral bankruptcy of its ideological control. The outlandish, ideology-driven nature of official propaganda has caused its contents to fall on deaf ears, and the media in their current state will not regain the confidence of the people.

INFORMATION REVOLUTION

No matter how harsh it may be, China's ideological control may have been exercised in vain. It may be rendered irrelevant by the emerging telecommunications revolution, which has internationalized media transmission and thereby weakened the protective effect of national boundaries. Even China's totalitarian regime cannot totally exterminate the incursions of outside information. This was indicated by the powerful signs of change during the years leading up to the Tiananmen crackdown when many CCP and state organs, including institutes in CASS and departments in the *People's Daily* circumvented official control mechanisms and introduced new ideas. Moreover, a crop of research institutes and publishing houses began to emerge whose operations were relatively independent from the government in spite of their nominal affiliation with various bureaucratic units. More importantly, the broad masses seem to have improvised creative and contemptuous means to subvert the stiff control imposed after the Tiananmen crackdown.[29]

In order to promote democratization in China, we must capitalize on the information revolution in our struggle to promote press freedom and tear down the tight walls of dogmatic ideology. Chinese journalists were said to have enjoyed a taste of press freedom for five short and confusing mid-May days during the 1989 democracy movement. But it was not, by any stretch of imagination, press freedom they enjoyed; it was at best a temporary relaxation of control by order of the beleaguered CCP General Secretary, Zhao Ziyang, who was desperately trying to rescue his own political life.[30] Despite its limited scope, however, this crack was enough to shake the Party's facade. No wonder press freedom is the CCP's primary fear and object of hatred.

The CCP has adopted a policy of ideological control in China which subjects one-fifth of the world's population to a state of perpetual ignorance. It is both repressive and anti-democratic. A prerequisite for democratization in China is the destruction of this system of ideological control—especially the information monopoly—and the exposure of fraudulent official propaganda. The important role of radio, television, fax communication, and satellite technology during the democratization of the formerly-Leninist states in eastern Europe and the former Soviet Union is encouraging. Our mandate is clear. While the CCP seeks to prolong its rule through maintaining ideological control, we must take advantage of the information revolution to supply real information to the Chinese people and expedite the collapse of that control.

NOTES

1. Translated by Su Shaozhi, Chin-Chuan Lee, and Karl W. Metzner.
2. *The Harper's Dictionary of Modern Thought* (New York: Harper & Row, 1988), p. 404.

3. Ibid., p. 830. The first side of the superstructure denotes institutional forms of the system such as the government, the state, and the legal system.

4. Stuart R. Schram, *Ideology and Policy in China Since the Third Plenum, 1978–84* (London: University of London, School of Oriental and African Studies, 1984), p. 2.

5. Moshe Lewin, *Gorbachev Phenomenon* (London: Radius, 1988), p. 112.

6. T. B. Bottomore (ed.), *A Dictionary of Marxist Thought* (Oxford: Blackwell, 1983), pp. 478–79.

7. See Yan Huai, "Understanding the Political System of Contemporary China" (Occasional paper, Princeton Center for Modern China, 1991), p. 8.

8. *Complete Works of Marx and Engels*, vols. 15, 16 (Beijing: People's Publishing House, n.d.).

9. See Li Shaojun, *Party and Reform* (Beijing: Chinese Academy of Social Sciences, Study Group of China's Political Reform, 1988), pp. 27–28.

10. *Complete Works of Stalin* (Beijing: People's Publishing House, n.d.), vol. 1, p. 88; vol. 5, p. 58.

11. Li, *Party and Reform*, pp. 47–48.

12. See Jan Feldman, "The Propagation and Impact of Ideology in the U.S.S.R.," *Problems of Communism* (Sept.–Oct. 1989): 87.

13. *China: 1949–1989* (Chinese) (Henan: Henan People's Publishing House, 1989), vol. 2, p. 512.

14. *Quotations from Vice Chairman*, from a speech given on 18 May 1966 and included in a work compiled by Red Guards (n.p, n.d.), p. 69.

15. Feldman, "The Propagation and Impact of Ideology," p. 88.

16. Schram, *Ideology and Policy in China*, p. 1.

17. Yan, "Understanding the Political System," p. 30.

18. Ibid., p. 31.

19. The propaganda system consists of the Ministry of Culture; the Ministry of Broadcasting, Television, and Movies; the Bureau of Information and Publication; the Chinese Academy of Social Sciences (CASS); New China News Agency (Xinhua) (under the State Council); the *People's Daily*; *Qiushi*, the official Party journal; and other mass media and cultural establishments. Ibid., pp. 6, 11.

20. This department is not subordinate to the Central Propaganda Department of the CCP.

21. Hu Qiaomu died on 29 September 1992, and events at the 14th Party Congress demonstrated that Deng Liqun has lost much of his power.

22. *China: 1949–1989*, p. 439.

23. Wu Xun was a beggar who collected money to open schools for poor people in the late Qing dynasty. Mao accused Wu Xun of fawning upon feudal rulers, rather than fighting against them, in order to gain a position previously beyond his reach. Mao Zedong, "Pay Serious Attention to the Discussion of the Film *The Life of Wu Hsun*," *Selected Works* (Beijing: Foreign Languages Press 1977), vol. 5, pp. 57–58.

24. *China: 1949–1989*, p. 437. This is based on a speech Zhou made at a symposium on art and literature.

25. See Mao, *Selected Works*, for a criticism of Liang Sumin, vol. 5, pp. 121–30; Yu Pingbo, pp. 150–51; and Hu Feng, pp. 176–83.

26. Mao, *Selected Works*, vol. 5, pp. 176–83.

27. Hu Jiwei, *The Moment of Awakening* (Beijing: Chinese and Foreign Culture Publishing Co., 1989), pp. 246–78.

28. Xiao Yenzhou, "A Description of Mao Zedong's Ideas on Political Morality," in Xiao Yenzhou (ed.), *Later Mao Zedong*, (Beijing: Spring and Autumn Publishing House, 1989), p. 261.

29. As the saying goes, "Even though you may issue a policy from above, we have counter-tactics [to cope with it] from below."

30. See Ruan Ming, "Press Freedom and Neoauthoritarianism: A Reflection on China's Democracy Movement," in Chin-Chuan Lee (ed.), *Voices of China: The Interplay of Politics and Journalism* (New York: Guilford Press, 1990).

6

THE POLITICS OF PUBLICITY IN REFORM CHINA

Lowell Dittmer[1]

The concept of "publicity" (*gongkai*) in contemporary China is derived from the age-old concept of the "public" (*gong*).[2] In the Confucian classics a prominent polarity exists between the terms "self" (*si*) and "public" (*gong*), which is linked to an opposition between selfishness (*zisi; sixin*) and selflessness (*wu si; wu sixin*). This is part of the Chinese antithesis between *yang* and *yin*, outer and inner, male and female, bright and dark, sun and moon, heaven and earth, and so forth—a set of polarities that actually antedates Confucius, going back at least as far as the *Book of Changes* and very likely to the very roots of Chinese civilization.

The juxtaposition corresponds to the Western public/private distinction, though it is more invidious. Selflessness is lauded for having the interests of all the people in mind, as selfishness is condemned for a cognitive or even a moral failure to perceive the self in terms of a more comprehensive social organism to which the person's fate is inextricably connected—such that "the universe and all things form one body."[3] Depending on the context and thinker, this larger entity is described as encompassing a network of social relationships, the physical matter of which all things are composed, and/or the natural patterns to which all things are subject.[4] The one-sided depiction of the two realms is perhaps at least partly due to the fact that the public realm happens to coincide politically with the formal institutional structure (i.e., the meritocratic Confucian bureaucracy, which monopolized the writing of the official histories), the private with the inner court (eunuchs, consorts, palace guard, and servants) and their informal organization (factional maneuvering and conspiracies for favor or succession).

The Western concept of the "private" is less pejoratively defined than the Chinese, with a strong strain going back at least to Adam Smith construing the private sector as making an almost necessarily positive contribution to public welfare. Private interests per se are sanctioned by the free market model in economic thought, by social contract theory in politics, and by the adversary tradition in jurisprudence. Analogies may be drawn from any of these realms to promote the free play of private interests throughout society (as in Mill's *On Liberty*, which first likens public discourse to a marketplace). The public is to be sure also positively evaluated in the West (e.g., "public interest," "public weal"), but it has subtly different connotations from the Chinese concept, as we seek to substantiate below.

If the Chinese Communist revolution endeavored to override and reverse certain elements of traditional Chinese political culture,[5] with regard to the public/private distinction and its implications the impact seems to have been rather to reinforce the momentum of the past. Despite the fact that Marx himself (in his critique of Hegel) denied the existence of a public interest, conceding sociological authenticity only to classes, CCP leaders for the most part fit rather comfortably into Chinese philosophical tradition on this issue. Actually, CCP discussions of public opinion use two terms: *yulun*, which refers to leadership views as reflected in the official media which the masses are expected to share, and *renmin qunzhong de yijian* (opinions of the masses), referring to the more or less spontaneous opinions of a range of people, as reflected in letters to the editor, big-character posters, and so forth. These two terms suggest an active impulse to build a consensus from above, on the one hand, but also an acknowledgment of indirect feedback from the masses below.

In "On the Correct Handling of Contradictions Among the People," Mao Zedong attempted to sort these out:

> Our People's Government is one that genuinely represents the people's interests, it is a government that serves the people. Nevertheless, there are still certain contradictions between the government and the people. These include contradictions among the interests of the state, the interests of the collective, and the interests of the individual. ...[6]

Mao then goes on to draw his famous distinction between "contradictions among the people" and "contradictions between the people and the enemies of the people," the latter to be resolved through "struggle" and the former through patient persuasion. Although Mao herewith seemed to be granting a measure of political autonomy to certain types of public contradictions, that autonomy is consistently lost in the act of realization. Resolution of either type of contradiction turns out to involve adaptation on the part of what might be called the private sector (the "masses") to the Party-state, which hence emerges as the sole proper repository of the public interest. The only difference is that the resolution to "nonantagonistic" contradictions is voluntary and pacific, whereas "antagonistic" contradictions involve violence and coercion. Moreover, Marx's denigration of "bourgeois privacy" reinforces the traditional Chinese scorn for "self-interest" (*liyi*), resulting in the Chinese Communist tendency to associate private interests with the selfish profit-maximizing (*liyizhuyi*) characteristics of capitalist economies—in contrast to their own alleged concern with the "great public" (*da gong*). The legitimacy of material interests must be accepted, in view of their centrality to Marx's theoretical schema, yet there is an underlying tendency to give them a negative connotation and to ascribe correspondingly idealistic motives to public concerns. There is also a tendency, particularly in the more radical version of Maoist ideology that emerged during the Cultural Revolution, to give paradigmatic status to those instances where public and private interests conflict, and to demand that the former prevail absolutely: "great public, nothing private" (*da gong, wu si*).[7]

CHINESE VERSUS WESTERN MEANINGS

What emerges, then, from the synthesis of traditional Chinese political culture and Marxist-Leninist ideology is a conception of the public that is recognizably parallel to that used in the West yet marked by subtle differences.

The Western concept of the public includes a connotation of *objectivity*—ultimately deriving, perhaps, from the methodology of scientific verification (according to which hypotheses, experiments, and theories had to be publicly exposed to possible refutation) that achieved such prestige during the European Enlightenment. This Western notion has been exacerbated in the course of centuries of religious secularization and economic commercialism, during which the public sector, initially imbued with the bourgeois values of "liberty, fraternity, and equality" from the French revolution, has progressively become eviscerated of any substantive content, aside from an essentially neutral set of "rules of the game" to govern the free play of private interests.[8] This nuance seems to be altogether lacking from the Chinese concept; to the Chinese, the concept of the public retains a distinct substantive content.

Precisely what is that content? This is a question that will require further research, but a few preliminary hypotheses may be suggested:

1. The Chinese concept has a more unambiguously positive moral value than in the West, deriving from both Confucian and Marxist-Leninist philosophical traditions. Moreover, since Chinese authorities deny the legitimacy of private interests, any claim made to the state must be expressed in terms of universal validity. It is perhaps partly because of this moral coloration that Chinese Communist "news" tends to be euphemis-

tic, whereas Western news, in contrast, seeks out sensation, scandal, the bizarre (man bites dog), and tends to be pejorative. Thus it is not just the lure of the limelight in the sense of an appeal to the human need for self-display that afflicts actors on the Chinese political stage, but the even more powerful urge to strike a heroic pose.

This pose involves a public emotional display of care for the people. Chinese refer to this display as "human feeling" (*renqing wei*).[9] In its absence, a public performance is apt to be rejected as "insincere." Thus during the Cultural Revolution Marshal Chen Yi was able to convince his Red Guard interrogators of his sincerity in a spirited and frankly combative defense, while the more emotionally withdrawn Liu Shaoqi and Deng Xiaoping were not.[10] In the West, in contrast, a line of distinction is drawn within the public sphere between politics and sports on the one hand, where rule-bound rationality is at a premium and the public display of emotion is constrained,[11] and theater and the performing arts on the other, where a full range of emotional display is appreciated.

2. The Western concept of the public presumes diversity and internal contradiction, particularly in the American "melting pot," but also in all systems with low economic and political entry barriers. To the Chinese, however, the public should represent unity and consensus (*yulun yizhi*); information that might mar this consensus should remain private. The Chinese (Communist) public realm is morally pure, hence relatively information-poor. This was particularly so during the late Maoist period, when detailed street maps or telephone directories were labelled "classified", government offices could be detected only by their oversized street number plates, and libraries were tightly restricted (important Chinese political events were often broken by the foreign media).[12] The West's relative tolerance for public diversity is to be sure tenuous and hard-won,[13] coming only after centuries of fierce religious and ideological strife, during which diverse creeds learned to tolerate each other *faute de mieux* because they could not destroy each other. Chinese politics, in contrast, has been characterized by a series of "winner-take-all" conflicts, in which disagreement is ruthlessly extirpated.[14]

3. The public sphere in China is proportionately larger and more pervasive than in the West. This is due in part to Chinese tradition, but also to the fact that the rather thorough "socialization of the means of production" carried out by the CCP in the 1950s included socialization of the means of communication. Not only the mass communications media in the conventional sense but public squares, statues, main streets, and public occasions (holidays, festivals, anniversaries, and other ceremonies)— even ostensibly private ceremonies, such as weddings or funerals—were coopted by the state and heavily regulated. Courtship, family planning, food consumption, child rearing, travel, belief systems—all aspects of life

became matters of legitimate public concern. Thus, on the one hand, Chinese ask in casual conversation what in the West would be deemed impertinent questions without any sense of intruding into "private" life. On the other hand, there is relatively little sense of responsibility for the public sector, because it has been monopolized by the "dictatorship of the proletariat" (now "people's democratic dictatorship") throughout the post-Liberation era.

4. Political elites have a much stronger claim to define the public sector than in the West. Even in the West there is often a tendency to confuse the governmental with the public realm, though even when the state is considered a necessary component of the public it is rarely deemed sufficient, given the prolific presence of nonstate actors contending to represent the public interest (political parties, public interest lobbies, religious denominations, the entertainment media, the market). Indeed, in the most recent period, there has been an increasing tendency to view the public as nothing but the interplay of private interests. In Chinese political culture, on the other hand, the state has been ceded much greater authority over the public sector; it is possible to conceive a distinction (as when the emperor is found to have violated the "mandate of heaven," or when a "clean official" (*qing guan*) confronts and upbraids a corrupt superior), but this is usually discernible only posthumously.[15] In contrast to the Western tendency to view the public as the playground of private interests, the Chinese inclination is to view it as the exclusive preserve of the state.

For the most part, these contrasts in the Chinese concept of the public held true under the empire and were reinforced rather than alleviated by the triumphant CCP's creation of a strong centralized state. The implication of these cumulative differences is that the whole context of meaning or cultural gestalt in which corollary and ancillary terms become articulated differs correspondingly. "Publicity" is not a morally neutral grilling in an openly competitive public arena whereby the objective truth will be sifted out, but rather a bright spotlight of virtue that gives prominence to superior individuals or achievements for others to observe and to follow. *"Publication" via the various media is in most cases merely a final confirmation of authoritative judgments*; it is not functionally necessary for different publication outlets to compete in the discovery of "news" or in the articulation of different editorial opinions—indeed, it does not normally make much sense for them to do so. That might confuse people unnecessarily, giving rise to "chaos" (*luan*). Once the authorities (those authorized to define the public interest) arrive at a consensus on a "correct" political agenda, the various media can be expected to relay this information more or less in unison. This typically gives rise to a "bandwagoning" process that contrasts with the more dialectical interplay of the media in the West.

Having outlined some of the broad cultural differences in the way Chinese understand their public sector, our purpose will now be to show how the distinction between public and private plays itself out in the political arena. We shall then review how the concept of the public has changed in the course of the last ten years of economic reform and political stalemate. Finally, we review the structure and history of the nonofficial mass movements that have arisen to fill an experienced void in the post-revolutionary public arena, culminating in the confrontation and crackdown at Tiananmen. The latter represents a climactic synthesis of many of the tendencies unleashed by the foregoing reform of the Chinese public sphere, bringing that reform to a crossroads.

POLITICAL PRIVATIZATION: FORMAL VERSUS INFORMAL

How does the public/private dichotomy relate to political power? While both realms are repositories of power, the former manifests itself in public, in the light of day, to widespread applause, whereas the latter is hatched in furtive plots, lurking in ambush, to emerge from hiding in surprise coups. Sun Tzu appreciated the potential of the private realm in his discussion of strategy (and Mao in turn appreciated Sun Tzu):

> All warfare is based on deception. Therefore, when capable, feign incapacity; when active, inactivity. When near, make it appear that you are far away; when far away, that you are near. Offer the enemy a bait to lure him; feign disorder and then strike him.[16]

In the tradeoff between public and private, the private sector relinquishes public legitimacy for offsetting gains in power, while the public realm manifests civil virtue but no power (in the sense of discretionary choice making a policy difference). The reason for this is that public behavior implies conformity with the public-regarding norms of selflessness and cannot tolerate discretionary choice that would permit conflict, not to mention the dirty tricks required for successful deal-making and power-mongering. Power per se can hence be effectively pursued only in private, to be publicly manifested in the form of impersonal, universalistic policy only after being cleansed of all trace of its self-aggrandizing, "unprincipled," and conflictual aspects. In the first stages of the political process "privatization" is indispensable, however unseemly.

The Chinese draw a rough distinction between two forms of political privatization: formal and informal. In formal privatization, the powerful meet in forums that have been officially sanctioned on a fairly routine basis with some sort of public disclosure of their activities. In this context, privatization means that the meeting must be closed to the public and procedurally open-ended. Closed forums shut out moralistic public scrutiny, permitting realpolitik to be conducted in a businesslike, sometimes brutal fashion; procedural open-endedness permits the "owner" (i.e., the chair or convener) to override various rules (e.g., agendas, voting rules, participant rosters) in order to cobble together a decision-making majority and crush any recalcitrant minority. In accord with the cultural assumption that publicity equals virtue, the CCP has historically opposed the privatization of meetings in principle,[17] a moral stance that only the supreme leadership has had the power to override, which it customarily does in the form of "expanded" sessions (those to which nonmembers have been invited). These sessions may have varying degrees of formality, from expanded Politburo meetings (marked only by a report that a meeting was held, with no information about its substance) and Politburo Standing Committee meetings (which are not marked by a report) to "work" or "report" conferences known only by the place and time they are held. All these meetings are procedurally open-ended, allowing the convener to set the agenda, designate speakers, shift the venue, and invite selected nonmembers.

Informally privatized meetings are even more closed to the public and procedurally open-ended, but have the disadvantage of lacking legal sanction (indeed, they are proscribed as "factions"), forcing them to meet clandestinely. Those excluded or anticipating exclusion from formally sanctioned forums may form such a privatized combat grouping as a last-ditch expedient, but their activities are likely to remain murky, win or lose, due to their illicit status. They, of course, honor no public disclosure requirement, and subsequent exposure of their activities is subject to polemical distortions. It is still not clear, for example, what Peng Dehuai and his "military club" did besides meet occasionally to complain of Mao's high-handedness. Similarly, the nature of Lin Biao's conspiratorial activities after the Second Plenum of the Ninth Party Congress which put him on the defensive remains shadowy. Deng Xiaoping seems to have formed a similar grouping with Ye Jianying, Xu Xiangqian, and others in southern China after falling from favor in Beijing in the spring of 1976, but precisely how they pursued their struggle has never been officially disclosed.[18]

Formal Communication: Mass Versus Internal Media

A policy emerging from a formally privatized forum must be heard and approved by an authoritative public forum—the Party Congress, the National People's Congress (NPC), or the Chinese People's Consultative Congress (CPPCC)—before it is deemed legitimate. The formally "correct" path of approval is for these meetings to meet seriatim, beginning with the Central Committee, then the Party Congress, NPC, and CPPCC; but during Mao's later years this sequence was frequently abridged, with the effect of many CCP policies were implemented without technically becoming laws. These assemblies' role has hitherto been essentially acclamatory, with a slight tendency to assuming a slightly more influential role in the course of reform.[19]

Following "congressional" approval the policy is announced to the public. Publication may flow through two channels, which have been termed routine-formal and enterprise-informal.[20] The formal channel in turn consists of a "dual communication network," consisting of the open mass media and the internal (neibu) communication system contained within the bureaucracy.[21]

The mass media are on the whole among the least informative avenues of publication, purveying general and euphemistic reports often discounted by their readership.[22] At least until the late 1980s the media prided themselves on their lack of prepublication censorship,[23] but the threat of post-publication sanctions (official or mass criticism, dismissal of editorial staff) has always been more or less present, resulting in fairly vigilant self-censorship.[24] The mass media are part of the propaganda "system" (xitong) which includes the Ministry of Culture; the Ministry of Broadcasting, Television, and Movies; the Bureau of Information and Publication; the Academy of Social Sciences, Xinhua News Agency, the official central newspaper (the People's Daily), and the official journal (Qiushi). This system is under the jurisdiction of the Central Propaganda Department of the CCP, which also controls the education system, the propaganda department in the military, scientific research, the Party school system, the "bourgeois democratic parties," and mass organizations. But a Politburo member outranks and may overrule the Propaganda Department: Mao himself wrote a number of key editorials,[25] and for a long time Hu Yaobang took a proprietary interest in the People's Daily.[26]

More detailed reports are parcelled out to the various bureaucratic "systems" on a need-to-know basis. The CCP divides the Chinese political structure into six systems: the military system, the political and legal system, the administrative system, the propaganda system, the united front system, and the mass organization system.[27] These systems, vertically integrated hierarchies between which lateral contact is minimized, then relay the information and directives downward through a wide variety of meetings including work conferences, symposia, transmission meetings, report-back meetings, and mobilization meetings.[28] This vertical communication system distributes by "dosage": knowledge is power, so those highest in the hierarchy get most fully briefed, while a stream trickles out to the lower strata. Although originally an exclusively oral network, the system has been supplemented over time by a wide variety of *neibu* printed media including, in ascending order of secrecy and restriction, *Reference News* (*Cankao Xiaoxi*), *Reference Information* (*Cankao Ziliao*), *Internal Reference* (*Neibu Cankao*), "red head reference" ("*hong tou cankao*"), and *Hand Copied Documents*, the latter two printed in large type so the "immortals" can read them and issued on an occasional basis to as few as a dozen people.[29] The political elite also have their own restricted television channels and special access to foreign movies.

At the base of these "systems" is a cellular matrix of "basic units" (*jiben danwei*). Even the mass organizations are subdivided into units. The basic unit, defined functionally and geographically, exercises relatively comprehensive control over its membership more through the calculated distribution of rewards than through disciplinary sanctions. The unit distributes salaries, housing, bonuses, rations, school attendance, and military service. During campaigns the unit organizes the killing of flies and rats or the designation and criticism of class enemies. The unit keeps score of its membership in a complete set of personnel files (*dangan*) and unit approval is needed to marry, have children, divorce, and form or dissolve a contractual relationship. Though the mechanisms of unit control have weakened in the course of reform, they remain formidable.

Informal Communication: Leaks, Rumors, Campaigns

Informal communication consists of leaks and rumors, and top-down campaigns. As defined here, the difference between a leak and rumor has to do with the amount of elite initiative. Leaks disseminated on a not-for-attribution basis by public officials are not just informal but illegal, according to the Official Secrets Act promulgated in the early 1950s and more recently reaffirmed. Enforcement has been strict but uneven, due to the troubled history of the rule of law and to the skill of the leaders at evading restrictions. The most flagrant violations took place during the Cultural Revolution, when leaks to the unofficial tabloid newspapers were widely used to smear factional opponents. Enterprising Red Guard reporters sometimes created their own leaks, breaking into the files and disseminating secrets to the public, smashing the distinction between public and private and creating "chaos."

During leadership disputes, leaders have their greatest incentive to attract a mass constituency by disseminating information favorable to themselves and damaging to their opponents, and they usually manage to do so without technically violating the official taboo on leaks by using symbolism or Aesopian language (*hansha sheying*—holding sand and throwing shadows). These communications transcend unit boundaries partly because high-level leaders are among the few whose careers have allowed them to assemble widespread "connections."[30] Mao Zedong was particularly artful at discovering (or even planting) an obscure article criticizing some untouchable bigwig and then proceeding to inflate its significance to devastating proportions; the critique of Wu Han's play *Hai Rui Ba Guan* with which he launched the Cultural Revolution is, of course, the most famous example, but he used the same technique recurrently. Mao wrote the *People's Daily* commentary that launched the criticism of the film "Wu Xun" in the spring of 1951, and in October 1954 stipulated to the publication of an obscure critique of Yu Pingbo's interpretation of *Dream of the Red Chamber*.

But Mao had imitators on either side of the ideological spectrum. Thus, when the radicals launched a campaign criticizing Confucius that implicated Zhou Enlai as the "Duke of Zhou" (*Zhou Gong*), Zhou seems to have instigated the discovery that the late Lin Biao had been an avid collector of Confucian scrolls, thereby redirecting the campaign against "Lin Biao and Confucius." The radicals attacked Deng in 1975 by denouncing the "capitulationist" Song Jiang in the novel *Water Margins,* and during the Tiananmen demonstrations a much older Deng was unflatteringly compared to the Empress Dowager; even the Great Helmsman was criticized during his lifetime as Qin Shihuang.[31] For his part, Deng Xiaoping made uncomplimentary speeches in the summer and fall of 1975 about Jiang Qing's handling of culture and propaganda which then circulated through the bureaucratic grapevine. Again in the summer of 1978 Deng paved the way for his comeback by arranging a nation-wide media campaign in support of the proposition that "practice is the sole criterion of truth" and by neglecting—for the first time in his life—to crack down on dissidents who were then making life difficult for Hua Guofeng.[32] When two or more sides engage in this type of manipulation, rival vertical coalitions are formed, each with its own informal information network.

There are both national and local rumors. The former subsist on leaks from the central political apparatus which monopolizes national political information. Because they are limited to word-of-mouth transmission, national rumors are usually limited to the capitol, although during mass movements intercity messengers (*chuanlian*) and telephones create a national grapevine. Local rumors or gossip (*xiaodao xiaoxi*) form a pervasive informal communications net within each unit from which few secrets are safe. Intraunit rumor networks, though much smaller, provide more opportunity for mass feedback than the public sector. Thus, while the big-character poster has appeared beyond unit compounds only episodically and accompanied by considerable turmoil, members of the unit have been more consistently permitted to write and post posters on a unit bulletin board for internal consumption. The rhetoric of "class struggle" has never fit well within the unit, where harmony is not only culturally consonant, but also a functional requisite.[33] Beyond the unit, in contrast, lies a jungle where civil culture easily breaks down.

CCP leaders have consistently supplied direction to the masses through a combination of symbolism and relatively ad hoc organizational techniques, known as the "mass movement."[34] Mass mobilization was deemed especially useful to implement new policies marking a radical departure from the status quo, which required active community commitment to foster an atmosphere conducive to deviation from traditional norms and commitment to new policies. But the CCP was perhaps unique among Communist movements in the resourcefulness with which it found new uses for the mass movement. Throughout the 1950s the mass movement played a major role in the transformation of the Chinese political landscape: mass movements socialized the means of production, ostracized and punished enemies of the "people," rectified the world of ideas and culture, and even facilitated public sanitation efforts. Despite considerable diversity, mass campaigns have tended to have a populist and specifically anti-intellectual animus. Between 1949 and 1966 around 16 nationwide campaigns were launched, at least eight of which singled out intellectuals.[35] By thus pitting the masses against the intellectuals most inclined to a critical perspective, the regime has kept a tighter reign on dissent than, for example, the Soviet Union.[36] In any event, mass movements typically provided an outlet for various and sundry mass grievances in the form of a scapegoat who was contraposed to a policy or value the regime wanted the masses to embrace.

The "public sphere" is thus segmented into relatively self-contained groupings, consisting of vertical hierarchies or "systems" on the one hand and units on the other. Although these are not without "windows" consisting of the mass media and certain cross-cutting communications (such as *Reference News*)—and although such interunit communication has improved considerably in the course of reform—communication within each unit or system is much more complete than communication between them. Only during campaigns or leadership disputes is this cellularization normally breached, creating a festive spirit of emancipation often quite at odds with the ostensible purpose of the movement. At this time one can vacate mundane concerns and engage on a voyage of mutual discovery, finding in the "great public" the gloriously abstract and anonymous collective purpose not found in workaday bureaucratic or unit routines.

THE IMPACT OF REFORM

After returning to power via the skilled use of every political trick in the trade, Deng Xiaoping proceeded to inaugurate a reform program that prudently disallowed many of those tricks. Although best known for legitimating a more generous accommodation of the private sector, Deng's reform program also foresaw a shift from private to public in the political arena. This program focused on promoting two trends: secularization and formalization. Considerable progress was achieved in both directions until the consequences of these trends precipitated a cleavage in the reform alignment and forced at least a partial and temporary retreat. Deng Xiaoping and his minions at this point reverted to the tactics they had been seeking to leave behind, ensuring their personal survival but posing questions about the future of the reforms.

Secularization

Secularization included, in the first instance, the systematic demolition of the cult of Mao as a way of undermining both a source of dogmatic resistance to policy innovation (the so-called "two whatevers") and the chief ideological pillar buttressing Deng's political nemesis Hua Guofeng. The cult was replaced at the elite level by the principle of "collective leadership," while its role in the public sphere as a sort of universal *a priori* criterion of truth was replaced by more empirical criteria under justificatory slogans such as "practice as the sole criterion of truth" and "emancipation of the mind." The new regime publicly condemned the imposition of a single political doctrine over every sphere of activity and fostered a certain autonomy for various scientific and professional activities under the rubric of "objective laws" which controlled, for example, economics, physics, and journalism. Various forums were thus sponsored to elicit the opinions of professionals on matters relevant to their area of expertise.

Inasmuch as the cult had formed the fountainhead of ideology, the almost magical efficacy attributed to Mao Zedong Thought, demolition of the cult resulted in a derogation of the almost sacrosanct status of ideology, making more room for pragmatic flexibility and innovation. The connection was most explicitly drawn in the "Resolution on Some Historical Questions in Our Party Since the Establishment of the Country" published by the Sixth Plenum of the 11th Party Congress in June 1981, which condemned Mao for "mistakes" (*cuowu*) in launching the Great Leap Forward and the Cultural Revolution (but not "serious mistakes," *yanzhong de cuowu*), as in the original draft). The Resolution also repudiated the theory of "continuing the revolution under the dictatorship of the proletariat," with which Mao had been closely identified, and redefined Mao Zedong Thought to make it compatible with the Party's unfolding modernization program. Whereas Mao had in the last decade of his life placed particular emphasis on the role of the ideological superstructure as an independent variable in historical change,[37] the post-Mao interpretation returned to a reflectionist view: the driving forces in history were those of production as reflected by the ideological superstructure.[38]

Into the empty spotlight left by ideology moved economics. Whereas during the Maoist era economics received very superficial (and often euphemistically inaccurate) attention,[39] it now began to take pride of place. The flagship *People's Daily*, expanded in January 1980 from four to eight pages, allotted more coverage to economic news. In January 1980, of the 29 news stories which were given greatest prominence on the front page, 21 were economic reports. In the corresponding month of 1979, only three out of 27 front-page headline stories focused on economics.[40] Reporting in other fields—politics, science, education, art, and literature—also tended to reflect the inherent logic or "objective laws" of those fields, rather than superimposing an extraneous ideological standard. Economic reform has also substantially expanded the diversity of China's media structure, content, and audience constituencies.[41]

Formalization

Formalization refers to a shift from factional intrigue in either officially sponsored or clandestine forums to regularly scheduled meetings by officially constituted political organs. Policy-making bodies were all placed on a more routinized schedule, meeting more frequently and in longer sessions. Beginning with larger forums such as the NPC plenary sessions, these organs began to open themselves to at least partial press coverage.

As far as information policy is concerned, this entailed putting the production of news on a more regular and "transparent" (the Chinese equivalent of *glasnost*) basis. News conferences began to be held for the first time with some regularity. The news media proliferated at a prodigious rate. Whereas routine-formal institutions of public relations won official blessing, the government proceeded energetically against enterprise-informal avenues of news disclosure. Deng introduced the "four cardinal principles," which set clear limits on public debate, immediately after his third resurrection in the fall of 1978. Although Hua Guofeng's downfall was facilitated by informal leaks and rumor-mongering, such circumstances have not yet repeated themselves. The big-character posters that had been sanctioned since their advent during the Hundred Flowers movement in 1957 were prohibited—indeed, the constitution was eventually amended to that effect. Tabloid newspapers were shut down and street activists were thrown into labor camps or prison. When the introduction of multi-candidate voting in 1980 permitted the advent of candidate-organized campaign committees, publication of pamphlets, and political rallies, the government amended the electoral laws to preclude this sort of entrepreneurship. Both the public media and the various intraelite communication systems prospered, but each pool of information was strictly segregated. To counter leaks by cadre children to the Hong Kong news media, the Official Secrets Act was reemphasized and the more prominent journals barred from import. By "formalization" the government clearly had an authoritatively controlled, top-down communications network in mind.

It is easy to forget that the Deng Xiaoping reform program achieved many of its objectives. Public life was freed of some of its pervasive ideological taboos, attention was shifted from the almost inquisitorial quest for ideological purity to economic construction, and private life became more autonomous and secure. Certain limitations and self-contradictions, however, soon became apparent. By secularizing ideology the leadership inadvertently divested itself of what had been a powerful instrument for legitimizing its rule and enforcing conformity with its policies. Introduction of the concept of a "socialist spiritual civilization" (and its negative corollary, "spiritual pollution"), which allegedly had an existence independent of the forces and relations of production, represented an attempt to retreat from the position of forthright advocacy of "emancipation of the mind" to a more controlled public sector. But efforts at enforcement were hamstrung by elite ambivalence. The intellectuals that comprised part of the reform movement's early core constituency became attached to the Hundred Flowers as an end in itself and resisted any encroachments on this freedom en masse even when it became somewhat troublesome. Thus when ideology was resuscitated in the late 1980s to shore up the regime's sagging authority intellectual resources on which the regime could previously rely were no longer available. The attempt to rationalize and formalize the public sector achieved impressive results, but only so long as the economy kept surging forward in relatively trouble-free fashion. When crises and leadership splits began to afflict the regime in the late 1980s, politics soon became reprivatized. Thus, the January 1987 decision to accept Hu Yaobang's resignation as General Secretary of the CCP and to crack down on "bourgeois liberalism" was made in an "expanded" meeting, as were the decisions in May 1989 to divest Zhao Ziyang of operational responsibility and invoke martial law, and then to use troops to clear Tiananmen Square.

The ideological secularization of the public realm provoked two quite different mass reactions. One was a businesslike preoccupation with professional careers and economic prosperity. Though seemingly logically consistent with the "moving from stone to stone to cross the stream" line, this ideologically anaesthetized outlook troubled many of the old revolutionaries in the regime, who complained of a "money is everything" (*wang qian kan*) mentality. The other reaction was a search for the lost "meaning of life" that invited voluntary submissions from the grass roots, or at any rate from outside the official hierarchy.

During periods of relative intellectual openness, the intellectuals responded with ideas from existentialism, Western Marxism (*xima*), structuralism, market economics, psychoanalysis, Western democratic theory, and norms of news objectivity.[42] Although the Party condemned "spiritual pollution," it became somewhat awkward to exclude such intellectual imports in the context of an economic opening to the outside world and avid promotion of Western tourism. The media became more independent, in the spirit of administrative decentralization and ideological secularization, publishing more elaborate and inclusive accounts of intellectual developments. In the absence of authoritatively sponsored mass movements consonant with the entrepreneurial spirit that drove the most dynamic sector of the economy, the younger generation seized upon public ceremonies as a plausible pretext for public entrepreneurship to sponsor spontaneous movements. These began in the fall of 1985 with a campaign against the Japanese commercial invasion, followed by the December 1986 demonstrations in support of reform and the enormous April-May 1989 demonstrations against corruption and in favor of democratization.

TIANANMEN

By May 1989 the reform leadership found itself with a public sector quite different from the one they had endeavored to create. How to deal with it became so controversial that part of the leadership split off rather than crush it. The moderate faction under Zhao leaned so far in its defense until their own careers were finally decimated because they viewed the new public sector, albeit somewhat difficult to manage, as an integral part of the reform package. The repudiation of the new public sector would deal reform policies a severe setback even if Zhao were to purchase personal survival by maintaining "organizational discipline." Deng and the hardliners were determined to crack down because they became convinced that these young people were not reformers, but Cultural Revolution-style radicals "objectively" opposed to reform who mouthed reform slogans to ward off punishment. The U.S. public became enamored of the movement that flowered in May 1989 because they saw in it a correlative of Western civil society, as symbolized by the Goddess of Democracy.

In fact, it was none of these things, though it shared characteristics with all of them. Although relatively sympathetic to Zhao and his reform grouping, the demonstrators were of no political use to Zhao because they could not be persuaded to leave once their point had been made, insisting on remaining until their illegal presence became an embarrassment to their would-be patrons. Although they employed certain Cultural Revolution tactics (such as public criticism of selected central leaders), this generation of young people espoused middle-class liberal—rather than radical proletarian—objectives and utilized nonviolent—if somewhat disruptive—media-conscious tactics. Although clearly entranced with democracy (and seemingly everything Western, including fashion, music, and technology) they were none too clear what it was, as indicated by their inability to make decisions concerning their own movement unless absolute consensus was obtained, resulting in marching orders repeatedly dictated by their most extreme contingent.[43] Just as their decision-making capacity was paralyzed by their need for consensus, their authoritative organization of the Square eerily echoed the CCP's organization of the central government. In Isaiah Berlin's terms, the demonstrators understood democracy in terms of "freedom from," not "freedom to." Having dared to be free, they seemed paralyzed by the next step.

Although perhaps a transitional or "emergent" phenomenon, the Chinese public sphere in 1989 was thus still recognizably a legatee of its unique historical pedigree. Its substantive dimension included a strong emphasis on selflessness. Thus, everyone engaged in the confrontation became ennobled—from the students, whose sincerity was most convincingly demonstrated by their hunger strike, which struck a chord among the food-obsessed Chinese,[44] to the highest leadership, where even Li Peng professed great solicitude for the students. It was perhaps in part due to the ennobling cast of the public spotlight that it proved so difficult for these amateur performers to leave the stage. After public negotiations were demanded and sometimes granted, the students would then quarrel about whether the right persons had been selected as negotiating partners and complain about lack of television coverage. Although by their own lights nothing was settled at these sessions, new sessions were repeatedly demanded. It was easy for the hardliners to conclude that negotiations would continue as long as there was an audience.

On the other hand, the regime's failure to show *renqing wei* when it excluded students from Hu Yaobang's state funeral was a serious public relations blunder, as was Li Peng's wooden public performance throughout the negotiations. Zhao Ziyang's emotional rendezvous with hunger strikers on the night of 19 May was in contrast quite "sincere" by Chinese standards, although too late for either side. Whereas leaks were, strictly speaking, avoided, elite-mass coalitions were tacitly formed via the nuances of public rhetoric, most notably when Zhao used his televised audience with Gorbachev to announce that Deng had made secret arrangements giving him veto power over all central decisions—an announcement calculated to infuriate the hardline contingent. Thus, a horizontal cleavage quickly became transformed into a vertical cleavage, as both sides sought constituencies for their position. The softliners placed their hopes in the NPC, while the hardliners mobilized the army.[45]

The emergent public sphere was also, however, marked by subtle differences from the recent past. Whereas both the Cultural Revolution and the Tiananmen demonstrations were marked by the jubilant, festive atmosphere that came partly from the ennoblement of selflessness and partly from being able to leap from small unit tawdriness to the great public, there was a difference in tone between the peace-loving, flower-child innocence of the Tiananmen demonstrators and the incendiary rhetoric of the Red Guards, who had wanted to "overthrow the king of hell and free all the little devils."[46] This may have been at least partly tactical—whereas the Red Guards had Mao on their side, in 1989 the demonstrators were quite aware—particularly after the 26 April *People's Daily* editorial denouncing "turmoil"—that the country's military strength would be arrayed against them if brought into the fray. Despite the tilt toward Zhao, elite-mass links were looser than during the Cultural Revolution—the vertical coalition with Zhao did not become activated until Zhao had become politically disabled and could no longer use it.[47] Even the link between the hardliners and their constituents was insecure—they seemed to have had some difficulty assembling the military units used to clear the Square. Although the ban on informal, lateral communication media such as big-character posters, tabloids, and intercity *chuanlian* held fairly well, more advanced communication techniques took their place. The telephone and fax machine became functional equivalents of *chuanlian;* students used beepers, walkie-talkies, megaphones, and even cellular telephones to facilitate local communications. When censorship was lifted by the moderates during the first two weeks of May, the Chinese press functioned as an effective nationwide communications network and the international media, particularly those with a Chinese audience (VOA and BBC), functioned indirectly in this capacity until transmissions were jammed.

The purge that was undertaken after Tiananmen—the most thorough since the fall of the Gang of Four—swept the public sector clear of opposition. Immediately after 4 June chief editors, prominent journalists, and any intellectuals who had been so indiscreet as to display their sympathy for the protesters were discharged and punished. A second purge was launched in mid-1990, focused on Shanghai. Media rhetoric became much more ideological and lockstep, and an attempt was made to revitalize the revolutionary institutions of criticism, self-criticism, mass line, and political "study"—with not altogether successful results. The public security apparatus has become more powerful, ubiquitous, and intrusive. The public space that the authorities lost control of had been recovered by brute force. A shocked public ceded the field to the regime's superior firepower and on subsequent occasions offered only tepid challenges—such as the shattering of small bottles—to the refurbished Maoist symbols displayed there. The regime, however, has not yet fully reclaimed control of the public arena, exposing its lack of confidence in its ability to do so by the obsessiveness with which it has fenced the people out of it.

CONCLUSION

Contrary to the impression of the Western popular press and certain Western scholars that the Chinese public sphere had by 1989 evolved into an analogue of Western civil society,[48] the Chinese concept of the public has retained certain culturally distinct features. Like the political economy in which it nested, the Chinese public sector was at best "half-reformed." The crucial flaw in the civil society analogy was the continuing dependence of the Chinese public sphere on leadership patronage.[49] During the Cultural Revolution, this had been provided by Mao Zedong. During the democracy demonstrations, the late Hu Yaobang provided the only acknowledged elite sponsorship. Zhao Ziyang seemed to be moving into this position, but the students were initially suspicious of Zhao, partly because his own family was tainted by the corruption they were protesting against, and partly because of Zhao's role in bringing down the martyr whose death they were mourning. Thus, the linkage was not formed until it could do neither side any good. In the absence of operational elite sponsorship, the protesters turned increasingly to their own internal leadership, an odd combination of authoritarian organization and ultrademocratic decision-making that proved incapable of making responsible decisions about the issues facing the movement. Thereby stripped of politically effective patronage or responsible internal leadership, the movement stubbornly, passively awaited its own destruction.

Part of the reason for the continuing dependency of the Chinese public sphere is undoubtedly economic. An independent public sphere presupposes an independent media and a middle class capable of supporting it,[50] and although the decentralization of the economy in the context of reform had given rise to distinct tendencies in this direction,[51] both the publicly owned but administratively decentralized and relatively autonomous enterprises, such as Shanghai's *World Economic Herald*, and the collectively or privately owned enterprises, such as the Stone Corporation, retained ties to the regime that made it quite easy to whip them back into line once the chips were down. Hard-won progress toward press autonomy was, therefore, quickly relinquished once martial law was imposed.[52]

Another part of the reason was, however, conceptual. One of the major distinguishing features of the Chinese notion of the public is that it is a substantively as well as procedurally defined space. The broad outlines of that substantive content, including the emphasis on selflessness and the demand for "human feeling," are inherited from Chinese cultural tradition. But this does not supply the specific strategy and tactics implied by service to those ideals. Historically, it has been the role of the charismatic leader to step into the public spotlight and provide that strategy, as Mao did, for better or for worse, during the Cultural Revolution. The Western conception of a pluralistic and substantively undefined public sector is alien to the Chinese dedication to the movement as a realization of specific substantive objectives. Ironically, China's partial reform, with its denigration of the cult and emphasis on peace, democracy, and consensual decision-making, tended to inhibit the emergence of such a leader. The movement's leadership vacuum proved its Achilles' heel when confronted by a determined and ruthless opposition. Lacking leadership, the movement became an organism in and for itself—rather than a rational means to its participants' ends—whose maintenance and enhancement needs proved all-consuming, ultimately sacrificing participants to its blind craving for growth.

NOTES

1. I wish to thank Chin-Chuan Lee for inspiring me to write this piece and the other participants in the symposium sponsored by the China Times Center, as well as the anonymous reader, for their helpful comments. A more elaborate version of this chapter appears in my book *China Under Reform* (Boulder, CO: Westview, 1994).

2. Chang Hao, *Liang Ch'i-ch'ao and Intellectual Transition in China* (Cambridge, MA: Harvard University Press, 1971); I-fan Cheng, "'Kung' as an Ethos in Late Nineteenth Century China: The Case of Wang Hsien-ch'ien (1842–1918)," in Paul A. Cohen and John Schrecker (eds.), *Reform in Nineteenth-Century China* (Cambridge, MA: East Asian Research Center, Harvard University, 1976); Prasenjit Duara, *Culture, Power, and the State: North China Villages, 1900–1942* (Stanford, CA: Stanford University Press, 1988); Keith Schoppa, *Chinese Elites and Political Change: Zhejiang Province in the Early Twentieth Century* (Cambridge, MA: Harvard University Press, 1982); Mary Backus Rankin, "'Public Opinion' and Political Power: *Qingyi* in Late Nineteenth Century China," *Journal of Asian Studies* 41, no. 3 (May 1982): 453-84; William T. Rowe, *Hankow: Conflict and Community in a Chinese City, 1796–1895* (Stanford: Stanford University Press, 1989); William T. Rowe, "The Public Sphere in Modern China," *Modern China* 16, no. 3 (July 1990): 309–329.

3. Although in principle the public/private juxtaposition is stark, in practice it is less so. Given the relatively modest bureaucratic resources available, it was practically impossible to compel compliance. Individuals had substantial autonomy within their nuclear or extended family, guild, *Landsmannschaft*, religious sect, secret society, or literary club. Much social activity took place with little active regard for how it conformed to official orthodoxy, leading Whyte to infer the existence of a "de facto civil society" in late imperial China. Martin K. Whyte, "Urban China: A Civil Society in the Making?" in Arthur Rosenbaum (ed.), *State and Society in China: The Consequences of Reform* (Boulder, CO: Westview, 1992), pp. 77–103.

4. Donald J. Munro, "The Concept of 'Interest' in Chinese Thought" (Paper prepared for the Workshop on the Pursuit of Political Interest in the People's Republic of China, Ann Arbor, Michigan, 10–17 August 1977).

5. As most cogently argued (outside the CCP canon itself) in Richard Solomon, *Mao's Revolution and the Chinese Political Culture* (Berkeley: University of California Press, 1971).

6. Mao Zedong, "On the Correct Handling of Contradictions Among the People," in Mao Tse-tung, *Four Essays in Philosophy* (Beijing: Foreign Languages Press, 1966), p. 81; as cited in Munro, "The Concept of Interest," p. 14, n. 27.

7. Ding Danian, *Gongchanzhuyi Renshengguan* (*Communist Life View*) (Shanghai: Huadong Renmin Chubanshe, 1953), p. 22; as cited in Munro, "The Concept of Interest," p. 17.

8. See Jürgen Habermas, *The Structural Transformation of the Public Sphere*, trans. Thomas Burger (Cambridge: MIT Press, 1989); John Keane, *Public Life and Late Capitalism: Toward a Socialist Theory of Democracy* (Cambridge, MA: Cambridge University Press, 1984). Independent reinforcement for this general argument may be found in Robert N. Bellah, et al., *Habits of the Heart: Individualism and Commitment in American Life* (Berkeley, CA: University of California Press, 1985).

9. See the interesting article by Chung-fang Yang, "Conformity and Defiance on Tiananmen Square: A Social Psychological Perspective," in Peter Li, Steven Mark and Marjorie H. Li (eds.), *Culture and Politics in China: An Anatomy of Tiananmen Square* (New Brunswick, NJ: Transaction, 1991), pp. 46–56.

10. True, other factors may have played a role—Zhou Enlai came to Chen's defense and Mao may have had it in for Liu and Deng. But the different public performances of these "human targets" also affected the outcomes.

11. See for example the case of Senator Edmund Muskie, whose emotional response to a newspaper attack proved politically suicidal to his 1975 presidential candidacy. In the world of sports, tennis player John MacEnroe's notoriously emotional public outbursts incurred severe financial penalties. It is perhaps not coincidental that sports metaphors are so common in the political realm.

12. News of the fall of the Gang of Four was first announced by a British News Agency dispatch. The VOA broke the story of the 1986 student demonstrations. Liu Binyan, *China's Crisis, China's Hope*, trans. Howard Goldblatt (Cambridge, MA: Harvard University Press, 1990), p. 95.

13. Indeed, there is also a tendency in the West, perhaps more dominant in continental (e.g., Rousseau, Hegel, Croce) than in Anglo-American philosophical traditions, to define public opinion as "pressure toward conformity." According to this way of thinking, the "public" media are not neutral instruments of enlightenment, but tools whereby elites manipulate and enforce mass conformity. Elisabeth Noelle-Neumann, *The Spiral of Silence: Public Opinion—Our Social Skin* (Chicago: University of Chicago Press, 1980); Alvin Gouldner, *The Dialectic of Ideology and Technology* (New York: Oxford University Press, 1978), esp. chap. 4; Friederich Pollock, "Empirical Research into Public Opinion," in Paul Connerton (ed.), *Critical Sociology* (New York: Penguin, 1976), pp. 225–36.

14. Tang Tsou, "Twentieth Century Chinese Politics: The Game to Win All—A Theoretical Perspective and a Research Design" (Unpublished paper, University of Chicago, Dec. 1991).

15. For an articulate defense of the dissident tradition, see Franklin W. Houn, "Rejection of Blind Obedience as a Traditional Chinese and Maoist Concept," *Asian Thought and Society* 7, no. 19 (Mar. 1982): 18–31; Ibid. 7, no. 21 (May 1982): 264–79.

16. Sun Tzu, *The Art of War*, trans. Samuel B. Griffith (New York: Oxford University Press, 1971), p. 66. See also Douglas Stuart and William Tow, "The Role of Deception in Chinese Strategic Calculus," in Donald Daniel and Katheryn Herbig (eds.), *Military Deception* (New York: Pergamon, 1982), pp. 292–316.

17. Mao, for example, complained bitterly about Peng Zhen's privatization of the Beijing municipal Party committee when he was mayor in the early 1960s, referring to it as an "independent kingdom" so tightly controlled that one could not stick a pin in. Mao himself was not, however, immune from similar tendencies, having first his secretary and then his wife promoted to the Party Politburo itself.

18. See, however, Lin Qinshan, *Fengyun Shinian yu Deng Xiaoping* (*A Chaotic Decade and Deng Xiaoping*) (Beijing: PLA Press, 1989), pp. 216, 219, 220, 223, 230–31.

19. See Kevin J. O'Brien, *Reform without Liberalization: China's National People's Congress and the Politics of Institutional Change* (New York: Cambridge University Press, 1990).

20. Tsan-kuo Chang, "Reporting U.S.-China Policy, 1950-1984: Presumptions of Legitimacy and Hierarchy," in Chin-Chuan Lee, (ed.), *Voices of China: The Interplay of Politics and Journalism* (New York: Guilford Press, 1990), pp. 180–202.

21. Michel Oksenberg, "Methods of Communication within the Chinese Bureaucracy," *China Quarterly* (Jan.-Mar. 1974): 1–39.

22. At least for that segment of the population lacking access to the *neibu* publications enumerated below, the media remain the major source of information about national affairs. As Friedman's chapter makes clear in this volume, however, many have become expert at extracting meaning from the glittering generalities they read.

23. This tradition seems to have been broken by the establishment of a State Media and Publications Office (*Xinwen Chuban She*) on 27 January 1987 (during the high tide of the anti-bourgeois liberalization campaign), under the direction of Du Daozheng, former editor of *Guangming Ribao*. Although its precise functions are unclear, this agency seems to have been modeled on the censorship bureaus of Eastern Europe. See *China Directory, 1988* (Tokyo: Radio Press, Nov. 1987), p. 111.

24. Party organ newspapers' editors are appointed by the organization department after discussion and decision by the standing committee of the Party committee at that level, and normally the managing editor and editor-in-chief are members of that Party committee. When necessary, they may attend standing committee meetings of the same level Party committee as non-voting delegates to make sure they understand the intentions of the Party committee on sensitive issues. Party newspaper workers join the Party committee's unit and are "national cadres" paid by the central government. All newspapers on the national level have members from the Politburo or Secretariat who are assigned supervisory responsibilities as well as ideological supervision. Any member of the Central Committee is permitted to criticize articles in the national papers, and the latter are usually obliged to recant. See Liu, *China's Crisis*, p. 84.

25. A number of Xinhua and *People's Daily* editorials were penned by Mao, the most famous being "Press Du Yuming to Surrender," "Carry the Revolution Through to the End," and "Five Criticisms White Paper."

26. During the 1981 public criticism of Bai Hua, for example, although the *Liberation Daily* (*Jiefang Ribao*) published one criticism after another, the *People's Daily* remained on the sidelines, not publishing a single criticism of Bai Hua. A former *People's Daily* reporter says everyone knew this, and knew that it was politically feasible because the campaign was not led by Deng Xiaoping. But as Hu Yaobang's influence declined, so did the degree of freedom. Liu, *China's Crisis*, pp. 88–89.

27. Yan Huai, "Understanding the Political System of Contemporary China," (Princeton: Center for Modern China, 1991), p. 30; as cited in Su Shaozhi, "Chinese Communist Ideology and Media Control," in this volume.

28. Oksenberg, "Methods": 1–3.

29. *Cankao Xiaoxi* was introduced in the late 1950s amid some controversy—Mao Zedong once called it "the Communist Party running a newspaper for the bourgeoisie"—because it contained international news as well as fragments of Hong Kong and Taiwan news that could not be published in newspapers for sale to the general public. At first, a regulation limited access to cadres at or above the agency level. Later, because the CCP decreed that "the working class is the leadership class," access was expanded to include factory workers. When, after the rise of Deng Xiaoping, the CCP decided that "intellectuals are part of the working class," even secondary school teachers could read it. It is now simultaneously printed in 25 Chinese cities, and each copy is read by several people. See Lu Keng, "Press Control in 'New China' and 'Old China'," and Marlowe Hood, "The Use and Abuse of Mass Media by Chinese Leaders During the 1980s," in this volume; Jennifer Grant, "Internal Reporting by Investigative Journalists in China and Its Influence on Government Policy," *Gazette* 41, no. 1 (1988): 53–65.

30. Lowell Dittmer, "Bases of Power in Chinese Politics: A Theory and an Analysis of the Fall of the 'Gang of Four,'" *World Politics*, 31 (Oct. 1978): 26–61.

31. For a translation of the famous big-character poster of Li Yizhe, posted in Canton in the 1974, see Li I-che, "Concerning Socialist Democracy and Legal System," *Issues and Studies* 12, no. 1 (Jan. 1976): 110–48.

32. See Merle Goldman, "The Role of the Press in Post-Mao Political Struggles," in this volume.

33. To say that it does not "fit well" within the unit is not to say that it does not occur, but that when it does the unit's efficient functioning is adversely affected. There are many studies that show how this transpires. See Yue Daiyun, *To the Storm* (Berkeley: University of California Press, 1985).

34. For a relatively systematic attempt to analyze mass mobilization, see Charles Cell, *Revolution at Work: Mobilization Campaigns in China* (New York: Basic Books, 1977).

35. See Su Shaozhi, "Chinese Communist Ideology and Media Control," in this volume.

36. Thus there have been no underground newspapers or *samizdat* or mass political organizations in China (except during brief breakdowns of public control, such as the Cultural Revolution). Underground periodicals existed in the Soviet Union during the 18 years of the Brezhnev era, and there are currently 30,000 pop-

ular organizations there, including fishing and hunting clubs. Liu, *China's Crisis*, p. 24.

37. Tang Tsou, *The Cultural Revolution and Post-Mao Reforms: A Historical Perspective* (Chicago: University of Chicago Press, 1986), pp. 112–43.

38. See Brantly Womack, "Politics and Epistemology in China Since Mao," *China Quarterly* (Dec. 1979): 768–92; Charles Burton, *Political and Social Change in China Since 1978* (New York: Greenwood Press, 1990).

39. In the early 1950s, only two newspapers were assigned by the government to cover economic news: *Dagong Bao* (Beijing) and *Xinwen Bao* (Shanghai). But in 1960, *Xinwen Bao* merged with *Jiefang Ribao*, leaving only one specialized economic newspaper left in the country. Its coverage, moreover, was not particularly "economic", focussing on current political and international news. Bangtai Xu, "Press Freedom in China: A Case Study of *World Economic Herald* before 1989" (M.A. thesis, Asian Studies, University of California-Berkeley, 1989).

40. Of the total of 151 stories appearing on the first page of the same paper in January 1979, only 49 were economic reports. In January 1980, the corresponding figures were 173 economic stories out of a total of 312. Bangtai Xu, "Press Freedom."

41. See Lynn T. White III, "All the News: Structure and Politics in Shanghai's Reform Media," and Jinglu Yu "The Structure and Function of Chinese Television, 1979-1989," in Lee (ed.), *Voices of China*.

42. For more on the struggle over news objectivity during the 1980s, see Li Liangrong, "The Historical Fate of 'Objective Reporting' in China," in this volume.

43. See Dorothy J. Solinger, "Democracy with Chinese Characteristics," *World Policy Journal* (Fall 1989): 621–32.

44. See Sun Longqi, *Zhongguo Wenhua de "Shenceng Jiegou"* (*The Deep Structure of Chinese Culture*) (Taipei: Gufeng, 1986).

45. "It was clear that Zhao was trying to betray Deng in public," wrote one eyewitness. "The response was enormous—on 17 May, more than one million people, consisting of Chinese of all walks of life as well as students, demonstrated. For the first time, slogans in great numbers were directed at Deng, demanding his retirement." King K. Tsao, "Civil Disobedience and Dissent Against the Party-State: An Eyewitness Account of the 1989 Chinese Student Movement," in Li, *Culture and Politics in China*, pp. 153–71.

46. Although the students themselves were in principle nonviolent and sufficiently well-organized to enforce that commitment, they did attract a considerable following of workers, *getihu*, and assorted local and transient citizens. This heterogeneous "rabble" showed a willingness to use (and did use) violent resistance in the context of military suppression and a collapse of the movement's leadership.

47. He seems to have been closely chaperoned by colleagues during the week of 13–20 May when his position was in question.

48. See Rowe, "Public Sphere"; David Strand, "Protest in Beijing: Civil Society and Public Sphere in China," in *Problems of Communism* 39, no. 3 (May-June 1990): 1–19.

49. See Lee Feigon, *China Rising: The Meaning of Tiananmen* (Chicago: I.R. Dee, 1990).

50. Habermas, *The Structural Transformation*.

51. Mayfair Mei-hui Yang, "Between State and Society: The Construction of Corporateness in a Chinese Socialist Factory," *Australian Journal of Chinese Affairs* (July 1989): 35–40, 55.

52. Seth Faison, "The Changing Role of the Chinese Media," in Tony Saich (ed.), *The Chinese People's Movement: Perspectives on Spring 1989* (Armonk, NY: M.E. Sharpe, 1990), pp. 145–64.

7

STRIVING FOR PREDICTABILITY: THE BUREAUCRATIZATION OF MEDIA MANAGEMENT IN CHINA

Judy Polumbaum

In his classic study of modern bureaucracies, French scholar Michel Cro-zier observed that adaptability is a key to the functioning and survival of complex organizations. He identified the challenge of striking a balance between the conflicting goals of predictability on the one hand and flexi-bility on the other as the central dilemma of modern institutional life.[1]

Crozier's framework arose from his research on industrial and govern-ment bureaucracies, but it readily translates to mass media organizations and institutions—indeed, it fits the journalistic enterprise perhaps better than any other type of endeavor. The news media in any society must cap-ture and construct coherent stories from the infinite possibilities pre-sented by events and issues in a manner that fills allotted space or time and suits the demands of daily, hourly, or even minute-by-minute pro-duction schedules. It is not surprising that much of the scholarly literature on newsmaking identifies ideologies, strategies, rules, routines, and ritu-als by which journalists and news organizations tame the subjective and unpredictable nature of news.[2]

Does this framework apply to the state-controlled news apparatus of the People's Republic of China? If so, how might tensions between pre-dictability and flexibility play out in that system? This chapter examines the changing balance between concerns for predictability and allowances for flexibility in Chinese news management since the launching of eco-nomic reforms in the late 1970s. It argues, firstly, that predictability is an essential objective of newswork in China, as it must be for any industry that operates according to clocks and timetables, depends on steady sup-plies of raw materials, and seeks ongoing acceptance by a mass of con-sumers; secondly, that flexibility became an additional necessity of newswork during the post-Mao reform period, when existing adaptive capacities in the system began to be exercised; and thirdly, that in the course of the reforms, inherent contradictions between the drive for predictability and the requisites of flexibility which had laid dormant for decades—the quandary pinpointed by Crozier—emerged as a salient predicament for those seeking to manage the news as well as for those who collect, process, and present it.

The discussion pivots on an examination of recent developments in Chinese press control which promise to enhance predictability and hamper flexibility in crucial arenas of newswork. There is considerable empirical evidence that, starting in the late 1980s, Chinese leaders embarked on a new strategy for controlling the news media which represented a marked departure from the Chinese Communist Party's (CCP) approach to press management in the past. Most importantly, the new approach involved a shift from informal to formal regulatory mechanisms. It allowed for flexibility in certain realms of information, such as "service," entertainment, and economic coverage, while making predictability paramount in other realms, notably political coverage. The new strategy easily could have been interpreted as a backlash against the domestic news media's energizing role in the political protest movement that spread across urban China in the spring of 1989,[3] but this was only partly the case. In fact, the redirection of media management had been well underway before the protests occurred.

The first part of this chapter reviews changes in mainland Chinese journalism during the reform period that helped bring requisites of flexibility to the fore and highlights paradoxical characteristics of CCP press control that facilitated adaptations to changing circumstances. The second part focuses on the ongoing reorientation of Chinese authorities' approach to news management. It provides evidence of the transition from a largely informal control structure to a more formalized structure and discusses the implications of this shift.

THE CONTEXT OF CONTINUITY AND CHANGE

At first glance, the premises and protocols of mainland China's mass communication system seem designed to reinforce regularity and uniformity. In philosophy and organization, the system is centralized and hierarchical: news outlets at all levels are expected to promote policies and priorities set at the top, and Communist Party and government officials, although far from exercising monolithic control over the media, remain chief arbiters of how "news" is defined.[4] These conditions suggest that predictability is the overriding dynamic of mainland Chinese journalism.

Upon closer scrutiny, however, China's news apparatus exhibits far more flexibility than a strictly totalitarian model would lead one to expect.[5] The media control system has never been as watertight as China's authorities would wish; messages emanating from the center have always been subject to leaks, interference, and distortion en route to the periphery.[6] But the impossibility of communicating official messages with precision became especially obvious after the launching of China's economic reform program. Rigid concepts and practices in newswork that had withstood the Maoist era proved dysfunctional in the post-Mao period, and flexibility became essential to the maintenance of the system itself.

The redirection of China's development policy in the late 1970s—away from class struggle and continuing revolution in favor of modernization via market-oriented means—brought unprecedented pressures to bear on Chinese journalism. The resulting changes, amply documented in the predecessor to this volume,[7] constitute the context in which flexibility emerged as an important and desirable aspect of newswork.

At an institutional level, the news media quickly began to respond to new economic and social strains. In mass communication as in other fields, economic experimentation and sociopolitical change worked upon each other synergistically. The expansion of China's media marketplace in terms of number of outlets and variety of offerings spurred journalistic competitiveness and strengthened responsiveness to consumer demand. Cuts in state subsidies and the rise of advertising and other alternative forms of financing pointed the way toward greater economic independence, which in turn helped lay the groundwork for more editorial autonomy.

The reforms also generated changes in the cultural climate of media organizations, perspectives of individual journalists, and attitudes among the media audience. The same open-door policies that brought foreign investment into China also admitted foreign correspondents, alien ideas about journalism, and the wide world of information overload. China's domestic press corps swelled with a younger generation of journalists who looked askance at the docility and conformity which marked their predecessors. Unwilling to placidly accept the conventions that equated propaganda with news, these young people, backed by intrepid veterans among the older generation, began to experiment with new perspectives, new genres, and new techniques. Meanwhile, the Chinese media audience grew ever more variegated, demanding, and discriminating. For these and other reasons, adaptation was not a choice—it was an inevitability.

Paradoxically, the old paved the way for the new in this process: Timeworn characteristics of Chinese Communist journalism no less than newly-emerging tendencies facilitated the news media's adaptation to the changing environment. China's media system already possessed a capacity for flexibility, albeit one seldom exercised in the past. For decades Chinese news management had operated through a complex and changeable mix of general policy pronouncements, official instructions, ideological suasion, personalized channels, and varying levels of prospective punishment for transgressing ill-defined boundaries. To use Curry's terminology, the CCP preferred a broad and implicit "directive mode" of media supervision rather than specific, explicit methods such as prepublication censorship.[8]

This was in character with the Party's general approach to organizational and ideological supervision, which rested on informal, fluid, and even ambiguous forms of control as much as on formal means.[9] Express or implied coercion usually was an element in the mix—one particularly hard to ignore at times such as the anti-Rightist movement in the late 1950s, the Cultural Revolution decade of 1966–1976, and the suppression of the protest movement of 1989. But even in restrictive periods media controls were far from absolute, and in times of political liberalization controls were often ignored or waived.

The People's Republic had never had a routinized system of institutional censorship; rather, education, socialization, and ad hoc directives guided political functionaries, chief editors, and news staff in figuring out what should or should not get into the news. As Chinese society opened up during the 1980s, it became clearer that the decisive factors in whether information or ideas were released or suppressed, and in where and how they were presented, tended to be situational rather than fixed.[10]

The lack of firm, predictable rules about what was permitted or proscribed meant that amidst the loosening of economic and ideological restraints, Chinese journalists faced opportunities to pursue news more assertively. Those bold enough to throw caution into the wind might get away with a lot more than they would if the boundaries of behavior were clearly defined. And indeed they did: even those who see the "journalism reform" movement of the 1980s as more talk than action agree that the reform ethos emboldened many editors and reporters to challenge the habitual and ideological constraints on selection, coverage, and presentation of news.[11] The late Qin Benli, editor of the ill-fated *World Economic Herald*, a maverick Shanghai weekly that became a prominent casualty of the 1989 government crackdown, was one of the most audacious challengers. He called it "hitting line balls," a reference to the risky and difficult table tennis strategy of aiming the ball so it barely nicks the far edge of the opponent's side.[12]

The elasticity of Chinese press controls became glaringly evident during the height of the 1989 demonstrations, when journalists pressed their luck to the utmost. In urban centers across the country large contingents of reporters, editors, journalism educators, and media scholars joined marches and signed petitions calling for greater democracy and openness. The foreign press corps descended and the whole world watched during April, May, and June, but for a time in mid-May the domestic news media also covered the movement with unprecedented thoroughness and obvious enthusiasm.[13] Ironically, this newfound spirit of press freedom had been unleashed by the very sociopolitical forces which then sought to crush it.

OLD RHETORIC, NEW RIGOR

The press corps constituted a convenient scapegoat after the debacle of 3–4 June 1989, when martial law troops in Beijing converged on the heart of the city to reclaim Tiananmen Square from student demonstrators, killing hundreds of civilians and wounding probably thousands en route. Arrests of journalists and the closing of several especially rambunctious publications constituted only one dimension of the retribution directed at the news media. Party leaders accused journalists of fanning the flames of what now was dubbed a "counterrevolutionary rebellion." They instructed news organizations to review all their coverage of the protest movement and subject it to appropriate criticism, and reshuffled editorial leadership and staff assignments at media outlets which had exhibited the greatest activism.[14]

A conspicuous aspect of press policy in the immediate post-Tiananmen period was the revival of old rhetoric, or what might be called a return to strict constructionism in the definition of the news media's mission. The orthodox view that the press was first and foremost a "mouthpiece" of the Communist Party and government had been discredited by the late 1980s, when freewheeling debates about "journalism reform" reached their peak.[15] Even top leaders had come to stress informational and watchdog ideals for the press, as then-Premier (later Party General Secretary, and after the 1989 reversal, *former* General Secretary) Zhao Ziyang did in his speech to the 13th Party Congress in October 1987. From mid-1989 on, however, the doctrinaire delimitation of news returned. Once again, journalism's primary role was to serve as an official mouthpiece, adhering unquestioningly to the Party line.

The months after the military occupation of Tiananmen Square saw a flurry of speeches, newspaper articles, and commentaries condemning the role of the press during the demonstrations and resurrecting the simplistic formula that service to officialdom automatically equated with service to the people—a formula which a press corps schooled in the contradictions of the Great Leap Forward, the Cultural Revolution, and other instances in which the Party had led the people down paths later deemed erroneous had been questioning openly for several years.

In July 1989, for instance, Shao Huaze, newly transferred from the army's daily newspaper to become chief editor of the *People's Daily*, chastised journalists for undermining policy and "misleading" the public during the previous months.[16] At a journalism forum in November 1989 Zhao Ziyang's replacement as Party General Secretary, Jiang Zemin, observed that many journalists had "turned their backs on the Party and the people" in the upheaval of 1989, and that some had "encouraged the turmoil and the counterrevolutionary rebellion."[17] The reputedly more liberal Politburo member Li Ruihuan, in a somewhat milder speech, declared, "The Party is the exclusive representative of the people's interests. Therefore, the Party's mouthpiece is naturally the mouthpiece of the people."[18]

Simply put, it would seem that the old-guard leadership that emerged in command from the confrontation of 1989 was orchestrating a universally familiar scenario, and one particularly common in the Chinese political tradition: Those who win a contest go about establishing their correctness while exacting penalties and confessions from those who have lost.

Given the recurrence of this pattern throughout the history of the People's Republic, the post-Tiananmen diatribes against the media could be seen as merely products of another pendulum swing. Additionally, the resurgence of a crude rhetoric of propaganda could be seen as laughable; such declarations sounded more anachronistic than ever in a world where Communist-led systems long professing the same principles were falling like ninepins.

Besides resurrecting old refrains, however, this drive to reconsolidate Party authority over the press had a novel aspect. This time, the old rhetoric was accompanied by a burgeoning of new administrative and regulatory efforts. The most important features were not the most obvious; indeed, some developments were hardly perceptible. But, taken together, they portended a radical reshaping of press management. Evidence of the change included the creation of new administrative agencies for press management; the promulgation of formal codes and regulations governing the activities of media organizations and news practitioners; newly-imposed or newly-enforced registration and licensing requirements for journalism outlets and journalists; and the resort to ostensibly neutral bureaucratic mechanisms to mask political actions such as the closing of troublesome newspapers and the punitive demotion or transfer of key news personnel.

In short, the controls in what used to be a fairly fluid and manipulatable system were becoming increasingly formalized and regularized. The overall pattern suggested a subtle, gradual, and still-evolving institutionalization of media management.

REGULARIZATION AS A PRODUCT
OF REFORM AND REALISM

The shift in media management strategy belonged to the larger movement toward rationalization spawned by the reform program. The notion that a tradition of "rule by men, not by law" had visited countless ills upon Chinese society was broadly accepted in post-Mao China, and the reforms ushered in efforts to codify and regularize human conduct in many realms. This was most evident in the rebuilding of the legal system.[19] In part, this agenda grew out of a yearning for predictability and certainty in the wake of the Cultural Revolution, when arbitrary use and abuse of power reached ludicrous and tragic extremes. In part, it reflected the changing nature of political legitimacy in China: in Weber's terms, the new emphasis on laws and rules could be seen as part of a standard evolutionary pattern in which "rational" authority replaces authority resting on "charismatic" grounds.[20]

In the context of China's ambitions to modernize, however, the rationalization urge represented a double-edged sword. On the one hand, development of a modern system of laws and regulations could advance development at home and also bolster the country's position in international affairs and global commerce. On the other hand, legal structures in some respects might reinforce conservatism instead of spurring progress.

The distinction between China's ongoing legislative efforts in economic and political matters highlighted this pitfall. As legal scholar Margaret Woo notes, while the focus of Chinese legislative activity in the economic arena after mid-1989 remained promotion of economic activity, especially foreign investment, the main thrust of legislative initiatives in the political arena was to maintain "stability" rather than to promote reform.[21] In other words, various legal efforts were working at cross-purposes—to simultaneously foster change and preserve the status quo.

The developments in Chinese press control provided further illustration of tendencies operating at cross-purposes. On the one hand, the creation of specialized agencies and detailed regulations dealing with the news media continued an evolutionary process set in motion by the reforms, with ostensibly progressive intent, and initially with broad support among journalists distressed over the mercurial nature of press control and editorial decision-making. On the other hand, the regularization of press control also grew out of conservative impulses in China's leadership. The accentuation of the process after mid-1989 indicated the ascendancy of these impulses in response to changes wrought upon the national psyche by the reforms themselves and compounded by the trauma of Tiananmen.

The assumption that progressive and conservative motivations can co-alesce in the cause of journalism reform might seem untenable in hind-sight, but such a notion was implicit at the outset of the reform period. It began to unravel in the debates of the 1980s, and especially in the contro-versy over the drafting of a national press law. Reformist journalists, edu-cators, and researchers sought remedy from arbitrary exercise of political power and protection from frivolous libel suits through passage of such a law. They hoped the law would carve out explicit safeguards beyond the vague "freedom of the press" provision in Article 35 of the Chinese Con-stitution, as well as clearly spell out the limits of press freedom. For differ-ent reasons, functionaries concerned with the news media's potential to hamper official business and harm reputations also harbored hopes for such a law—mainly the hope that it might restrain the press from excess zeal. Ideological differences over the press law proved a tremendous drag on the drafting process, and the latest draft in circulation was indefinitely shelved following the demonstrations of spring 1989, while consolidation of media management with an emphasis on proscription rather than pro-tection picked up speed.[22]

The expansion and fortification of institutionalized press controls re-flected a new realism on the part of Chinese political authorities, includ-ing a realistic appraisal of journalistic propensities in the aftermath of Tiananmen. The limits of ideological exhortation—a crucial method of in-fluence and control in earlier periods—became especially obvious follow-ing the brutality of 3–4 June 1989. To journalists of reformist bent, to those with fond memories of the relatively relaxed and open climate of the late 1980s, to those for whom the military occupation of the symbolic heart of the nation was an unimaginable shock, exhortations now carried little weight. Even journalists who previously felt confident that reforms could unfold under Party leadership were inclined to balk at official efforts to reinspire their faith. Thus, the leaders who emerged as self-proclaimed victors in the struggle against "counterrevolution" faced the need for new methods to engineer consent, or at least compliance.

Coercive measures such as the heightened presence of soldiers in and around central news organizations, the detention of renegade journalists, and the trials of several political activists associated with reformist publi-cations constituted part of "killing the chicken to scare the monkeys," as the Chinese say. But coercion had limited utility as a management device over a press corps saturated with reformist sentiment—and now with confusion and outrage as well. Papers still had to be published and broad-casts aired, and coercion alone would not bring the news media back into line in fulfilling these tasks. Nor would continuation of heavy-handed tac-tics against journalists or others improve China's blighted image in the world. Another approach was required.

ADMINISTRATIVE INNOVATIONS SINCE TIANANMEN

An apparatus for tightening up administrative supervision of the press was already in place in the form of the State Press and Publications Administration (SPPA), a ministry-level agency set up in the spring of 1987 with corresponding agencies at provincial and municipal levels. The next few years saw the elaboration of news management through bureaucratic organs, and the adoption of a succession of legal measures, administrative regulations, and occupational codes directed at the news media and their personnel.

The SPPA was an important agent in the regularization process. In 1987–1988 the agency carried out its first nationwide review of the politics, rationales, and management of publishing houses, newspapers, and other periodicals; more than 600 publications were shut down or merged in this drive. Authorization for new publications also tightened up, with only 50 new newspapers approved in 1988, along with 35 that switched from internal to open publication.[23] A directive issued in October 1989 launched a second consolidation drive, resulting in the closing or merger of 190 newspapers, nearly 12% of the total nationwide. Additionally, some 600 magazines had to cease publication in 1990.[24] These sweeps evidently combined political audits with scrutiny of the business side—by official accounting, most of the closings and mergers had a financial or managerial rationale. In the first round, for instance, only five newspapers were said to have been closed for political errors, while in the latest reevaluation only eight closings were acknowledged as political.[25]

The SPPA's promulgation of the first set of formal detailed regulations governing newspaper registration, operation, and content represented further evidence of the new managerial rigor.[26] Adopted in December 1990 and publicized in early 1991, the regulations highlight how a restrictive posture prevailed over demands for expanded protection for the press—the major controversy fueling debates on the draft press law in preceding years. Aside from specifying bureaucratic requirements and procedures that formerly had been left largely up to happenstance and human whim, the regulations explicitly enshrined the preeminence of Party leadership over the press—a statement whose necessity, but not reality, had been hotly disputed in earlier discussions of the draft press law.[27]

Checks on the professional practice of journalism were tightened up considerably. The SPPA came to oversee issuance of press credentials as well as permissions for news organizations to operate "journalism stations," or local news bureaus. As of 15 November 1990 all journalists were required to have SPPA press cards. By the end of 1990 74,254 journalists were accredited, with the process not yet completed. Another 6,335 temporary credentials had been issued as well. In addition, there were 939 news bureaus registered nationwide.[28]

The establishment of a special central government "information office" to supervise propaganda aimed at foreign audiences—a move that received tangential reference in the Chinese press for many months before being formally announced in mid-1991—was another expression of administrative elaboration.[29] Previously, the assembly and dissemination of material for foreign audiences were overseen in a looser, ad hoc manner. Policy emanated in part from a working group in charge of overseas propaganda directly under the Party's Central Secretariat, but when it came to interpretation and enforcement of policy, lines of command were fuzzy. Editors of the English-language *China Daily*, for instance, often reported to the Central Committee Propaganda Department and the Foreign Ministry, but the newspaper was not formally or exclusively in the charge of either. The new office under the State Council potentially created a more specialized and visible locus of coordination.

Yet another relevant development was the adoption of a code of ethics by the All-China Journalism Federation in January 1991 and its subsequent ratification by the Federation's new, conservative board.[30] The key point is not the contents of the code. In fact, numerous elements Western journalists might applaud, such as a call for "authenticity" in journalism and a ban on running advertisements in the guise of news, accompanied the emphasis in the code on Party loyalty. More significantly, the code, while not technically binding, formalized many ideas that used to be part of a fluid debate over the rights and responsibilities of journalists.

In the aftermath of Tiananmen administrative strategies provided a peculiar cosmetic gloss for how personnel decisions at news organizations were justified. An initial wave of replacements of top personnel at some key news organizations soon after 4 June 1989 was nothing surprising; this is a common response to insubordination, and not only in China. Additional reshuffling was carried out later, however, and in a seemingly more methodical manner, although the precise scope of this development is unclear. The Hong Kong press reported the demotions and reassignments of 20 or so upper- and mid-level editors at the *People's Daily* in the spring of 1991, with some being transferred out of Beijing. Other informal estimates of those affected at this one news organization ranged as high as 40 or 60. These reassignments could be interpreted as punishment for the newspaper's irrepressible behavior during the spring of 1989. Chinese officials, however, offered a bureaucratic rationale: the moves simply "rationalized" a deployment of personnel under new provisions dealing with cadre assignment and were motivated by labor needs rather than by politics.

As the Tiananmen episode receded in time, if not in memory, the repercussions for newsworkers continued to reverberate in smaller incidents. The Hong Kong press reported numerous cases of newsworkers being arrested, tried, and sentenced to prison for divulging confidential information to foreigners. Typically, such cases would be handled under the 1989 law on state secrets, superseding an earlier set of vague, catch-all regulations. Reformers had welcomed the update since it narrowed authorities' discretion in defining what materials were confidential; nonetheless, it still may serve to restrict dissemination of a broad range of materials, particularly military information, economic data, and Party documents.[31]

At the same time, however, the Chinese government was relaxing its grip on some of the high-profile troublemakers in journalism circles.[32] The fact that former *People's Daily* editor Hu Jiwei, who had objected to the imposition of martial law during the 1989 protests, was merely disciplined within the Party, rather than arrested, is a case in point. And a former *Beijing Daily* editor imprisoned for revealing the suspension of Hu's Party membership in an article published abroad reportedly was released early for medical reasons. Several prominent journalists were allowed to accept research fellowships in the United States, including former *Guangming Daily* reporter Dai Qing, who had been imprisoned for nine months as a result of her sympathies toward student demonstrators; Wang Ruoshui and his wife Feng Yuan, both formerly of the *People's Daily*; and former *World Economic Herald* reporter Zhang Weiguo, who also had been in prison. These developments could indicate another aspect of realism, namely, the leadership's recognition that heavy-handed treatment of mavericks who were well-known at home and abroad would cause more trouble than it was worth.

Such apparent concessions to international public opinion, however, did not presage abandonment of the underlying strategy for press control. In fact, the goal of strengthening media management was pursued with even greater sophistication. Press supervision underwent a bifurcation of sorts in 1992, most noticeably since the end of that year, when Ding Guanggen replaced Li Ruihuan as the Politburo member in charge of propaganda. On the one hand, the Party and government seemed willing to relinquish control over certain categories of specialized, professional, lifestyle, and entertainment publications. On the other hand, the authorities seemed determined to get a better grip on media that trafficked in political content. Some observers even predicted the establishment of a formal censorship system for the latter, with articles vetted by bureaucrats in administrative departments in accord with specified criteria.[33]

One of Ding's first actions in his new role was to issue a document on publications management calling for tightened supervision over books, journals, and newspapers.[34] Noting that many new periodicals had received approval to publish beginning in the second half of 1992, the document instructed local authorities to be especially vigilant with respect to newspapers and journals of a political nature. It advocated a moratorium on approval of additional publications of this type, along with improved oversight of existing ones.

The Ding document reportedly warned against permitting theorists of "bourgeois liberalization" to sneak their ideas into professional or entertainment papers. This brings to mind the bimonthly *Future and Development*, published by the official Chinese Association for Science and Technology, and closed after its October 1992 issue ran two articles by elderly scholars advocating greater democratization.[35] Apparently, official auspices did not protect unofficial ideas.

Efforts to stamp out what officials consider "pornography" were continuing in tandem with the consolidation of controls over political content; sometimes the two drives were hard to disentangle. During 1992, according to official figures, authorities confiscated 160,000 copies of "obscene" publications and 100,000 with "reactionary" content, as well as more than two million videotapes, including 120,000 defined as pornographic. They shut down 8,400 sales stalls and 5,400 printing units dealing in these materials and arrested some 3,000 persons in connection with such cases.[36]

When it comes to moral scruples, again, official auspices did not necessarily offer protection. The Ministry of Culture's newspaper *China Culture News* was barred from putting out a new weekend edition after the debut issue, published 1 January 1993, carried several photographs of nudes. Many readers must have been disappointed, for the 300,000 copies of the first *China Culture News* weekend supplement sold out in a matter of days.[37]

THE TEMPTATIONS OF CERTAINTY

In China, one might conclude, certain categories of publications and subject matter are vulnerable to restriction not merely because of their inherent "undesirable" character, but perhaps even more because they are likely to attract a following. This brings to light contradictions confronting the Chinese media under market reforms. As the push for economic expansion resumed with renewed vigor in 1992, news and publishing units were expected to redouble their efforts as publicists for the marketplace and, increasingly, to plunge into the marketplace themselves. They were being encouraged to operate as businesses, and ultimately many would be *forced* to do so. With two-thirds of the 1,750 newspapers registered at the end of 1992 still reliant on state support, the government was planning to phase out virtually all newspaper subsidies, with exceptions for a few central Party organs, beginning in 1994.[38] Yet, in the face of growing inducements to print anything that would sell, publications still couldn't print *everything* that would sell. Entrepreneurs and reformers who might have made common cause out of ambiguities in the system had to recognize not only that certain types of content remained off-limits, but that the limits were clearer, and that the grey areas of maneuverability were correspondingly shrinking.

In their efforts to make the most of the marketplace, many Chinese newspapers added pages as well as weekend editions and specialized subsidiary publications, thus creating more space and additional vehicles for advertising. As of early 1993 several official municipal papers put out issues of 8 or 12 broadsheet pages, and the *Guangzhou Daily* had gone as high as 20, in contrast to the previous standard of four. Newspapers in southern China pioneered the publishing of weekend papers and other spin-offs in the 1980s, and the trend has taken hold in the North in the 1990s. A rosy prediction might be that such growth in publication numbers and size necessitates increased content, inevitably leading to pluralism, but this is not necessarily the case. Under conditions of tightened political supervision over the press, expansion does not equate with press freedom: it is more aptly described as a means to increase advertising revenue.

Certainly, the boundaries of newswork were firmer after 1989, even if the efficacy of the new strategy for news management had yet to be proven. Ironically, the formalization of press controls could be said to fulfill reformist aspirations because it introduced greater regularity and predictability into what was a terribly uncertain, arbitrary, and capricious environment. But reformers could not feel happy that much of the regulatory framework was laid in the post-Tiananmen climate of coercion, conservatism, and timidity. One could also argue that Chinese leaders have grown shrewder about managing the media; but the smoothly oiled machine some might envision remains an elusive goal. And in elevating the allure of predictability over the necessity of flexibility, the regularization process planted the seeds of new problems.

Crozier recognized the dangers of such a situation. "[I]n any kind of organization," he observed, "there is a constant pressure to escape from reality. This tendency corresponds to what popular sentiment calls 'bureaucratic tendencies.' Centralization is one of the ways to achieve it; completely impersonal rules are another. Both permit escape from otherwise necessary adjustments."[39]

Both are expressed in the history of press controls in contemporary China. For several decades journalism was directed in a centralized and hierarchical manner, although through informal and irregular means. During the 1980s centralized command broke down under the pressures of reform. In the 1990s the proliferation of formal administrative structures and rules might ensure greater predictability in the short run, but in the long run the new approach is likely to produce fatal results, namely, the inability to adapt to social change.

NOTES

1. Michel Crozier, *The Bureaucratic Phenomenon* (Chicago: University of Chicago Press, 1964), esp. pp. 183–87.

2. Examples from the U.S. context include Warren Breed, "Social Control in the Newsroom," *Social Forces* 33 (1955): 326–35; Leon V. Sigal, *Reporters and Officials* (Lexington, MA: D.C. Heath, 1973); Bernard Roshco, *Newsmaking* (Chicago: University of Chicago Press, 1975); Gaye Tuchman, *Making News* (New York: Free Press, 1978); Herbert J. Gans, *Deciding What's News* (New York: Pantheon, 1979); Mark Fishman, *Manufacturing the News* (Austin, TX: University of Texas Press, 1980); Todd Gitlin, *The Whole World is Watching* (Berkeley: University of California Press, 1980). British and Canadian examples include Peter Schlesinger, *Putting 'Reality' Together: BBC News* (London: Constable, 1978); and Richard V. Ericson, Patricia M. Baranek and Janet B.L. Chan, *Visualizing Deviance* (Toronto: University of Toronto Press, 1987). See also Stanely Cohen and Jock Young (eds.), *The Manufacture of News* (Beverly Hills, CA: Sage, 1981); and Robert Karl Manoff and Michael Schudson (eds.), *Reading the News* (New York: Pantheon, 1986).

3. The journalistic activism of the spring of 1989 and some of the aftereffects are described by Michael J. Berlin, "Chinese Journalists Cover (and Join) the Revolution," *Washington Journalism Review* (Sept. 1989): 31–37; Donald R. Shanor, "The 'Hundred Flowers' of Tiananmen," *Gannett Center Journal* (Fall 1989): 128-36; and Frank Tan, "The *People's Daily*: Politics and Popular Will—Journalistic Defiance in China During the Spring of 1989," *Pacific Affairs* 63, no. 2, (Summer 1990): 151–69.

4. Brantly Womack, "Editor's Introduction," *Media and the Chinese Public: A Survey of the Beijing Media Audience* (Armonk, NY: M.E. Sharpe, 1986).

5. For an elaboration of this point, see Judy Polumbaum, "China's Press: Behind the Stereotype," *Nieman Reports* 46, no. 5 (Spring 1992).

6. Lynn T. White III, "Local Newspapers and Community Change, 1949–1969," in Godwin C. Chu and Francis L.K. Hsu (eds.), *Moving a Mountain: Cultural Change in China* (Honolulu, HI: University Press of Hawaii, 1979).

7. Chin-Chuan Lee (ed.), *Voices of China: The Interplay of Media and Politics* (New York: Guilford Press, 1990).

8. Jane Leftwich Curry, "Media Control in Eastern Europe: Holding the Tide on Opposition," in Curry and Joan R. Dassin (eds.), *Press Control Around the World* (New York: Praeger, 1982), p. 105.

9. Franz Schurmann, *Ideology and Organization in Communist China*, 2nd ed. (Berkeley: University of California Press, 1968).

10. Informal press controls are discussed in detail in Judy Polumbaum, "The Tribulations of China's Journalists After a Decade of Reform," in Lee, *Voices of China*, pp. 33–68.

11. Kenneth Starck and Yu Xu, "Loud Thunder, Small Raindrops: The Reform Movement and the Press in China," *Gazette* 42 (1988): 143–59.

12. Hsiao Ching-chang and Yang Mei-rong, "'Don't Force Us to Lie': The Case of the *World Economic Herald*," in Lee, *Voices of China*, p. 116.

13. See Berlin, "Chinese Journalists," pp. 31–37; Shanor, "The 'Hundred Flowers' of Tiananmen," pp. 128–30; Tan, "The *People's Daily*," pp. 151–69.

14. For more on the post-Tiananmen retribution, see Allison Liu Jernow, *"Don't Force Us to Lie": The Struggle of Chinese Journalists in the Reform Era* (New York: Committee for the Protection of Journalists, 1993), esp. pp. 69–102.

15. On the journalism reform movement, see Stark and Yu, "Loud Thunder"; Polumbaum, "The Tribulations"; Timothy Cheek, "Redefining Propaganda: Debates on the Role of Journalism in post-Mao Mainland China," *Issues and Studies* 25, no. 2 (Feb. 1989): 47–74; and Seth Faison, "The Changing Role of the Chinese Media," in Tony Saich (ed.), *The Chinese People's Movement: Perspectives on Spring 1989* (Armonk, NY: M.E. Sharpe, 1990).

16. Shao Huaze, "Press Reform Must Adhere to the Correct Orientation," *Xinwen Zhanxian (Journalism Battlefront)*, no. 7/8 (30 June 1989): 3–5.

17. Jiang Zemin, "On Several Questions in the Party's Journalism Work," 28 Nov. 1989, published in *People's Daily*, 2 Mar. 1990, pp. 1,4.

18. Li Ruihuan, "Persist in the Guiding Principle of Taking Positive Propaganda as the Main Thrust," 25 Nov. 1989, published in *People's Daily*, 3 Mar. 1990, pp. 1, 2.

19. See Jingshan Wang, "The Role of Law in Contemporary China: Theory and Practice" (Ph.D. dissertation, Cornell University, 1988), esp. pp. 75–81; Ralph H. Folsom and John H. Minan, *Law in the People's Republic of China* (Dordrecht: Martinus Nijhoff Publishers, 1989), pp. 13–17; and Anthony Dicks, "The Chinese Legal System: Reforms in the Balance," *China Quarterly*, no. 119 (Sept. 1989): 545–46.

20. Max Weber, *The Theory of Social and Economic Organization*, A.M. Henderson and Talcott Parsons (ed. and trans.) (New York: Macmillan, 1947), p. 328.

21. Margaret Y.K. Woo, "Legal Reforms in the Aftermath of Tiananmen Square," in Bih-jaw Lin (ed.), *The Aftermath of the 1989 Tiananmen Crisis in Mainland China* (Boulder, CO: Westview, 1992), p. 215.

22. This discussion draws on Judy Polumbaum, "To Protect or Restrict: Points of Contention in China's Draft Press Law," in Pitman B. Potter (ed.), *Domestic Law Reforms in Post-Mao China* (Armonk, NY: M.E. Sharpe, 1993).

23. Zheng Zhongxiang, "Talking Freely About the State Press and Publications Administration in the Midst of Reform" (interview with Du Daozheng), *Xinwen Jizhe (The Journalist)*, no. 2 (1988): 4–9.

24. Zu Yi, "Let the Publications of Newspapers and Periodicals Develop in a Healthy Way," *Banyue Tan (Fortnightly Chats)*, 25 Aug. 1990, pp. 12–14.

25. These included the *World Economic Herald*, whose distribution had been held up, and its chief editor, the late Qin Benli, suspended for content sympathetic to the views of student protesters; the Beijing-based *Economic Weekly*, two of whose editors, Chen Ziming and Wang Juntao, were arrested in connection with the protest movement and subsequently convicted and sentenced to prison terms; and the Beijing-based magazine *New Observer*, whose editor, Ge Yang, a feisty elderly woman and one-time "rightist", had left for the United States.

26. Text in *Xinwen Chubanbao* (*Press and Publishing Journal*), 6 Feb. 1991, p. 2.

27. See "Journalists: Waiting for the Press Law?" *China News Analysis* (Hong Kong), no. 1384 (1 May 1989).

28. *Zhongguo Xinwen Nianjian 1991* (*China Journalism Yearbook* 1991) (Beijing: Chinese Academy of Social Sciences Press, 1991), p. 3.

29. "Information Office to Promote Understanding of China," Xinhua Overseas Service, 13 June 1991; see also Tsai Wen, "Dual Leadership Over External Propaganda Work," *Tangtai* (Hong Kong), 17 Nov. 1990, p. 5.

30. Text in *Xinwen Zhanxian*, no. 5 (1991): 3–4.

31. Timothy A. Gelatt, "The New Chinese State Secrets Law," *Cornell International Law Journal* 22, no. 2 (Spring 1989): 255–62.

32. This occurred with respect to other selected "dissidents" as well. For instance, several imprisoned activists from student and religious circles were released early.

33. *South China Morning Post* (Hong Kong), 28 Dec. 1992, p. 8, reprinted in Foreign Broadcast Information Service/China Daily Report (FBIS), 29 Dec. 1993, pp. 27–28.

34. *Cheng Ming* (Hong Kong), 1 Feb. 1993, pp. 42–44, translated in FBIS, 1 Feb. 1993, pp. 21–24.

35. AFP, 11 Dec. 1992, reprinted in FBIS, 11 Dec. 1992, pp. 15–16.

36. Xinhua Domestic Service, 19 Jan. 1993, translated in FBIS, 28 Jan. 1993, p. 5.

37. *Ming Pao* (Hong Kong), 18 Jan. 1993, p. 7, translated in FBIS, 28 Jan. 1993, pp. 6–7.

38. *Ming Pao* (Hong Kong), 9 Dec. 1992, p. 7, translated in FBIS, 10 Dec. 1992, p. 21.

39. Crozier, *The Bureaucratic Phenomenon*, p. 186.

8

THE OPPOSITIONAL DECODING OF CHINA'S LENINIST MEDIA

Edward Friedman

As recent critical scholarship known as the "reader/response school" informs analysts that authorial intent and reader response need have little or nothing in common, similarly, non-written popular culture cannot be taken at face value in an effort to comprehend popular oppositional possibilities. This is true of all societies and times. Throughout history, Chinese were well versed in attack by innuendo (*hansha sheying*). Symbols, even those made out of cement, are plastic in their meaning. In the American depression of the 1930s, when banks seemed unjustly to foreclose unpaid mortgages and seize the land of virtuous, hard-working farmers, popular consciousness turned even the sadistic robber-killers, Bonnie and Clyde, into popular and protected social bandits who supposedly robbed the unjust banks and helped poor people. In retrospect, popular mythologizing served to indicate support that could come to a reform leader who would oppose the financial moguls, as Franklin Roosevelt did. Consequently, decoding popular mythologies can offer a methodology that provides clues to prospects for a democratic or reform opposition even in the particular situation of contemporary China.

   In Leninist dictatorships,[1] public opinion is inordinately volatile because people must manufacture a good conscience, the result of their daily complicity with an oppressive system required to protect and advance family interests.[2] Typical of this opinion volatility, a poll of people in the Ukraine in the last year of the Soviet Union showed 90% in favor of staying in the Union, whereas only 11 months after free speech and press began, over 90% voted for an independent Ukraine. With opinion so volatile and much of Leninist consciousness very superficial and transient, a scholar needs clues to deeper realities. Decoding popular response in Leninist China is most useful if it pays less attention to the momentary and manifest that merely gives good conscience to compelled complicity and instead probes the latent meaning of popular response in a search for underlying trends, as is done in the scholarship on political symbolism in the work of Murray Edelman.[3]

In mid-1986 the old guard of elder rulers in China was moving against a weakened and isolated leader of expansive reforms, Hu Yaobang. After Party General Secretary Hu was not seen in public for a few days, a rumor spread that he was preparing to flee to the Soviet Union. People gossiped that Moscow was threatening China's anti-reform elders with nuclear attack should the reactionaries try to block the progressive Hu's escape. Although unsupported, this rumor spread a myth that ruling reactionaries would someday, somehow, be defeated by the forces of good. Symptomatically, Chinese readers flocked to tales of good conquering evil, of chivalry and swordsmanship based on China's fabulous outlaw-heroes and knights-errant.

Also in the 1980s tales were recounted about the massively corrupt behavior of the unaccountable children of the senior leadership. A story spread that a son of China's paramount leader was in cahoots with officials in the northwestern city of Xian, making gobs of ill-begotten wealth by illegally cornering a monopoly on grossly marked-up, high-priced luxury television sets. Amazingly, the son cut his ties to the firm, which was disbanded. This dialogue and reaction occurred with no muckraking exposures in the official press, with the discourse occurring at the level of rumor and gossip. Political reality lies beyond the printed word.

DISCREDITING OPPRESSORS

Outsiders who only read the official story cannot hear the words in the minds of reader respondents that give meaning to symbols, turning cement into moldable plastic. Throughout the universe of Leninist nations, people who have been fooled and cheated in the past read subsequent official stories to protect themselves from being played again for chumps. Once nationals in Leninist states know that the regime is split, they read the media seeking signs of support for their worldview. Starting right after the establishment of the People's Republic in 1949, Mao Zedong launched one attack after another against an allegedly hidden opposition which supposedly used the popular media to undermine what Mao called socialism. Mao's group found, revealed, and denounced essays, books, and movies full of anti-regime messages. Chinese consequently could presume that even the official media were replete with Aesopian or hidden messages on the side of the people. Chinese became expert decoders, eagerly believing that a sculptor had depicted Mao as a Buddha with one eye slightly open because he wanted to see who did and did not worship him.

On a university campus where a statue of Mao Zedong, the leader of the Great Leap Forward and the Cultural Revolution—the one responsible for massive famine and pervasive oppression—remained standing, passersby in 1991 did not comment that a hero was being celebrated, but that a culprit was finally being punished. People said, "In the summer, he burns; in the winter, he freezes; year-round, birds shit all over him."

Throughout history, in all parts of the world, outraged people find similar ways to turn a discredited regime's propaganda against itself. The issue here is not Mao himself. At the very same moment that some cursed Mao, other Chinese could put up pictures of Mao as a way of saying that even Mao—whose son died in the Korean War—was better than the post-Mao crowd whose sons were getting rich in foreign deals. What was shared, rather, was a popular response that turned a legitimizing symbol for the regime into one that opposed the dictators. The very nature of being human, of seeking some dignity, limits the capacity of repression and propaganda to fill people's heads with the ideas, categories, and worldview of discredited despots.

Another extraordinary instance of decoding and recoding occurred in a political prison on the outskirts of the capital right after the Beijing massacre of 4 June 1989. The authorities' tactics, in using their control of information for reprogramming democratic opponents of the Leninist dictatorship, included playing the national anthem and compelling prisoners to stand and sing that hymn to the regime. But the prisoners sang it with enthusiasm. The prisoners sang with gusto, "Arise! Refuse to be enslaved! … The Chinese nation has reached its most crucial hour. … Arise! Arise! Arise! … Onward! In the face of the enemies' fire, Onward! Onward! Onward!" They believed that this song, composed during the patriotic resistance to Japan, also expressed their patriotic resolve against armed tyrants who had enslaved the people. The authorities dropped their ritual of disciplining degradation. The decoders had prevailed, even in prison.

HEGEMONY QUESTIONED

Popular, oppositional decoding may run counter to the expectations of those who accept the work on ideological hegemony of the powerful Italian Leninist theorist Antonio Gramsci.[4] This is because Gramsci's entire *problematique* is misconceived. He wrote in an era and a nation where liberal democracy seemed to turn into police-state fascism when challenged from below. He wrote to legitimate Leninism. He assumed that democracy was a deception masking a bourgeois dictatorship and that there was something false in the consciousness of industrial workers that kept the proletariat from finding the goals of Leninist Marxism attractive and compelling. Gramsci concluded that ideological presuppositions of the dominant capitalist class project so pervaded consciousness as to be hegemonic, that is, the rulers' ideology precluded the people from critically comprehending their plight and the creation of an oppositional mind set.

Yet, in retrospect, it makes more sense to ask why Gramsci was misled by the actualities of the Leninist project. Given the economic disaster and political barbarism embedded in the Leninist project from Albania to Angola, it seems more sensible to ask what is wrong with the minds of Leninist intellectuals who are still attracted to that inhuman Leninist project. Why can't misguided intellectuals free themselves more readily from Marxist-Leninist ideological hegemony? In contrast to the ideological blinders of such elites, people outside of the ruling culture tend to construct an oppositional culture.

As James Scott has shown in two superb studies,[5] subordinated groups, in contrast to misled Leninist intellectuals, have little trouble turning the ideologies of oppressive rulers against the tyrants. Stories abound in China about how audiences in darkened movie houses and live theaters applaud at the inauspicious moment—inauspicious as defined by regime propaganda. So people applaud on hearing "What if the Nationalist Party came back?" before an answer with a negative assessment can be given in the film. People delight in recounting how such films had to be withdrawn for better editing or how runs of plays were cut short. Despite the repressive dictatorship, people recount instances when their will prevailed. The Gramscian notion of hegemony and Marxist false consciousness are approaches that underestimate the power of people to see through the camouflage of dictators.

In autumn 1991, for example, the dictatorship in Beijing sought to relegitimate itself by appealing to the symbolism of Mao Zedong, who also had struggled to prevent democratization. Students at Beijing University, seeing through the veil of deception, immediately plastered the campus with portraits of Mao. Students decoded the message as victims of despots, manipulating a symbol in their own oppositional interest rather than in support of Mao and in opposition to democracy. The portrait represented the students' cry against today's despots and put Mao in a relatively favorable light. To embrace Mao, for the popular opposition, meant delegitimating the regime. Chauffeurs hung a small image of Mao from the rear view mirror seeking good fortune, as gamblers prayed to him hoping that their number would turn up. Mao, who inveighed against superstition, became the god of the superstitious.

This ordinary mode of oppositional decoding or silent resistance reflects the impossibility of ideological hegemony. Gramsci had everything virtually backwards. China's oppositional decoders, who readily reject the hegemonic project of those who monopolize the media, thereby convey a hopeful message about the human capacity to resist the self-serving myths of an intended ideological hegemony and struggle for something better.

Two stories spread after the crushing of the 1989 democracy movement, both of which testified to the isolated and transient character of the Leninist dictatorship. One story centered on Cui Guozhen, a peasant-soldier said to have been burned, crucified, and tortured by the demonstrators. Such a corpse existed. It was publicly displayed in Beijing as proof of the injustice of the democracy movement. But in the story that spread, when Cui's father was offered a sizeable monetary reward by President Yang Shangkun, believed to be one of the architects of the massacre, the father refused the money, worrying out loud that he feared what might happen when the verdict on the democracy struggle was reversed and Cui was no longer a martyr. Indeed, Cui's father was said to have insisted that, given the unrecognizable corpse, he believed his son was still alive. It was supposedly soon discovered (and covered up by the authorities) that Cui was indeed alive and well, home in Jilin province, where he had been transferred just prior to the Tiananmen Square incident. Thus there was, at least in popular mythology, no martyr of opposition to the democratic struggle.

Another story told of the fate of a junior officer at a military academy in Shanghai who wanted to send the central authorities a telegram saying that the enemies of the people were those declaring martial law. His commander promised to protect this outraged officer, but beseeched him not to send the cable. Instead, the junior officer sent his declaration of support for the democratizers to Shanghai's Fudan University democrats, who then transferred it to Beijing. Although higher authorities decided to arrest and try the officer, his local unit won approval for a two-year sentence to be served in their lockup, the equivalent of a nice hotel. Subsequently, the officer was given a cushy job supervising Shanghai nightclubs, while Beijing was told that the culprit had been mustered out of the military. The premise of the story was that popular unity would win eventual victory for the democrats. Putting the two stories together creates an oppositional mythos in which the real Chinese army is with the democratic cause of the people that will ultimately triumph.

POPULAR CYNICISM

This demythologizing and remythologizing, however, is often misleadingly idealized. In fact, the decoding does not guarantee that the popular opposition either gets the facts straight or organizes reinterpreted information in its own political best interest. The consequences of popular cynicism should not be romanticized. Despite social bandit mythology,

Bonnie and Clyde, after all, were only vicious criminals who were no help to the poor.

Oppressed people incapable of political action often grow cynical about all political views and actors. Hence, if they hear a propaganda lie from Beijing and a different story on the Voice of America, they often assume that the truth must be somewhere in the middle. Consequently, cynical consciousness unintentionally lends some credit to the regime's lies. Cynical, powerless, and outraged people tend to believe the worst about all political actors, including potential political friends within the divided ruling groups. Thus China's 1989 democracy movement condemned Party General Secretary Zhao Ziyang for the corruption of his offspring, thereby furthering a dismissive popular attitude that obstructed any mass politics of reaching out from movement democrats to ally with regime reformers. As with a similar condemnation of Deng Xiaoping's physically handicapped son, pure moral outrage and cynicism self-defeatingly precluded accepting a broad alliance of popular democrats and regime reformers that might have replaced the Leninist dictatorship.

The focus of this study, however, is not on the creation of politically useful truth for a democratic movement, but on the limits of propaganda effectiveness by the dictatorship. Hsiao Ching-chang and Yang Mei-rong report that people treat

> a story in the newspaper saying, "the students' patriotism is running high in the universities, and the Anti-Bourgeois Liberalization campaign has obtained vital achievements"... [to mean] that students have lost confidence in the leadership of the Communist Party and yearn for democracy and freedom.[6]

In other words, because the people have their defenses, the regime cannot act in a hegemonic manner. It is, therefore, worth decoding the oppositional culture for clues about future Chinese politics.

The crushing of the democracy movement in 1989 and the subsequent purge of 24 of 25 section heads of the *People's Daily* was not part of a process of unrestrained tyranny in which a ruling group had unlimited power to impose its will and policies on a hapless population. Such a description would incorrectly describe the state system as totalitarian, one in which the political elites have all the power. This analysis leads to a projection of no end to the discredited dictatorship.

But because China's rulers lack legitimacy, the alienated citizenry decode government propaganda to harmonize it with popular oppositional presuppositions. There are such contradictions within the system, and between power holders and the people, that to classify the state system as totalitarian obscures potentially powerful popular opposition. An idea of a society's ability to defend itself against the Leninist system can come from looking at a realm of state secrecy and apparent total state control—foreign policy. This examination reveals great limits on Leninist power and potential for a transformation of the system.

If the rulers did control a totalitarian system, they would be able to manage information and passions so that a manipulated people applauded the purported heroics of leaders who claimed to protect the people against dangerous enemies at home and abroad. In reality, policy is experienced by most politically conscious Chinese outside the ruling group as anti-people, almost despite any of its particulars.

The regime tries to woo public opinion by propagandizing a policy the populace should like while executing a contradictory policy of hidden purposes defined only in the cloakrooms of power. The regime fears to make its true aims known, but reiterates the slogan of "openness" as the essence of its foreign policy. It is silent on its goal of relegitimating its power by siding with all remaining Leninist dictatorships.[7] Its priority foreign policy goal is not to serve citizen needs but to hold on to power. Consequently, the government attempts to rigidly control the media in order to persuade the public, while hiding a deep policy direction that is inherently objectionable to a politically conscious citizenry that seeks economic exchanges to improve living conditions.

A foreign policy priority of China's rulers, in the wake of the democratization of Leninist systems from East Germany to Mongolia, is to help surviving Leninist-type dictatorships that resist political reform. What do Chinese think of such friends? It is absurd to believe that Chinese support the mass murderers who rule the miserable nation of Myanmar (Burma). It is likewise inconceivable that ties to Kim Il Sung win applause. In fact, stories spread in China of North Korea as an ingrate that would be poverty-stricken if not for Chinese aid. Normalization of relations with Vietnam will persuade Chinese, including the military, that sending Chinese to die there in 1979 was an unnecessary sacrifice of life, thus further undermining the regime's nationalistic legitimacy. With the rulers perceived to be narrowly self-serving, citizens decode the media to ferret out the hidden truth from the media, in advance of any real facts, as to how the rulers sacrifice the people.

The government acts as if public opinion mattered, that the media are powerful shapers of public opinion, and that the media as powerful shapers of public opinion cannot be allowed to reveal the regime's actual foreign policy purposes. Popular oppositional presuppositions, however, impose limits on the capacity of the dictators to carry out a "non-propagandized" foreign policy that mainly serves their closed, corporate power interests. Having seen journalists and broadcasters in the 1989 democracy movement demonstrate behind such slogans as "Don't force us to lie," regime opponents assume that "The vast majority of CCP news workers ... have not been content with the CCP's obliteration of press freedom. ..."[8] Viewers and readers, therefore, assume that media workers will find ways to provide data that actually subvert the illegitimate, hidden purposes and policies of the super-secretive Leninist system. Despite propaganda, censorship, control, and manipulation, the media are also experienced by alienated Chinese as an instrument of truth, delegitimation, and even democratization.

At times journalists do plant Aesopian messages against the dictatorship. There is no doubt that the diagonal reading of one poem in the overseas edition of *People's Daily* did indeed say "Down with Li Peng." With the 1989 democracy movement having shown the isolation of the rulers, ever more people assume that all good people only pay lip service to the state, while actually thinking for themselves. Consequently, there is a virtual mass movement to decode the Aesopian anti-regime messages that people assume must be hidden in that mere lip service to the regime. This attitude of decoding the anti-regime content of propaganda is a contagion that even spreads to non-native readers of Chinese who stay in the country for any length of time.

DEMOCRATIC POTENTIAL

One reason Chinese so often interpret media events to prove that the media reveal the truth about the regime, despite censorship and severe punishment for media democrats, is Chinese culture. Far from being uniformly anti-democratic, Chinese culture contains democratic potential. Chinese culture teaches that an ethical, educated Chinese must stand up for justice and the people even at the cost of career or life. When Wang Ruoshui was removed as managing editor of the *People's Daily* for his Marxist-humanistic writings analyzing the alienating nature of leader-led relations in Leninist China, many young people showed up at his office the day he had to move out.[9] One told me that Wang was surprised to see them and asked, "Don't you know I have been criticized and punished by the Party?" Someone answered that that was precisely why the people were there to help him. In like manner, right after Liu Binyan was booted out of the Party and attacked in the press in 1987, a stream of visitors went to see Liu and a torrent of signed letters poured in despite secret police surveillance. Rather than being cowed by the 1989 martial law crackdown, politically aware people found that very few people informed for the authorities. Consequently, people speak freely to friends in ever larger numbers.

The illegitimacy of the regime and a change in values cause people to decode regime lies and thereby reveal unspoken truths. With regime ideologist He Xin a laughing stock and regime spokesman Yuan Mu a target of cursing, people often assume that the real truth is probably closer to the opposite of what the regime claims. Because a discredited ruling group is seen as selling out the people for private gain while people who know how to buy and sell get wealthy outside the state sector, Southerners can even revel in a northern pun aimed against them. People understand the attack in a way that defuses it. Hence Southerners laughingly repeat the canard, "Northerners love the country; Southerners sell the country," implying that the northern-based regime, in fact, is but a group of hypocrites, while southerners have the ability to make money and survive in the competitive world economy. I overheard gossip about how southern anti-Communist leader Chiang Kai-shek knew how to get money from the rich Americans, a trick the discredited regime in the North cannot perform.

HEROES AND VICTIMS

When the regime attacks a muckraking writer, Liu Binyan, or a courageous democrat, Fang Lizhi, Chinese who read the attacks understand them as attempts by the media to publicize the anti-regime ideas of those under attack. The citations of the words of those under attack are treated as the hidden and real message. The metaphysical presupposition of the decoding ontology is that China's cultural heroes are bravely standing with an unjustly victimized people against selfish and outmoded rulers. Given the way the people insist on understanding the media and their messages, the regime is damned whether or not it censors and punishes. Insiders assert that the rulers have decided not to attack hidden messages for fear it will make them seem weak and out of control. The media are consequently seen as doing their best to reveal the hidden truth. Hence, similar to a Rorschach test, people project what they want to see—the Chinese people and their media standing up against an unjust order.

Consequently, press censorship cannot achieve its purposes. The regime gave great publicity to flooding in the summer of 1991 in order to trumpet relief funds from Taiwan and Hong Kong to enhance the image of rulers in Beijing as the respected leaders of all Chinese. Chinese, however, noted that the stories hid both the human suffering and the culpability of rulers for the floods. Hence, stories of people in Taiwan and Hong Kong helping the victims were taken as proof that even outsiders cared more about mainland Chinese than their rulers.

This popular decoding makes the rulers seem destined to fall. People say that when heads of military units give lectures, they comment that their unit was not in Beijing during the June 1989 massacre. The evidence of popular decoding suggests that the military, to prosper as a proud and patriotic institution, already distances itself from the perpetrators of the Beijing massacre and insists that it never would have used such tactics on its own. The ridiculous and meretricious official interpretation of the massacre will eventually be corrected formally, culminating in the targeting of a few worst culprits and an acknowledgment of the patriotism of the demonstrators. History, people think, is not on the side of the rulers.

The issue, however, is not the 4 June massacre or any other single event. As mentioned earlier, public opinion is inordinately volatile in Leninist systems. Even 4 June can quickly pass from popular consciousness. What continues is a discredited system that forces people to a live complicitous, two-faced existences that outrage people because the regime has lost its legitimacy. Chinese, refusing to be made fools of again by government propaganda, assume that the official story is the big lie. This belief puts a limit on the regime's ability to legitimate policy.

Thus one could have known in advance that the Chinese people would not believe that disaster relief from Taiwan and Hong Kong was a manifestation of respect for rulers in Beijing, as the media claimed. Media propaganda on the flood changed rapidly, as if in a silent dialogue with regime critics. At first, the flood was said to prove the need for more power to collectives. Later, it was used as evidence that the army, in charge of flood relief, loves the people. By the fall, however, the new media line on the flood, to counter the daily gossip by a distrustful populace about the disaster having had political causes, was that disasters *also* have natural causes. Once again, oppositional decoding was so loud and clear that ruling groups felt a need to respond.

PATRIOTISM, CHAOS, AND NATIVISM

Is there any popular credibility for the accounts in the press of the happiness of scholars and scientists who have returned from abroad, presented as proof that the better future is in China? People usually consider the returnees crazy and mock such stories. Do Chinese believe the accounts of life in America in terms of crime, drugs, homelessness, AIDS, racism, and unemployment? While a few may believe such accounts, a story that spread in China during the Gulf War reflects different thinking among Chinese. Chinese rulers condemned a hegemonic United States for picking on Iraq, portrayed as a small oppressed Third World nation. Ordinary Chinese, on the other hand, volunteered to fight on the American side in Kuwait. This reflects a profound split in the military and in society in general where the young see their elders as hurting China's national dignity by acting on irrational Maoist categories of bad big and good small states. A craving for a new, true, and pure patriotism results.

This does not mean that Chinese automatically embrace democracy—a patriotism of the Constitution—as a superior alternative. They tend, rather, to identify with American strength crushing weak Iraq. They seem to long for similar Chinese strength. Such popular tendencies could be satisfied by nativistic, ascetic militarism in China. The younger military officers know that China's Maoists isolated China from advanced science, technology, and weaponry, thus making China weaker. Propaganda is reinterpreted to harmonize with the popular presupposition that an *ancien régime* is out of touch with China's future needs. Whether the preferred alternative will be open democracy, nativistic militarism, or something worse remains unknown. Oppositional decoding, however, suggests a lot of popular tendencies in the anti-democratic direction.

Importantly, this decoding suggests that despite extraordinary economic growth in the post-Mao era, Chinese remain disenchanted with the Leninist rulers, even in the countryside where the economic boom is mind-boggling. The rural Party tends to be corrupt and hated. Economic success is experienced by ordinary villagers as occurring *despite the system*—as success in *getting around the system*. Villagers do not credit the rulers in Beijing for post-Mao economic gains. Change is assumed to be needed in Beijing's powerholders and policies regardless of the specifics surrounding the 4 June massacre.

Has the constant media barrage indicating that democratization in other Leninist states has resulted in chaos, decline, and division served the rulers' purpose of legitimizing the anti-democratic Chinese regime? Do Chinese believe that they are fortunate to enjoy a Leninist system that delivers both stability and economic growth, a combination said to make China the envy of frightened, suffering people in post-Leninist states all around the world? In China there *is* great fear of chaos and making things worse by premature or ill-conceived attempts at political reform. This anxiety, however, surrounds the death of the ruling elders; it does not credit the Leninist system for China's recent economic success. Indicatively, politically conscious Chinese citizens, in contrast to the ruling elders, celebrated the fall of Ceausescu in Romania and the failure of the coup orchestrated by the old guard in Russia. None tout other surviving Leninist regimes in Havana, Pyongyang, and Hanoi as models for the future. Leninist dictatorship seems an anachronism.

Chinese benefited greatly from the openness and partial decollectivization which accompanied post-Mao reforms, just as did people in Yugoslavia and Hungary in the 1950s and 1960s. But reform within Leninist state institutions is limited. The Chinese Leninist state guarantees polarization between people and rulers, an intensifying budget crisis, economic viability moving outside of the control of wasteful and misguided central ministries, worsening corruption, and the existence of useless—

and, therefore, experientially hypocritical—state enterprises. The regime continues to be delegitimated while regional identities strengthen. Alienated citizens are not grateful for Leninist rule in China, even when faced with post-Leninist chaos elsewhere. The continuation of a counter-productive Leninist system in China is taken to block progress and even make a regression possible. In short, people decode regime propaganda in ways that can legitimate and activate future anti-regime action.

Fear of chaos, disorder, and disintegration could in the future serve the demagogic interests of a tough, anti-corruption military despotism that would appeal also to nativistic sentiments. In 1992 I heard numerous individuals mock patriotism and then, in the next breath, long for a regime they could be proud of such as an America whose rulers smashed Iraq and supposedly proved their concern for the American people by crushing rioters in Los Angeles. Such supposed goodness is contrasted with betrayal of the people by rulers in Beijing, alleged to allow African blacks in China to run riot over Chinese. This methodology of decoding reveals some strong anti-democratic nativism in the opposition. Perhaps this comes from Chinese thinking as anti-regime patriots, trying to believe the regime's chauvinistic propaganda but interpreting the material against the regime.

REINTERPRETING REGIME PROPAGANDA

Many Chinese do accept some regime propaganda as partially true, but do so to discredit the regime. The people tend to add on what they know from experience—overseas Chinese come from places doing much better than people in China, students who return from abroad are treated as carriers of truths that are unavailable in China, and people who stand up to the regime are regarded as heroes. Thus, the regime's propaganda lies are, by and large, irrelevant. Chinese who read official newspapers seriously are mocked for wasting their time. Chinese who pass on news from foreign radio broadcasts, foreign travelers, VOA, BBC, Taiwan, and other foreign sources are treated as purveyors of truth. At times word spreads that a particular journal—the English language *China Daily* or a paper covering the international economy—can be read for hard information. A combination of quotidian daily experience, the corrupt and false system, and the deep personal desire not to be fooled induce people to construct "truth" from preferred, non-official sources that discredit the system.

One of the most twisted outcomes of reinterpreting government propaganda occurred in the Nanjing race riots of December 1988.[10] Chinese students, having read endless denunciations by their leaders of America's anti-black racism, experienced blacks from Africa as part of the undeserving privileged in China. The official Chinese media, which decried American racism against blacks, were discredited. The Chinese, therefore, assumed that white American students, as representatives of a system which properly treated blacks with contempt, would naturally join Chinese students in their outrage at the Chinese government's unfair privileging of African students, "humiliating" ties between Chinese women and African men, and a rumored unpunished murder of a Chinese by an African. Chinese student demonstrators perceived a common goal with white Americans: rewarding merit by punishing the undeserving. The Chinese anti-African mob displayed especial anger toward an American teacher in Nanjing who condemned the Chinese students, seeing him as a dupe, fink, and apologist for a tyranny that privileges the incompetent. Popular decoding reveals a receptiveness to meritocratic and democratic values replacing the regime's privileging of political loyalty. Concomitantly, however, a powerful, ongoing dispute between a primordial "us" and the regime could reinforce nasty communalist tendencies, as developments in other post-Leninist states have already shown.

Still, people try to counter what they assume are regime lies. Regime propaganda on foreign policy and popular desires, moreover, is taken to be in conflict. People tie southern China, Shenzhen, Hong Kong, Taiwan, and the United States to a happier future. The rulers, however, warn that cultural pollution and bourgeois liberalization come from these places, far from the supposed good, solid northern loess soil that sprouted the Confucian Chinese values of mutuality and self-discipline. Popular decoders, however, see a ruling group whose children are set up in cushy jobs, given a foreign education, and provided lucrative foreign trade contacts.

In the permanent succession crisis that shapes the politics of Leninist states, large sectors of the governing apparatuses begin to wonder about their careers once the elders are gone. What should they as individuals, family members, and corporate entities do to survive and prosper? The military has to worry about its corporate prestige. Its junior officer corps is well aware that the 1979 intervention in Vietnam, wars on the Chinese people by the military in various Cultural Revolution campaigns starting in 1966, and the June 1989 massacre have turned public opinion somewhat against them. More actions are not seen as in the military's long-term corporate interest.

Remembering when Albania was China's only ally, officers tend to see the embrace of the few remaining weak Leninist dictatorships—scoffed at by the Chinese people—as an indication that China's elders are trying to live outside of international norms. Because membership in the international scientific and technological communities benefits China economically, politically aware people reject regime policies that threaten China with international censure. The military and citizenry in general, therefore, tend not to support the current regime's nuclear proliferation and missile sales policies, which threaten China's access to the global economy and international prestige. Readers of the press, noting the headlining of pro-China praise by minor officials in a small African states, can not help but get the message that the regime has painfully isolated China from happier global possibilities by ignoring international norms. The endless declarations that China has friends all over the world often seems an attempt to obscure the regime's self-imposed isolation. Even Chinese in official sectors have learned to decode meaning into media propaganda that discredits the regime and could legitimate a process of political reform into democracy or a tough, military authoritarianism.

The frightened ruling clique in post-Mao China focuses great attention on public opinion, thereby tacitly accepting the power of democratic legitimation while subverting the Leninist doctrine that the vanguard leadership knows the way to the future. Apparent quiet and stability, however, are false clues of a momentary hiatus in political action that call attention away from decoding evidence that a crisis of legitimation defines the Chinese political system. Unseen and unheard, China's people share musings about alternatives to what is detested.

Chinese media heroes have contributed mightily to this new potential; Chinese cultural creators have furthered despotism's delegitimation. Journalists such as Deng Tuo, Wang Ruoshui, and Liu Binyan have tried to tell the truth about Mao's irrationality, the inhuman essence of the Leninist socialist system, and the outmoded, feudal nature of the Party-state. The editors and staff of the *World Economic Herald* in Shanghai, including the renowned Qin Benli, also contributed greatly to letting truth into China. Viewers were captivated by the six-part television series "River Elegy" that frontally attacked the worldview of elders who opposed Zhao Ziyang's attempt to push much further with reforms. People experience a daily struggle against censors in all areas of reporting in China, from movie makers to fiction writers and journalists.

CREATING OPPOSITIONAL SYMBOLS

People seek and find hidden truths in media headlines or story juxtapositions and then spread the 'true' story to undermine the regime's lies. For example, a story spread about the symbol of the 1990 Asian Games hosted in China (Figure 8.1). The symbol was said to be an A (for Asia) on its side, the better to look like an open, welcoming Great Wall. But is that an A? Looked at sideways, taxi drivers in Beijing told me that it contained a commemoration to the democratic martyrs of 4 June 1989, or 6–4–89, as it is put in Chinese. One can see to the right a distinct 6 and on the left, a distinct 4. From a left side view of the symbol, one can see the whole as a distinct 8 and the left side as 9, hence 6–4–89.

FIGURE 8.1   Symbol of the 1990 Asian Games

Did the creator of the symbol intend this, or did people read anti-regime decoding into a neutral sign? What then is the regime to do? If it tears down the Asian Games posters, it reveals it was tricked and displays weakness. If it lets the posters stay up, then the story of a successful popular protest mocks the regime. The regime tends to feel that strength means publicly ignoring attacks. Rumors consequently spread with details of the creator of the symbol and his successful flight from regime police, gossip that further ridicules regime ineptness and isolation.

In like manner, the regime banned the V for victory symbol of the democratic protesters. When a television advertisement ran for a product that highlighted two of something—symbolized by a jutting out of the same two fingers that make the V, people merely mentioned the product instead of making the sign.

Delegitimation is such that even media repression and censorship further delegitimate the rulers. Tee shirts with totally apolitical slogans such as the English word "bored" were banned as subversive. A story spread of a cartoon in which three people were sitting. Balloons above their heads carried their repressed conversation:

Person One: Sigh.

Person Two: Sigh.

Person Three: Stop that bourgeois liberalization propaganda.

Even when the regime tries to be at one with popular meanings, its efforts are mocked. A story spread of paramount leader Deng Xiaoping reading a televised speech in which he tried to appeal to cultural pride by using an ancient slogan once forbidden. It was said that he was so new to the historically-valued idiom that he said the old phrase backwards and had to return to the television studio to retape the talk. People swore that a close view of the tape proved the fraud and indicated that the regime was not at one with the Chinese people.

SURFACE TRANQUILITY, VOLCANIC ERUPTION

Chinese are creating space in society where the truth may get through. People talk and visit and share truths they claim to have garnered from the media, thereby breaking what Hannah Arendt labeled "the deadly spell of impotent apathy." A burgeoning literature on the growth of civil society in late Leninist regimes explores this topic.[11] Thus, regardless of recent economic gains and stepped-up appeals to chauvinism, people insist on the truth and put freedom on their political agenda when they know they are living amidst lies.[12] That, of course, was the agenda of the spring 1989 democracy movement that seemed impossible to those who had believed that surface tranquility reflected success for regime propaganda and economic reform. In fact, decoding reveals that the surface tranquility hides volcanic forces seeking an outlet through which to transform the political landscape.

What then is the true foreign policy of the Chinese government—as understood by politically conscious Chinese who look for hidden, delegitimating, decoded messages? It is neither the proclaimed purpose of openness to the world market nor the hidden purpose of allying with other Leninist regimes in the hope that China and socialism can save one another. Rather, the hidden foreign policy of the rulers is taken to be selling the fruit of the people's hard work for the private benefit of the isolated regime and its friends.

In 1988–1989 new Mercedes-Benzes in Beijing were taken as the essence of China's foreign policy. The people's work won foreign exchange which was then monopolized by the ruling strata. Aid from and trade with Japan are taken to demonstrate that rulers are selling out China to the Japanese for the private benefit of the elite. Arms sales by firms led by the family members of the ruling group are not seen as winning foreign exchange for China's modernization or pridefully circumventing American attempts to limit military escalation, but as seizing corrupt opportunities for the highest members of the feudal monarchy's court to enjoy personally the most expensive luxuries of a corrupt life at the people's expense. China's foreign policy is decoded as a crime, almost treason.

None of this means that a popular uprising will soon topple the Leninist dictatorship and build a popular, liberal democracy. It does not even mean that people clearly see or now know how to act against the discredited dictatorship. What the decoding means is that, over time, the dynamics of the Leninist dictatorship alienate most of the people and persuade them that they can see through the propaganda of a corrupt, incompetent, and unconscionable regime. This combines with a Chinese historical tradition that expects courageous ethical acts by the intellectuals who work in cultural spheres such as journalism, fiction, movies, and television and creates an extraordinary anti-regime, oppositional potential in China.

Still, the existence of that potential does not guarantee victory, let alone democracy. Inertia, anxiety, and the discrediting of all politics can maintain the status quo. Moreover, a strong anti-regime tendency that is quite anti-democratic also exists.

Yet there is more: Democratization—the danger that Leninist rulers define as "peaceful evolution." It is supposed to undermine a moral socialism. The rulers endlessly inveigh against peaceful evolution. Yet, virtually all Chinese I have talked with in China about that slogan ironically see "peaceful evolution" as the regime's actual policy and only worthy legitimation. When the regime invokes peaceful evolution it boasts that, in contrast to post-Leninist transitions elsewhere that have led to violence and chaos, China's rulers are moving China gradually into a market-oriented economy, a merit-based society and, as people decode the message, a democratic polity, but that Chinese are doing so without disorder or decline. The regime is popularly praised for democratization by evolution, the policy direction it most fears and attacks. Chinese experience their media and their cultural heroes as contributing to the democratic evolution that so terrifies many of China's Leninist powerholders. Propaganda is turned against the propagandists. What Chinese insist on decoding from their media is a message and a hope, a portent that Chinese too may one day know freedom.

NOTES

1. A Leninist dictatorship combines four institutional networks: a secret, hierarchical, and militarized party, a command economy, a pervasive police, and a *nomenklatura* system of appointments and promotions by political loyalty.

2. The writings of Vaclav Havel are an excellent critical introduction to this complicitous mentality.

3. See Edelman, *Politics as Symbolic Action* (Chicago: Markham, 1971). For insight on "the kind of code breaker we need," see Salmon Rushdie, *Imaginary Homelands* (London: Granta Books, 1991), pp. 203–6. For an application to China, see Jeffery Wasserstrom and Elizabeth Perry (eds.), *Popular Protest and Political Culture in Modern China* (Boulder, CO: Westview, 1992).

4. For a good critique of Gramsci, see James Scott, *Domination and the Arts of Resistance* (New Haven, CT: Yale University Press, 1990), pp. 9off., and Leszek Kolakawski, *Main Currents of Marxism*, vol. 3 (Oxford University Press, 1978), pp. 240–44.

5. James Scott, *Weapons of the Weak* (New Haven, CT: Yale University Press, 1988) and *Domination and the Arts of Resistance*.

6. Hsiao Ching-chang and Yang Mei-rong, "American Press Coverage of the Cultural Revolution" (Paper delivered at China Times Center Conference, "Voices of China: Ambiguities and Contradictions in China Reporting and Scholarship," Minneapolis, Minnesota, 4–6 Oct. 1991.)

7. Thus it gives friendship aid to Cuba.

8. Lu Keng, "Press Control in 'New China' and 'Old China'," in this volume.

Political philosopher Hannah Arendt found that this insistence on truth eventually undermines and explodes Leninist states that impose a hypocritical existence on people. For an application of Arendt's insights to China's Democracy Movement, see Edward Friedman, "Was Mao Zedong A Revolutionary?" in Bih-jaw Lin (ed.), *The Aftermath of the 1989 Tiananmen Crisis in Mainland China* (Boulder, CO: Westview, 1992), pp. 39–66.

9. Wang Ruoshui, *In Defense of Humanism* (Beijing: Joint Publications, 1986).

10. The following material is from Michael Sullivan, whose article on the Nanjing riot appears in the 1993 *China Quarterly*, but who wrote a longer and more detailed version, from which this paragraph also draws.

11. See Lawrence Sullivan, "The Emergence of Civil Society in China," in Tony Saich (ed.), *The Chinese People's Movement* (Armonk, NY: M. E. Sharpe, 1990), pp. 126–44; Barret McCormick, Su Shaozhi, and Xiao Xiaoming, "The 1989 Democracy Movement: A Review of the Prospects for Civil Society in China," *Pacific Affairs* 65, no. 2 (Summer 1992): 182–202.

12. Arendt, "Reflections on the Hungarian Revolution," *Journal of Politics* 20 (1958): 5–43.

9

PRESS CONTROL IN "NEW CHINA" AND "OLD CHINA"

Lu Keng[1]

> *To be honest, under the Kuomintang our fight for freedom is really over the question of "how much freedom." If the Communists come to power, the question is going to be "will we have freedom at all?"*
>
> —Chu Anping (1906–1966)[2]

JAILS AND BLACKLISTS: A PERSONAL STORY

I have witnessed China's struggle for press freedom under both the Nationalist (KMT) and Communist (CCP) regimes for half a century. In fact, I have spent my entire life alternating between the status of reporter and criminal, the latter marked by 22 years of imprisonment—a result of fighting for press freedom. At 76, I am still on the front line gathering news and look upon press freedom as the source of my vitality.

I was sent to Europe during the final stages of World War II and served as a broadcast journalist for "Voice of China." In July 1945 I followed General Dwight D. Eisenhower's advance on Berlin and eight months later returned to China to take a position as deputy editor-in-chief of Nanjing's *Central Daily News* (*Zhongyang Ribao*), a chief organ of the KMT. I then set up the Lu Shan (Mount Lu) edition of this paper in central China's Jiangxi province. The publication of this paper provided Generalissimo Chiang Kai-shek with information on the eight trips General George Marshall made to Lu Shan to mediate the Nationalist-Communist conflict.[3] In this position, I came into contact with upper-level KMT officials and members of the Communist Party delegation headed by Zhou Enlai. The delegation made a strenuous attempt to accommodate reporters—including KMT reporters—in order to improve its public relations image. Not only did Zhou answer all questions asked during press interviews, he also invited Chinese and foreign reporters to watch the Yangge-style dance, *Brother and Sister Pioneers*, at Nanjing's New Plum Garden Village where the CCP delegation was staying. He even gave each reporter a length of Shandong silk produced in a Communist-controlled "liberated district."

This contrasted with the impression given by the Nationalist's chief representative to the peace talks, Xu Yongchang, who was minister of the Chinese Military Affairs Department and had previously represented China at the acceptance of the Japanese surrender on the battleship *Missouri*. Xu went to great lengths to avoid reporters and would not even meet with reporters from Nationalist-controlled newspapers. Xu's attitude prompted me to impetuously publish an article in an April 1946 issue of the *Central Daily News* caricaturing Xu under the headline, "Xu Yongchang is Missing." This forced Xu to grant me an interview. Peng Xuepei, the Minister of Propaganda for the KMT Central Committee, arranged a meeting with the support of Chiang Kai-shek. The three of us agreed that Xu would update me after each mediation session held between himself, General Marshall, and Zhou Enlai, after which I would be allowed to write related news articles for the *Central Daily News*. In exchange, I would be held personally responsible for the content of my articles.

This anecdote illustrates that the KMT, unlike the CCP, had no organized system to rein in, let alone destroy, press freedom. Rather, each official could handle matters with a relatively large degree of autonomy. Moreover, it demonstrates that when everything was going well for the KMT, it was fairly tolerant toward the media.

In 1946 the *Central Daily News* in Nanjing candidly reported various scandals during the first National Constitutional Convention in Nanjing, including a morbid demonstration during which people carried coffins to protest election fraud. Papers published a large volume of news beneficial to the Communists vis-à-vis the Nationalists, including criticism of the sincerity of the Nationalists at peace talks held with the Communists. The KMT tolerated the assaults of press freedom when it held the upper hand.

Incivility, however, accompanied the descent of the Nationalists. As deputy editor-in-chief at the *Central Daily News*, I published an article on 31 July 1947 in which H.H. Kung and T.V. Soong (Chiang Kai-shek's top lieutenants and brothers-in-law) were accused of embezzling over U.S. $300 million from China's foreign exchange reserves, which at that time totaled less than $500 million. The KMT, however, claimed that the decimal point had been mistakenly moved two places, which changed $300 million into $3 million![4] The KMT threatened to punish me if I did not reveal my source, but I flatly refused. Just when the situation had become quite serious for me, General Albert Wedemeyer, who was on a fact-finding mission to China as President Truman's special envoy, heard of this matter from a brief report by John Leighton Stuart, the American ambassador to China. Chiang Kai-shek did not pursue the matter after Wedemeyer praised the *Central Daily News'* exposure of corruption among high-ranking Nationalist officials—an event later recorded in the appendix of a White Paper on U.S.-China relations.

The KMT tried to settle old scores with me in April 1949 after I had resigned from the *Central Daily News* and established the independent *Heaven and Earth Daily News* (*Tiandi Xinwen Ribao*) with some friends in Guangzhou. This publication invoked the ire of the KMT and prompted Guangdong KMT Chairman Gao Xin to threaten, "Lu Keng may think that he has crossed all the mighty rivers in China, but his boat will surely capsize in the Pearl River this time."

On 21 April the *Heaven and Earth Daily News* predicted where Communist forces might breach Nationalist lines to make their first crossing of the Yangtze River, including one point at Di Harbor in Anhui Province, and published a map of this latter scenario. When Mao Zedong's "million bold lions" crossed the Yangtze two days later, Di Harbor was indeed one of the chosen crossing points. Nationalist officials who had already retreated to Guangzhou held a meeting at which, based on the aforementioned article, I was declared a "Communist bandit" and "plotter." My paper was closed and a sealed order was soon issued for my arrest. If not for Chinese and overseas public opinion and the rescue efforts of senior Nationalist statesmen Yu Youren and Yan Xishan, my head might have been lopped off by Guangzhou garrison commander Ye "the Razor" Zhao.

The Nationalists, after retreating to Taiwan, learned the wrong lesson from their defeat. They attributed it to an overly-tolerant attitude on the mainland: More people should have been killed and arrested. Therefore, in the 1950s, they drew up a publishing law to limit press freedom. Using Taiwan's limited paper supplies as an excuse, the KMT restricted each daily newspaper to one and a half sheets of newsprint. The KMT furthermore forbade the establishment of any new newspapers. This "news prohibition" (*baojin*) policy lasted for more than 30 years.

Even though there were no direct legal controls on reporters' activities, Nationalist authorities jailed many who were inexplicably accused of being Communist sympathizers and arrested many more based on groundless suspicion. Even reporters for the KMT Central Committee organ newspapers were implicated. Reporter Shen Yuanchang of the Taiwan provincial government newspaper *New Life Daily News* (*Hsin Sheng Pao*) and her husband, editor Yao Yonglai, were both arrested, charged with sedition, and savagely tortured. (Shen's ten fingernails reportedly were pulled out and she eventually died in prison.) *New Life's* editorial director Tong Chang was also executed as a "(Communist) bandit spy" (*fei die*). Li Ching-sun, editor of the *Central Daily News* in Nanjing and later Taiwan, also invoked the wrath of the KMT. Although extremely loyal to the KMT, he was branded a bandit spy and sentenced to life in prison after publishing some short critical commentaries in the paper he and others had established, the *Grand China Evening Post* (*Ta-Hua Wan Pao*). Li's sentence was reduced to 15 years after Chiang Kai-shek's death, but he died of a heart attack soon after his release from Green Island Prison off the coast of Taiwan. These examples reveal the high price many news workers paid during the hard-won battle for press freedom in contemporary Taiwan.[5]

Returning to my own experience, I chose to base myself as a reporter in Tokyo in the late 1940s after some confrontations with Nationalist authorities. On 21 December 1949, when the Communists were scoring one military victory after another in China, I decided to risk flying back to my hometown, Kunming (Yunnan province), intending to bring out my stranded family. Although I had also planned to interview General Lu Han—the governor of Yunnan province and a close acquaintance who had just submitted himself to the Communists—I was instead arrested for being a "KMT infiltrator" and spent the next four years in prison.

During the Hundred Flowers period in 1957, which peaked soon after my release from prison, I was cordially invited to "offer advice" to the CCP. I suggested that China reconsider its policy toward the United States with the intention of improving Sino-U.S. relations, that English replace Russian as the main foreign language taught in colleges in order to meet the needs of modernization, and that old journalists like me be allowed to run a private newspaper and put on a "rival show" with the CCP.

The heavy price I paid for these suggestions began with my new label: "Pro-American and anti-Soviet ultrarightist." After nine months of harsh struggle sessions, I was sentenced in March 1958 to a ten-year prison term and was concurrently deprived of political rights for five years. Even though my prison term expired in 1968, when the Cultural Revolution was rampaging, the CCP detained me for another eight years, ostensibly because my "anti-revolutionary capacity was too great to lead a social life." I went to Hong Kong in 1978, two years after my release. From there, I visited Taiwan briefly three times between 1980 and 1981 and was warmly welcomed. After publishing an article in 1982 urging Chiang Ching-kuo not to serve another term as president, however, I was blacklisted in Taiwan and barred from entry for nine years. After being removed from Taiwan's blacklist in October 1990, I subsequently found myself added to the CCP's blacklist for having criticized Prime Minister Li Peng's Tiananmen crackdown and have been unable to visit mainland China since then. This is the fate of many modern Chinese—barred from Chinese soil on the basis of an article, discussion, or interview.

PRESS CONTROL: NATIONALISTS VERSUS COMMUNISTS

The KMT and CCP are two of a kind, both armed by Leninism in conception and in methods. Both publicly profess to use the Party to govern the country (*yi dang zhi guo*), though in reality they take the Party *to embody* the country (*yi dang dai guo*). Thus, although the authorities profess to represent Party and nation, their interest has been limited to the Party alone. Ultimately, the parties themselves are merely hollow shells that enclose a dictator or a dictatorial regime. Discussing press freedom with these two parties, therefore, has been no different from "playing a fiddle to a cow." Political organizations established according to the Leninist model sacrifice human considerations to the interests of the party. The "democratic centralism" they claim as their guiding principle consists of centralism without democracy. They also speak of collective leadership while supporting autocracy. Beginning in 1927, the KMT progressively evolved into the Chiang family party, and 30 years later the CCP began its transformation into the Mao family party.[6]

Within the CCP, secrecy is strictly maintained, orders are uniformly dispatched, and the supremacy of ideology is carefully preserved. The CCP, therefore, looks upon the dissemination of news as a battle, and has scrupulously obeyed Lenin's dictum that newspapers are a tool of class struggle. Before coming to power, the CCP used press freedom to defeat the KMT. After attaining power, the CCP strengthened press control and hence prevented opposition.

The Nationalists' tolerance of major politically-nonaffiliated periodicals such as the *Impartial Daily* (*Da Gong Bao*), the *New People's Paper* (*Xin Min Bao*), *Newsdom* (*Xinwen Tiandi*), and *The Observer* (*Guancha*)—publications which undoubtedly would have been forbidden by the CCP—reflected their less stringent press control policy. The KMT strayed from its normally lax treatment of the press only when the regime's tangible interests were violated, such as when it closed down the privately owned *New People's Daily* in Nanjing in 1948. Though infrequent, such actions were taken with explosive ferocity. Rather than use the Party to carry out press control, the KMT typically relied on special agents to keep watch over pro-Communist expressions.

The KMT gave less weight to ideology than the CCP and thereby allowed greater journalistic freedom. When I was working at the *Central Daily News* in Nanjing, my office would receive "propaganda directives" (*xuanchuan zhishi*) from the KMT Central Committee's Propaganda Department, but we seldom gave them much consideration. The chief or deputy chief of the KMT Propaganda Ministry presided over weekly meetings attended by our editorial board and personnel from major KMT organs to set the upcoming editorial policy.[7] They discussed themes for the next week's editorials and sometimes the latest instructions from Chiang Kai-shek. The editorials, which reflected the official line of the KMT and were distributed to KMT newspapers across China twice a week, proved quite useful during the Sino-Japanese War, but were thereafter considered irrelevant. Even KMT newspapers were allowed considerable autonomy over news releases. Between 1946 and 1948, for example, the *Central Daily News* rarely reprinted official Central News Agency copy. Rather, the autonomy of the *Central Daily News* was proudly expressed by the addition of "special to this paper" or "dispatch by our correspondent" to the vast majority of its bylines. Interestingly, the KMT conveyed neither instructions nor criticisms regarding this practice during these two years. The CCP would have found such a decentralized management style inconceivable.

Factionalism within the KMT inhibited successful interference in journalistic affairs. Although a party organ in name, the *Central Daily News* was in fact controlled by the "CC Faction" (the Chen brothers), which vied for power with other factions. The publisher and managing editor were nominated by the Chens' staff and approved by Chiang Kai-shek rather than the KMT's Propaganda Department or Organization Department. Only scandals such as criticism of Xu Yongchang and the Kong-Soong affair led to investigations by Chiang Kai-shek's staff; the bulk of the daily news was not tightly controlled. Both Party and non-Party members worked at the paper, which was devoid of an "organization life" (*zuzhi shenghuo*).

CCP newspapers have always been vastly different—publication content is predetermined[8] and individual decision-making is not possible. Consequently, during the middle of the Cultural Revolution all provincial CCP newspapers attempted to emulate the "correct" page layout of the *People's Daily* (*Renmin Ribao*) and most phoned the editorial department of the *People's Daily* in Beijing every day to ask about the lead story, second story, number of columns used by each story, size of the typeface, type style (e.g. boldface or standard), and the total number of articles and their arrangement on the page. The *People's Daily* eventually assigned a team of editors to answer the voluminous questions of the provincial newspapers and the mainland Chinese press further became "a thousand newspapers with one face."

Originally, I knew only that small papers watched big papers and big papers watched "Liang Xiao," a writing team made up of people at Beijing and Qinghua universities.[9] Their signed articles were carried simultaneously by the *People's Daily*, the *Liberation Army Daily* (*Jiefangjun Bao*) and *Red Flag* (*Hongqi*). Ma Rong, a CCP newsworker, wrote,

> In enacting their "universal press freedom," the Gang of Four defiled public opinion and attempted to follow Chairman Mao's instruction that public opinion should be uniform. Small "rebel" newspapers ran rampant and were full of counter-revolutionary clamor for complete dictatorship. Even the feudal and religious tribunals of the Middle Ages could not compare to

such unrelenting intellectual repression. Under these circumstances, the yearning for human rights and bourgeois press freedom (*zichan jieji xinwen ziyou*) is not surprising.[10]

The nature of press control in China revealed by the examples above seems absurd in its intensity and form—such massive imitation has been unheard of in the history of the world's newspaper industry. Such extreme press control has indeed been one of the greatest insults to press freedom.

Communist press control has always been much stricter than Nationalist press control. Those who view circumstances during the Cultural Revolution as atypical and inapplicable to journalism in China today should note the observations of veteran mainland broadcast journalist Cheng Kai:

> Mainland newspaper editorials will never contain independent opinions. Every editorial, critique, commentary, and signed article is written according to the desires of the powerholders. Moreover, when writing their articles, some journalists just copy Central Committee or provincial committee documents, or the speeches of their leaders. The newspapers have a strict editing system—the Central Committee Secretariat inspects important manuscripts at the *People's Daily* and the provincial CCP secretary or the secretary in charge of supervising propaganda work inspects provincial newspaper articles.[11]

I once witnessed an event demonstrating this system in 1956 when Zhou Enlai arranged for me to participate in the Yunnan Province People's Political Consultative Meeting in Kunming. During a dance party following the plenary session, I saw a person suddenly pick up a *Yunnan Daily* editorial to be published the next day. The person asked Ma Jikong, the secretary of the provincial committee responsible for propaganda, to examine it. Ma had no choice but to stop dancing and immediately go over the manuscript. He saw me cast a curious glance toward him and half-jokingly said, "I'm afraid your KMT newspapers weren't like ours!" "Absolutely no comparison (*wang lu mou ji*)!" I shot back.

CHIANG KAI-SHEK AND MAO ZEDONG

Chiang and Mao were both dictators. From the perspective of press control, however, Chiang was confused, while Mao was an unequivocal master who had a theory he put into practice. Chiang, however, still could be ruthless. For example, one of Chiang's special agents assassinated Shi Liangcai, owner of China's largest paper in the 1930s, the *Shanghai News* (*Shen Bao*), because it relentlessly exposed and criticized Nationalist corruption.[12] News of this murder caused an international stir and demonstrated that when press freedom impinged upon the foundation of his rule, Chiang could be absolutely merciless.

Mao, however, was even more ruthless than Chiang. Chiang only understood how to use a gun. Mao, however, used two weapons—the gun and the pen—to do battle. Mao's literary background allowed him to study in depth how Chinese feudal dynasties encouraged the indiscriminate killing of intellectuals during literary inquisitions in order to consolidate their authority. His schooling in Leninist ideology and appreciation for the central role of the dictatorship also contributed to an ability to control thought and expression that will remain without comparison. The scope and depth of harm done to intellectuals by his political movements are also unrivaled in modern times.

Mao's form of press control was basically a policy of keeping the people fooled. The traditional saying, "ignorance assures obedience to the emperor," accurately describes his tyrannical policy. Further embellishing Lenin's concept of press control, Mao declared, "All those who want to topple a regime must first do ideological work and mold public opinion. This is the case for both the revolutionary class and the counter-revolutionary class."[13] Mao acted in line with this conviction. When handling issues ranging from the victory over Chiang Kai-shek to the downfall of President Liu Shaoqi, Mao always first worked on public opinion.

Mao had perhaps the best understanding of the importance of news and public opinion of any twentieth-century world leader. When the Communists were not in power, he made every effort to gain press freedom from the Nationalists. In February 1942 Mao demanded that the KMT "follow public opinion by lifting the ban" on opposition parties and criticized the KMT for its "lack of editorial freedom." In 1945, at the Seventh Congress of the CCP, he emphasized that "the people's freedom of expression, publication, assembly, association, thought, belief, and bodily integrity are the most important freedoms."[14] Mao's demands for democracy and freedom prior to obtaining power were the same as those of the majority of people.

The tactics used by the CCP in their battle against KMT-organized press control were effective. Nationalist censors took their scissors to the final article proofs of newspapers published in the wartime capital of Chongqing. Staff at the CCP's *New China Daily* (*Xin Hua Ribao*), however, would sometimes leave a section blank to demonstrate the result of the censorship—a practice known as "opening a skylight" (*kai tian kong*). Skirting the KMT press restriction, the paper printed an article that covered the annihilation of the CCP New Fourth Army and the capture of its commander, Ye Ting, by KMT forces when a truce was in effect.[15] The paper further avoided the KMT censors by switching the original printing plate with one that included a couplet by Zhou Enlai just before going to print. The inscription read: "One thousand strange injustices, General Ye superbly unmatched in South China. Family members draw swords on each other and brothers slaughter one another." After the issue came off the press, Zhou Enlai and the entire staff went out on the streets with the paper boys to distribute the paper, an act which won them widespread public sympathy.

The CCP's attitude toward press freedom changed dramatically after it came to power. Under its Leninist interpretation of the ideal of "proletarian democracy"—as opposed to "bourgeois democracy"—the CCP recognized freedom of "the People" but prohibited "reactionary cliques" and forced newspapers to carry out "the will of the dictatorship of the proletariat." Newspapers in China were turned into political bulletin boards, propaganda trumpets, and announcers of CCP combat orders. The CCP called upon the press to spread falsehoods in its capacity as a propaganda instrument. A most transparent example occurred after thousands of people poured onto Tiananmen Square on 5 April 1976—traditionally a day to honor the dead (*Qing Ming Jie*)—to mourn the death of Zhou Enlai, China's popular premier. The demonstration, an allegorical denouncement of the Maoist Gang of Four and endorsement of the reform-minded Deng Xiaoping, was summarily crushed. A *People's Daily* article published two days later which denounced the demonstration as a "pre-planned, organized, and engineered counter-revolutionary political event" remained unchallenged by other Chinese newspapers. One commentator has noted that this incident indicates the achievement of a higher level of "fascist despotism" in China.[16]

Mao Zedong was an effective writer continuously involved in journalistic matters. Chiang Kai-shek, in contrast, was only interested in intensely correcting speeches penned by others, including those ghostwritten by Chen Bulei or Tao Xisheng and delivered by Chiang via radio on New Year's Day and National Day. (I once saw Chiang correcting his speech with red and blue pencils as he was about to sit down at a microphone in Chongqing.) Chiang or his staff would even sometimes phone in modifications after the speech had been broadcast, but before the Central News Agency sent out its dispatches. On 31 December 1943, while Central News Agency editor Gu Jianping was proofreading Chiang's New Year's address, he received a call from Chiang asking him to change a few words. After Gu hung up the phone—still so nervous that his face was bathed in sweat despite the December weather—he exclaimed, "That was the Generalissimo calling!"[17] It was also widely known that Chiang treated the editor-in-chief of the *Impartial Daily* (*Da Gong Bao*), Zhang Jiluan, with the utmost respect, which Zhang reciprocated by heaping compliments on Chiang in his commentaries.

Mao Zedong, in contrast, crafted numerous Xinhua (New China News Service) and *People's Daily* editorials, including "Press [General] Du Yuming to Surrender," "Carry Through Revolution To The End," and "Five Criticisms of the White Paper." The influence of these editorials has been long-lived. Consider, for example, the story of Fu Jingbo (Philip Fu), a confidant of John Leighton Stewart, a former U.S. ambassador to China and president of Yenching University (now merged into Beijing University). Fu confided in me that his fellow Yenching alum, former Foreign Minister Huang Hua, had helped obtain permission from the CCP Central Committee to fulfill Stewart's wish that his remains be placed near Lake Weiming on the University campus. The crackdown on the democracy movement in 1989 disrupted these plans and Fu died soon thereafter. Someone else approached Jiang Zemin, the new Party General Secretary, in 1990, but was rebuffed when Jiang emphasized the "historical assessment" of the matter, unexpectedly drawing upon Mao Zedong's article, "Begone J. Leighton Stewart!"

Nary a shadow of press freedom remained in China during Mao's reign. Mao expressed his dictatorial tendencies when he attempted to refute Hu Feng's criticism of the uniformity of public opinion by stating,

> The great majority of readers belong to some organization—this is excellent. In thousands of years nothing like this has ever happened. It was only after the Communist Party led the people in waging a long and arduous struggle that they were able to change to being united from being like loose sand, a condition which favored the reactionaries' exploitation and oppression, and that the people achieved this great unity among themselves. ... By "coercion" (*qiang po ren*), Hu Feng means our coercing those on the side of counter-revolution. Yes, they tremble with fear, feeling "like the miserable daughter-in-law always afraid of being beaten", or worrying that "a mere cough is being recorded". We consider this excellent too. Nothing like this had ever happened in thousands of years either. Only after the Communist Party led the people through a long and arduous struggle were these scoundrels made to feel uncomfortable. In a word, the day of joy for the people is a day of woe for the counter-revolutionaries. This, above all, is what we celebrate each year when National Day comes around.[18]

INFORMATION-POOR PUBLIC, INFORMATION-RICH POWER HOLDERS

The CCP's effective rule in China has been the result of not only omnipotent organizational control, but also strict press control. During particularly xenophobic periods of China's recent history, anyone caught listening to foreign broadcasts—or merely selling a shortwave radio—risked spending time in prison. Later, after the pathetic understanding of world affairs among CCP cadres was revealed, Xinhua began distributing *Reference News* (*Cankao Xiaoxi*). Mao sarcastically described this as "the CCP running a newspaper for the bourgeoisie" (*gongdang ti zichan jieji ban bao*). *Reference News* contains international news unavailable to the general public, including commentary from media sources in Hong Kong and Taiwan. Initially limited to cadres at or above the agency level (*jiguan ganbu*), access to *Reference News* was later expanded to include factory workers— members of the highly-touted working class. Although its circulation at one time reached nine million and included secondary school teachers— members of the intellectual class, which eventually also constituted a section of the working class—the existence of *Reference News* demonstrates the lack of press freedom in China.

The vast majority of Chinese have been barred from a basic understanding of major international issues. They accepted the CCP's declaration that the Korean War was started by "South Korean reactionaries" in collusion with American imperialists, not Kim Il Sung, and remain unaware of Nikita Khrushchev's confidential report to the 20th Communist Party Congress which implicated the North Korean leader. Even today, although intellectuals in China may be aware of the report's existence, they know little of its contents.

Similarly, the Chinese have had the wool pulled over their eyes regarding domestic affairs such as the Great Leap Forward. Information on this utopian experiment, including evidence of over 20 million deaths due to starvation—including about six million in Anhui Province alone—has only recently become known. Very few people in China know how many people died in this famine, and even fewer know how many people Pol Pot killed in Cambodia with Chinese support.[19] Nothing was published about the 300,000 people who drowned when a thunderstorm in southern Henan Province caused the Banqiao Reservoir's dam to burst in 1974, and it took ten years for the CCP to produce an estimate of the number of people killed after the Tangshan earthquake struck. The CCP also prohibited reporting on a severe plague of locusts which hit Hainan Island in 1988. These examples illustrate what Mao Zedong referred to as the "unified state of the people" (*renmin dachuanjie zhuangtai*), which could only be presented favorably. Media control in China has contributed to a "bamboo curtain" more rigid and less penetrable than the "iron curtain" which surrounded Eastern Europe and the Soviet Union, and continues to inhibit gradual political change.

The wealth of information enjoyed by the CCP leadership contrasts with the limited access allowed the common people. This includes "internal reference materials" (*neibu cankao* or *neibu*), compiled and graded according to content by almost all of China's press organizations and selectively distributed to cadres.

In addition to *Reference News*, Xinhua also supplies *Reference Materials* (*Cankao Ziliao*) to upper-level county cadres and Youth League cadres. Published in morning and evening editions until 1988 but now distributed as a daily, *Reference Materials* contains not only restricted news of local origin but also overseas editorials about the CCP. Xinhua also compiles and prints *Xinhua Internal Reference* (*Xinhua Shenei Can*) and *Outline of Trends* (*Dongtai Qingyang*) and distributes them to military commanders (*junji ganbu*). In addition, the CCP provided a kind of "special publication" ("*te kan*") which contains classified materials to Politburo and Secretariat members. More recently, these materials have been provided to the deputy premier of the State Council, the deputy chairman of the Standing Committee of the National People's Congress, and the chairman of the Chinese People's Political Consultative Conference. Central Committee members who do not fall under one of the categories above, military cadres, and provincial cadres are barred access from this information. Lastly, *Hand-copied Documents* (*Shouchao Jian*)—highly-classified documents printed in large type—are meant to accommodate "the dim-sighted old eyes" of a tiny octogenarian elite within the leadership.

The *People's Daily* publishes an internal reference publication, *Situation Compilations* (*Qingkuang Huibian*), which contains reports from journalists stationed in various places and are only supplied to upper-level provincial and military cadres. *Reflected Trends* (*Dongtai Fanying*), an analogous but more highly-classified *People's Daily* compilation, is distributed to the same readership as Xinhua's "special publication." The *Hand-copied Edition* (*Shouchao Ben*), the most highly classified publication put out by the *People's Daily*, is for a tiny elite. All restricted-access publications—whether originating from the Xinhua or the *People's Daily*—are printed at the "classified print shop," where all the workers are CCP members who have been granted the highest-level security clearance.

This system creates a news privilege pyramid. The higher the privilege, the richer the news, the more comprehensive the secrets contained, and the more authoritative the ideas. Press centralization replaces press freedom. Those who have been guests at Zhongnanhai, the Beijing compound where top officials live, will discover that the Communist leadership not only enjoys the special "large-print edition" of the *People's Daily*, but also watches television programming unavailable to other Chinese. Zhongnanhai has a special television unit that translates and comments on important international news. In addition, the programming is divided into categories such as politics, economics, military affairs, foreign relations, culture, and sports. Some of the leaders' homes even have four or five big televisions all tuned to different channels at the same time, accommodating the different wishes of family members—the leadership, perhaps, following the socialist dictum "to each according to his needs."

The CCP Central Committee leaders' modernized news and entertainment privileges are just a couple of examples of their wanton extravagance and the preferential treatment denied common people, regardless of their economic circumstances. Comparing the CCP leadership's enjoyment of press freedom to the strict press control implemented against the people under their rule clearly indicates a gross injustice.

The vast majority of CCP news workers, however, particularly after the reforms of the 1980s, have not been content with the CCP's obliteration of press freedom and its comprehensive control of the press. The brief phenomenon of three days of press freedom during the 1989 democracy movement demonstrated the aspirations of news workers. As China is confronted with an information explosion, it is obvious that this lack of press freedom in China must change.

The former director of the *People's Daily* and China Press Institute, Hu Jiwei, took the lead in press reform by proposing to draft a "press law." He studied press freedom in developed countries and integrated his findings with China's realities. The lack of a political component in Deng Xiaoping's reforms and the blockage of a proposed press freedom law by some elderly conservatives prevented the publication of a completed draft of his work and thereby hindered the growth of press freedom.

Political reform accompanied by genuine press freedom, however, eventually will arrive in China. The rapid changes in electronic media technology have created too many difficulties for totalitarian countries which attempt to control the press and will hasten an inevitable trend. History will be the last judge. It will show that the old news warhorse Hu Jiwei and his group of young comrades-in-arms did not waste their efforts struggling to obtain press freedom in mainland China. I invite all to listen for a sudden clap of thunder to ring out from the silence!

NOTES

1. Translated by Joseph Dennis, Chin-Chuan Lee, and Karl W. Metzner.

2. A liberal journalist and publisher who was purged during the Anti-Rightist movement. He said this in the late 1940s. See Dai Qing, *My Imprisonment* (Hong Kong: Ming Pao Press, 1990), p. 186.

3. The truce negotiations were held in a resort at the summit of Mount Lu, one of China's most famous mountains. The negotiations began to unravel as soon as Marshall returned to America.

4. Tao Xisheng, Deputy Chief of the Central Committee Propaganda Bureau and editorial director of the *Central Daily News*, was responsible for this ploy. See Chi Ching-yao, "The Decimal-Point Trick that Solved a Political Storm," *Biographical Literature* (*Zhuangji Wenxue*) 54, no. 1 (1989): 63-67.

5. See Chin-Chuan Lee, "Sparking a Fire," in this volume.

6. I am thus reminded of the antithetical couplets which hang in the study of University of North Carolina political scientist Qi Xisheng. They read, "In every generation, China has had heroes surface, but each hero [e.g. Chiang and Mao] has ended up harming the people for 30 years."

7. Other personnel included the director of the Propaganda Ministry's Bureau of Journalism; the publisher, editorial director, and deputy editorial director of the *Central Daily News*; the managing editor and editorial director of the *Peace Daily* (*Heping Ribao*); and the editor-in-chief of the Central News Agency. Sometimes the editor-in-chief and deputy editor-in-chief of the *Central Daily News* were called in to observe.

8. According to Cheng Kai, editor-in-chief of the *Hainan Daily*:

> Party organ newspapers' editors-in-chief and managing editors are appointed by the Organization Department after discussion and decisions by the standing committees of the same level CCP committees. Under normal circumstances such staff are all at the same grade in their CCP committees. When necessary, they can attend meetings of the standing committees of the same level CCP committees as non-voting delegates so that they will always understand the intentions of the CCP committee regarding the carrying out of propaganda. CCP newspaper workers have all joined the CCP committee's unit and are "national cadres" paid by the national government.
>
> The Propaganda Department oversees newspaper, radio, and television editorial policy and, when needed, passes on and supervises the implementation of CCP committee propaganda instructions. Problems, including inappropriate page layout and improper article content, are resolved by the Propaganda Department through criticism, correction, or other means.

9. Mao Zedong's wife, Jiang Qing, had formed this group of ideological dogmatists during the Cultural Revolution.

10. See "What I See of Socialism's Press Freedom," in *Anthology of Press Freedom* (Beijing: Chinese News Institute, n.d.).

11. Personal communication.

12. Shi was assassinated on 14 November 1934 on the road from Shanghai to Hangzhou near Bo Ai Township in Haining County. Shen Zui, an important captured KMT military agent who is now a member of the Chinese People's Political Consultative Conference, told me and three former KMT generals (Bai Tianmin, Tang Yuzong, and Luo Chunbo) in detail about the assassination while we were imprisoned in Kunming in 1950.

13. Quoted in *Red Flag*, no. 9 (1967).

14. This is from Mao's report entitled, "Discussion of a United Government." He also wrote in this report that the Nationalist government should "eliminate all reactionary decrees which suppress the people's freedom of expression, publication, assembly, association, thought, belief, and bodily integrity, so that the people may enjoy an abundance of freedom and rights."

15. This has been known as the Southern Anhui Incident (*Wannan Shibian*). The commander of the headquarters of the KMT Third Military District, Gu Zhutong, sent a KMT army led by Shangguan Yunxiang to ambush the Communist troops.

16. See Sun Xupei, "On Press Freedom in Socialism," in the Chinese Journalism Institute's *Collected Essays on Press Freedom* (Shanghai: Wenhui Press, 1988). Sun is Director of the Institute of Journalism at the Chinese Academy of Social Sciences.

17. See Chou Pei-ching, *The Story of the Central News Agency* (Taipei: Sanmin, 1991).

18. Mao Zedong, "In Refutation of 'Uniformity of Public Opinion'," vol. 5, *Selected Works of Mao Zedong.* (Beijing: Foreign Languages Press, 1977), pp. 173–74.

19. Liu Binyan, "Press Freedom: Particles in the Air," in Chin-Chuan Lee (ed.), *Voices of China* (New York: Guilford, 1990), p. 134.

10

SPARKING A FIRE: THE PRESS AND THE FERMENT OF DEMOCRATIC CHANGE IN TAIWAN

Chin-Chuan Lee

THE ANALYTICAL PROBLEM

Taiwan, an island nation of 21 million people, is said to be one of the few Third World countries that have had some success in transforming authoritarian rule to democracy. Riddled with complex contradictions, this transformation marks perhaps the first democratic experiment in Chinese history. Embedded within this process is Taiwan's struggle over press freedom, both in the sense of freedom *from* state censorship of the press and freedom *for* the use of the press to further political participation. In this struggle, political magazines (small media) have played a crucial role in subverting the state domination of newspapers and television channels (big media). This case study aims to achieve a broad historical and interpretative understanding of Taiwan's struggle over press freedom—with special reference to the vital role of political magazines—in the interplay between the state and the press.[1]

Broadly put, this quest for press freedom is seen as part of the broader cultural contradictions in Taiwan's political economy—it is a cultural struggle fought against the larger backdrop of the conflict between Taiwan's political illusion (what John K. Fairbank referred to as a "Continental China") and its economic realism (a "Maritime China").[2] This paper addresses two main themes. First, how have the political and economic strategies adopted by the state to combat internal and external challenges to its legitimacy conditioned Taiwan's press control mechanisms and determined its cultural dynamics? Second, as the state exercised strict control of newspaper and television operations, how did reformist intellectuals and opposition politicians take advantage of political magazines to air their grievances and organize activities for change? Within this second theme, several related questions arise. What characterized the mutual influences between big media and small media? As the functions of political magazines changed over time, how did they help subvert official ideology and act as a catalyst for democratic change? Conversely, how did the democratic change impact political magazines? These questions will be examined historically.

This chapter represents part of a larger theoretical concern with one of the most enduring issues in the field of communication: the role of the mass media in societies undergoing rapid and vast transformation.[3] There has been very little theoretically-informed literature examining the structural link between the mass media and political transition. Having stood in the forefront of change, Taiwan offers a rare social laboratory for observing the dynamics of political communication. Moreover, Taiwan's experience may foreshadow that of some Third World countries (especially the People's Republic of China) and hence contribute to the development of comparative studies. Finally, this study will challenge some of the conventional wisdom in the field that favors big media for social change.

Because there is so little groundwork, this project faces obstacles akin to those articulated in Franz Schurmann's work: "There is almost no secondary literature to be used as a guide, in the sense that such literature often points out major problems, introduces concepts, and does the spade work by organizing a confused mass of materials."[4] Although Schurmann took recourse to the theoretical and comparative literature, he relied primarily on his intuition for sensing problems and constructing patterns. A perceptive intuition—as an ordering capacity of the mind—is by no means haphazard; it can only be acquired through painstaking cultivation and long-term empathetic understanding.[5]

In the present case, the interpretative capacity—what Michael Polanyi calls "tacit knowledge" or "subsidiary awareness"[6]—is partly based on hundreds of Chinese articles (including press accounts, memoirs, analyses, and interviews), from which larger patterns emerge. Because press freedom as an area of inquiry was a taboo under martial law, trickles of relevant information—even from some of the most unlikely and seemingly unrelated sources—have had to be unearthed and pieced together. Further insight is derived from two decades of extensive interaction with journalists and policy makers in Taiwan and from numerous interviews conducted under the promise of anonymity for over a decade.

All analyses of Taiwan's media must hinge on the behavior of a state that encompasses a "triple alliance" of the ruling Kuomintang (the KMT, or the Chinese Nationalist Party), the government, and the military. Because control of this triple alliance was exercised by two successive supreme leaders—Chiang Kai-shek and his son, Chiang Ching-kuo—under the mantle of the Leninist-style KMT organization, the KMT, in some cases, became synonymous with the state, making Taiwan a "bureau-cratic-authoritarian regime."[7]

Taiwan has historically been part of China, but significant settlement by the Chinese did not take place until the mid-seventeenth century when supporters of the defeated Ming dynasty migrated to the island and used it as a center of opposition to the invading Manchu (Ching) dynasty. In 1683, however, Taiwan fell to the Ching dynasty, which further ceded Taiwan to Japan in 1895 after losing the Sino-Japanese war. Having overthrown the Ching dynasty to establish the Republic of China in 1911, the KMT reclaimed sovereignty over Taiwan from Japan in 1945 after the Second World War. The descendants of these mid-seventeenth century Chinese immigrants, known as Taiwanese, grew large in number. Many of them welcomed liberation from Japanese rule only to discover that the KMT local authorities were intent on maintaining Japanese colonial institutions on the island and exploiting it for rebuilding the war-torn mainland. Ethnic protests resulted in the KMT's killing of thousands of Taiwanese on 28 February 1947.[8] Two years later the central government of Nationalist China, along with the entire KMT apparatuses, retreated to Taiwan after being defeated by the Communists on mainland China. Since then the local Taiwanese majority (85%) have been deprived of their full political rights, while the three million mainlander minority (15%)—those who fled to Taiwan with the KMT in 1949—have dominated Taiwan's political power.[9] This mainlander-Taiwanese division was to develop as a major source of friction in the decades to come.

But the legitimacy of Nationalist rule has been under constant challenge—externally by a potential Communist threat and international isolation, and internally by a resentful and insurgent majority local population. In the name of anti-Communism, the KMT imposed the world's longest-lasting martial law on the island between 1949 and 1987. Martial law legalized the KMT's reliance on military and police forces to suppress the press, restrict civil liberties, and diminish political participation by prohibiting mass strikes or protests. Suppression was indeed severe, although melded with persuasion.[10] The KMT had to control both the "gun barrel" and the "ink barrel" to prevail on the public to accept autocracy either as a natural way of life or as a necessary price to pay to prevent Communist domination.

Toward this end, the KMT adopted a press policy of "incorporation," as distinct from repression or cooptation. Conceptually, repression (as in Communist China) means that a central authority coerces the press into becoming its mouthpiece without delivering inducements. Cooptation (as in Hong Kong) is marked by a coexistence of high inducements and low constraints. Pre-1987 Taiwan, under martial law, was a case of incorporation involving a simultaneous and intermittent interplay of state repression and cooptation—with obvious, rigorous rewards and punishments accrued to press owners. The press was kept as a weak, auxiliary, and dependent organ of the state but not strictly as its mouthpiece. While politically subservient to the state, the press had substantial room to maneuver in nonpolitical areas. Those who willingly acceded to state inducements relished vast economic benefits and political status while those who contested the power structure were suppressed.[11]

In Taiwan, the state monopolized television channels (with the Party, the government, and the military each controlling one channel) and most radio stations.[12] In addition, a press ban was declared in 1951 which foreclosed registration of new press licenses and only allowed existing certificates to be traded. The total number of newspapers in Taiwan was thus frozen at 31 until 1987 (see Table 10.1), effectively preventing press ownership from falling into the hands of KMT challengers. The high price of these scarce licenses kept them out of reach for the usually resource-poor social movement groups. Only the party-state and the two main private publishers had the requisite financial means to acquire such licenses.[13] The government-Party-military complex consequently amassed more than half of the total 31 newspapers. Although a few of the state-controlled papers were financially self-reliant, most others depended heavily on public subsidies.

The two most profitable private newspapers, on the other hand, developed into pro-KMT conglomerates through gradual consolidation of press certificates and came to garner two-thirds of Taiwan's newspaper circulation and advertising revenue. As this oligopolistic structure was taking shape in the 1970s, the party-state promptly struck what political scientists call a "patron-client relationship," bestowing immense political and economic benefits on the two conglomerates in exchange for their loyalty.[14] Both publishers were recruited into the Standing Committee of the KMT's Central Committee, the equivalent of the Leninist politburo. While the *United Daily News* group sides with the conservative wing of the KMT hierarchy, the *China Times* group leans toward its liberal faction.[15]

In sum, the KMT has effectively controlled big media (newspapers and television). Owing presumably to their modest circulations, however, the KMT did not consider political magazines a serious threat and exempted them from the press ban. Deprived of access to big media, dissidents had no other alternative than to fall back on political magazines. Table 10.2 summarizes a succession of the most significant political magazines, whose role will be examined chronologically.

But a general point has to be made here: Although political magazines have been catalysts for change, virtually all of them led a precarious life. They possessed small circulations (between 2,000 and 10,000 copies) and drew virtually no advertising support because of advertisers' fear of KMT

TABLE 10.1   Ownership Pattern of Taiwan's Television Stations and Newspapers Under the Press Ban (1949–1987)

Name	Year Founded	Ownership
Television		
Taiwan TV	1962	Taiwan Provincial Government
China TV	1969	KMT
Chinese TV	1971	Department of National Defense
Newspapers		
Central Daily News	1928	The KMT's organ
Taiwan Hsin Sheng Pao	1945	Taiwan Provincial Government
Chung Hua Jih Pao (Taipei)	1946	KMT
Chung Hua Jih Pao (Tainan)	1946	KMT
Ming Sheng Jih Pao	1946	Private; very insignificant
Keng Shen Jih Pao	1947	Private; very insignificant
Independent Evening Post	1947	Private; most independent
Chung Cheng Pao	1948	Department of National Defense
Kuo Yu Jih Pao	1948	Private; caters to school children; non-political
Taiwan Hsin Wen Pao	1949	Taiwan Provincial Government
China News	1949	English-language; nominally private; heavy KMT capital and personnel
Ta Hua Evening Post	1950	Nominally private; a spinoff of the KMT's *Central Daily News*
Ming Chung Jih Pao	1950	Private; relied on the KMT's financial support from time to time
China Times	1950	English language; private; pro-KMT; one of the two largest newspaper groups
Ming Chu Evening Post	1950	Nominally private; owned by Chiang Kai-shek's former guard; relied on the KMT's financial aid
United Daily News	1951	Private; pro-KMT; one of the two largest newspaper groups
China Post	1952	English language; private; pro-KMT
Shang Kung Jih Pao	1953	KMT
Chung Kuo Evening News	1955	Private; very insignificant; relied on gov't support
Chung Kuo Jih Pao	1956	Private; very insignificant; relied on gov't support
Taiwan Jih Pao	1964	Department of National Defense
Economic Daily News	1967	Private; part of the *United Daily News* group
Taiwan Shih Pao	1971	Private
Ming Sheng Pao	1978	Private; part of the *United Daily News* group
Liberty Jih Pao	1978	Private
Commercial Times	1978	Private; part of the *China Times* group
Youth Jih Pao	1984	Department of National Defense
Hsin Wen Evening News	1985	Taiwan Provincial Government
Ta Chung Pao	1986	Department of National Defense
Quemoy Jih Pao	1986	Department of National Defense; internal circulation
Mah-tsu Jih Pao	1986	Department of National Defense; internal circulation

NOTE: Although the government ceased to grant new newspaper licenses, the existing certificates were allowed to be traded or transferred. Arranged chronologically according to information contained in *Global View Monthly*, 1 January 1987, this table indicates the year in which the paper was founded under its present name.

TABLE 10.2   Major Political Magazines in Taiwan, 1949–1986

Name	Background Events	Composition	Appeal
Free China (1949–1960)	The KMT's withdrawal to Taiwan	Older KMT liberals; U.S.-educated intellectuals; older Taiwanese politicians. Aimed at urban intellectuals	Democratic values and two-party system; freedom of speech. Ended with Lei Chen's jailing
Ta Hsueh (1970–1973)	Chiang-Ching-kuo's rise in power; Taiwan's U.N. ouster; Nixon's visit to Beijing	Young U.S.-educated professors; some KMT liberals; children of high KMT officials	"Save Taiwan through Reform," including liberal-democratic norms and better treatment of farmers and workers
Taiwan Political Review (1976)	Death of Chiang Kai-shek; second oil crisis; Indochina's downfall; recognition of Beijing by Manila and Bangkok	Taiwanese politicians & middle-class intellectuals (legacy of Ta Hsueh). Aimed at middle-class and small/medium entrepreneurs	Equitable power sharing and political opportunities; political realism; fair elections; parliamentary reform; banned after five issues
Formosa (1979)	Explosion of electoral participation after the Chungli protest (1976), U.S.'s recognition of Beijing; Beijing's stepped- up propaganda	Taiwanese politicians & intellectuals. Organized "service stations." Grassroots support	Liberal reform and electoral activism. More radical wing of the Dangwai movement, ended with the Kaoshiung Incident
Eighties[a] (1979–1986)	Same as above	Taiwanese politicians/journalists. Middle-class support	Continued to uphold the appeals of the Taiwan Political Review. Moderate wing of the Dangwai movement.
Over a dozen Dangwai magazines (1981–1986)[b]	Rise of more professional Dangwai workers, discontent with the Dangwai's parliamentary route	Mostly young Taiwanese journalists & politicians; family members of political victims	Mostly exposure of the KMT's scandals & inside stories. Market-driven, lacking in-depth political analysis or critique[c]

[a]Includes The Asian and Current magazines, published by Kang Ning-hsiang.

[b]Many of them changed names frequently because of censorship. The list included Chien Chin (March), Peng-lai Tao (Taiwan), Fa Chan (Development), Cheng Chi Chia (Statesmen), Hsin Tsao Liu (The Movement), Hsin Huo (Torch), Taiwan Square, Lei Sheng (Thunder), Kuan Huai (Care), and the Tzu-yu Shih Tai (Freedom Times) series. See "The Yesterday, Today, and Tomorrow of the Dangwai Magazines," Hsia Tsao Forum, Oct. 1984, pp. 2–32.

[c]Exceptions to the rule include the Chien-chin (March) series published by Lin Cheng-chieh and numerous journalists and Hsin Tsao Liu (The Movement), ideologically most critical of the Dangwai's fervor for elections.

reprisals. When allowed to publish, they did so at the pleasure of the censors and risked abrupt confiscation. Few of these journals could boast of graceful writing, slick production, or eminent professionalism—in fact, most of them suffered from a high staff turnover rate, lack of audience research, and political uncertainty. Nevertheless, the fugitive information and alterative interpretations they carried were widely circulated through interpersonal networks and occasionally prompted mainstream media reactions. Political magazines thus proved to be a mainspring of social dissent, a center of political opposition, and an indispensable wedge that finally led to the rupture of official ideology.[16] They pushed political boundaries, broadened press coverage, and gradually chipped away at state ideological hegemony as a standard yardstick of reality in times of confusion. To a certain extent, the history of Taiwan's political change can be said to be tantamount to the history of its political magazines—their rise, struggles, and fall.

This analysis will thus challenge conventional wisdom in the communication literature that favors the development of technologically advanced big media in the Third World. Stated more generally, big media tend to reinforce the status quo and create foreign dependence while small media may be more suitable to foster change at the margins.[17] Because of their low capital requirement and high flexibility, small media could well be the most potent and, in many cases, the only resources for waging battles against state domination.

THE 1950S: WHITE TERROR

When the KMT withdrew to Taiwan in 1949, party leaders attributed the cause of its failure on the mainland to rancorous intraparty rivalry rather than a lack of constitutional and democratic rule. Amidst the Communists' vow to "liberate Taiwan by bloodbath," the KMT was determined to resurrect an authoritarian system revolving around the charismatic leadership of Chiang Kai-shek. Chiang was vested with an unchecked power to command the tripartite of the military, the Party, and the government bureaucracy.

Martial law was imposed. The KMT, emulating Leninist organizations, had posted political commissars in every company of the armed forces on the mainland since the 1930s. Now with Taiwan under martial law, security officers and Party workers spread further to each echelon of government offices and educational institutions, and to hundreds of sub-county Party branches in the name of "public service stations." No viable challenges were permitted to arise. For survival's sake, the KMT regime made it known that it would rather strike out thousands of "innocent" Communist suspects than let a single true Communist escape unpunished.

In what is now characterized as the "white terror" of the 1950s (as opposed to Communist "red terror"), a large but undisclosed number of people—many presumably innocent—were executed on the slightest hint of suspicion. The state took no heed of warrants or due process of law, and constitutionally guaranteed rights—including freedoms of speech, publication, and assembly—were frozen. Naturally, journalists bore the brunt of brutal assaults. Some of them disappeared; many others were detained, interrogated, or imprisoned. They were usually either entrapped or turned in by informers. Some were implicated because they had—years ago, perhaps beyond their recall—joined a study club, read a left-leaning book, uttered a casual remark, or simply because their names somehow found their way into the wrong person's address book.[18] Journalists lived in constant fear.

With U.S. President Harry Truman ready to abandon Chiang Kai-shek's Nationalist forces in 1949, Taiwan was virtually ostracized from the world community. While committing an internal terror campaign Chiang thus had to present Taiwan outwardly as a "Free China," as distinct from Communist China, in order to regain vital American support. After a period of indecision the United States did resume its aid, although with the condition that Chiang must implement reform on the island.[19] Within the first few years of Chiang's refuge in Taiwan, therefore, some degree of criticism by the press was tolerated. Chiang had not completely consolidated his personal power and thus exhibited "a sense of solidarity and common fate with the people;" the press was allowed to "break taboos and cut to the core of issues."[20] Even the party organ, the *Central Daily News*, was somewhat bold in criticizing corrupt officials.[21] As will be documented, *Free China* semimonthly (1949–1960) stood out as a symbol of courage and commitment in Taiwan's struggle for democracy.

The Korean War soon broke out, which unexpectedly saved Taiwan's fortune in the redrawn world power landscape. The United States, having endured the "Who Lost China" debate and the Red Scare of the McCarthy era, abhorred the role of Communist China in the Korean War. Washington thus resumed its support of Chiang and backed his seat as a permanent member of the United Nations Security Council. In appreciation of Taiwan's geomilitary importance to combatting global anti-Communism, the United States signed a mutual defense treaty with Taiwan in 1954, empowering the Seventh Fleet to patrol the Taiwan Strait. Taiwan finally found itself under the protective umbrella of the free world's leader. The treaty also, however, prohibited Chiang from attacking the Communists without Washington's approval.[22]

Owing to the escalated East-West conflict, Taiwan boasted that it served as Washington's "unsinkable aircraft carrier" in the Pacific. When heavy Communist bombing of the Quemoy Island outpost broke out in

1958 to greet President Eisenhower's visit to Taiwan, Chiang's China gained both readmission into the world community and full sponsorship from the United States.[23] The easing of immediate external menaces did not push Chiang toward openness and democracy but strengthened his hand in purging domestic critics and adversaries. Chiang submitted Taiwan to his absolute personal will and used the press, as *Free China* described, to paint "an illusive, paper image of peace and prosperity in Taiwan" and quickly collected a faithful pack of political actors— "professional liars, collaborators who did evil to serve their self-interest, and clever SOBs chanting 'Long Live (Chiang)' to advance their careers."[24]

The "Free China" Movement

The rise and fall of *Free China* magazine graphically illustrated the acute predicament of Taiwan's liberal advocates in the 1950s. The magazine was founded in 1949 partially with funding from the KMT and the Asia Foundation, a front agency of the U.S. government. Revered as the magazine's spiritual leader was Hu Shih, China's wartime ambassador to the United States and perhaps the most renowned liberal intellectual in modern China, while main editorial and financial responsibilities fell upon Lei Chen, who was once a trusted aid of Chiang Kai-shek. Having initially aspired to rally anti-Communist forces around Chiang, the magazine gradually became disillusioned by what it perceived to be the KMT's failure to learn a lesson from the mainland debacle. Arguing that democratic reform was the KMT's last and best hope, the magazine took the regime to task for its transgressions against human rights and disregard for constitutional procedures. The secret police should be curbed, the magazine insisted, while Chiang Ching-kuo's power bases (such as the Chinese Youth Corps) should be held accountable to the national legislature because of their total dependence on government funding. The Party's liberal wing, mostly western-educated and protective of Taiwan's image, had envisioned the magazine as a showcase of press freedom, but Chiang's security squad, indifferent to the outside world, began to launch relentless assaults on Lei.

Lei was expelled from the party in 1954. Once *Free China* struck a chord in the public's conscience and provoked the wrath of the authorities, there was no turning away from democratic principles and reformist impulses, and Lei showed little sign of indecision or retreat amidst harassment from the Taiwan Garrison Command. Chiang Kai-shek insisted that national security necessitated postponing democratic rule until after a defeat of Communism. *Free China* demanded, however, that democracy should be implemented here and now, because immediate recovery of the mainland had been blunted by the Sino-American Mutual Defense Treaty of 1954 that forbade the KMT to launch military attacks against Communist China without U.S. approval.[25]

In 1956 Chiang Kai-shek implored the nation to offer him "advice" as a gift for his 77th birthday, so *Free China* published a special issue containing 16 articles on 31 October in his honor. Major themes in this issue, which was reprinted 11 times, included pleas to the paramount leader that he pick a successor and restrain the KMT's interference in the military. The political staff of the military directed by Chiang Ching-kuo, however, immediately issued a 61-page "top secret document"—entitled "A Total Attack on the Poisonous Thought!"—harshly accusing Lei and his writers of being anti-government.[26]

From 1959 to 1960 *Free China* tried in vain to dissuade Chiang from his bid for constitutional amendments that would make him a life-long president.[27] Moreover, Lei concluded that unless there was an effective opposition party, little reform would come to fruition. Disregarding alarming threats from the KMT authorities and friendly advice from his former colleagues in the government, Lei committed his worst offense in Chiang's eyes by advocating the formation of a viable opposition party. Lei set out in 1959 to assemble an alliance of mainlanders and local Taiwanese politicians (who had managed to survive the KMT's 1947 massacre of Taiwanese) for organizing the Chinese Democratic Party. Two days before its inauguration, however, Lei was abruptly arrested by the Taiwan Garrison Command on sedition charges. He spent the next decade in solitary confinement in a military prison.[28] An experiment of mainlander-Taiwanese cooperation failed and the torch of reform dimmed. But the seeds of democratic values inspired generations of reformists to come.

Fighting Against the Odds

In the 1950s, the state-owned press claimed more than 80% of newspaper circulation, with the KMT organ, the *Central Daily News*, being most influential. Most private papers were struggling to survive. Commercial advertising was so inconsequential that government publicity provided for 70% of newspaper advertising revenues, primarily reserved for state-owned papers. Since the state held a monopoly over the banking sector, state-owned papers easily secured credit to upgrade printing facilities.[29]

Even under such unfavorable conditions, the press in the 1950s—in contrast to the succeeding two decades—did not completely back away from the KMT's stepped-up control attempts. The Ministry of Interior decreed a policy in 1954 authorizing government bureaucrats to unilaterally impose wide-ranging restrictions on press coverage in the name of national security. Under instant and intense crossfire from the press and the

Legislative Yuan (Taiwan's national legislature), the Minister of the Interior abandoned this policy after five days.

The Executive Yuan (the Premier's office) again requested in 1958 that the Legislative Yuan bypass a full-house debate and approve publication law amendments it submitted. The amendments would empower government units to enact publishing bans and rescind newspaper licenses in disregard of court decisions. This plain contempt of due process provoked intense resentment in the Legislative Yuan, where more than 100 legislators tried in vain to halt the KMT's offensive. Cheng She-wuo, a renowned journalist-legislator, commented that while the mainland warlords whom Chiang Kai-shek had defeated years ago might have detained individual journalists, none of them would have dared revoke press licenses.

The infuriated Chiang ordered that the bills be approved in the KMT-controlled Legislative Yuan with a minimum of delay. But even when it looked certain that the amendments would be rubber-stamped as instructed, the press—in the spirit of Confucian moral obligation—made a last-ditch effort to plead with the government for the bill's "wise withdrawal." After this plea fell on deaf ears, the press, including the submissive Taipei Newspaper Association, advised against the bill's unimpeded voyage through the Legislative Yuan. But all to no avail. Newspapers condemned timid KMT legislators for the bills' passage, as typified by the tone of the *Independent Evening Post*'s editorial: "History will punish you!"[30] After losing this battle, the press remained tame until the mid-1970s when a nascent democratic movement emerged. Some of the same publications, warriors of press freedom in the 1950s, had by then become entrenched in the established interest and disparaged members of the opposition forces and press freedom advocates.

The Case of Li Wanchu

Another symbol of the liberal struggle in the 1950s was Li Wanchu. A Taiwan-born intellectual, Li's dream of Chinese democracy took him to the Chinese mainland in the 1930s, where he established close ties with the Nationalist authorities. He returned to Taiwan in 1946. Even though he was a native Taiwanese, Li was trusted enough to be appointed director of the *Taiwan Hsin Sheng Pao* (*Taiwan New Life Daily*), a newspaper inherited from Japanese colonialists. But Li became increasingly critical of the KMT after the tragic 28 February 1947 uprisings, in which thousands of Taiwanese were massacred by KMT troops. Li decided to launch his own liberal and outspoken *Kung Lun Pao* (*Public Commentary Daily*).

Much like Lei Chen's *Free China*, Li's *Kung Lun Pao* initially professed allegiance to Chiang's leadership but soon reflected his disillusion. Elected as a member of the Taiwan Assembly, Li had a legitimate forum in which to deliver speech after speech condemning the KMT's anti-democratic conduct, which he then published in his paper. This open and irreverent defiance of Chiang's control cost Li his security and wealth, if not fame. The paper was a target of constant surveillance by the secret police; his reporters and editors were known to have been unlawfully arrested, and his personal secretary reportedly was an infiltrating security agent.[31] Both Li and Lei Chen devoted their lives to establishing the Chinese Democratic Party, only to have their efforts suppressed by the KMT authorities at the last minute. The KMT wrested control of *Kung Lun Pao* from Li and entangled him in drawn-out court cases.[32] A decade of liberal uprising ended.

THE 1960S: INSTITUTIONALIZED CENSORSHIP

The KMT regime, having weathered the stormy 1950s, now settled into the more stable and quieter 1960s. This decade saw the apex of East-West conflicts and an escalated Vietnam war, both conducive to the KMT's effort to seek U.S. patronage. With U.S. backing, Chiang upheld his claim as the sole representative of China at the United Nations and other international organizations. Internally, after the "white terror" had eliminated many potential threats, the remaining opponents were brought under effective control.[33] Equally important, Taiwan's economy was at this time "taking off." The land reform program initiated in the late 1950s showed visible benefits to a wide section of the middle and lower peasantry, and by the mid-1960s the export-led industry further prompted Taiwan's gross national product to rise annually at a rate of 10%. The growth of advertising revenues in this decade—averaging 21% annually—was even more striking; the total size of advertising revenues was approximately U.S. $27 million in 1969, half of which were claimed by newspapers.

These factors, alone or combined, did not seem to kindle greater political participation but instead provided a justification for the KMT's authoritarian rule. Asserting that economic growth and political stability were inseparable, the government showed neither tolerance for dissent nor enthusiasm to broaden popular access to power. Like the British colonial regime in Hong Kong, the KMT was determined to maintain political dominance in Taiwan while funneling public energy away from the political field to the pursuit of economic wealth.[34] As the press gained financial maturity, it became editorially timid.

Meanwhile, the KMT's control was increasingly systematized. In an address to the second KMT conference on the press in 1964, Chiang Kai-shek said that propaganda must be treated as equal in importance to military action. The conference ratified resolutions aimed at mobilizing the press, literature, and public opinion as powerful instruments of spiritual armament among the populace.[35] Strict political control led to the steady decline of the *Central Daily News*, whose lead in circulation was overtaken by two emerging privately-owned papers: the *United Daily News* and the *China Times*. Both private papers avoided challenging official policies, developed considerable expertise in local coverage, and owed much of their success to vivid, detailed crime accounts. In contrast, the KMT organ declined because it rigidly reflected Party rhetoric, neither providing authoritative information about government policies nor resorting to sensational crime reports.[36]

A cultural vacuum engulfed Taiwan throughout the 1960s. Exposure to foreign influences was limited, while an umbilical cord to mainland progressive (mostly anti-KMT) writings of the 1930s and 1940s had long been severed. *Wen Hsin* (*Literary Star*), the most significant magazine during this period (1957-1965), announced its aims as not political, but cultural. Although it did not directly attack the KMT regime, this monthly magazine concentrated its fire on traditional Chinese culture and thus antagonized many conservative elites who called for the government to ban it. While the KMT denounced Western liberalism as soft on Communism, *Wen Hsin* actively promoted such values as human rights, due process, and democracy. After 98 issues, the magazine was ordered closed.[37] The United States Information Agency, with branches around the island, was a major point of contact with the outside world for young minds.[38] Appleton found in his survey that most students were politically apathetic during this period and their cherished hope was to study—and stay—in the United States.[39]

With the decade-long Cultural Revolution launched in 1966, Communist China was too absorbed in relentless power struggles to menace Taiwan's security. Now that the KMT's power was firmly entrenched on the island, various overlapping security units were brought under the more unified control of the augmented Taiwan Garrison Command. State repression of the press came to be better institutionalized and more discriminating, but no less ruthless. At *Taiwan Hsin Sheng Pao*, a paper owned by the provincial government, scores of reporters and editors were charged with treason in 1966, each receiving a sentence ranging from several years to capital punishment.[40] And in 1968, the famed radio-play director in a KMT-controlled station, Tsui Hsiao-ping, was charged with treason.[41] Chen Ying-chen, a novelist noted for his leftist, anti-imperialist, nationalistic sympathies, was also indicted along with 35 other people for his alleged participation in a reading club whose topics included the works of Mao Zedong. Chen was imprisoned for ten years.

The popular newspaper satirist and editor Bo Yang was sentenced in 1968 to 12 years in prison for printing a syndicated Popeye cartoon on the women's page of the newspaper he edited—a comic strip that the Taiwan

Garrison Command interpreted as a disguised caricature of Chiang Kai-shek and his son stranded on an island on an extended fishing trip with little hope of returning home.[42] Then in 1970, Li Ao, a mainland-born writer and former editor of *Wen Hsin*, whose biting criticisms had earned him notoriety and a myriad of intellectual and political foes, was confined in a military prison on charges that he had taken part in advocating Taiwan's secession from China.

Most intriguing was the case of Li Ching-sun, whose liberal editorship made the *Central Daily News* rank among the boldest, liveliest, and most outspoken publications during both the late-1940s in Nanjing and the early 1950s in Taipei. Under his stewardship in the waning years of the KMT's mainland rule, the paper embarrassed Chiang Kai-shek and handed the Communists anti-Chiang propaganda when it exposed a judiciously guarded financial scandal committed by two of Chiang's top advisers and brothers-in-law. Despite this political transgression, Li continued to serve as the paper's editor-in-chief in the first years after its relocation to Taipei. Detained in 1971 without warning, Li was sentenced to life imprisonment for his alleged participation in a left-leaning reading club during his youth. At the time of his arrest, Li was holding three concurrent positions: publisher of the pro-KMT *Ta-Hua Wan Pao* (*Great China Evening Post*), news director of the KMT-controlled Broadcasting Corporation of China, and a senior adviser to General Chou Chi-rou, head of the powerful National Security Conference and a chief rival of the ascending of Chiang Ching-kuo.[43]

Each of these martial-law casualties was convicted by the Taiwan Garrison Command to at least ten years in military prison. They were all prosecuted on vaguely worded sedition charges, crimes that many of the victims continued to disavow years after their release. This literary inquisition was, however, only part of a much larger purge orchestrated from the center which left Taiwan with many broken families, scarred hearts, and an impotent press.

THE 1970S: FERMENT OF THE OPPOSITION

The KMT's legitimacy was severely undermined in 1971 when the United Nations seated the People's Republic of China at the expense of the Republic of China. Taiwan was once more relegated to world-orphan status. President Richard Nixon, an anti-Communist ally, added insult to injury in 1972 by visiting Communist China and proclaiming in the Shanghai Communique that the United States recognized Beijing as the sole legitimate government of China, including Taiwan.[44]

At a loss to justify these diplomatic setbacks to its doubting people, Taiwan found its succession problems looming ever larger. The aging Generalissimo Chiang Kai-shek was preparing to transfer power to his son Chiang Ching-kuo, only to incur resistance among the old guard. Between 1970 and 1972 the young Chiang opted to bypass his father's supporters and reach out directly to young reformist intellectuals. Most notably, he requested private audiences with the editorial board of *Ta Hsueh* (*University*) magazine, numbering about 50 to 60 reform-minded intellectuals, many of whom had studied abroad, primarily in the United States. As Chiang Ching-kuo gained power, a more open press was briefly tolerated. Rallying around the cause of "saving Taiwan through reforms," *Ta Hsueh* upheld democratic values as espoused by *Free China* on the one hand, and advocated a sounder welfare policy for farmers and workers on the other.

These young intellectuals, the self-appointed conscience of the people, did not seek to marshal grass-roots support. Nor did they move to organize an opposition party despite their endorsement of such a countervailing force. In a self-congratulatory way they touted access to Chiang Ching-kuo as genuine cooperation between "the wise" (themselves) and "the powerful" (Chiang), but the dialogue ended abruptly with the young Chiang assuming the premiership in 1972. Some of "the wise" (children of prominent KMT officials and a select few Taiwanese who rose from oblivion) were drafted into the cabinet, while some leftist-leaning intellectuals who had expressed sympathy for student movements were briefly detained and then stripped of university positions, and other Taiwanese burned their bridges to the KMT by taking up the cause of the nascent opposition movement.[45]

In the 1970s Taiwan's economy continued to soar at an annual rate of 10%, compared with advertising's 22% annual growth rate (with total revenues reaching U.S. $224 million in 1979).[46] By the end of the decade both Wang Ti-wu's *United Daily News* and Yu Chi-chung's *China Times* surpassed the one million mark in circulation, whereas the *Central Daily News* continued to lose influence. The press ban policy had excluded potential adversaries from the market, and now further strengthened the hand of these two private papers on their road to conglomeration through acquisition of licenses from failing operations.[47] Both publishers were recruited by Chiang Ching-kuo in the late 1970s to serve on the standing central committee of the KMT. While Yu sided with the Party's liberal wing, Wang allied himself with the conservatives.[48] The KMT, meanwhile, bought other press licenses.

The Rise of the *Dangwai*

The KMT government had anachronistically clung to a two-track power structure in Taiwan. While elections were regularly held for local offices (mayors, county, and provincial assembly persons), citizens of Taiwan could not choose national level officials or legislators. High government positions remained the special enclave of the KMT's mainlander loyalists. Claiming to be the sole repository of power for all of China, the regime insisted that those elected to the national legislature during the 1940s in China be allowed to serve until the KMT's recovery of the mainland. Taiwan was considered one of the smallest of the 35 Chinese provinces and entitled to limited seats in the three chamber national legislature (the National Assembly, the Legislative Yuan, and the Control Yuan).[49]

It became increasingly unjustifiable, however, for the Taiwanese to be denied more delegates in the national legislature when the KMT was desperate to find enough qualified people to replenish the mainlander seats lost to natural deaths.[50] Premier Chiang Ching-kuo undertook some much needed administrative reforms, and recruited younger technocrats and more Taiwanese into high governmental positions. Without impairing the fundamental basis of the token legislature, he also authorized a limited election that would give the province of Taiwan's representation a symbolic boost in 1972.[51] This modicum of openness was a first taste of the forbidden fruit for aspiring Taiwan-born politicians and thus enough to spark an indigenous democracy movement. It also unexpectedly paved the way for political magazines to become a powerful organizer and information disseminator.

Chiang Kai-shek died in 1975. Taiwan's economic growth was temporarily hampered by the second world oil crisis. As Indochina was falling into Communist hands, Thailand and the Philippines switched recognition from Taipei to Beijing. Overcoming feelings of gloom and despair, Chiang Ching-kuo committed an unprecedented, huge sum of public funds to initiate ten massive construction projects. These projects not only relieved Taiwan from economic hardship but upgraded its industrial infrastructure to sustain export growth.

Since the demise of *Free China* and *Ta Hsueh*, there was no voice of press dissent until the *Taiwan Political Review* appeared in 1976. Published by opposition leaders Huang Hsin-chieh and Kang Ning-hsiang, the *Review* inherited the earlier democratic struggles of *Free China* and *Ta Hsueh*. But the *Review* also proceeded further to express profound yearnings for more equal power-sharing between mainlanders and Taiwanese. Toward that end, the magazine argued that it was imperative to open up all seats in the national legislature for popular vote as well as to lift martial law and press bans. The *Review* also urged the KMT to pursue a realistic foreign policy instead of inflexible adherence to the regime's "one China" claim that abused the political rights of Taiwanese. After only five issues of publication, the magazine was ordered closed by the irate Taiwan Garrison Command, but it was enough to set the tone for other journals to follow.[52]

Formosa *Magazine*

The watershed point of political development in Taiwan was crossed with the outbreak of the Chungli Incident in 1977. A mayoral candidate for the first time took a vast crowd to the streets to protest against what seemed to be election irregularities engineered by the KMT.[53] This year also marked the first time opposition candidates won a significant victory in island-wide elections, capturing five mayoral seats, 21 of 77 seats in the Taiwan Assembly, and 6 seats in the Taipei Assembly. These victories represented about 30% of the popular vote. This taste of conquest injected self-confidence into the formerly scattered anti-KMT politicians, and precipitated the advent of a loose organization which they euphemistically labeled *Dangwai* ("outside the party"). Since the KMT was determined to crack down on any new political party, oppositional politicians chose the name *Dangwai* to suggest that they were members of neither a formal party (thus to avoid persecution) nor the KMT (thus to distance themselves from the regime). But because the term *Dangwai* indicated Taiwan was a one-party state, the KMT referred to members of the *Dangwai* as *Wu-tang-chi* ("the partyless").

The *Dangwai* movement became synonymous with *Dangwai* magazines, which served as their chief organizational and ideological instrument. Huang Hsin-chieh published *Formosa* (*Meilitao*, or *Beautiful Island*) in 1979, which was the most conspicuous early crystallization of the *Dangwai* movement. Bolder than its predecessors and sharper in its oppositional identity, *Formosa* was impatient with words and eager for action. Its members quickly established an island-wide network of 11 "service stations" headed by prominent members of the *Dangwai* movement, including newly elected members of the Legislative Yuan or the Taiwan Provincial Assembly. These service stations were organized primarily to coalesce political rallies and secondarily to promote the magazine's circulation, which soared to 80,000 copies a month. Meanwhile, Kang Ninghsiang, leader of a more moderate *Dangwai* faction, published *Eighties Monthly* as a voice of reform.

Formosa was the *Dangwai*'s indispensable propaganda and organizational apparatus. It refuted the regime's assertions, coordinated practical action, and nurtured collective oppositional consciousness among its members. The *Dangwai* concluded that the time had come to hold the KMT accountable to its own laws and constitution. For this reason, many lawyers joined hands with professional politicians to push the *Dangwai* movement to the limits of the permissible. The lingering trauma of pre-1949 Communist uprisings conditioned the KMT to react with extreme sensitivity to mass-oriented movements (banned under martial law) such as demonstrations organized by the *Dangwai*. Skirmishes erupted and

came to a head on 10 December 1979 in what is now referred to as the
Kaoshiung Incident, the significance of which exceeded the earlier
Chungli Incident. On this International Human Rights Day the *Dangwai*
defied police orders to stage an outdoor torchlight parade in the southern
seaport city of Kaoshiung, resulting in clashes with the police. All but two
major leaders of the *Dangwai* were arrested and tried in a military court.

So much doubt was raised at home and abroad about this mass arrest
that Chiang decided to let the press print, for the first time in the island's
history, full texts of the court proceeding.[54] This policy backfired, however, as the public read such texts more as evidence of exoneration than
guilt. *Formosa* magazine was nonetheless dissolved; their leaders were
sentenced to prison terms ranging from several years to life.[55] This was
followed by a major reshuffle within the KMT hierarchy, ushering in
hardline control. Feeling encircled and embattled, the KMT tightened its
grip on the press.

From Free China *to* Formosa

There were sharp differences in style, appeal and tactics between *Free
China* of the 1950s and *Formosa* of the 1980s. *Free China* initially assumed a
traditional role of *chien cheng*, whereby Confucian intellectuals dutifully
made earnest but totally non-binding pleas to the authorities, hoping that
for the good of the country their advice would be heeded. Lei Chen and
his followers, mostly reform-minded politicians rather than professors
and editorialists, later became convinced that reform efforts would be futile without institutional checks and balances. Lei's enthusiasm for organizing an opposition party stood in ironic contrast to the general passivity
of the otherwise outspoken intellectuals. Most notably, the U.S.-educated
symbol of liberalism, Hu Shih, advised Lei that the emerging party should
act primarily as a candid advisor (rather than an adversary) to the KMT
and should not seek to offend Chiang Kai-shek.[56] This traditional style of
chien cheng was also followed by *Ta Hsueh* in the early 1970s, with intellectual reformers presenting themselves as a social conscience that made no
attempt to rally mass support.[57]

The titles of these two magazines disclosed a decided shift of interest
from abstract China to concrete Taiwan. *Free China* primarily represented
the views of liberal mainlander intellectual elites who believed that if
democracy could take root in the temporary Nationalist base of Taiwan,
then it could serve as a model for post-Communist China. Toward that
end, the magazine maintained that the system should be rectified to allow
the development of an equal and genuine partnership between mainlanders and Taiwanese.[58] Lost with the failed *Free China* movement was an opportunity for mainlanders and Taiwanese to forge a political coalition.
The ethnic cleavage between them became excruciatingly entrenched.

Just as *Free China* was elite-oriented, *Formosa* was mass-oriented. The former was an intellectual project, the latter a politician's ambition. The reading circle of *Free China* was limited primarily to urban intellectuals, teachers, and government workers. By the mid-1970s, however, oppositional magazines such as *Formosa*, which were almost exclusively undertaken by indigenous Taiwanese, reached downward to attract a sizeable middle-class and grassroots following that yearned for more equitable power sharing and greater political participation to complement their newly-elevated economic status. Political magazines tested the limits of the KMT's tolerance, contested the official monopoly on truth, and openly negotiated new rules of the political game with the regime. In the mystique-debunking process they educated the public, provided it with information otherwise unavailable from official channels, and expanded press boundaries. Ironically, many of the reformist mainlanders who had resented the KMT's suppression in earlier decades now took offense at the *Dangwai*'s demand that they too—lifetime legislators or officials—should resign or retire. But as the *Dangwai* movement garnered widespread support, it would not settle for rhetorical niceties; its leaders were not pleaders, but power challengers.

THE 1980S: CLOSING DOWN AND OPENING UP

President Jimmy Carter in 1979 normalized diplomatic relations between the United States and the People's Republic of China and severed ties with Taiwan. But Taiwan's dependence on Washington for weapons procurement and trade deepened, and the Carter Administration's pointed criticisms of Taiwan's human rights violations increased. Meanwhile, Beijing extended the olive branch to Taiwan by calling for mutual contacts and direct negotiations toward eventual reunification under the newly conceived "one country, two systems" policy.[59] Rejecting this overture as a "Communist united-front conspiracy," Taiwan's press echoed the government policy of "no contact, no negotiation, and no withdrawal."

While Chiang Ching-kuo resorted to administrative reforms and broadened political participation in the early 1970s, he opted for an opposite course in the late 1970s to tackle the KMT's legitimacy crisis. He conferred greater power on the secret police, more conspicuously coopted (to divide and rule) various local Taiwanese factions, and moved to internationalize the economy.[60] These tactics represented Chiang Ching-kuo's "soft" authoritarianism, which never matched the supreme power his father's "hard" authoritarianism commanded.[61]

In what seems in retrospect to be the last hardline hurrah, however, Chiang approved the establishment of a "Shao-kang Office" (1979-1983) to coordinate Taiwan's interdepartmental anti-Communist and anti-

Dangwai operation.[62] Headed by Chiang's student and confidant, General Wang Sheng, director of political warfare for the Ministry of Defense, the Shao-kang Office was supposedly an ad hoc agency but actually surpassed all government and party apparatuses in power, if not in stature.[63] The Shao-kang office victimized intellectual critics, journalists, writers, and members of the *Dangwai*, whom the KMT compared to seditious advocates of the Taiwanese Independence Movement and Communist fellow-travellers.[64]

The Dangwai's Revival and Infighting

With all but two *Dangwai* leaders imprisoned in the Kaoshiung Incident, it was generally believed that at least several years would pass before the opposition could regroup itself. But no sooner had a year elapsed than family members of the Kaoshiung Incident victims and their defense lawyers, provoked by what they perceived to have been unfair trials, came to the forefront of the opposition. They offered themselves as candidates for the Legislative Yuan in the 1980 race, urging the electorate to "retry the *Formosa* case" and repudiate official verdicts. As the *Dangwai* magazines multiplied, campaign leaflets were also heavily used to condemn the KMT. As an unmistakable sign of the changing times, those who earlier would have been ostracized because of their ties to political offenders scored a resounding triumph in elections beginning in 1980. Some of them won simply by assaulting the KMT or pleading for public sympathy, rather than by stating their issue positions.

Elections were the lifeblood of political magazines, which became firmly established in Taiwan's marketplace of opinions, notwithstanding harassments from the authorities. Besides serving as the *Dangwai*'s propaganda arm, political magazines were an informal command post and a chief organizational mechanism for the loosely dispersed anti-KMT aspirants. To bolster their credibility, the two newspaper oligopolies were forced to follow suit and publish their own political magazines, which were editorially less stringent than their parent organizations though still within the KMT-prescribed confines.

Different ideologies and conflicting interests, however, began to divide the *Dangwai*.[65] The moderate opposition leader Kang Ning-hsiang, who escaped a jail term in the Kaoshiung Incident due to President Chiang's personal clemency, continued to publish his *Eighties Monthly* and participate in electoral politics. But a crop of young radical professional *Dangwai* workers, along with family members of their jailed leaders, began to issue their own magazines with derogatory references to Kang's suspected accommodation with the KMT. Kang was defeated in a reelection attempt.

The young radicals decided that the opposition figures, even wives of the jailed leaders, should refuse to play the electoral game with the KMT because low number of seats open to election gave the opposition no hope of beating the KMT's voting machine. They felt that the opposition should seek a change *of* the system instead of a change *within* the system, and only by mobilizing mass rallies—or people power—could the unrepentant KMT be pressured to change. This splintering of factions gave rise to a proliferation of *Dangwai* magazines, pointing fingers not only at the KMT but also at each other.[66] All of these publications were totally consumed by political fights in Taiwan, displaying little or no interest in mainland China. The Kaoshiung Incident did not chill political activism but seemed rather to accelerate it.

Seizing the Dangwai *Magazines*

The Taiwan Garrison Command issued a confidential "An-chi [base-stabilizing] Document No.3" in 1981, outlining how the security forces and the media should be mobilized to level a serious blow at the *Dangwai* candidates (called "conspirators") and their campaign offices.[67] In October 1982 Chiang Ching-kuo himself told the KMT standing central committee that the motives of those journalists and dissidents who expressed discontent with the government should be scrutinized.[68] Following his instructions, the KMT set up special committees whose primary purpose was to gain the support of various assemblies, social groups, radio, television, newspapers, and magazines, thereby launching an organized campaign which denounced the *Dangwai*'s demand for the right to form a formal political party because it "disturbed the social peace."[69]

Dangwai magazines were being confiscated more frequently and more randomly by the Taiwan Garrison Command, often on the basis of the vague, unexplained charge of "misleading public opinion." Many were impounded in the printing house or at the bindery. Even according to the martial law regulations that empowered the cultural police to censor publications, the *Dangwai* magazines should have been allowed to circulate after the deletion of disagreeable articles or passages. Moreover, only seizure in finished form, not at the printing stage, was permissible under the regulations. The *Dangwai* protested against the Taiwan Garrison Command's disregard of its own regulations to no avail. Moreover, General Wang Sheng's security forces created numerous magazines to confront the *Dangwai* journals. Among them *Chi-feng* (*Strong Wind*) stood out, whose editors were Red Guards who had defected from mainland China. They not only assaulted the *Dangwai* in their magazine but employed physical violence to intimidate crowds at *Dangwai* rallies.[70] Military generals were named managing directors of three television stations, and General Wang's former students occupied high editorial positions at many newspapers.[71]

Once the military's political staff had assumed a more prominent role, the Taiwan Garrison Command acquired more power in the triple alliance of cultural censors which also included the Government Information Office and the KMT's Committee on Cultural Work. It was widely known that the KMT's censors (some of whom were former journalists) would dutifully make a round of nightly phone calls before deadlines to newspaper editors and publishers (especially to KMT members) with instructions to kill or edit a particular news item the KMT deemed sensitive or embarrassing. The Taiwan Garrison Command tailed *Dangwai* leaders, watched their activities, and confiscated their magazines, but its chief commander (a three-star general) was exempted by martial law from having to answer questions before the Legislative Yuan about these actions. The director of the Government Information Office was instead summoned to bear the brunt of public outrage. When Kang Ning-hsiang, an opposition legislator whose *Eighties Monthly* was a constant target of confiscation, once demanded an exact definition of "misleading public opinion," the official was at a loss to give one. The official awkwardly denied that the Government Information Office had ever used such a reason to censor publications. Although he made no reference to the Taiwan Garrison Command, his resentment toward having to be blamed for the conduct of the secret police seemed thinly veiled.[72]

Indiscriminate seizure of *Dangwai* magazines bred resentment and spiraled radicalism, but could not discourage low-cost publications from cropping up. There would have been an explosion of public outrage if any attempts had been made at this time to subjugate political magazines to the press ban policy. Political magazines were now an institution not to be uprooted by force. Moreover, *Dangwai* publishers, who had been accustomed to the idea that each could only publish one magazine, grew adept at developing tactics to get around the censors' unanticipated interruption of their publication schedule.

Kang Ning-hsiang, for example, capitalized on a legal loophole and applied to the Government Information Office for three separate licenses, so whenever *Eighties Monthly* was suspended, *Asian* or *Current* could be called upon to fill the void. This developed into a guerilla-war strategy whereby *Asian* could be published as a monthly or a semi-monthly, and *Current* as a weekly or a biweekly, as the situation warranted. Many magazine publishers—who had been recently elected by popular vote into the national legislature and were thus shielded from persecution—also became more eager to openly confront the regime.

Struggles Within the KMT

In view of the censorship, Tao Pai-tsuan, the well-respected senior counsel to the president, wrote a newspaper article in 1982 arguing for transfer of power in cultural matters from the Taiwan Garrison Command to the Government Information Office. He also maintained that the media should be treated according to the Publication Law instead of the harsher martial law. The beleaguered Taiwan Garrison Command responded by running a covert operation in which writers would be recruited, with promises of handsome payment for articles which systematically cast Tao's motives into doubt. Internal documents outlining this operation were leaked to a member of the Legislative Yuan, who demanded an explanation from Premier Sun Yun-hsuan.[73] The premier pleaded ignorance. No sooner had he pledged an investigation into it, however, than the KMT censors campaigned to black out the news.

But the *China Times* and the *Independent Evening Post* refused to withhold the news.[74] As a member of the KMT's standing central committee, Yu Chi-chung allowed his mildly liberal *China Times* to lend overall support to the KMT's authority while holding its specific policies under criticism. Once the scandal was disclosed, General Wang Sheng had to make an apology to Tao. Already a target of attack by some conservative members (including his press rivals) in the Party's standing central committee, Yu made himself even more vulnerable to harassment campaigns.[75] Yu had to lie low, even taking temporary refuge for several months in New York, where he had just launched a successful American edition of his paper. That paper's liberal orientation, however, also antagonized conservative KMT leaders in Taipei.[76] Under martial law the inflow and outflow of hard currencies had to be officially approved, and Yu's request for authorization to furnish his New York paper with funds from its parent organization in Taipei was rebuffed. Told to either relinquish his editorial control or close the paper, Yu opted for the latter.[77]

Disenchantment

As the secret police hardened its control, the civil society in Taiwan underwent what Max Weber called the process of disenchantment.[78] The Shaokang Office was dissolved in 1983, indicating that state-imposed terror had lost some of its magic power. People had little fear of going to jail, and in fact imprisonment was viewed as a prerequisite for getting oneself elected. Kang Ning-hsiang had a lot of explaining to do about President Chiang's pardon for his role in the Kaoshiung incident.

In the years that followed resentment toward cultural censors raged so fiercely that the *Dangwai* magazines displayed little inhibition in washing KMT officials' dirty linen in public—including stories involving two public figures said (and confirmed) to be Chiang Ching-kuo's sons born out of wedlock. The low capital requirements enabled political magazines to survive in the market and play "hide and seek" with censors. Acting on tips from informants planted within these publications, censors usually waited at the bindery to seize a "questionable" issue. But violations occurred with such a high frequency that it later became feasible for *Dangwai* publishers to negotiate with overworked censors on the number of copies to be confiscated. Official restrictions were disregarded and taboos broken at an alarming rate. In anticipation of a ban, the magazines could quickly shift to different printers and continue to circulate that particular issue underground.

Censorship whetted such public curiosity that some magazines deliberately published a certain article to court censorship, only to hoard an issue en masse for consumption at a higher price. Public interest in sensational exposure pressured some *Dangwai* magazines to produce many ethically and journalistically dubious accounts to the neglect of serious political analysis and critique, thus undermining their own credibility and sowing the seeds of self-destruction. As state censorship finally began to break down by 1986, they were also deprived of their *raison d'être*. Political magazines had outlived their historical usefulness and embarked on their demise.

The KMT now had to choose between a policy of continued repression or more democracy. For several years the liberal wing of the KMT had engaged in open strife and veiled struggle with the conservative wing. The media radically shifted their editorial lines to accommodate the erratic political winds. In 1985 the KMT found itself unable to cope with the confidence gap created by a major financial scandal that cost two government ministers and many other officials their careers and nearly wrecked Taiwan's vaunted financial stability.[79] In that year the head of a military intelligence unit had Taipei hoodlums assassinate Henry Liu, a Chinese-American writer based in San Francisco and suspected of being a triple informant for Taiwan, Communist China, and the United States. As if the KMT were not amply embarrassed, the Taiwan Garrison Command proceeded to arrest Li Ya-ping, a Los Angeles publisher, during her trip to Taiwan. A naturalized U.S. citizen from Taiwan, Li owed her early ascendancy in wealth and power to the KMT's crucial support, but now her *International Daily News* was turning opportunistically pro-Beijing.[80] The U.S. State Department demanded her immediate release, hence hastening the demise of the demoralized Taiwan Garrison Command, where resentment against public criticism ran high.[81]

In 1986 a ripple effect was felt in Taiwan as the tide of democracy toppled the neighboring autocratic regimes of Chun Do-hwan in South Korea and Ferdinand Marcos in the Philippines.[82] Realizing that repression could be ineffective and even explosive, the ailing Chiang Ching-kuo finally came around to cast his lot in with the democratic forces.[83] Once the decision was made—in 1986—Chiang rose to the forefront of reform and, with his supreme authority, cleared the remaining stumbling blocks to democracy. He ordered that preparatory studies be made to restore constitutional rule, preached restraint to the secret police, and authorized a dialogue between the KMT and *Dangwai* leaders (with the aforementioned Tao Pai-tsuan as a chief mediator). As a further act of defiance, the impatient *Dangwai* leaders refused to wait for the KMT's formal approval and declared the formation of the Democratic Progressive Party (DPP) on 28 September 1986.

Although the government had warned that any attempt to organize a political party without its approval was a breach of martial law and would be severely punished, *Dangwai* leaders refused to be intimidated; more than 120 of them announced their collective resolve to go to prison. A news blackout effort was mounted and again aborted by the *China Times* and the *Independent Evening Post*, and for weeks tension grew.[84] Finally, Chiang Ching-kuo decided that the new party would be allowed to exist as long as it adhered to the constitution and renounced Taiwan's secession from China. Chiang had obviously concluded that terror was no longer effective, and he seemed reluctant to sacrifice Taiwan's image by spilling blood, as had been done a few months earlier in South Korea.[85] From then on, the pace of reform accelerated.

In the following year, 1987, the government terminated martial law imposed 38 years earlier, stripped the Taiwan Garrison Command of its vast power, and lifted the press ban. Chiang Ching-kuo died in early 1988, and the specter of the Chiang dynasty gradually began to vanish from the stage. Taiwan moved on to a new era. Regulations based on martial law were abolished and new laws were written. The legislative body was fully elected by popular will, while the press was finally free from the yoke of state censorship. The government for the first time acknowledged its intention to seek rapprochement with Beijing and hundreds of journalists have visited mainland China. Trade between Taiwan and China reached U.S. $10 billion in 1993, not including Taiwan's direct investment on the mainland, and continues to grow. Even Bo Yang, the once imprisoned (1968-1977) satirist and social critic, credited the birth of political and press freedoms in Taiwan as a "golden age," notwithstanding its lingering problems and fresh challenges. "China has 4,000, maybe 5,000, years of history, but it has never had an era like Taiwan today," he said, "There has never been a time when people were so wealthy and so free."[86]

IMPLICATIONS

Small Media in Social Movements

The early literature on the mass media and national development counseled the Third World to seek technologically advanced big media to the

exclusion of traditional and small media.[87] This advice is empirically untenable because the development of big media may strain financial resources of the Third World and create acute foreign dependence.[88]
Schramm also noted that little media were superior to big media as tools
for instruction in the developing countries.[89]

From the perspective of social movements, as this study shows, owners
of big media in Taiwan tended to be integrated into the established interests, imbued with the dominant ideology, and unlikely to challenge the
status quo. Social movement groups in Taiwan—generally resource-poor
and with little access to big media—were forced to take recourse to alternative small media, which are usually less susceptible to both financial
and technological constraints. Small media, especially political magazines, became a center of organized intelligence for the opposition movement.

Parallel examples can be found elsewhere. During the Iranian Revolution the powerful broadcasting institution loyal to the Shah was overcome
by Khomeini's interpersonal network of clergy, merchants, and students
who circulated *samizdat* and audio cassettes.[90] *Samizdat* had always been
important for dissidents in Eastern Europe and the Soviet Union. Ironically, Mao Zedong also mobilized the young Chinese Red Guards who
used crude wall-posters at the start of the Cultural Revolution to circum-
vent the newspaper and radio institutions controlled by his rivals.[91] These
alternative forms of communication are termed either "guerrilla media"
or "radical media."[92] In recent years a self-styled "Green Team" has
emerged in Taiwan to present, with the help of mobile VCR cameras, "a
people's perspective" on social conflicts in contrast to state-controlled
television. Democratic change has also stimulated a vast number of alternative small media, such as local periodicals and "popular video," in
South Korea and Brazil.

But the subversive small media suffer from inherent limitations. Their
audience reach is often limited to a small group of people highly committed to political causes, and the diffusion of their message tends to be indirect and slow. Because they are resource-poor and constantly denied access to official sources, their credibility may be cast in doubt. In general,
they are most effective when fighting against control from a position of
moral strength which compensates for their lack of technical slickness and
occasional lapses in coverage. When small media become substantially
market-driven and cater to the mainstream public and their often vulgar
tastes, however, they run the risk of losing both their idealism and audience: they cannot compete successfully with the established media on
those terms. This study shows that political magazines in Taiwan exhibited such moral strength in the 1950s when state suppression was harsh.
Conversely, with the erosion of state control in the mid-1980s, many of the

political magazines were driven by market pressure to pursue sensationalism. Since 1987 their political functions have been replaced by more effective channels of public opinion: elections, rallies, legitimate political parties, and a troop of suddenly reinvigorated mainstream newspapers.

Public Space for Struggle

The loosening of censorship and broadening of participation in Taiwan have also been related to the duality of the KMT's control: while authoritarian, it has failed to fully close off the public space from liberal struggle. Significant leakages in its ideological control have arisen from the glaring incongruity between the regime's official ideology and its autocratic rule. This incongruity was a constant target of criticism from opposition magazines.

Ideologically, the KMT proclaims to be a committed disciple of Sun Yat-sen's "Principles of the Three Peoples," which loosely embody turn-of-the-century Western concepts of nationalism, people's democracy, and the Fabian social-democratic economy. While the regime has never renounced democracy and freedom in the abstract, neither has it done more to pay lip service to them. Abridgement of political rights was primarily justified on national security concerns. This gap between words and deeds, in the long run, provided a fertile battleground for the struggle against state censorship of the press and the renewal of civil society. The emergent opposition, thus, continually challenged the regime's behavior with political magazines and mass rallies in light of a liberal constitution drafted in accordance with Sun's teachings.

From a comparative perspective, while the left-wing Chinese Communist regime has sought to *politicize* the civil society, the right-wing KMT regime has sought to *depoliticize* it. In Communist China, the party-state attempts to act as the main provider of livelihood and correct thought, omnipotently and omnipresently assaulting the whole range of civil life. The press, leisure, and even sports are nationalized and brought into the ideological struggle.[93] In contrast, the KMT has traditionally mobilized the media to justify its rule and shield its power from challenges by depoliticizing the civil society. Potential power seekers were encouraged to realize their personal ambitions in economic activities.[94] The KMT safely rode through decades of social demobilization until sustained economic prosperity and the enlightening role of oppositional political magazines awakened civil society. In sum, political participation was antithetical to—and submerged by—economic profit-making motives in the short run, but, in the end, economic affluence vitally contributed to the growth of a civil society, a more defiant press, and political participation. Similarly, a gradual, albeit limited, loosening of totalistic control has also accompanied economic reform in China.

Newspapers, the KMT, and the Opposition

In Taiwan's case, however, it would be unfair to give all the credit to the opposition movement and their magazines. They needed allies. The strict control of radio and television made them natural enemies of democratic reform. The same can be said about the state-owned press.[95] The role of major private newspapers was much more complex and contradictory: while the *United Daily News* and the *China Times* displayed an ideological kinship with the KMT's conservative and liberal wings respectively, they closely followed the political winds. When the liberal wing had an upper hand, the press was allowed more latitude, otherwise it was timid. Examples of critical reporting of politically sensitive issues such as the *China Times*'s disclosure over the cultural police's abuse of Tao Pai-tsuan were few and far between.

Like the KMT, these main newspapers espoused an ideology marked by democracy, freedom, and anti-Communism. Since the onset of the 1970s the main papers regularly featured contributions from respected intellectuals at home and abroad, whose prestige put them in a position to mildly and subtly criticize the KMT's continued imposition of martial law and its press ban. For two decades there was scarcely a day that went by without the major newspapers carrying at least one such professorial analysis. Some writers were ideologically compatible with both of these two rival papers, but most of them were aligned with either but not both outlets. The party, state, and military papers also commissioned articles—largely unpersuasive—from far-right writers to rebut the liberal commentary. Selection of writers obviously reflected the papers' ideological leaning within the KMT. Within each of the two largest newspapers a "special column" unit was dedicated to cultivating ties with these writers and, in fact, making stars out of them.

These "stars" selectively quoted ancient Chinese philosophers (especially Confucius) and contemporary Western political theorists (such as Samuel Huntington of Harvard, who stressed the importance of stability). They preached such liberal concepts as checks and balances, human rights, and constitutional rule, thus making the irony of the KMT's control more glaring. The two major newspapers, capitalizing on the high public stature of these intellectuals—including many university professors—and their own wide audience (each with a circulation of more than one million copies), were critical in legitimizing democratic values and the ideology of press freedom. The values these major papers helped to disseminate and legitimize laid the groundwork for broad-based democratic change.

The major newspapers made strange bedfellows for opposition magazines in their common embrace of democratic ideology. But in practice major newspapers (with occasional exceptions) did not morally defend the opposition movement against the iron fist of martial law censors. Some of them (such as the *China Times*) found their hands kept full by the censors, but in most cases they seemed to collaborate with the KMT in ambushing the opposition. Ironically, however, these papers did supply, against their will, the *Dangwai* magazines with crucial manpower and articles in an unexpected and surreptitious way. Too understaffed and financially stricken to mount a journalistic operation on their own (not to mention legal restrictions that denied them access to official news sources), the *Dangwai* magazines were able to secretly enlist the assistance of reporters who were frustrated by their own newspapers' timidity. Whatever the newspapers refused to publish found its way into the *Dangwai* magazines.[96]

Journalists in Taiwan undoubtedly based their decision to publish in the *Dangwai* magazines on their educational background. Journalism education in Taiwan is a wholesale importation from the United States, whose media are closely followed and whose norms of professionalism and press freedom have long been almost uncritically accepted by working journalists in Taiwan as the cardinal principles of their craft. Although absorption of the "watchdog" rhetoric was spotty, it eventually did have an impact on coverage. Having their journalistic pride ridiculed daily by political reality prompted a small corp of young, committed, liberal-minded reporters to gradually find in the *Dangwai* magazines their soul mates. These reporters lived in two seemingly separate zones of experience, writing something "proper" for their own rich papers to earn their livelihood, and submitting something else to the poor *Dangwai* publications to soothe their consciences. Without these contributions—written under pseudonyms—many of the inside stories and biting criticisms of the KMT would not have seen the light of day.[97] In this sense the *Dangwai* magazines were living in symbiosis with their strange bedfellows for 15 years, until their functions were taken over by a liberated press in 1986. Since then the mainstream conservative newspapers have continued to abuse the now legalized opposition party, whereas their more progressive counterparts have legitimized it within the two-party framework.

Market Censorship

This chapter has focused on *state* censorship.[98] But as Jansen and other writers point out, state censorship is not the only source of the threat to press freedom; another threat comes from the market, especially when media ownership is highly concentrated.[99] In Taiwan, with the sharp decline of state censorship in 1987, the hazard of market concentration has become more visible. Even though more than 50 newspaper licenses have been granted since 1987, none of these newer newspapers have gained a significant foothold. Barriers to market entry were so insurmountable that the *Capital Daily*, published by Kang Ning-hsiang (publisher of *Eighties* magazines under martial law), was forced to close after 15 months of operation and at a loss of U.S. $16 million.[100] Other papers have also failed.[101] The two press conglomerates have meanwhile ventured into the evening newspaper market and threatened the position of the once politically influential *Independent Evening Post*.

Major newspapers have a considerable capacity for appropriating or incorporating various perspectives to the exclusion of fringe views. The opposition party, now legitimized, is financially too impoverished and internally too divided to run a daily newspaper. The opposition came to realize that perhaps a radio station (a small medium) rather than a newspaper (a big medium) could better suit its needs. The two major papers continue to dominate and the three television stations remain state-owned. The opposition party's weekly organ has a trivial presence at best, while the *Central Daily News* has sunk to an all-time low (under 100,000 copies). Kang Ning-hsiang and others (such as the popular KMT legislator-turned-official Chao Shao-kang) were denied applications for radio licenses, but the opposition party has nonetheless disregarded official restrictions to establish an island-wide network of radio and low-power television stations.

Meanwhile, Taiwan's telecommunications policies for VCR, cable television, public television, and satellite transmission are being written and rewritten. Direct satellite broadcast signals from Japan and mainland China have penetrated Taiwan's television screens. New technology has rendered state monopoly of television irrelevant and called Taiwan's cultural sovereignty into question. Democratic change also has brought the question of national identity to the surface: Should Taiwan remain in or secede from China? Just as Taiwan has won a major battle for political and press freedom, questions about national identity have gained momentum. The media in Taiwan will have to use their dearly-won press freedom to meet four main practical and conceptual challenges: the trend toward media concentration; technological developments that may defy national borders and subvert state authority; cultural "spillover" from Japan and China; and the question of national identity.

NOTES

Reproduced from *Journalism Monographs* 38 (April 1993), with permission of the Association for Education in Journalism and Mass Communication.

1. Earlier versions of this article were presented (in Chinese) at the Chinese University of Hong Kong on 31 March 1991 and (in English) at the conference on

"Voices of China: Ambiguities and Contradictions in China Reporting and Scholarship," held 4–6 October 1991 under the auspices of the China Times Center for Media and Social Studies at the University of Minnesota. The responsibility of English translations from the original Chinese sources in this article is solely mine. I am indebted to Leonard Chu for encouraging me to write this paper's first draft for the conference he organized; the Shaw College of the Chinese University of Hong Kong for a travel grant; Tsan-kuo Chang and Eddie Kuo for commenting on a number of substantive issues; Laurie Dennis and Karl Metzner for skilled editorial assistance; David Hess, who served as a U.S. journalist and diplomat in Taiwan, for an informed critique of my paper.

2. John K. Fairbank, "Our One-China Problem," *Atlantic Monthly*, no. 328 (Sept. 1976), pp. 4–12. Fairbank argues that "Continental China," inheriting the Chinese imperial tradition of government, is an agrarian-bureaucratic empire busily engaged in updating itself. In Maritime China, individual enterprise, venture capital, and commercial calculations are essential. For an application of Fairbank's insights to Taiwan's television culture, see Chin-Chuan Lee, *Media Imperialism Reconsidered* (Beverly Hills, CA: Sage, 1980), pp. 143–72.

3. Chin-Chuan Lee (ed.), *Voices of China: The Interplay of Politics and Journalism* (New York: Guilford Press, 1990); Joseph Man Chan and Chin-Chuan Lee, *Mass Media and Political Transition: The Hong Kong Press in China's Orbit* (New York: Guilford Press, 1991).

4. Franz Schurmann, *Ideology and Organization in Communist China*, new and enl. ed. (Berkeley: University of California Press, 1968), pp. 13–16.

5. For a most penetrating discussion on intuition, see Thomas S. Kuhn, *The Essential Tension* (Chicago: University of Chicago Press, 1977), pp. 225–39.

6. Michael Polanyi, *Personal Knowledge* (Chicago: University of Chicago Press, 1958).

7. This concept was developed in Guillermo A. O'Donnell, *Modernization and Bureaucratic-Authoritarianism* (Berkeley: Institute of International Studies, University of California, 1973); Guillermo A. O'Donnell, "Reflections on the Pattern of Change in the Bureaucratic-Authoritarian State," *Latin American Studies* 8 (1978): 3–38. For coverage of Brazil, see Fernando H. Cardoso and Enzo Faletto, *Dependency and Development in Latin America* (Berkeley: University of California Press, 1979) and Peter Evans, *Dependent Development* (Princeton: Princeton University Press, 1979). Thomas B. Gold's *Taiwan Miracle* (Armonk, NY: M.E. Sharpe, 1986) used the Brazilian model to analyze Taiwan.

8. The Taiwanese, who had aspired to Chinese rule after the Japanese relinquished their colonial control, came to resent the KMT's corruption and oppression. The KMT banned both Japanese and local Taiwanese dialects upon its arrival. See Wang I-ting, *Walking Through the Crucial Years: A Memoir* (Taipei: Business Week, 1991), pp. 33–73. Until recently open discussion of this incident was considered a punishable crime.

9. *Encyclopædia Britannica*, vol. 28., (Chicago: University of Chicago Press, 1991), pp. 292–93. See also, notes 49 and 50.

10. For a conceptual distinction between "state repressive apparatuses" (such as the police and the military) and "state ideological apparatuses" (such as the me-

dia and schools), see Louis Althusser, *Lenin and Philosophy and Other Essays* (New York: Monthly Review Press, 1972).

11. Chan and Lee, *Mass Media and Political Transition*, pp. 26–29; Youngchul Yoon, "Political Transition and Press Ideology in South Korea, 1980–1988" (Ph.D. diss., University of Minnesota-Minneapolis, 1989).

12. For further analysis on television control, see Lee, *Media Imperialism Reconsidered*, pp. 143–72.

13. Each license was worth U.S. $2–3 million in the mid-1980s. With access to the national treasury (the KMT's chief financial officer has always been a government minister of finance or a president of the central bank), the KMT had funds to purchase licenses of failing newspapers. Opponents of the regime were thus precluded from owning their own press organ.

14. For a conceptual discussion on patron-client relations, see S. N. Eisenstadt and Rene Lernarchand (eds.), *Political Clientelism, Patronage and Development* (Beverly Hills, CA: Sage, 1981). This concept has been applied in analyzing the Taiwan case. See Nai-teh Wu, "The Politics of a Regime Patronage System: Mobilization and Control within an Authoritarian Regime" (Ph.D. diss., University of Chicago, 1987). Wu's excellent analysis did not, however, touch on the press. A preliminary analysis of patron-client relations is available in Chin-Chuan Lee, *The Politics of Journalism, the Journalism of Politics* (Chinese) (Taipei: Yuansheng, 1987).

15. Some argue that power control is exercised not through reward and punishment, but through ideological conditioning so that submission to authority is unquestioned or unrecognized. See John K. Galbraith, *The Anatomy of Power* (Boston: Houghton Mifflin, 1983); Steven Lukes, *Power: A Radical View* (London: Macmillan, 1974). It can be argued that this also applies to the patron-client relationship that characterizes state-press interaction in Taiwan.

16. Research shows, for example, that 90% of those who regularly read two sampled *Dangwai* magazines expressed their lack of trust in political information given by the conventional big-media of newspapers, radio, and television. (Based on a M.A. thesis by Fung Chien-san done at National Chengchi University, this figure was quoted in *Eighties Monthly*, 3 Apr. 1984, p. 13.)

17. See Jeremy Tunstall, *The Media Are American* (New York: Columbia University Press, 1977); Wilbur Schramm, *Big Media, Small Media* (Beverly Hills, CA: Sage, 1977).

18. Gung Hsuan-wu, *Memoir*. More and more information about the period of persecution and excesses is being made public, and the descriptions are quite consistent. But it will take many years for a fuller picture to be drawn.

19. Peng Huai-eng, *A Political-Economic Analysis of Taiwan's Development* (Taipei: Feng-yun, 1990), pp. 211–21.

20. "The Reflection of the Opinion Circle," *Free China* 16 Nov. 1953.

21. See Gung, *Memoir*. For example, national legislators were said to have demanded privileges in exchange for their support of Chiang Kai-shek. The *Central Daily News* condemned them as "political garbage," urging the public to sweep them into the heap of historical ashes. But its director, Ma Hsing-yeh, was soon criticized for blurring the distinction between a party newspaper and a privately-owned newspaper.

22. *China: U.S. Policy Since 1945* (Washington, D.C.: Congressional Quarterly, 1980), p. 9.

23. At that time, the Sino-Soviet rift was emerging. It has been argued that Mao's decision to bomb Quemoy was not only aimed at Eisenhower's visit, but also to test Moscow's guarantee. It turned out that the Soviets did not back Mao up.

24. "Our Press Freedom," *Free China*, 16 Dec. 1957; "The River of No Return," *Free China*, 1 Sept. 1960.

25. Refusing to abide by the restrictions placed on him by the Mutual Defense Treaty, Chiang Kai-shek was, however, launching small-scale military provocations against the Communists behind the back of the United States. Lei's dim assessment of Chiang's quick return to the mainland was to constitute one of his seditious crimes, that of "spreading defeatism."

26. Lei Chen, *Memoir* (Hong Kong: Seventies Monthly, 1978), pp. 106–45. Chiang Kai-shek's calls for advice on Taiwan paralleled the "Hundred Flowers" policy that Mao Zedong launched on the mainland in 1956. When the "advice" exceeded the limits of their tolerance, both leaders ordered crackdowns. A lengthy memoir Lei dedicated to his mother was confiscated by military prison officers. After his release from prison he reconstructed the present shorter version and smuggled it into Hong Kong for publication.

27. Lei Chen, *Memoir*; Wei Cheng-tung, "The Process of Pursuit for Freedom and Democracy by the Intellectuals in the Past Thirty Years," in Editorial Committee of the *China Forum, Social Change and Cultural Development in Taiwan* (Taipei: Lien-ching, 1985).

28. Ibid.

29. Chen Kuo-hsiang and Chu Ping, *Forty Years of Newspaper Evolution in Taiwan* (Taipei: Independent Evening Post, 1987), pp. 62–64, 85.

30. Chen and Chu, *Forty Years of Newspaper Evolution in Taiwan*, pp. 65–71; Lee, *Politics of Journalism*, pp. 87–94.

31. Deferring to Li's local influence, the KMT sought to punish his associates instead. His chief editorialist, Ni Shi-tan, had joined a leftist (but not Communist) study group in Fujian province when he was young. Ni then withdrew from the group and cleared his record with the authorities, but decades later was arrested in Taipei for his earlier activities. Li Wanchu angrily attacked the KMT's witch hunt in his editorials, thus worsening Ni's situation. Ni died in 1965. See Wang, *Walking Through the Crucial Years*, pp. 77–82.

32. Yang Jinlin, *Li Wan-chu: A Critical Portrait* (*Liwanchu Pingzhuang*) (Xiamen, China: Xiamen University Press, 1992) is a valuable mainland source. Ironically, no credible work on Li has yet appeared on Taiwan. See also, Chen and Chu, *Forty Years of Newspaper Evolution*, pp. 78–83.

33. In 1964 Kao Yu-shu defeated a KMT candidate to become mayor of Taipei. He won on a platform attacking mainlanders' political privileges over Taiwanese. Opposition candidates also won mayorships in Keelung and Kaoshiung. The KMT decided to close off elections in Taipei (and later Kaoshiung), and both mayors were to be appointed, and replaced, by the government. No elections have since been held for these two posts.

34. Chan and Lee, *Mass Media and Political Transition*.

35. Chen and Chu, *Forty Years of Newspaper Evolution*, pp. 113–14.

36. Ibid., pp. 72–77, 114–15. While figures for the 1960s are unavailable, it is clear that by 1971 the *United Daily News* already led all other papers in circulation (260,000 copies), followed by the *China Times* (240,000 copies), with the *Central Daily News* (140,000 copies) far behind.

37. Li Hsiao-feng, *Forty Years of the Democratic Movement in Taiwan* (Taipei: Independent Evening Post, 1987), pp. 85–89.

38. Yang Suo, "Is the American Moon Thrown Off the Stairs?" *China Times*, 7 Sept. 1991, p. 19.

39. Sheldon Appleton, "Silent Students and the Future of Taiwan," *Pacific Affairs* 43 (1970): 227–39.

40. This and the next paragraphs are partly based on Nan Fang-suo, "We Had a Dark Age," *The Journalist* 23 Jan. 1989, pp. 68–70; Chen Ying-chen, "A Warm Torch: In Memory of Paul Angels," *China Times Express* 14 Apr. 1991, p. 10.

41. New revelations attributed Tsui's imprisonment to a personal vendetta. Nan Ming, "Tsui Hsiao-ping Wants the History to Vindicate Her," *The Journalist*, 16 Jan. 1989, pp. 77–78.

42. This was, however, not the official reason for Bo Yang's imprisonment. Instead, he was beaten during the interrogations until he "admitted" to the crime of having previously joined the pro-Communist Front for United Democracy on the Mainland. Bo Yang, *Home* (Taipei: Lin-pai, 1989), pp. 135–38. At one point during the interrogations, Bo Yang asked that a friend of his, Sun Chien-chang, with whom he had fled Communist troops to Taiwan in 1949, be allowed to testify on his behalf. Refusing to collaborate with the authorities to implicate Bo Yang, Sun was fired as a senior police officer and imprisoned for four years. Ibid., pp. 156–58.

43. Sheng Tsu-yang, "A Newspaperman Returned from the Green Island," *The Journalist*, 23 Feb. 1987, pp. 66–68.

44. Richard M. Nixon, *RN: The Memoirs of Richard Nixon* (New York: Simon & Schuster, 1978), pp. 544–80; Henry Kissinger, *White House Years* (Boston: Little, Brown, 1979), pp. 684-787, 1049–96.

45. Mab Huang, "Intellectual Ferment for Political Reforms in Taiwan, 1971–1973," *Michigan Papers in Chinese Studies*, no. 28 (Ann Arbor, MI: University of Michigan, 1976); Wei, "The Process of Pursuit for Freedom and Democracy"; Chang Chun-hung, *My Reflections and Struggles* (Taipei: Author, 1977); Li Hsiao-feng, *Forty Years of the Democratic Movement*, pp. 89–108.

46. Calculated from Yen Po-ching, "Economic Development and Advertising Growth in Taiwan" (Paper presented at the Chinese University of Hong Kong, 29 April–1 May 1991).

47. By the mid-1980s the *United Daily News* group owned three newspapers, seven magazines, one publishing house and one news agency in Taiwan. It also published the *World Journal* in New York. The *China Times* group owned two newspapers, four magazines, and one publishing house in Taiwan.

48. For example, in the mid-1970s the *China Times* promoted the *hsiang-tu* (native soil) literature which critically reflected on both the plight of the underprivileged and Taiwan's cultural autonomy. Attributing this literary movement to Communist influence, the *United Daily News* and the *Central Daily News* called for government suppression and the movement was officially suppressed in 1979.

49. According to Sun Yat-sen's design, there are five Yuans in the government of the Republic of China, of which the Legislative Yuan is the Congress and the Executive Yuan is the cabinet. The Examination Yuan administers tests for potential government workers and the Control Yuan monitors the conduct of government officials. Neither, however, has exerted much authority in Taiwan. The Judicial Yuan is the highest agency of justice and law enforcement.

The national legislature consists of the Legislative Yuan, the Control Yuan, and the National Assembly. First-term members of these three bodies were elected in 1948 and their terms should have ended in 1951, but 557 Legislative Yuan members who fled to Taiwan with the KMT in 1949 unilaterally passed three resolutions (in 1950, 1951, 1952) to extend their own terms, with a provision that the government should recover mainland China when their terms were extended. In 1954 the KMT government, to avoid further embarrassment, asked the Judicial Yuan's Grand Justices Conference (the equivalent of the Supreme Court) for a constitutional interpretation that legitimized an indefinite extension of their service until it became feasible to form the second-term Legislative Yuan.

Meanwhile, the unwieldy National Assembly, the equivalent of an electoral college, had no official business other than convening every six years to elect the president. Instead of being dissolved as the Constitution required, it was made a regular chamber of the national legislature. The 2,000-odd members of the National Assembly, virtually all mainlanders, thus dutifully elected Chiang Kai-shek (four times) and Chiang Ching-kuo (twice).

Pressure built up after the lifting of martial law in 1987 to reform the national legislature. This time the Grand Justices Conference interpreted it as "constitutional" to ask these old-guard delegates to "retire" at the end of 1991. Having held seats for nearly forty years, most of them were in their 80s or 90s when they retired. In exchange, each retiree received U.S. $200,000 and other fringe benefits.

50. For delegates who failed to escape to Taiwan or died, replacements were first chosen from a small pool of trusted people from the same original provinces or counties. Even so, as time went by, delegates died at a pace faster than the KMT could find replacements. This resulted later in a "no replacement" policy which shrank the number of members in those legislative bodies. As of 1991 more than 400 of the 557 Legislative Yuan members—including those elected in 1948 and their replacements—died during their term of service. See *China Times*, 24 Sept. 1991, p. 3. Taiwanese delegates, however, continued to be dwarfed in number by the overwhelmingly pro-KMT mainlander delegates, whom opposition politicians denounced as nothing but "a voting brigade." Taiwanese finally outnumbered mainlanders in the National Assembly and the Legislative Yuan, in 1992 and 1993 respectively, when full-scale elections were held.

51. The residents of Taiwan were only entitled to elect just over 50 members of the 900-member National Assembly and just over 50 members of the 380-member Legislative Yuan. These newly elected members carried six-year and three-year terms, respectively, while the "old" members in both chambers could keep their positions indefinitely.

52. Wei, "The Process of Pursuit for Freedom and Democracy."

53. Hsu Hsin-liang, who quit the KMT to protest against its favoritism toward the other candidate, won the mayorship of Taoyuan. He became a central figure in

the *Dangwai* movement and *Formosa* magazine, and his relations with the authorities worsened. Forced to a decade-long exile in the United States, he advocated Taiwan's independence from China. He made several unsuccessful attempts, by air and sea, to return to Taiwan. Captured for trying to land in Taiwan aboard a fishing boat from mainland China, Hsu was briefly imprisoned after the death of Chiang Ching-kuo. Pardoned by President Lee Teng-huei, Hsu was released from prison and was elected chairman of the opposition Democratic Progressive Party (DPP) in 1991.

54. For the press coverage of the trial, see *The Kaoshiung Incident: A Special Collection* (Hong Kong: n.p., n.d.), believed to be put together by an ad hoc dissident group. The Kaoshiung incident coincided with the arrest of Wei Jingsheng—a leader of the democracy wall movement in Beijing—marking two tragic setbacks for Chinese democracy. The best researched work on the Kaohsiung Incident to date is Lu Hsiu-lien, *Retry Formosa* (Taipei: Independent Evening Post, 1991). Lu herself was jailed for four years in this incident.

55. All of them were released, paroled, and pardoned in the late 1980s. They are now leaders of the DPP. More than half of the 51 DPP members in the Legislative Yuan in 1993 had been political prisoners.

56. Chang Chung-tung, *Five Essays on Hu Shih* (Taipei: Yun-chen, 1987) offers a more sympathetic portrait of Hu Shih.

57. Huang, "Political Ferment for Political Reforms," pp. 103–4.

58. See Eighties Monthly (ed.), *On the Question of the Opposition Party*, vol. 4, *Selections from "Free China"* (Taipei: Eighties Monthly, 1979).

59. For information on China's "one country, two systems" policy that has broader implications for resolving problems pertaining to Hong Kong and Taiwan, see Chan and Lee, *Mass Media and Political Transition*.

60. Wang Jenn-hwan, "Political Transition and Oppositional Movement in Taiwan," *Taiwan: A Radical Quarterly in Social Studies* 2, no. 1 (1989): 71–116.

61. Edwin A. Winckler, "Institutionalization and Participation on Taiwan: From Hard to Soft Authoritarianism?" *China Quarterly* 99 (1984): 481–99.

62. Shao-kang was a prehistoric legendary king-heir who led 500 troops to crush a coup and revive the Hsia Dynasty, and this office symbolized the KMT's anti-Communist aspirations.

63. Chen Che-ming, "Wang Sheng and the Sudden Rise and Fall of the Shao-kang Office," *The Journalist*, 19 Nov. 1990, pp. 32–35; Chu Ming-huei, "We Are Like an Oppressed Daughter-in-Law: An Interview with Wang Sheng," *The Journalist*, 19 Nov. 1990, pp. 36–38. Seven years after his loss of power, Wang defended himself by saying that he was careful not to exert power in the Shao-kang office, which he said was nothing more than an intergovernmental coordinating agency.

64. Prior to 1977 the Sixth Division (later renamed the Mainland China Affairs Committee) of the KMT central committee was responsible for dealing with the Communists, two other nominal parties in Taiwan (the Chinese Youth Party and the Chinese Democratic Socialist Party), and the loosely organized *Dangwai* members. See the November 1982 issue of *The Asian*.

65. For an analysis of the *Dangwai*, see Jürgen Domes, "Political Differentiation in Taiwan: Group Formations within the Ruling Party and the Opposition Circles, 1979–1980," *Asian Survey* 21 (1981): 1029–39.

66. More than a dozen *Dangwai* magazines were published between 1981 and 1986. For information about their infighting, see Kang Ning-hsiang, *Crisis and Hope* (Taipei: Eighties Monthly, 1983), pp. 135–51; Li Wang-tai, "Not Even a Prairie Fire Can Destroy the Grass; It Grows Again When the Spring Breeze Blows," *Eighties Monthly*, 3 Apr. 1984, pp. 11–18; "The Yesterday, Today, and Tomorrow of the *Dangwai* Magazines," *Hsia Tsao Forum*, October 1984, pp. 2–32.

67. The document was leaked to Kang Ning-hsiang, who showed it to Premier Sun and asked for an explanation in the Legislative Yuan. Sun acknowledged that it was the first time he had seen the document, implying that his power did not reach into the security units. See Kang, *Crisis and Hope*, pp. 213–24.

68. He said, "Internally we have a very few people who do not fully understand our country's current situation, who intentionally or unintentionally become the tool of internal division, who even harbor the thought of opposing the government." Eighties Monthly, *The Might and Reason of Politics* (Taipei: Eighties Monthly, 1983), p. 193.

69. "The 'China Spring' and the 'Taiwan Spring'," *The Asian*, Dec. 1982.

70. *Chi-feng* was taken from a famous poem that reads "The force of the wind (*chi-feng*) tests the strength of the grass," thus suggesting the far right's strength of character and loyalty to the KMT. It also implied that *Dangwai* members were traitors.

71. In the early 1980s, for example, four of the eight deputy editors-in-chief at the *United Daily News* had graduated from the Academy of Political Warfare, which was General Wang Sheng's power base.

72. Kang, *Crisis and Hope*, pp. 259–83.

73. Tao Pai-tsuan, *Political Torchlight* (Taipei: Independent Evening Post, 1983).

74. The secret police's abuse of the revered Tao Pai-tsuan, a close friend of Yu's, was such an outrage that Yu decided to run the story. In the process he discarded social etiquette and refused phone calls trying to change his decision—including one made by the powerful KMT Secretary-General Chiang Yen-shih—after others had failed to reach Yu. See Chu Sou, "Taiwan's Largest Newspaper Under Attack: An Inside Story," *Seventies Monthly* (Hong Kong), 1 Apr. 1983.

75. Some of these operations were known to have been masterminded by General Wang's office; the right wing *Lung-chi* (*Dragon Flag*) magazine carried many articles and distributed anonymous letters, all portraying Yu as an unpatriotic opportunist.

76. Decidedly more liberal than the more established *World Journal* (a New York-based sister paper of the *China Times*'s arch rival in Taipei—the *United Daily News*), Yu's New York-based *China Times* irked the KMT authorities in 1984 when it prominently featured on its front page the mainland Chinese team's victories at the Olympic Games in Los Angeles and a critical editorial of President Ronald Reagan, based largely on a published commentary by James Reston of the *New York Times*. See China Times, *The Forty Years of the China Times* (Taipei: China Times, 1990), pp. 40–45, 80–94. The president has always been fair game for criticism in the United States, although when this was reported out of context to Taipei, Yu was at once made a scapegoat by his foes as someone unworthy of the Party's expectations, someone who aided the enemy's cause and made trouble for

Taiwan's diplomacy. General Wang's conduct had by now caused President Chiang to reduce his power, but Yu had other opponents.

77. Ibid.

78. In Weber's historical writing, the spread of rationalization means the progressive "disenchantment of the world"—the elimination of magic thought and practice. These concepts enter so extensively into Webster's writing that it is difficult to elucidate the exact sphere of their application. See, for example, Max Weber, *The Protestant Ethic and the Spirit of Capitalism*, trans. Talcott Parsons (New York: Scribners, 1958).

79. A member of the Legislative Yuan, Tsai Chen-chou, illegally borrowed U.S. $175 million from the trust funds of a financial cooperative he controlled. Even more shocking was that Tsai embezzled additional U.S. $100 million from the coffers in January 1985—the whereabouts of which remain undisclosed—presumably under the watchful eye of a government team assigned to oversee the cooperative's transactions. As a result, the government had to pour in U.S. $275 million to save millions of small investors from bankruptcy. Huang Kuang-kuo, "Clouds over the Tenth Cooperative Must Be Cleared Up," *United Daily News*, 27 Feb. 1985.

80. Chuang Feng-ho, "A Chameleon Newspaper Owner," *Eighties Monthly*, 21 Sept. 1985, pp. 4–9; Hsueh Tsuen-sheng, "Another KMT Traitor?" *Eighties Monthly*, 21 Sept. 1985, pp. 10–13. Li and her husband (a retired intelligence staffer) had profiteered from a junior college operation in Kaoshiung with the KMT looking the other way, and it was also with the authorities' special permission under martial law that she was able to transfer assets to the United States for publishing the *International Daily News*.

81. Sima Wen-wu, "A Talk with Martial-Law Officers," *Eighties Monthly*, 21 Sept. 1985, pp. 18–21; Chiang Liang-ren, "The 'Black Face' [Taiwan Garrison Command] Will No Longer Be a Scapegoat," *The Journalist*, 11 May 1987, pp. 40–41.

82. The *Dangwai* magazines attempted to link Taiwan to larger developments in South Korea and the Philippines. But my interviews revealed that the KMT was not concerned about a ripple effect, because it felt that control in South Korea was more ruthless and the Korean student culture was more radical, and that the Philippines was ruined by poverty and a corrupt dictator. Extensive press coverage of both events in Taiwan partly demonstrated the KMT's lack of concern.

At about the same time a student movement erupted in China which engulfed many major cities and provinces and finally led to the downfall of Hu Yaobang, General Secretary of the CCP. The press in Taiwan initially reported on this movement rather openly because it served anti-Communist rhetoric. But the press was subsequently told to tone down its coverage for fear that students in Taiwan might question why mainland students were allowed to protest and they themselves could not. The *Dangwai* magazines noted this irony but did not pursue it with vigor.

83. It was widely believed, although difficult to confirm, that the U.S. government had exerted strong pressure on Chiang to democratize Taiwan.

84. *Forty Years of the China Times*, pp. 46–49. Yu explained to the KMT's general secretary that his newspaper was obligated to report about an event of this magnitude, but also that he was willing to urge caution in the editorial. The *United Daily News* was editorially very derogatory toward the new party and, for some time, refused to address it by its own name.

85. Chiang reportedly told his personal secretary, "What should we do with them after we arrest them?" He realized that demand for democratization could not be suppressed forever.

86. Nicholas D. Kristof, "A Dictatorship that Grew Up: In Taiwan, Despotism Passes Posthaste into Democracy," *New York Times Magazine*, 16 Feb. 1992, pp. 16–21, 53, 56–57.

87. For example, Wilbur Schramm, *Mass Media and National Development* (Stanford: Stanford University Press, 1964); Daniel Lerner and Wilbur Schramm (eds.), *Communication and Change in the Developing Countries* (Honolulu, HI: University of Hawaii Press, 1967).

88. See a critique in Tunstall, *The Media are American*.

89. Schramm, *Big Media, Little Media*.

90. Majid Tehranian, "Iran: Communication, Alienation and Revolution," *Intermedia* 7, no. 2 (1979): 6–12.

91. Alan P. L. Liu, *Communications and National Integration in Communist China* (Berkeley: University of California Press, 1971).

92. See David Hoffman and Will Duggan, *Guerrilla Media: A Citizen's Guide to Using Electronic Media for Social Change, The Inside Story From Tony Schwartz*. (A video program produced by Varied Directions, Inc., 1988); John Downing, *Radical Media: The Political Experience of Alternative Communication* (Boston: South End Press, 1988).

93. Lee, *Voices of China*.

94. Myers argued that Taiwan had an "inhibited center" whose power was checked by a society made up of private associations, business firms, and households, whereas Communist China had an "uninhibited center" where the state had considerable control over households. R. H. Myers, "Political Theory and Recent Political Developments in the Republic of China," *Asian Survey* 27, no. 9 (1987): 1003–22.

95. Lee, "Taiwan: Wither the Culture Drifts?"; Lee, *Politics of Journalism*.

96. Personal interviews with, among others, Sima Wenwu, former editor of *Eighties Monthly*; Lin Chen-yi, former deputy editor of the *Freedom Times* (*Tzu-yu Shih Tai*); Keng Jung-shui, former editor of *Torch* (*Hsin Huo*).

97. Ibid.

98. Taiwan, of course, is not immune from the five interlocking types of political censorship found to exist in Western democracies: emergency powers, armed secrecy, lying, state advertising, and corporatism. See John Keane, *The Media and Democracy* (Cambridge, England: Polity, 1991), pp. 95–109.

99. Sue Curry Jansen, *Censorship* (New York: Oxford University Press, 1991); Nicholas Garnham, *Capitalism and Communication* (Newbury Park, CA: Sage, 1990); Edward S. Herman and Noam Chomsky, *Manufacturing Consent* (New York: Pantheon, 1988); Graham Murdock, "Large Corporations and the Control of the Communications Industry," in Michael Gurevitch et. al. (eds.), *Culture, Society, and the Media* (New York: Methuen, 1982); Ben Bagdikian, *Media Monopoly* (Boston: Beacon, 1982).

100. *The Journalist*, 3 Sept. 1990, pp. 56–61; *Wealth Magazine*, no. 103 (Oct. 1990), pp. 160–74.

101. *Wealth Magazine*, no. 103 (Oct. 1990), pp. 175–83.

PART THREE

IDEOLOGY, KNOWLEDGE, AND PROFESSIONALISM

11

THE AMERICAN CORRESPONDENT IN CHINA

Michel Oksenberg

American newspaper, magazine, radio, and television correspondents abroad confront a challenging task. They must make developments abroad intelligible to the American public. They serve as bridges between cultures. The most renowned have had considerable influence upon public policy and opinion in the United States and abroad, including Edward Murrow, John Reed, Harrison Salisbury, William Shirer, Edgar Snow, David Halberstram, Leland Stowe, and, more recently, Thomas Friedman, Bernard Shaw, and Peter Arnett.

Reflecting their global imperial position, the British led the world prior to World War I in the posting of energetic and enterprising correspondents abroad. In fact, British journalists established the initial norms of the profession, especially William Henry Russell who covered the Crimean War for the *London Times*. Russell pioneered the idea of rugged and independent coverage of a foreign war. His forthright coverage earned him the enmity of British troops—who once demonstrated their views of him by burying his tent—and his reports inspired Lord Tennyson's epic, "Charge of the Light Brigade." The tradition continued with Winston Churchill's coverage of the Boer War and Stanley's search for David Livingston. The tradition spawned classic British novels as well, such as Evelyn Waugh's *Scoop*.

Not surprisingly, British journalists led in the coverage of China at the turn of the century. G.H.C. Morrison was the particularly well-known and influential *London Times* correspondent. Britain also supplied arguably the greatest rogue foreign correspondent in China, Edmund Backhouse. The full extent of Backhouse's deceptions was not revealed until Hugh Trevor-Roper published his study of the Englishman's shenanigans. Backhouse let it be rumored that he was having an affair with the Empress Dowager to enhance the credibility of his reporting on the Boxer Rebellion. He donated a collection of allegedly rare Chinese manuscripts to the Bodelein Library that later proved to be forgeries and extracted large sums from the British government in World War I in exchange for muskets promised to him by warlords who never appeared.

After World War I American newspapers began to surpass the British press in foreign coverage. Such papers as the *New York Herald-Tribune* and the *Chicago Sun-Times* had the resources to station correspondents throughout the world and were able to record the worldwide economic depression and the path to World War II.

American correspondents in China came of age in the late 1930s and during World War II. Perhaps one can be more precise: Their day arrived when Edgar Snow journeyed to Yanan, where Mao Zedong and his Long March survivors had only recently arrived. Mao brilliantly seized the opportunity to convey his message to the world, and Snow brilliantly used his interviews to write his account of the Communist movement. In his interviews with Snow, Mao greatly exaggerated his position within the Chinese Communist movement at the time, distorted aspects of the Long March, and veiled the more brutal and autocratic dimensions of the movement and his personality. Snow's *Red Star Over China* became the vehicle through which Mao's varnished image was conveyed to the world and disseminated within China.[1]

During World War II a number of other outstanding reporters sought to reduce the complexity of the China scene to manageable proportions: Theodore White, Harrison Froman, Graham Peck, and Jack Belden, to name a few. With the advantage of considerable hindsight, we can say their reportage, as Snow's earlier account from Yanan, slighted the darker side of the Chinese Communist Party (CCP)—its totalitarian impulses, anti-intellectualism, and violent streak. But many of the intellectuals who joined the movement in those days and indeed many of the Communist leaders themselves did not see or understand these dimensions of the Party. The American journalists did capture the ineptitude of the Nationalist government, perhaps in exaggerated form and with insufficient stress upon the reasons for the government's problems. They also correctly portrayed the growing gap between the two Chinas—one under CCP leadership and the other under the Kuomintang (KMT). Reporting from 1941 to 1945 pointed in a clear direction: A civil war loomed ahead for China and, despite the military strength at the KMT's disposal, the CCP would enter the fray with many advantages.[2]

The 1945-1949 civil war was also well covered by a group of talented journalists, such as Tillman Durdin, Seymour Topping, Doak Barnett, and Keyes Beech. Next came those hardy correspondents ensconced in Hong Kong, usually on three- to five-year assignments. From the early 1950s through the late 1970s, between five and 15 or 20 such people were based in Hong Kong, their numbers ebbing when the China story was not very exciting or growing when it heated up, especially during the Cultural Revolution. Since Hong Kong-based journalists frequently covered other parts of Asia as well, their numbers peaked during the Vietnam War.

Many young American scholars then embarking on careers as China specialists spent one or two years of their training in Hong Kong doing research about the mainland. While there, we formed lifelong friendships with journalists who regaled us with stories upon their return to Hong Kong from covering the September 1965 coup in Indonesia, the 1971 Indo-Pakistani war, or the unfolding tragedy in Pnomh Penh.

Such correspondents as Stanley Karnow, Robert Elegant, Joseph Lelyveld, Loren Festor, Tillman Durdin, and Henry Bradsher paraded across the Hong Kong stage, peering through the Bamboo Curtain to decipher developments on the mainland. They relied on local China-watchers whom they employed on a long-term basis such as the knowledgeable Sydney Liu at *Newsweek*. They also turned to the U.S. consulate which for years was second to Munich as the United States' largest foreign consulate, housing successive cohorts of younger China specialists who subsequently had distinguished careers in the Foreign Service. Such future ambassadors and consuls general as Donald Anderson, John Holdridge, Paul Kreisberg, Nicholas Platt, and Morton Abramowitz cut their teeth briefing the Hong Kong-based journalist corps, debriefing recent travelers returning from the mainland, and running the Chinese mainland press monitoring and translation service on which much of the analysis was based. The common Hong Kong experience forged bonds of friendship among academics, journalists, and government analysts that have lasted to the present day.

Ping-pong diplomacy in 1971 ushered in a new era of press coverage of China. Following the American table tennis team's invitation to tour China in the spring of 1971, invitations were extended to and accepted by such leading journalists as James Reston, Joseph Alsop, and Theodore White. These visits were preceded by an Edgar Snow journey in late 1969 that was meant to signal to the Nixon administration Mao's interest in improving relations with the United States. The favorable reportage helped ease the initiatives of the Nixon administration. Although journalists did not accompany Henry Kissinger on his secret July 1971 trip, President Nixon's February 1972 journey was the occasion of a media spectacular. From then until the establishment of diplomatic relations in March 1979, American coverage drew on two sources: reports filed by non-specialists based on short trips to China, and the ongoing dispatches of the Hong Kong-based China hands. The Hong Kong reporters, who were skilled China-watchers or Pekingologists, focused on power struggles, factional strife, and the disruptive effect of such ideological campaigns as the 1973 criticism of Lin Biao and Confucius. Short-term visitors and correspondents accompanying American government officials, in contrast, were introduced to a different China. Prior to succumbing to cancer in 1976, Zhou Enlai gave virtuoso performances in his many midnight interviews, almost single-handedly transforming the popular interpretation of Chinese foreign policy in the United States from one of threat and irrationality to one of caution, subtlety, and sophistication.

The establishment of full diplomatic relations between China and the United States in 1979 opened a new chapter, as it became possible for American journalists to open bureaus in Beijing. Since that time an increasingly long list of distinguished journalists have been assigned to the People's Republic: Fox Butterfield, Linda Mathews, Jay Mathews, Michael Parks, Frank Ching, Takaski Oka, Daniel Southerland, Melinda Liu, John Woodruff, Nicholas Kristoff, Sheryl WuDunn, and Michael Chinoy, to name a few.

THE CHINA JOURNALISTS: A PORTRAIT

To oversimplify, three generations of journalists have covered China: the wartime generation who covered World War II and the civil war on the mainland, the Hong Kong-based China watchers from 1950 to 1978, and the evolving contingent based in the People's Republic since 1979. Throughout this period of over 50 years, correspondents have visited China briefly, often to cover the journey of a top official. The total number of those who have served in one of these roles reaches into the thousands. They are a diverse lot, sharing only one quality: They all wrote about China.

Some have been career journalists assigned to China for a two- or three-year stint, having earlier covered, for example, Baltimore city hall or the Detroit auto industry. Upon their return to the United States, they may have been assigned to the political scene in Washington, the academic world in Cambridge, or Wall Street. These career journalists acquired a modicum of competence in China.

Others have been career foreign correspondents who have moved from the Soviet Union to China to South Africa—to recall one pattern—or from the Middle East to China to Ottawa. The China assignment was part of an ongoing career. Yet others, such as Tillman Durdin of the *New York Times*, have spent their entire career primarily on China. Others, such as Fox Butterfield, Jay Mathews, Linda Mathews, and Richard Bernstein, can be expected to return to the China moorings periodically through their careers.

Another type has surfaced through the years: adventurers who set off for East Asia with perhaps a smattering of journalistic and/or area training, stumble upon China, and become writers to earn a living. Edgar Snow is, of course, the best-known journalist with this career pattern, but many others have gone to Hong Kong, Taiwan, and the China mainland to seek their fortune or discover themselves, but discover journalism instead.

Then there are the career journalists—often quite prestigious ones— who have taken maximum advantage of one or several short-term trips to China to do some reporting or write a book. Harrison Salisbury probably best fits that category, though Salisbury brought a unique perspective through his deep knowledge of the Soviet Union. James Reston, Joseph Kraft, and Joseph Alsop are among American journalists who wrote extensively on the basis of brief visits in the early 1970s. Edgar Snow himself returned to China for brief visits in 1960, 1969, and 1973, with each journey resulting in both magazine articles and books.

Before the crushing of the democracy movement in 1989, accompanying the entourages that descended upon the Chinese during a visit by the president, vice president, or secretary of state probably provided the best opportunity for a large number of journalists to journey to China. These visits also provided the opportunity for China to intrude upon the American consciousness. On such occasions American politicians used China as a photogenic backdrop through which to portray their statesmanship. In the television era state banquets in Beijing were timed to coincide with NBC's "Today Show" and ABC's "Good Morning America." But the most important gathering of the media for an epic journey was not for an American politician. It was for Mikhail Gorbachev's May 1989 Beijing trip. The amassing of American journalists coincided with demonstrations on Tiananmen Square, thus allowing the student movement and its fate to capture world attention.

Finally, some journalists end up working for the Chinese. This interesting group of people includes the influential George Sokolsky and Sydney Rittenberg. Sokolsky, a prominent journalist in Shanghai in the 1920s and 1930s, drifted into the KMT camp, for whom he eventually worked. After the war he immigrated to the United States where he became a major voice for the Taiwan lobby. Rittenberg, a South Carolinian, went to China during the war and ended up in the Communist camp. Remaining on the mainland after the Communist victory, he had a checkered career until the Cultural Revolution when he became head of the Chinese broadcast and television network. At the time Rittenberg had close ties with the extreme leftists of the Cultural Revolution. He was subsequently jailed, released in the post-Mao era, and today works in Sino-American trade. Gerald Tannenbaum was another American who remained on the mainland after

1949, working as a journalist. He worked for a long time with Madame Soong Qingling on the journal *China Reconstructs*. Perhaps the most famous writer-journalists who produced sympathetic accounts of the Communists were Agnes Smedley and Anna Louise Strong, while more recently American journalists have worked for Beijing television and the *China Daily*.

In short, American journalists in China have been a diverse lot, each facing his or her own unique problems and opportunities. The most influential among them, however, have been the career journalists—either generalists or China specialists—assigned to China for a substantial length of time. In contrast to the various backgrounds of journalists who have covered China, some of the salient problems and issues that they face exhibit considerable commonality and continuity.

THE DISTINCTIVE PROBLEMS OF CHINA COVERAGE

Size and Diversity

Covering China poses a greater challenge than that faced by correspondents in most other places. Its sheer size and diversity is daunting. How can one correspondent cover a nation of a billion? China in many respects is more a continent than a country. It is no more possible for a single journalist to fully understand and portray China's complexity than for a single correspondent to cover all of Latin America from Tijuana to Punta del Este or the whole Moslem world from Morocco to Pakistan and Indonesia.

To be sure, China's political unity and certain common cultural features of the Han ethnic group—94% of the total population—justify certain generalizations about the country. Nonetheless, the present regionalization and fragmentation of the economic and political system constitute an important trend in China. As the political anthropologist G. William Skinner has so frequently stressed, China must be analyzed in regional terms. It consists of several macro-regions: the Lingnan region of Guangdong and Guangxi commercially centering on Guangzhou and Hong Kong; the lower Yangtze (Changjiang) centering on Wuhan; the Red River basin of Sichuan; the north China plain centering on Beijing and Tianjin; and the Manchurian corridor.[3] Added to these large macro-regions, each home to over 100 million people, are the enclaves on the Fujian coast linked historically to Taiwan and the plateau of Yunnan and Guizhou. Finally, there are the pastoral and desert areas of the northwest inhabited by various Moslem Turkic and Uighur peoples, and the Tibetan regions of the southwest.

If journalists neglect this diversity and rarely report on it, their readers will not understand the fragility and tenuousness of China's political unity. This theme is likely to become even more pronounced in the 1990s as China's periphery—its coastal cities, Taiwan, Hong Kong, perhaps even Tibet—become larger factors in shaping its core. From the 1950s through the 1970s Beijing and the core acted upon and shaped the country's fate; that process is now more complicated. One of the major challenges in covering China will be to capture this complexity, including growing ties between regional China and the outside world: south China and U.S., European, and Southeast Asian markets; Fujian and Taiwan; Shanghai and the United States and Japan; and northern and northeastern China with Japan, Korea, and Siberia.

History

Beyond size and regionalism, Chinese culture and history present an even greater challenge. China's leaders are greatly influenced by their sense of history, and not only by their perceptions of Western and Japanese aggression and memories of the revolution. They also learned as youth about power struggles at court in previous dynasties, tales told in popular novels and operas. Their own political plans and their strategies in political struggle are based in part on their memories of how different emperors and courtiers acted under similar circumstances. The high drama of succession to an aged ruler has been played out in dozens of well-known instances in Chinese history. Today's handling of Deng's succession is occurring against the backdrop of these memories, and today's actors pick their parts and veil their strategies based on this common knowledge. But which American journalist has been trained to penetrate this arcane world? And even if a brilliant journalist were able to unmask the actors, how could he describe the drama to an American audience?

The uproar over the concept of sovereignty, for example, can only be understood in a historical context. Beijing ideologues condemned former U.S. Ambassador James Lilly for asserting that China clung to an outmoded concept of sovereignty, an observation similar to my reflections on the current leaders' reluctance to embrace the idea of interdependence. But the Chinese sentiments should not simply be derided as expressions of xenophobia and fear, nor should the Chinese alarm at American designs to ensure China's "peaceful evolution" be seen as stemming solely from its leaders' tenacious desire to cling to power. Rather, the views of the octogenarian leaders and their ideologues spring from memories and a worldview which categorize the notion of interdependence as a clever attempt by the powerful and wealthy nations to justify new forms of domination. They believe that the vigorous assertion of national independence is a precondition for an equitable world order. Only the tight organization of the people by the governments of the developing worlds can prevent their exploitation by outside forces.

Culture

The problems of China's cultural distinctiveness call upon American journalists to try and interpret a society whose values differ from ours. The same words may have different meanings in American and Chinese societies. Democracy, freedom, and individualism—concepts intertwined in the American mind—are notable in this regard. These concepts, however, stem from ideas deeply rooted in Judeo-Christian and Greco-Roman philosophical traditions, and are based on fundamental assumptions about the nature of human beings and the purposes of governance. While a liberal tradition also exists in Chinese thought that could sustain benevolent rule responsive to popular aspirations,[4] it is not supported by ancillary beliefs in the rule of law, the virtues of pluralism, tolerance of diversity, the inalienable rights of individuals, and the equal participation of citizens in their own governance. These beliefs, many political theorists would argue, are important to sustain a meaningful democracy. Thus, it is natural to ask what the demonstrators had in mind when they called for democracy in April–May 1989. Were they calling for a system such as ours—a pluralistic system with universal enfranchisement and the rule of law—or simply a more liberal regime based upon authoritarian-meritocratic principles? Beijing-based American correspondents must keep complex questions such as these in mind when interpreting Chinese reality.

Remaining sensitive to China's diversity, history, and cultural nuances is a huge challenge. As bridges between two cultures, American journalists cannot lose their national American identities in the process. They must make Chinese views intelligible to an American audience, and that necessitates remaining well-anchored in American society. They cannot lose their American audience by appearing to have been absorbed by China or becoming one of them. Covering the democracy movement provides a good example. To have reminded American readers in spring 1989 that China's unity is fragile and its order tenuous, that the West behaved rapaciously toward China in the past, and that China's "democrats" may not be democratic would have been to echo the views of hardliners in Zhongnanhai. Journalists stressing such themes would very likely have been seen by their readers and listeners as spokesmen for repression; their credibility would have eroded. When the intellectual chasm separating the United States from a foreign country is great, China being an example, the challenge confronting the correspondent or scholar is at its maximum.

Language

Finally, there is the difficulty of the Chinese language. Few American journalists in China have had truly excellent language proficiency. Many may speak Mandarin, but few can read with speed or are proficient in regional dialects. Reading different types of calligraphy, including the poetry in Chinese scrolls or the handwriting script (grass or running style) used in letters and wall posters, presents a further challenge. When wall posters have gone up or a handwritten manuscript has fallen into their hands, most American journalists have been unable to read the material swiftly and accurately without the assistance of a native speaker. Nor should one assume that Chinese-Americans have the requisite language capability. Adding to the barriers of coverage is ethnicity. It is impossible for Caucasian or Black Americans to meld with the population; keeping surveillance over them is relatively easy. As a result of these considerations, as we will note below, American correspondents usually must rely on local Chinese, especially one or a few with excellent fluency in English, to introduce them to Chinese society.

THE COMMON PROBLEMS

In addition to the distinctive problems in the coverage of China, many problems our journalists in China face are common to the profession of foreign correspondent. Those include the difficulties of covering an authoritarian political system: surveillance, censorship, and concern with protection of sources. Then there are problems with editors back home. Frequently, correspondents file insightful dispatches only to see them go unprinted or severely altered and edited. Theodore White at *Time* under Henry Luce faced an extreme instance of this. In the case of China, however, the gap between the bureau and headquarters seems to have arisen rather frequently. Images of China—both favorable or unfavorable—have taken hold of the public, including editors, and dispatches that have not accorded with this mood have been more prone to rejection, heavy editing, or being accompanied by a misleading headline. Differences in perceptions of China held by headquarters and the people in the field pertain not only to journalism; foundations, corporations, and religions are often chronicled in accounts of the China activities of such organizations as the Rockefeller Foundation, the YMCA, and Yale-in-China. Americans at home repeatedly have created a China that accords with their images of the world and the United States which they then press upon their reluctant agents in the field.

   This phenomenon is obviously related to Harold Isaac's classic observations about the love-hate relationship between China and the United States, but it is more than that.[5] The American mood has fluctuated between periods of self-adulation and self-flagellation, between periods of self-confidence that the world is becoming safe for democracy and fear that evil foreign forces are about to engulf us. To what extent the domestic media are responsible for fostering these oscillations is an interesting but irrelevant question for the purposes of this chapter.[6] But what is relevant—to return to our metaphor of foreign correspondents serving as a bridge between cultures—is that the American foundation anchoring one side of the bridge is embedded in an earthquake zone, not firm granite.

Managing the ceaseless tension between reporting the news and providing background for it is another challenge journalists must face. What is necessary to put the current developments in context? What is the proper balance between simply reporting the latest news and using the story to make a broader point? If the article gives undue emphasis to background material, the reader may wonder why the paper carries this story today, or the editor may conclude the dispatch contains little "news." But if the foreign correspondent gives a lean account, the reader may be baffled.

THE CHOICES CONFRONTING JOURNALISTS

The objective difficulties mentioned above arise from the nature of China and journalism as a profession. As one reflects on the issues that three generations of China journalists have confronted, one is particularly struck by the continuity in the challenges. Although the telecommunications transformation present journalists with new problems and opportunities, the continuities deserve special attention.

Filing Dispatches and Writing Books

Although journalists are in China to cover the contemporary scene, they are remembered for the books they write. Edgar Snow is not remembered so much for his various articles in newspapers or *The Saturday Evening Post* as for *Red Star Over China*. Theodore White is not remembered for the dispatches he sent to *Time*, but rather *Thunder Out of China*.[7] Doak Barnett's columns in the *Chicago Daily News* do not have a lingering influence, but his *China on the Eve of Communist Takeover* is memorable.[8] Jay and Linda Mathews, for all of their excellent reporting in the *Washington Post* and the *Los Angeles Times*, will be read in the years ahead not through their columns but for their book, *One Billion*.[9] China offers an opportunity to write memorable and lucrative books which can also enhance careers.

Reporters, therefore, confront a most difficult issue: how to balance their obligations to their contemporary readers with their desire to serve a more enduring audience. Several American journalists stationed in Beijing after 1979 deliberately decided prior to going to China not to write a book. They decided to concentrate their energy on the current story and not to retain or gather material for their books. Others arrived in China with a contract knowing that at the end of their stay, they were to produce a volume. Without sacrificing their daily or weekly duties, they therefore simultaneously were thinking about this other assignment. Yet others, midway through or toward the end of their stay, became tempted to write a book.

Both approaches to the task of reporting merit respect. But it is useful for the newspaper reader to know whether the correspondent plans to write a book and is burrowing quietly and more deeply into the society than their current stories might suggest, in order to accumulate material for an in-depth study. Such writers might be prone to be more cautious in contemporary coverage in order not to risk the larger project, but their contemporaneous coverage also should be particularly strong in those areas that the forthcoming book will dwell upon. In any case, journalists in Beijing must decide what mix of publications will emanate from their stay in China, and that decision will have a major effect on the kind of contemporary coverage they produce.

The China Audience

American correspondents can have enormous influence not only upon the United States but upon China. While Edgar Snow affected American thinking about China, he had an even a greater impact within China through *Red Star Over China*. That book was published at a time when the Kuomintang exercised strict censorship over stories about the Communists. The American correspondent became an indirect channel enabling the Communists to reach the Chinese public, and when the book became available in Chinese, its impact was even greater. Ironically, at the same time in the early days of World War II, American journalists helped Chiang Kai-shek strengthen his own position within China by building up his reputation outside China. His designation as *Time*'s Man-of-the-Year helped legitimate his position among certain segments of Chinese society, as did the same magazine's selection of Deng Xiaoping in 1978 and 1988.

In today's China internal, classified bulletins that contain reprinted news dispatches of foreign journalists based in China circulate among officials and privileged members of the public. These bulletins have been widely perceived in China as more informative about internal developments than Chinese newspapers. In fact, the bulletins can be deliberately used to inform the public about developments that are ignored or downplayed in the official propaganda. For example, in the Chinese coverage of President Nixon's trip to China, part of the press plan was to make deliberate use of foreign reporting on Nixon's visit via *Reference News* rather than informing the public through the open Chinese press. Thus, Chinese newspapers purposely did not initially give the Nixon visit banner headlines as part of the signaling strategy for the Western audience. The Chinese wanted the Nixon party and the Western press to feel that their presence in China was not the most important event taking place in China. Meanwhile, the Chinese leaders informed their people about the trip through Western press reports reproduced in *Reference News*, thereby conveying to the Chinese populace a sense of how important this event was in Western eyes.

Many other instances illustrate the domestic importance of foreign coverage about China.[10] There is no question that foreign reporting on the Democracy Wall movement in 1978-1979 had stimulated developments within China. The reports were beamed back to China by the Voice of America (VOA), to which many Chinese listen. One American journalist, for example, has insisted to me on several occasions—revealing the specifics—that a foreign journalist advised one dissident in the preparation of a poster that the journalist subsequently wrote about. My source tells me such a violation of journalistic norms was very unusual, but also claims that journalists influenced the course of the movement through close linkages with dissidents. Yet, the code of honor among the journalists prevented reporting on these linkages. The Democracy Wall movement was probably halted in part because these connections came to the attention of the authorities and because the VOA and other news sources amplified the effect of the movement.

A second incident involved the 1979 oil rig disaster in the Bohai Gulf. The disaster initially received no mention in the Chinese media, and months later the story was leaked to an American correspondent whose coverage was then replayed in China. The leak probably accelerated the dissemination of the information and had adverse political implications for the source's targets within China.

The 1983-1984 spiritual pollution campaign and the 1987 campaign against bourgeois liberalism were modified in part by foreign coverage and reporting by the VOA. Foreign journalists raised a sense of alarm in the West over the implications of the campaigns. Perhaps encouraged by Chinese who also saw advantage in heightening Western concern that China was sliding toward another Cultural Revolution, Western and Japanese coverage soon affected investor confidence in Chinese stability. Would it be safe to do business in China when Western businessmen were accused of corrupting the nation? By swiftly raising such issues, the Western journalist played a role in moderating such campaigns.

Thus, although the primary audience of American journalists may be the United States, they often are perceived to have a greater short-term influence on China. Journalists therefore become obvious targets for manipulation. And there is tremendous temptation to use one's influence to become an actor in the Chinese political system. Foreign coverage of the

1989 democracy movement and its crushing was the most dramatic instance of this set of issues. One senses that perhaps some journalists became caught up in the movement and succumbed to the opportunity to accelerate—rather than report on—the processes of Chinese history. Believing their reporting was beneficially affecting China's course and knowing that their accounts then returned to China via fax and radio, the correspondents may have even subconsciously highlighted the idealism of the youths while neglecting their less savory and hypocritical dimensions. Their heart was with the movement, and it was impossible for the heart to not affect the mind.

Instances in which journalists have inadvertently or purposely become actors in Chinese politics have often been counterproductive, resulting in coverage which has created illusions that the outside world was more engaged, concerned, and willing to assist than reality warranted. Has reporting ever beclouded the true balance of power in China? Repeatedly over the past century, Westerners have underestimated the strength of conservatives and anti-foreign sentiment. Is one reason for this that Chinese reformers and cosmopolitans strike up informal alliances with unwitting foreigners—including businesspeople, scholars, and government officials—whom they draw into their quest for power? While I do not know the answer to these questions, they are certainly worth pondering. Edgar Snow may have eased Mao's ascent, but Mao probably would have risen had he never met Snow or any other foreign journalist. Wuer Kaixi and Chai Ling, however, may have ended up in the United States through their journalist contacts, while others languish in prison. In the final analysis, perhaps the ability of foreign journalists to influence China's course is marginal and illusory, even though the involvement may fleetingly or permanently assist the Chinese who lure the journalist into playing this role and may appeal to the ego of the journalist.

Chinese Assistants and Chinese Sources

A third issue has long confronted the American corespondent in China. What does one do with one's Chinese assistant? As already mentioned, few correspondents have the language capability or indeed the energy and time to cover the story on their own. The memoirs of Edgar Snow and Teddy White and Fox Butterfield's introduction to his book make clear that their Chinese assistants were crucial to their work. They become, in part, the eyes and ears of the foreign journalist, inevitably doing more than surveying the Chinese press. In effect, many aids play the role of the taxi cab drivers and chauffeurs of New York City. They illuminate the conditions in the country, the public mood, and political attitudes.

Yet under both the Nationalist and Communist regimes, these assistants often were either KMT or Communist agents and informants. Even if not on the payroll, they nonetheless frequently were expected to report on their employers. Despite these considerations, such assistants have played an invaluable role in increasing the quality of reporting on China, sometimes developing loyalty to their foreign correspondent while reporting to authorities.

Correspondents with Chinese assistants face a series of issues: training them, confiding in them, compensating for potential distortion and bias, and protecting other sources. For example, Beijing bookstores frequently contain revealing publications about both the past and present. In recent years my own scouring has yielded a massive study of juvenile delinquency throughout China, including detailed data on organizations and personnel in the departments of all provincial government agencies, and specific budget data from the provinces. Rarely, however, have the assistants hired by the government service bureau possessed the requisite skills, energy, and understanding to ferret out such nuggets. Meanwhile, sources such as the New China News Agency (Xinhua) and the *China Daily* give no indication of the information available through books, journals, and the provincial press.

The Government Spokesperson

In both Nationalist and Communist China, foreign correspondents typically are expected to direct their inquiries to the official government spokesperson. A recurring theme in the coverage of China, however—be it Shanghai or Nanjing in the 1930s, Chongqing in the 1940s, or present-day Taipei or Beijing—is that the Chinese government has not been well served by its spokespersons. The inadequacy of the spokesperson, however, may be traced to his or her position in an authoritarian regime which both produces inadequate or misleading official stories and tightly restricts efforts at independent investigation. Authoritarian regimes have not fully understood the needs of American journalists and how the role of the spokesperson can be performed effectively. Tight strictures on the autonomy of the spokesperson combine with the high expectations of journalists to result in painful briefing sessions. As the spokesperson loses credibility, a sense of hostility develops, not so much against the spokesperson (although this can happen), as against the regime he or she represents.

The stakes are quite high. The dynamics of the situation remind one of reporters' reactions to the afternoon USMAG (United States Military Advisory Group) briefings in Vietnam. A cynicism about the system begins to pervade the journalist corps. Neither the Nationalists nor the Communists have ever learned how much influence they could gain through the intelligent handling of the Western media. But the techniques perfected by such communicators as Marlin Fitzwater probably are inapplicable in an authoritarian system. First of all, docile in-house Chinese journalists might be harder to contain if they saw Westerners treated far more openly than themselves. Second, the leaders would have to be more open to scrutiny. And third, damaging and sometimes embarrassing information would have to be released in an official forum.

Other Sources

Since the official sources are inadequate, journalists must develop alternative sources. Embassy personnel are a natural source. American diplomats have played a very important role in shaping popular American perceptions of China, since most American journalists rely upon the Embassy for leads and background. Another source is the American community in China, such as students, businesspeople, and English language teachers. American students in particular have played a crucial role in the shaping of journalists' views. Edgar Snow, Doak Barnett, and Fox Butterfield, to cite three examples, all maintained close contact with the American scholarly community as a way of penetrating the society. American journalists also gravitate to Chinese intellectuals, particularly those who speak English, have a pro- American orientation, and are willing to meet with Americans. (This is not, one must stress, a representative sample of China's intellectual community. Many intellectuals, for various reasons, have little interest in meeting American journalists.) Journalists also drift toward artists and dissidents. They are willing to take risks, are perhaps more likely to perceive benefits arising from foreign contacts, and often seek ways to disseminate their message. Finally, journalists make an effort to meet officials under informal, off-the-record circumstances, or to befriend the children of high-level officials. Such contacts, however, are not easily made.

This list of the usual contacts outside official government channels prompts several observations. Farmers, peddlers, workers—the bulk of the population—are not among the group. Almost all of these contacts take place in Beijing and the coastal cities. (Recall that Edgar Snow grabbed the prize because he had the sense to leave the capital; the big story of the decade was in the remote areas of northwest China.) The community of Chinese that enters the journalists' orbit, therefore, is selective and not representative of the total society. Chinese outside government channels talk to journalists for reasons other than generosity, friendliness, and a desire to be helpful. They usually have an interest in using the journalist to get some story across for their own purpose. Journalists in China, as elsewhere, must try to figure out the source's interest: What is the motive for the assistance which the Chinese is giving? The answer is not always obvious.

Circumstances even further beyond the control of Western journalists have led to reportorial inaccuracy and omissions. No Western journalist was freely able to roam the country during the two episodes from 1960–1962, when perhaps as many as 20–30 million Chinese died of malnutrition or starvation (depending on how one measures the effects of the famine). Several foreign journalists briefly visited areas in 1960–1961, including Edgar Snow, but none of them sensed the dimensions of the tragedy. Neither was the extent of the terror and bloodshed during the Cultural Revolution of 1966–1969 well understood. In both instances, Taiwan authorities and those who had confidence in Taiwan reporting (such as Kurt London) were on the mark. Unfortunately, their information was discounted, since Taiwan spokespersons had been exclusively reporting starvation and terror in China from the early 1950s. When the situation corresponded to their worst claims, they were no longer credible. Nor did the Hong Kong listening post, with its refugee influx, prove adequate for capturing the 1960–1962 and 1966–1969 disasters.

The implications are clear: Unfettered travel through rural areas and the ability to interview privately and in-depth are necessary. One suspects that the situation after 4 June is the same. What are the peasants and industrial workers in such provinces as Sichuan, Henan, and Zhejiang thinking and planning? What fears and aspirations, demands and expectations in the countryside and the new industrial cities are transmitted to the top leaders via Communist Party channels? What pressures from the interior buffet the top leaders and shape their views? To what extent, indeed, are the leaders in control of their agenda, and to what extent are their options constrained by the demands emanating from their primary constituencies? To what extent, for example, has the crackdown on Beijing intellectuals and students since 4 June 1989 been encouraged or supported by local officials demanding unity and stability? Or have the rapid spread of television, the decollectivization of agriculture, and the increased mobility of peasants begun to change the rural political culture and created a yearning for more freedom? The constraints on the foreign journalist preclude careful answers to these questions. As with 1960–1962 and 1966–1969, journalists may be missing the big story of China in the 1990s.

Even so, a major rationale exists for remaining in Beijing. The journalist takes a big risk in leaving the capital for extended periods. That is where fast breaking stories occur. Pity the journalist who is in a peasant hut on the day that Deng Xiaoping passes from the scene! Covering Deng's death and the initial jostling for the succession would be worth weeks if not months of boredom.

Fellow Journalists and Oneself

American journalists must also decide on their posture toward their fellow correspondents. Are they competitors or colleagues? Do they assist one another and share information, or do they hoard it for the stories that they are building? Different journalists approach this issue in very different ways. In fact, an interesting story remains to be written about American journalists in China, including the factionalism within the community and the different, overlapping sources they draw upon. Nor should the secretive loner be denigrated. Indeed, one problem in Beijing arises from the collegiality of journalists: They accredit gossip by rapidly spreading unsubstantiated rumors.

But no matter how collegial, the community cannot carry a weak journalist. Eventually, the journalist must rely on her own innate skills, judgment, and character. In many respects a journalist's stay in China has always been a rather personal statement, as revealing about herself as about China. What are her values, emotional balance, and capacity to withstand stress? Journalists in China—flattered by some and reviled by others—also see their integrity taxed to the maximum. It is too easy to become jaded, corrupt, petty, or enmeshed in Chinese society, and objectivity under such circumstances is difficult to retain.

The Evaluative Yardstick

Finally, any coverage of China involves judgments and evaluations of the system's performance. What yardstick does the correspondent use to measure Chinese performance? Should China be implicitly or explicitly compared with Taiwan, the United States, the former Soviet Union, developing countries, the goals of Chinese leaders, the aspirations of the Chinese people, China's immediate past, or the ideals of the correspondent? All are legitimate yardsticks from which the journalist may choose, but he must make his choice clear to his readers so that they may evaluate the story and place it in context.

This, however, is a tricky matter. There seems to be a herd instinct among the journalist community, and every so often they adopt a new implicit comparison, causing either detriment or advantage to China. The consequence is that China appears to have changed when in reality it has changed very little. The Communists in Yanan, for example, were often explicitly compared with the KMT in Chongqing; they benefited from the comparison. But in the 1950s similarities between Communists in Beijing and their counterparts in Stalinist Russia were stressed. In the Cultural Revolution years, coinciding with America's Vietnam War era and civil rights turbulence, China frequently was compared with the United States. James Reston, for example, remarked that Maoist China exhibited some of the virtues that the United States had lost.[11] The yardsticks of the 1980s were the Cultural Revolution and the Soviet Union, and the contrasting portrait was of an open, reforming, and liberal China. But in the 1990s, it appears, the comparison will be with an Eastern Europe or Soviet Union that has abandoned Communism or with a democratizing Taiwan or South Korea. Now China appears oppressive and anachronistic, one of the last Communist states. Through it all, the Communists have exhibited greater continuity than changing perceptions suggest.[12]

An interesting but unanswerable question is the extent to which the media select the preferred comparison of the moment, reflect broader intellectual currents emanating from universities and think tanks, and their interaction with American foreign policy. This also addresses the role of world affairs in shaping perception. The changed yardstick of the 1990s, a change that has placed China in a more negative light, must be ascribed to both sweeping changes in the world as well as developments in China.

THE DEFICIENCIES AND OPPORTUNITIES

To draw the strands of this chapter together, I suggest that the major deficiency in American media coverage of China has been its oscillating quality. For generations the United States and China have been locked in a love-hate relationship, including periods of intense friendship during which undue expectations are aroused. Mutual recriminations occur as expectations go unmet, prompting periods of estrangement.

The media have not been responsible for the unsteadiness in Sino-American relations and the swings in public mood. The reasons go much deeper. But for reasons that have been enumerated in this chapter, the media perhaps have been more confined to the oscillations than they should have been. Nor is this problem attributable to the China-based correspondents, often trapped between the perceptions of their home office and the bureaucratic rigidities of the Chinese government, a position which prevents them from developing and presenting a portrait of China's enduring and complex qualities.

Recognizing these difficulties, it seems that certain areas in particular merit improvement. First, neither journalists nor scholars nor government analysts have penetrated the politics at the top. While we understand the issues leaders debate, we do not understand the nature of the power struggles and how the issues become intertwined, if at all, with succession politics. As a result, Americans have continually been surprised by high-level politics in China.

Neither high-level Kuomintang politics from the 1930s through the 1940s nor the politics surrounding the succession to Chiang Ching-kuo on Taiwan were well covered, and the present travails of Lee Teng-hui are almost ignored. The significance of the Lushan Conference of July-August 1959, at which Mao purged his Minister of Defense, Peng Dehuai, was not effectively reported in the West for many years. Yet this decisive event in the evolution of high-level leadership contributed in the long run to the occurrence of the Cultural Revolution itself. Hong Kong-based journalists missed Mao's growing disenchantment with his successors in 1963–1965 and the intense political strife that broke out over a whole range of issues in late 1964 and 1965. The purge launching the Cultural Revolution, therefore, came as a great surprise. Journalists later missed the growing schism between Mao Zedong and Lin Biao from 1969 to 1971 which led to Lin's alleged failed coup attempt.

Western coverage from Hong Kong in Mao's last years, including criticism of Zhou Enlai in 1974–1975 and the machinations of the Gang of Four, was better. For that reason Deng Xiaoping's 1977 re-emergence after his second fall in 1975–1976, the arrest of the Gang of Four, and the revelation of deep divisions within the leadership did not come as a total surprise to the outside world. In the post-Mao era Beijing-based journalists have not yet penetrated the veil cloaking top-level politics and have been unable to chart one of the great political performances of recent decades, despite their valiant efforts. Deng Xiaoping's rule has been one of the great attempts at political reform, comparable to Cardenas in Mexico in the 1930s or Kemal Ataturk. Deng has faced opposition at every stage, and he has had to maintain a shifting coalition of supporters which contains people of various views and beliefs. On occasion he has had to abandon programs to placate strong foes. Despite its importance, no journalist or academic has really understood the political dynamics of this era.

A second and more manageable task is to capture the diversity of China, the developments outside the capital, and the growing impact of the outside world and the periphery upon the core. I have already dwelled on this challenge. It necessitates travel and more coverage of the China story from Japan, Korea, Taiwan, and Hong Kong. In fact, the *Wall Street Journal*, the *New York Times*, and the *Washington Post* are doing this, but the electronic media are not following suit.

Finally, there is a new challenge. China is becoming a global actor, and coverage of the China story is becoming a global task. Such developments as the negotiations for China's full participation in the General Agreement on Tariffs and Trade (GATT) and its membership in the World Bank are stories occurring not only in Beijing, but also in Geneva and Washington. China's arms sales in the Mideast are both China and Mideast stories that also involve Washington. Moreover, certain worldwide stories are penetrating China: its involvement in the narcotics trade, an incipient AIDS problem, and severe environmental problems. To cover such stories well, China-based journalists must acquire some sophistication in their understanding of the global problems now affecting China. Covering the Chinese angle on stories breaking in Geneva, New York, or Washington requires journalists based outside China to acquire a greater understanding of China.

In sum, American journalists who cover China have confronted a great professional challenge. Given the difficulties and complex choices they face, over the past 50 years they have done remarkably well, as their books demonstrate. But there is room for improvement, and China's changing role in world affairs suggests that the challenges ahead will be even greater.

NOTES

1. Edgar Snow, *Red Star Over China* (New York: Random House, 1938).

2. Peter Rand, "A Quixotic Adventure: The American Press in China, 1900-1950," in Chin-Chuan Lee (ed.), *Voices of China: The Interplay of Politics and Journalism* (New York: Guilford Press, 1990); Stephen R. MacKinnon and Oris Friesen, *China Reporting: An Oral History of American Journalism in the 1930s and 1940s* (Berkeley: University of California Press, 1987).

3. See G. William Skinner (ed.), *The City in Late Imperial China* (Stanford: Stanford University Press, 1977).

4. Wm. Theodore DeBary, *The Liberal Tradition in China* (New York: Columbia University Press, 1983).

5. Harold Issacs, *Images of Asia: American Views of China and India* (New York: Capricorn, 1962).

6. For detailed and sophisticated discussions on this issue, see Lee, *Voices of China*, esp. part III.

7. Theodore H. White and Annalee Jacoby, *Thunder Out of China* (New York: William Sloane, 1946).

8. Doak Barnett, *China on the Eve of Communist Takeover* (New York: Praeger, 1963).

9. Jay Mathews and Linda Mathews, *One Billion: The China Chronicle* (New York: Harper and Row, 1983).

10. See Marlowe Hood, "The Use and Abuse of Mass Media by China's Leaders During the 1980s," in this volume.

11. Frank Ching (ed.), *The New York Times Report from Red China* (New York: Quadrangle Books, 1971).

12. Interestingly, perhaps the most insightful comparison has also been rather sparingly employed: China in comparison to other large developing countries such as India, Indonesia, Brazil, Nigeria, and Egypt. In this league, China's performance is mixed, but certainly not an unmitigated disaster.

12

THE HISTORICAL FATE OF "OBJECTIVE REPORTING" IN CHINA

Li Liangrong[1]

"Objective reporting"—a journalistic adherence to facts and an attempt to separate facts from value—arrived in China from the West at the end of the nineteenth century. Since then it has both enjoyed popularity and suffered decline; it has been sometimes praised and sometimes censured. In the People's Republic of China, objective reporting has remained a particularly controversial subject. The checkered history of objective reporting in China reflects a clashing and fusing of Chinese and Western cultures as well an intense dispute over the function of the media within different political factions and their place in the context of ideological trends. This history is a profile of the changing political winds in China. This chapter aims to review the development of objective reporting during the latter half of this century. In order to give the reader a more comprehensive understanding, however, I shall first give a brief overview of the emergence and development of objective reporting in China before the 1940s.

THE EARLY YEARS OF OBJECTIVE REPORTING

Modern Chinese newspapers were transplanted from the West. Before the 1890s Chinese papers were usually run by foreigners—first missionaries and subsequently businessmen. Although these newspapers were started for various purposes, they were all directed at a Chinese audience and invited Chinese intellectuals to serve as editors. These intellectuals were accustomed to writing news according to the methods of traditional Chinese chroniclers, whose methods can be broadly divided into the Spring and Autumn (*chun qiu*) and the Historical Records (*shi ji*) styles.

In the Spring and Autumn writing style, derived from Confucius, the writer neither explicitly expresses his own emotions toward his subject nor clearly reveals his own judgment of the truth or falsehood of events.

Instead, the writer subtly suggests such information through nuanced language, rank-titles which serve as a form of moral judgment, and a level of detail commensurate with the importance of the subject. The Historical Records style, named after the work of the Western Han Dynasty historian, Sima Qian (145 B.C.–?), uses a narrative style to register historical events and personages, followed by a critical commentary at the end of each passage. At the turn of the century, the Historical Records style was the dominant mode of Chinese newspaper reporting. In such writing, people characteristically took precedence over events, causes over consequences, a broad perspective over close scrutiny, and narration over commentary.

The principles of objective reporting, like the form of the modern Chinese press, were also introduced from the West. Early in this century, Chinese students studying abroad came into contact with Western news media and treatises on Western journalism. Upon returning home, these students introduced the methods of running Western-style newspapers to China. In 1905 the *Times* of Shanghai was established as "the *London Times* of the East," vowing to follow a "five character" policy of *bo* (abundant information), *su* (timely news), *que* (reliable reporting), *zhi* (honest treatment), and *zheng* (unbiased articles). Concurrently, China began to translate foreign scholarship on journalism.[2]

China's harsh sociopolitical climate, however, hindered the successful introduction of objective reporting in China. The first two decades of this century witnessed intense political struggles and social turbulence in China, making it impossible for Chinese newspapers to maintain their autonomy. Nearly every newspaper was either overtly or covertly controlled by a political faction and thus became immersed in a political whirlpool. Many of the most significant politicians-cum-journalists in modern China—including Liang Qichao, Zhang Taiyan, and Zhang Shizhao—had advocated the principles of separating reportage from commentary, but even they exhibited political overtones in their articles, which were marked by a Confucian style.[3]

The May Fourth Movement in 1919 marked the first wave of intellectual liberation in modern China and inspired a large-scale effort to learn from the West. Some students who had returned from studying abroad began to publish works in Chinese on reporting. Among these, Xu Baohuang's *Journalism* (1918) and Shao Piaoping's *Practical Journalism* (1923) both gave prominence to objective reporting.

The coming of age of objective reporting was coterminous with the emergence of the first financially and politically independent newspapers in China, including *Da Gong Bao* (the *Impartial Daily*), established in the northern port city of Tianjin in 1926. In an attempt to model their paper after the *New York Times*, its editors upheld as fundamental principles *bu dang* (no alignment with any political party), *bu si* (no service of private ends), *bu mai* (no falling sway to commercial influence) and *bu mang* (no blind following of any ideology). Objective reporting had thus revealed its potential and become the main trend in the 1920s.

Objective reporting, whether in theory or in practice, was summarily suffocated by Nationalist (KMT) censorship in the 1930s. Soon after the KMT gained control over China in 1927, it promulgated a news policy aimed at enforcing strict censorship and subjugating the press into "following the Party's doctrine and policies as the highest principle."[4]

OBJECTIVE REPORTING—CHINESE STYLE?

Beginning in the early 1940s, the Chinese Communist Party (CCP) established newspapers and radio stations in its guerrilla bases. Already at this early stage of development, the CCP set basic news policies governing media function and structure. These policies, principled on allegiance to the CCP, paved the way for future journalistic practices. The overriding policy was clearly enunciated in the editorial, "To the Reader," which appeared in the CCP organ *Jiefang Ribao* (*Liberation Daily*) on 1 April 1942. It remarked that all editorials, news articles, and analyses must "faithfully follow the Party's perspective" and "closely correspond to Party policies" so that newspapers could act as the CCP's sentry and advocate. This philosophy turned the press into a mere tool of the CCP and foreclosed any opportunity for objective reporting. Nevertheless, some of the CCP leaders in charge of propaganda work had studied Western journalism and acutely knew that news should provide facts. The problem of integrating the media's roles as provider of facts and propagandist for the CCP remained.

In the 1940s the CCP set forth its news reporting model, that of "seeking to speak (ideology) through facts," as typified by Hu Qiaomu's article, "[Let's] Learn How to Write News" (1 September 1946):

Today news has become a most important and most effective propaganda method . .... News writing teaches us how to use facts to express our opinions. Such expression used to be explicit, but now the news consists of implicit ideas. Literally, it looks as if the speaker were describing what he has seen and heard quite objectively, truthfully, and plainly. But since reportage is based on a certain point of view, when the readers accept those facts, they also accept the embedded point of view.

Hu's article, which soon became the guideline for news practice, powerfully discloses five vital differences between Chinese-style news reporting and Western "objective journalism." First, Western reporting regards information dissemination as its central task, whereas Chinese-style reporting focuses on the use of news as a form of propaganda. Second, the Western press aims at providing news to help readers understand their world, while Chinese reporting seeks to impose CCP views on its audience. Third, Western editors select stories to suit their readers' interests, while Chinese editors select information according to the intentions of the propagandists. Fourth, Western journalists pursue facts and try to avoid their own inclinations and emotions, whereas Chinese reporters express a predetermined perspective through carefully sifted facts. Finally, Western reporting purports to include the facts in a balanced manner, make clear which sources are used, and select presumably unbiased quotes. Chinese reporting, however, relates the facts from an explicit ideological perspective.

Western and Chinese objective reporting methods first clashed in 1948. On 10 October the *People's Daily* ran a news article titled, "Everyone Must Unite in Struggle to Overcome Calamities!," reporting on several natural disasters in northern China that destroyed 30% of that year's agricultural crop. Three days later, the Central Propaganda Department of the CCP repudiated the article for presenting only a dark picture of the disasters rather than showing people how to successfully organize themselves to recover losses. This news, the department sternly pointed out, manifested a kind of "objective tendency not to be allowed in our propaganda work." As a result, the *People's Daily* published an editorial criticizing its own "bourgeois objective reporting" as purposeless, hollow, and superficial. This criticism of objective reporting left a profound and long-term mark on China's media.

TWO STEPS BACKWARD, 1949–1979

The two supreme leaders of the CCP—Mao Zedong and Liu Shaoqi—officially proposed their ideologies of journalism in 1948. They both urged journalists to adhere to Marxism and to stand on the side of the CCP, but they differed on the function of the media and on the requirements of news reporting. *The Selected Works of Mao Zedong on Journalism*, published posthumously, included dozens of articles on journalism which clearly showed Mao's disdain for objective reporting. In only one article, though, did Mao mention objective reporting by name, where he stated that "[t]here is no such thing as completely objective reporting."[5] Mao himself wrote about ten news stories in his own vivid writing style, mixing facts with personal commentary. Some were actually political analyses rather than news reports, written according to neither Western nor Chinese principles of objective reporting. Mao's contempt of objective reporting came from his conviction that the news media should be the tool of the CCP. On

12 January 1958 Mao wrote in a letter that provincial newspapers should organize, encourage, agitate, criticize, and promote provincial work to the people.[6] Newspapers should, in sum, propagandize. Mao never mentioned the press functions of conveying information, cultivating knowledge, or providing entertainment.

Liu Shaoqi's "A Talk With the North China Journalists' Delegation" reflected his core ideas on journalism.[7] Liu insisted that the media should serve as a *two-way* communication conduit between the CCP leadership and the people; they should not only be the CCP's mouthpiece, but also its eyes and ears. Liu considered the reflection of objective reality as conducive to the interests of the proletariat. Therefore, he opposed the idea of reporters trying to find facts in practical life to fit their predispositions. For Liu, the reporter's first responsibility was to reflect public opinion truthfully, and he saw this as consistent with CCP policy. He noted:

> Your first job is to be truthful. Avoid inflammatory exaggeration (*jia you jia cu*). Don't wear colored glasses. If the masses oppose us, they oppose us; if they welcome us, they welcome us; if they misunderstand us, they misunderstand us. Don't be afraid to reflect such attitudes faithfully. ... If our policies are correct, say so based on facts; if they are not, say so also based on facts.[8]

If Liu's news concept had been carried out, China's media would have acquired a totally new face. But within the CCP and the military, Mao Zedong's reputation and influence far exceeded Liu's. The Chinese media, therefore, embodied Mao's news concepts.

The CCP established a CCP-centered media structure and totally extinguished the private press after the founding of the People's Republic in 1949, but maintained the same newspaper style and layout. Amidst waves of political movements aimed at purging "bourgeois thought," the principles of news objectivity came under severe criticism, eventually becoming taboo.

In the early 1950s China's media copied the Soviet Union's Tass and *Pravda*, insisting that every word and every sentence encompass the Party's position. As a result, newspapers were filled with page after page of reports on conferences, production statistics, and leadership activities. Newspapers read like conference bulletins. Liu Shaoqi criticized this phenomenon by saying, "Our news reports copy Tass style—deadly dull, not lively at all. ... There is no concern about readers' ideas and feelings. We just put [the news] out, whether they like it or not."[9]

As part of the Hundred Flowers policy, during which Mao invited intellectuals to speak out in 1956, the *People's Daily* published the editorial, "To the Reader," which marked the onset of news reform. "The name of our newspaper is 'the *People's Daily*'," the editorial said, "which means that it is the public weapon of the people, the public's property."

During that period, Liu Shaoqi's talks with the staff of the New China News Service (Xinhua) staff on 28 May and 19 June 1956, at which he promoted journalistic truthfulness, completeness, objectivity, and fairness, were particularly influential. Liu said that even though the Chinese news agency could take its own editorial position, the news reports must respect facts. He remarked:

> Foreign reporters emphasize that their news reports are objective, truthful, and fair. These are their slogans. ... If we dare not emphasize objective and truthful reports and emphasize nothing but [CCP] positions, then our reports would be subjective and one-sided. ... If Xinhua is to be a global news agency, Xinhua's news must be objective, truthful, fair, and complete; meanwhile, it should represent a certain position. ...[Only in such a way can we] establish credibility in the world.[10]

Both the *People's Daily* editorial and Liu's talks helped open up certain taboo areas in journalism scholarship. The second half of 1956 and the first half of 1957 saw an outpouring of discussion about the news media's social functions, the media-audience relationship, and evaluations of Western journalism studies and the party-press tradition. The principle of objective reporting earned a certain amount of respect.

These discussions were cut short by the Anti-Rightist Movement, when Mao authored a series of three editorials for the *People's Daily* severely attacking the press for opposing the leadership of the CCP, deviating from the CCP's positions on class, and endorsing bourgeois liberalism.[11] In one of his well-known arguments, Mao said, "As long as class distinction still exists in the world, the press will always be an instrument of class struggle."[12] From July 1957 Mao's three editorials became required reading in newsrooms and classrooms throughout the nation. The logic that newspapers must stand firmly for class positions advocated by the CCP leadership resulted in severe attacks on objective reporting as being "supraclass" and led to the expulsion of thousands of reporters—labelled "rightists"—from their profession.

Excessive emphasis on class positions and the denunciation of objectivity produced disastrous distortions of reality during the utopian Great Leap Forward between 1958 and 1960, when readers thought that the world record for food production per acre was being broken every day. These three years brought China to the brink of economic collapse. Liu Shaoqi later twice criticized the *People's Daily* for exaggerating economic achievements and distorting CCP propaganda, once stating, "[y]ou only report pleasant news and withhold the unpleasant. You only give the positive side, and do not publish any negative news or report [government] mistakes." Liu maintained that reporters must work independently, "seek truth from facts," and undertake in-depth investigative projects.[13] Although no one mentioned objective reporting, *People's Daily* reports began to contain less exaggeration after Liu's talks.

Soon after these talks, however, the political turbulence of the Cultural Revolution swept through China. Liu became a prime target of attack— one of his "crimes" being the advocacy of objective reporting. On 1 April 1968 China's trinity of publications (the *People's Daily*, *Red Flag*, and the *Liberation Army Daily*) together prominently published an editorial, "We Should Carry Out the Great Revolution of the Press to the End!," which severely criticized Liu's news philosophy, including his remarks on objectivity and fairness. If objectivity, truthfulness, and fairness were patented by the bourgeoisie, then subjectivity, falseness, and bias were left for the proletariat. This attitude culminated in news reporting during the Cultural Revolution later characterized as *"jia* (false), *da* (exaggerated), and *kong* (empty)."

THE DECADE OF REFORM, 1979–1990

In October 1976 the Cultural Revolution finally came to an end, although by this time China had almost tortured itself to death. The CCP began to advocate "seeking truth from facts" and tried to emancipate itself from ideological rigidity, thus initiating a new period of news reform aimed at eliminating "false, exaggerated, and empty" reporting. The emphasis on newspapers as a tool of class struggle was reduced, while the importance of objective reporting gained recognition. On 17 January 1980 Hu Qiaomu, the director of ideology for the CCP, wrote a letter to Xinhua emphasizing that "news should always relate the facts objectively." Members of the Chinese press then tried once again, through discussions in publications such as *News Front*, to restore the reputation of objective reporting by emphasizing the following principles. First, bourgeois and proletarian media sources require both objectivity and fairness. Second, objective reporting can conform to a proletarian class view. Third, because the masses are supposed to be in control in "socialist China," truthful and objective reporting aids their participation in politics. Fourth, an increasingly pluralistic and complicated world which defies simplistic analysis requires objective reporting.

In the early 1980s there was virtually no opposition to objective reporting, although a major difference eventually arose as to whether journalists should advocate *Western* objective reporting principles. Although China had criticized objectivity for several decades, it had never seriously studied it. Objectivity was criticized almost solely because it came from the

West. Only in the 1980s did journalists begin to study the Western methods seriously, when around a hundred (mostly American) journalism publications and university textbooks were translated into Chinese. Many articles originally written in Chinese followed; students soon began to write dissertations and theses on objective reporting.[14] These articles discussed topics ranging from the social origins, development, and function of objective reporting to scholarly views on reporting principles.

Since then, many Chinese journalists have intensively studied and cautiously endorsed Western principles of objective reporting. For example, Ai Feng, while rejecting objectivity, noted:

> If objectivity means taking an "objective" attitude toward facts—that is, [if it means journalists] must respect the facts—then objectivity is an indispensable principle. … Objectivity and fairness issues grow out of news requirements. Since the news is about reporting the facts, this is what the readers are concerned with, making the journalist's own views unimportant. Even if the readers wanted to know the journalist's views, they still would want such views separated from the facts. Readers don't like to have the two mixed together.[15]

While approving of objective reporting in principle, however, Chinese journalists have also added a few ritualistic caveats, noting that there is no such thing as truly objective reporting and that even U.S. scholars—especially those on the left—have tried to demythify it.

During the 1980s discussions about objective reporting had a great impact on differentiating the news from propaganda and on questions about portraying the truth. Before the 1980s, however, the debate centered on the media's primary role as either propagandist or information provider. The earlier, orthodox view held that each news article was inherently endowed with its own propaganda purpose and each reporter should take a definite position. Reformists, on the other hand, argued that news should provide facts and the media should exist as simply an information conduit.[16] The socialist media, it was argued, should not allow the bourgeois media to monopolize the role of information provider.

This re-acknowledgment of the media's role as an information disseminator stood in sharp contrast to the CCP's insistence that the media should promote "authentic truth" (*benzhi zhenshi*), a characteristic of "proletarian news reporting."[17] Authentic truth has been described in two ways. First, it refers to the "laws," reason, impact, and character of a news event. Second, it represents a "reflection of the mainstream" (*fanying zhuliu*); reporting only positive news about China while disclosing the negative aspects of capitalism.

Starting in the 1980s authentic truth became a topic of academic controversy. Its opponents argued that in order for news reporting to reflect accurately complex human phenomena, news organizations must supplement the functions of scientific institutes, public security organs, judicial departments, and top authorities. They must place themselves in a position to study all sides of an issue. Supporters of the authentic truth view held that this was practically impossible and that it confounded news with history.[18]

Notwithstanding the commentary of professional critics, the media audience has given objective reporting its most potent impetus. Once post-Mao reform policies were in place, higher expectations for democratic participation fostered by China's media audience led to growing frustration with the existing news media. These expectations stimulated a demand for news reform from both popular and official audiences. In a survey of 2,000 prominent figures conducted in Beijing in February 1988, for example, 91.5% of the subjects complained that China's media failed to adequately reflect popular sentiments, while 87% felt the level of openness in reporting the political decision-making process was low. In the same survey, 75% believed the media gave undue emphasis to propagandizing rather than to a fair and complete evaluation of party policies, and 60.5% considered media coverage out of touch with real life.[19]

Other surveys taken in Beijing, Shanghai, Zhejiang, and Jiangsu between 1983 and 1984 reported that more than 30% of the audience did not consider Chinese media coverage credible.[20] These surveys engendered a sense of crisis among working journalists. In yet another survey of 4,000 news workers in early 1988, 76.3% acknowledged that the audience was dissatisfied with news reports and 78.9% admitted that the credibility of China's media was low. For this reason, journalists advocated "one freedom and three rights," including freedom to report the news within the limits of China's constitution and laws, and the right of the masses to know, to speak out, and to watch over the government through public opinion. This same survey indicated that more than half of the journalists would like to see more open reporting in ten areas: official replies to newspaper criticisms (85.9%); views on the law-making process (75.9%); different opinions expressed within the CCP and in the National People's Congress (NPC) (72.2%); evaluations of leaders at various levels considering their performance and political views (68.8%); mistakes committed by the CCP and the government in policy formulation and implementation (67.9%); conversations between Chinese leaders and foreign dignitaries and reporters (67.7%); analyses and commentaries by domestic and foreign sources regarding China's major policies and leadership changes (55.8%); major political, economic, and social events, including those unfavorable to the Party and government (53.3%); direct use of foreign wire copy and media reports (52.4%); and court decisions concerning controversial cases (51.3%).[21]

The media in China underwent notable changes between 1985 and 1988 and saw the rise of "neutral reporting" (*zhongli baodao*). What is neutral reporting?

> In reportage, journalists should not act as judges or educators. There are many events that have occurred during the reforms; the right or wrong of them remains unclear, and life itself has not provided answers. Therefore, reporters must faithfully tell their readers about the true conditions of these events. They should put aside their own opinions. They should not advocate, oppose, praise, criticize, but rather provide comprehensive facts and let readers themselves think, find answers, and make judgments.[22]

Neutral reporting, which gained popularity between 1978 and 1988, became basically indistinguishable from objective reporting.

Journalism scholarship was a catalyst for the rise of neutral reporting, but the determining factor was the demand for the effective diffusion of information about new trends at home and abroad as the market economy expanded. Media developments, however significant, fell far short of expectations among both media consumers and journalists of even broader and more insightful coverage. Nevertheless, neutral reporting once again came under harsh criticism during and after the Tiananmen incident in 1989 as a manifestation of "bourgeois liberalization." Beijing journalism groups twice convened to denounce news objectivity.[23] Similar criticisms were printed in other newspapers, notably the *People's Consultative Conference News*, which printed an article attacking journalistic bourgeois liberalization.[24] The press was blamed for promoting bourgeois functions such as reflecting mass opinion, maintaining surveillance on government, providing information, and covering entertainment. The press had allegedly spread bourgeois-liberal ideas though the use of neutral reporting in the name of "objectivity, fairness, and truthfulness to the masses."

These criticisms, however, do not represent those of most news workers. As the principles of objectivity and fairness have become an irreversible trend after over a decade of profound reforms, journalists continued to treat objective reporting favorably. Shortly after the two symposia held by Beijing journalism groups which condemned neutral reporting, Shanghai's *Liberation Daily*, in "Hitting the Wrong Target," argued that it was wrong to attribute the media's mistakes during the Tiananmen incident to the promulgation of news objectivity and fairness. In urging the critics to look for other scapegoats, the article supported following the principles of news objectivity and fairness. The Moral Code for Chinese Journalism Professionals, released in 1991, also reiterated these very principles.

CONCLUSION

China has seen considerable theoretical argument over Western principles of news objectivity, but issues remain regarding how objective reportage relates to the media's political stance and journalists' social responsibility. In the daily practice of news work, even more issues emerge. Even in the United States, where journalists strenuously attempt to abide by the principles of objectivity, research reveals that they still exhibit biases when covering issues such as race relations and politics in developing countries.

Objective reporting in China has undergone cycles of approval and opposition. These cycles, however, have not resulted in decisive changes in news work; the discussion has stood still. The criticisms of objective reporting in the 1980s have travelled full circle; they are the same as those in the 1940s. Even though the reintroduction of objective reporting accompanied the reforms of the 1980s and early 1990s, the general understanding of objective reporting has, nevertheless, remained shallow.

In China, objective reporting is not a problem of method or style, but rather is related to the media system and function. Since the mid-1800s China has witnessed a string of political struggles which have involved newspapers as a tool of various political factions. Information dissemination has not been the primary role of China's media; rather, their news coverage role has been in constant conflict with their propaganda role. This has resulted in a Chinese style of reporting which uses the appearance of objectivity while concealing underlying propagandistic motives.

After the Communists took control of China in 1949, the private ownership of papers was abolished and most general interest newspapers were turned into Party organs. The role of media as information provider and propagandist has remained. The greatest success of the 1956 news reform was the agreement over the importance of the information provider role. Objective reporting soon appeared, only to be crushed by the Anti-Rightist Campaign of 1957 and was dormant until the second news reform in 1979. The principles of objective reporting, therefore, could only be carried out with any thoroughness when China's news structure underwent change or when the focus was on information rather than propaganda.

The structure of China's news media takes the official Party organs as its core. Reports on Party guidelines, policies, and major decisions are expected to be carried in all Chinese papers according to party organ style. It will be impossible, therefore, for China to have independent news media and hence completely accept the principles of objective reporting in the near future. Changes in Eastern Europe and what is now the Commonwealth of Independent States have caused Chinese authorities to reemphasize the positive in Chinese reporting. These authorities cannot deny, however, that expectations of democratic reform and equality have been raised in China. The authorities, journalists, and readers have also come to recognize the information-provider role of the media, particularly in their coverage of topics such as foreign and economic news, social issues, and civil disputes. Thus, despite disheartening obstacles, we must still strive toward the goal set by Liu Shaoqi, namely, that the news media maintain an independent stance that does not compromise truthful, fair, and complete coverage.

NOTES

1. Translated by Laurie Dennis and Yang Meirong with the assistance of Chin-Chuan Lee and Karl W. Metzner.

2. Among these works, two of the most influential were *Journalism*, by Matsumoto, and *Practical Journalism* by Shulman, both of which introduced the principle of objective reporting to China.

Matsumoto obtained a doctorate in the United States, where journalism was one of his specialties. *Journalism* was published in Japan in 1899, and translated into Chinese in 1903. Shulman's book was published in the United States in 1905 and translated into Chinese in 1913.

3. Leo Oufan Lee and Andrew Nathan, "The Beginnings of Mass Culture: Journalism and Mass Culture in the Late Ch'ing and Beyond," in David Johnson, Andrew J. Nathan, and Evelyn S. Rawski et al. (eds.), *Popular Culture in Late Imperial China* (Berkeley, CA: University of California Press, 1985), pp. 360–95.

4. *Regulations Governing the Party Press* (*Zhidao Dang Bao Tiaoli*) (Nanjing: KMT Central Training Department, 1928).

5. *Selected Works of Mao Zedong on Journalism* (*Mao Zedong Xinwen Gongzuo Wenxuan*) (Beijing: Xinhua Publishing House, 1986 ed.), p. 113.

6. Ibid., p. 211.

7. Delivered on 2 October 1948. Contained in *The Collected Works of Liu Shaoqi* (Beijing: People's Publishing House, 1986), p. 215.

8. Ibid.

9. Liu's speech was given on 28 May 1956. "Instructions on Xinhua's Work," *Selected Documents of the Chinese Communist Party's Journalistic Work* (Beijing: Xinhua Publishing House, 1982).

10. Ibid.

11. "Situations in the Summer of this Year" (*Jin Nian Xiaji de Xingshi*), 26 June 1957; "Affairs are Undergoing Changes" (*Shiqing Zhengzai Bianhua*), 15 May 1957; "The Bourgeois Orientation of *Wen Wei Bao* Should be Criticized" (*Wen Hui Bao de Zichan Jieji Fangxiang Bixu Pipan*), 1 July 1957.

12. Mao Zedong, "The Bourgeois Orientation of *Wen Wei Bao* Should be Criticized," *Selected Works of Mao Zedong*, vol. 5 (Beijing: Foreign Languages Press, 1977), pp. 451–56.

13. See Hu Jiwei, *Essays on News Work* (*Xinwen Gongzuolun Shuoji*) (Beijing: Workers' Press, 1989), pp. 71–120.

14. For example, the first dissertation from Fudan University's School of Journalism was entitled "A Discussion of Several Basic Questions Regarding the Historical Evolution of American Journalism" (*Lun Meiguo Xinwenxue de Ruogan Jiben Wenti de Lishi Yanbian*), which examined the evolution of objective news reporting theory.

15. Ai Feng, *News Coverage Methods* (*Xinwen Caifang Fangfalun*) (Beijing: People's Daily Publishing House, 1984), p. 101. Ai Feng was a senior reporter for the *People's Daily*.

16. The earliest series of articles questioning previous criticisms of objectivity were published in *News Theory and Practice* (*Xinwen Lilun yu Shijian*), no. 5 (1981).

17. Kang Yin, *General Introduction to the News* (*Xinwen Gailun*) (Beijing: Beijing Broadcasting College Publishing House), p. 5.

18. Fudan University School of Journalism (ed.), *General Ideas on Journalism* (*Xinwenxue Gailun*) (Fujian Province: People's Publishing House, 1985).

19. The average age for the sample was 65.8 years and government leaders above the rank of minister accounted for 34.5% of the respondents. See *Perspectives on Communication Effects in China* (*Zhongguo Chuanbo Xiaoguo Toushi*) (Beijing: Xinhua Publishing House, 1988), p. 182. This survey was conducted by the Institute of Public Opinion at People's University in Beijing.

20. Ibid., p. 98.

21. Ibid., p. 195.

22. *Newswork* (*Xinwen Gongzuo*), no. 5 (1988), p. 6.

23. *Guangming Ribao*, 1 July 1989, 5 August 1989.

24. "The Function of Press Opinion Calls for Deep Reflection," 18 July 1989.

13

FIGHTING AGAINST THE ODDS: HONG KONG JOURNALISTS IN TRANSITION

Joseph Man Chan, Chin-Chuan Lee, and Paul Siu-nam Lee

Unlike the abrupt changes in Eastern Europe and the former Soviet Union, the transfer of Hong Kong from British colonial rule to Chinese Communist control—which will officially occur in 1997—has unfolded since 1984 on a graduated schedule. New China News Agency (Xinhua), China's command post in Hong Kong, has stepped forward to form a dualistic power structure with the British colonial regime. As a result, Hong Kong's press has undergone decisive, yet uneven, editorial paradigm shifts.[1] To wit, the mainstream press has tried to maintain a semblance of loyalty to both regimes, while the Communist press has moderated its anti-colonial rhetoric in the interest of a smooth transition, and the rightist press has had to balance Taiwan's ideological interests with its economic survival. The press had opposed China's takeover of Hong Kong, but is now acquiescing.[2]

But because the Sino-British Joint Declaration was a *fait accompli*, China is at best an unwelcome master lacking legitimacy or what Weber calls "the subjective *belief* in the validity of an order which constitutes the valid order itself."[3] In order to bolster its legitimacy in Hong Kong, China has tried to incorporate the press into the new political order with offers of benefits, resources, and status. In return, media organizations have accommodated China's power by adapting their *institutional* policies to the rapidly changing socioeconomic context.[4]

Theoretically, even though mass media may reflect a plurality of perspectives, they depend primarily on the dominant power structure as a legitimate point of reference. Structural control of the media by the power center is filtered through hierarchically ordered bureaucracies responsible for the production and distribution of information, through the political ideology of working journalists and their media organizations which tend to correspond to the consensual basis of mainstream ideology, and through interests the media share with the authorities in the maintenance of the existing order.[5] But when elite consensus collapses, the social environment turns unstable, or the fundamental political order is upset (as in Hong Kong), journalistic assumptions about reality become futile and must be redefined.[6]

From an organizational perspective, political transition produces environmental uncertainty for the media. Media organizations have to develop strategic interorganizational relations to cope with and reduce this uncertainty.[7] These responses vary from shifting editorial allegiance to modifying priorities in the allocation of resources, reconstituting the "news net," and ingratiating oneself with the power victors. The media take these measures to maximize their interests and minimize risks, but in this process interorganizational changes may necessitate *intraorganizational* changes,[8] as reflected in the norms and culture of the newsroom as well as in the journalistic paradigms held by journalists.[9]

This study is part of the only comprehensive survey examining the impact of political transition on working journalists in Hong Kong. Specifically, we explore the congruence between the political ideology of individual journalists and that of their news organizations. Political ideology is expected to exert a profound influence on journalists' definition of the transitional political reality, including their assessment of the transition itself, the future of press freedom, censorship, and the changing media role. This study of journalists complements those directed at media organizations.[10]

MASS MEDIA IN HONG KONG

Though ceded to Britain in 1842, Hong Kong has been closely linked with China in all aspects of life, including journalism. As a birthplace of the modern Chinese press, it has also been a focal point of relentless ideological struggles between contending political forces. These rifts reached their climax in the antagonism between the Kuomintang (KMT, or the Nationalist Party), which now controls Taiwan, and the Chinese Communist Party (CCP), which has ruled the mainland since 1949. The colony's stability has been threatened by the uncertainties of the Cold War world order and, particularly, by the political tumult in Communist China. But Hong Kong has nonetheless seen rapid economic growth, with its population of six million boasting a per capita income close to that of England, its political master. Thanks to the abundance of advertising revenue and purchasing power, this small island-city has developed a vibrant media industry, with four television channels, three radio operators (one public and two commercial) totaling 12 channels, more than 20 daily newspapers, and many more magazines. The territory is also a major regional center of the world's news and entertainment.

To fend off Communist influence, the colonial government of Hong Kong passed stringent laws in the 1950s, which, if enforced to the letter, would have severely curtailed press freedom.[11] In actuality, however, the Hong Kong press has enjoyed a level of freedom in Asia second only to Japan. In spite of the government's close watch, the print media are allowed to advocate opposing ideological doctrines as long as they do not undermine the legitimacy of British rule or provoke conflict. While only a handful of electronic media are licensed to operate, anyone can apply for a license to start a publication. Except for pornographic and politically sensitive materials, the government rarely practices overt censorship. The government's management of the media is far more subtle and sophisticated, relying on an efficient apparatus to control the flow of news and organize elite support for its policies.[12]

No indigenous political parties were allowed to exist in Hong Kong before 1990. Politics was thus sharply divided along the line of the struggle between the CCP and the KMT, that is, mainland China and Taiwan. The British have been content with establishing the rules of the game, granting both the rightist and leftist groups the freedom to organize trade unions, publish partisan newspapers, distribute propaganda, and engage in party polemics. The press has extended—and has been shaped by—the CCP-KMT rift. Not until the early 1970s did "centrist" newspapers gain their foothold in the market, professing their allegiance to Hong Kong rather than either Chinese regime. Benefiting from Hong Kong's rapidly expanding economy and advertising, the centrist papers are motivated by commercial profits and are, therefore, responsive to the law of the market. Although devoting significant coverage to Chinese politics, they focus on immediate local concerns in Hong Kong. Unlike juxtaposition of the full ideological spectrum in the print media, the electronic media tend to take a centrist and non-partisan position. Neither Beijing nor Taipei is allowed to own or run radio or television stations, even though individual owners may have economic or ideological ties with them.

POLITICAL IDEOLOGY AND JOURNALISTS

In adopting Plamenatz's definition, we define ideology as "a set of closely related beliefs or ideas, or even attitudes, characteristic of a group or community."[13] In contrast to what Converse calls the "know-nothings" characteristic of the general populace, journalists are usually well-educated, politically knowledgeable, and internally consistent in their beliefs.[14]

In the United States, the rise of a market democracy has been the main force in the replacement of partisanship by media professionalism since the 1930s.[15] Journalists adhere to canons of objectivity and neutrality, norms predicated, however, on a generally unarticulated commitment to the established order.[16] Journalists are active constructors of social reality within the mainstream ideology. Gans, for example, contends that American journalists ground their facts in an array of enduring values such as ethnocentrism, altruistic democracy, responsible capitalism, small-town pastoralism, and individualism.[17] Members of radical political groups, including leaders of the women's movement and antiwar protesters are, therefore, framed as "deviants."[18] U.S. media are also apt to reduce the rich complexity and contradictions of foreign countries and cultures to "us-against-them" in a Cold War context.[19]

These professional norms may not be universally shared or adopted.[20] In many European and Third World countries, the press system closely parallels the party system in terms of ideological commitment, organizational linkage, and audience membership despite the turn toward media professionalism in recent decades.[21] As the *party* press declines in Europe, a professional orientation remains juxtaposed with a strongly partisan tradition.[22] Concluding a comparative survey, Weaver and Wilhoit argue that there is some evidence of "similarity of professional attitudes of journalists across cultures."[23] McLeod and Rush also found similarities between the professional values of Latin American and U.S. journalists.[24]

But there is a major caveat. Weaver and Wilhoit note a wide range of ethical standards employed by journalists in the United States, Germany, and Britain.[25] By the same token, while German journalists tend to conceive of their professional role as an active and political element in a democracy, their colleagues in Britain, the United States, and Canada define the information function as their primary task.[26] Even among American "professional" journalists, political conservatives tend to emphasize the disseminator, rather than adversarial, role of the media.[27]

Informed by Kuhn's notion of a "paradigm," Chan and Lee define the concept of "journalistic paradigm" as a set of taken-for-granted and unspoken assumptions, cognitive maps, or gestalt worldviews that instruct the media which "social facts" to report (and which not to report) and how to interpret them.[28] It is thus a way of "seeing" that defines the entities of journalistic concern and results in patterns of selective coverage, interpretation, emphasis, and exclusion. Chan and Lee identify three major determinants that jointly and interactively shape the formation of journalistic paradigms: (a) the larger pattern of power distribution that defines the mode of media ownership and press control; (b) market forces (on an industrial-organizational level); and (c) press ideology.[29] The market-oriented press tends to be privately owned, motivated by profits, and inclined to adhere to mainstream ideology and canons of media professionalism. The partisan press is marked by its close organizational, financial, and ideological ties to political parties. Hong Kong journalists are often caught in the sharp tension between the ideals of media professionalism—the result of a Western education—and the political ideology or partisan allegiance to which they have been socialized through upbringing, schooling, or work. The resolution of this conflict depends on the social context, the type of media ownership, and the issue in question.

HYPOTHESES AND MEASUREMENTS

Hypothesis 1: *Journalists' political ideology tends to be congruent with that of their organizations.*

Siegleman observes a high degree of belief congruence between U.S. reporters and their newspapers due to processes of ideological self-selection and newsroom socialization.[30] Hong Kong's partisan press fits into the same pattern but goes a step beyond in its effort to ensure this belief conformity right from the point of staff recruitment, which is based primarily on political recommendation rather than open competition. A tightly controlled organizational culture which brings journalists' partisan affinity further in line with that of their newspapers cements this ideological homogeneity.[31] Radio and television, less ideologically polarized, tend to steer a neutral course.

With the colony being vigorously absorbed into China, the media as a whole have displayed patterns of organizational accommodation to China, acknowledging it as Hong Kong's new power center.[32] But the pace and direction of this accommodation vary with media ideology, and working journalists may feel enormously uncertain about acceptable norms and standards of behavior under this state of flux. They either have to bring their journalistic paradigms in line with their organizations' or else seek alternative employment with an ideologically more consonant organization. The journalist-media belief congruence is expected to remain high despite an overall restructuring of Hong Kong's ideological field.

We measured *journalists'* political ideology by asking them to identify their locations on a 11-point Likert scale with regard to (a) their affinity toward Taiwan or Beijing; (b) their preference for socialism or capitalism as a way of life; (c) their preference for slowing down or speeding up Hong Kong's democratization at present; and (d) their perception that the government should give its priority to the interests of the upper strata or those of the lower strata.[33] Statistics show that these dimensions of political ideology are related to one another systematically.[34] In testing hypothesis 1, similar patterns of results are found when either the journalists' regime identification or any of the other three dimensions are used as the indicator of political ideology. Because of the pervasive influence of regime identification on political ideology in the context of Hong Kong, and for the sake of concise reporting, only regime identification will be used in the testing of the hypotheses.

By the same token, regime identification of media *organizations* was treated as the objective indicator of their political ideology and was categorized on the basis of their (a) source of financial support and party affiliation; (b) place of registration (Beijing or Taipei, if not Hong Kong); (c) choice of national day celebration (Taiwan—10 October; China—1 October) and calendar system; and (d) ways of addressing the Beijing and Taipei regimes.[35]

Hypothesis 2: *Journalists whose political ideology follow the macropolitical trend tend to be more optimistic about the future of Hong Kong and the freedom of its press. Specifically, leftist journalists are more inclined than centrists or rightists to evaluate positively the future of Hong Kong and their profession in Hong Kong.*

Journalists' partisan identification with Beijing or Taipei proves most potent as a determinant of journalistic paradigms. This ideological effect is at its maximum when journalists cover controversial issues.[36] Facing the vast and rapid changes of political transition, journalists have to resort to political ideology to anchor their definition of news.

In this study, we asked journalists to respond to two 5-point Likert scales with regard to how they perceived (a) the future of Hong Kong; (b) the feasibility of China's "one country, two systems" policy;[37] (c) press freedom before 1997; and (d) press freedom after 1997.

Hypothesis 3: *Journalists working in news organizations ideologically closer to the power center tend to exercise greater self-censorship. Hence, journalists working in pro-Beijing media are more inclined to exercise self-censorship toward China than those in centrist and rightist media.*

Self-censorship as a form of information control is both anticipatory and preemptive. Journalists dilute or omit certain information to avert adverse consequences for themselves or their organizations. Journalists may act against their better professional judgment out of fear that full disclosure of such information runs counter to the interests of the power center and may invite its retaliation. The power structure usually need not exert overt pressure to get what it wants; a subjective perception or anticipatory fear by journalists or their superiors is enough. This perception is not entirely unfounded because China has periodically resorted to implied or explicit threats in its dealings with Hong Kong journalists. It is widely believed that China keeps dossiers on journalists and will not easily forget their offenses. Tension culminated in the wake of the Tiananmen crackdown when China singled out the Hong Kong media as manufacturers of falsehood and instigators of unrest.

Alongside threats, however, China has also woven an extensive web of bondage with journalists and publishers through skilled cooptation and united-front campaigns. Partly because Chinese culture inhibits criticizing authority figures who display cordiality or benevolence, this bondage induces self-censorship by journalists. Not to be overlooked is China's significant control over Hong Kong's business opportunities and advertising resources, which further deters media owners from taking too critical or adversarial a posture.[38] The goodwill fostered toward China was interrupted by Beijing's recriminations after the democracy movement in 1989.

Journalists have intensified their self-censorship since 1984, conscious of the risks involved and despite their expressed apprehension about the effects of outside political influences on the media and their own work. But self-censorship is not only practiced by individual journalists; it is also a function of the media's increased institutional affinity with the Chinese authorities. With the left-leaning media bearing the brunt of China's organizational and ideological pressure, they are expected to surpass others in their degree of self-censorship toward Beijing. In this study, we measure self-censorship by asking journalists to indicate their agreement or disagreement with the statement that they are "apprehensive when criticizing China."

Hypothesis 4: *Journalists whose political ideology differs from that of China's authorities are more likely to favor harnessing the media to protect Hong Kong's interests. Hence, rightist and centrist journalists are more inclined than leftist journalists to advocate harnessing the media to serve Hong Kong's interests both during and after the political transition.*

Even though the Hong Kong press has adjusted its journalistic paradigms toward China, local interests limit such shifts. Hong Kong's media must survive in a viable market environment fundamentally antithetical to Communist control. The press is, after all, a business deeply intertwined with local enterprises and other social institutions, entities fearful that China's words and deeds may hamper Hong Kong's well-being. Therefore, although the media in Hong Kong have acquiesced to China's reclamation of the territory, they may at times pit Hong Kong's local interests against Beijing's central control.[39]

In this survey, journalists were asked to indicate on two 5-point Likert scales (a) their approval or disapproval of using the media to advance local interest; and (b) their stance (pro-China, neutral, or pro-Hong Kong) when covering conflicts involving China and Hong Kong.

Hypothesis 5: *Non-partisan journalists tend to favor media professionalism more than partisan journalists.*

Although partisan (rightist or leftist) journalists differ in specific sympathies, they possess similarly intense levels of commitment, while centrists profess ideological "neutrality." We asked journalists to indicate on 5-point Likert scales (a) their approval or disapproval of the media taking on the role of informing, analyzing, being a government's adversary, or conveying public opinion, and (b) their approval or disapproval of such journalistic practices as objectivity, balanced reporting, and news source confidentiality.

THE SAMPLE

A list of 1,381 journalists was compiled from 25 Hong Kong news organizations in July 1990. This list covered news workers (reporters, editors, and news translators) at newspapers, magazines, radio stations, and television stations. Excluded were sports writers, entertainment writers, photographers, and foreign correspondents. Because political concerns cause Hong Kong's media to treat their staff roster with strict confidentiality, we had to compile this list with the aid of informants.

We distributed a total of 692 questionnaires to every other name on the list. Ninety-five are expatriates from two English-language newspapers or English news departments of the electronic media. Respondents could return the questionnaire directly to our informants or mail it back to us. A response rate of 75% (N=522) was obtained after follow-up phone calls and reminders. This rate is consistent across media (print versus broadcast), types of journalists (reporters versus editors), and journalists of different political persuasions.

Of the 522 respondents, 75% come from newspapers, 14% from television, 8% from radio, and 2% from magazines. Males constitute 65%. About seven in ten (67%) are reporters, one-fifth are editors (22%), and most of the rest are translators (4%). Journalism in Hong Kong is marked by low pay and a high number of inexperienced young workers. Although 78% of them have a tertiary education, six in ten make less than U.S. $1,300 monthly and four in ten hold a second part-time job. Also, 85%

are under age 41, while 68% have stayed at their present organization for less than four years.

FINDINGS

Hypothesis 1

Table 13.1 confirms that journalists' ideologies tend to match their organizations' (gamma=.72, chi-square=74.5, df=4, p<.001). The CCP-KMT conflict remains the most potent demarcator of political ideology for both journalists and media organizations. Only 39% of the leftist journalists, however, correspond ideologically with the pro-China media; the comparable figures are much higher for their centrist (68%) and rightist (77%) counterparts.[40]

In addition, media ideology also correlated with (a) preference for capitalism versus socialism (gamma=.52, chi-square=50.63, df=4, p<.001); (b) preference for capitalism versus socialism (gamma=.49, chi-square=51.6, df=4); (c) emphasis on upper-class versus lower-class interests (gamma=.18, chi-square=11.38, df=4, p<.02); and (d) sympathy for swifter or slower democratization (gamma=.52, chi-square=33.52, df=4, p<.001).

Hypothesis 2

Table 13.2 confirms that pro-Beijing journalists—whose ideology is more in line with the direction of political change—tend to be more optimistic than their centrist or rightist counterparts about (a) the future of Hong Kong (gamma=-.27, chi-square=20.05, df=6); (b) the feasibility of China's "one country, two systems" policy (gamma=-.45, chi-square=53.05, df=4); (c) press freedom before 1997 (gamma=-.24, chi-square=13.4, df=6); and (d) press freedom after 1997 (gamma=-.40, chi-square=22.9, df=4). All these correlations obtain statistical significance at .001.

The survey shows, however, that a preponderance of journalists across the ideological boundary feel uncertain about Hong Kong's future (Table 13.2a). Although 46% of leftists agree that China's "one country, two systems" policy will be feasible, most of the centrist and rightist journalists express doubt (Table 13.2b). Furthermore, one out of two leftists, six out of ten centrists, and seven out of ten rightists believe that press freedom in Hong Kong's will be curtailed even before China's takeover in 1997 (Table 13.2c). These journalists are even more in agreement—across the partisan divide—in voicing anxiety about the curtailment of Hong Kong's press freedom *after* 1997. None in the sample thinks that press freedom will be enhanced (Table 13.2d).

TABLE 13.1   Media and Journalist Ideology

	Pro-China Media	Neutral Media	Pro-Taiwan Media
Pro-China journalists	39[a]	14	0
Neutral journalists	59	68	24
Pro-Taiwan journalists	1	19	77
(N)	(71)	(395)	(17)

Gamma = .72, chi-square = 74.5, df = 4, p <.001

[a]Numbers are percentage of respondents

NOTE: Percentages have been rounded. Pro-China media include *Wen Wei Pao, Ta Kung Pao*, the *New Evening Post, Ching Pao* and the *Commercial Daily*, whereas the *Hong Kong Times*, closed in 1993, was the only pro-Taiwan outlet. The rest (including broadcast journalists) are categorized as centrists. Journalists' ideologies are collapsed from an 11-point Likert scale.

TABLE 13.2   Journalists' Ideologies and Their Social Outlook

	Leftist	Centrist	Rightist
(a) Hong Kong's future in 10 years will be			
Better	22[a]	12	7
Unchanged	18	12	13
Uncertain	43	52	42
Worse	17	25	38
(N)	(86)	(311)	(86)

Gamma = −.27, chi-square = 20.5, df = 6, p < .003

	Leftist	Centrist	Rightist
(b) "One country, two systems" is feasible			
Agree			
Uncertain	41	51	26
Disagree	13	27	57
(N)	(70)	(288)	(82)

Gamma = −.45, chi-square = 53.05, df = 4, p <.001

	Leftist	Centrist	Rightist
(c) Press freedom before 1997 will be			
Reduced			
Hard to say	27	22	15
Unchanged	18	15	14
Increased	7	4	0
(N)	(83)	(306)	(87)

Gamma = −.24, chi-square=13.4, df = 6, p <.05

	Leftist	Centrist	Rightist
(d) Press freedom after 1997 will be			
Reduced			
Unchanged	33	26	12
Hard to say	9	2	1
Increased	0	0	0
(N)	(82)	(306)	(87)

Gamma = −.40, chi-square=22.9, df = 4, p <.001

[a]Numbers are percentage of respondents

Control variables (age, gender, educational level, and professional rank) do not weaken the correlation between journalists' regime identification and their appraisal of press freedom in Hong Kong after 1997 (Table 13.2d) or the "one country, two systems" policy (Table 13.2b). The elaboration procedure shows, however, that the other two sets of correlations (Tables 13.2a and 13.2c) only hold under some conditions. This shows that political ideology exerts an uneven impact on how journalists evaluate or construct different aspects of reality.

Hypothesis 3

Table 13.3 confirms that journalists working in news organizations that are ideologically closer to the power center (i.e., those in leftist media) exhibit a higher propensity to exercise self-censorship toward that power center (as measured by the degree of "apprehension about criticizing China") (gamma= .37, chi-square=17.0, df=4, p < .002). As expected, journalists in leftist media surpass their colleagues in rightist and centrist media (in that order) in expressing such "apprehension." This relationship holds up well when controlling for journalists' age, gender, educational level, and occupational rank.

While journalists who work in leftist media are evenly split between those expressing and not expressing "apprehension," those in rightist and centrist media who disavow any apprehension about criticizing China constitute a clear majority. Since self-censorship is considered professionally despicable, we suspect these self-reported figures to be somewhat understated. This suspicion gains credence because as many as 54% of all journalists agreed with the statement that "journalists at large" (not including themselves) have exhibited apprehension. Moreover, there is a significant correlation between the media's regime identification and the extent to which journalists perceive that China meddles in news operation (gamma=.41, chi-square=36.10, df=4, p < .001). A higher proportion of leftist-media journalists have reportedly experienced pressure from the Chinese authorities to modify news stories.

Hypothesis 4

Table 13.4 shows no empirical support for the hypothesis that journalists whose political ideology differs from China's are more likely to advocate using the media to stress local interests (gamma=.10, chi-square=7.2, df=4, p <.13). Table 13.4b, however, provides moderate evidence to show that rightists are more prone to advocate using the media to fight for the maximization of Hong Kong's autonomy beyond 1997 (gamma=−.29, chi-square=5.98, df=4, p <.02). Upon closer scrutiny, it seems clear that these correlations have been suppressed because journalists' endorsement of using the media to achieve such goals overwhelms partisan differences.

TABLE 13.3   Self-Censorship and Journalists Working in News Media with Different Ideologies

	Journalists in Pro-China Media	Journalists in Centrist Media	Journalists in Pro-Taiwan Media
Agree	42[a]	22	13
Uncertain	18	15	19
Disagree	39	63	69
(N)	(71)	(395)	(16)

Gamma = .37, chi-square = 17.0, p <.002

[a]Numbers are percentage of respondents

TABLE 13.4   Journalists' Ideologies and Their Perceived Media Roles

	Leftist Journalists	Centrist Journalists	Rightist Journalists
(a) To pressure China and UK for Hong Kong interests			
Agree	84[a]	79	88
Uncertain	6	14	6
Disagree	10	8	6
(N)	(81)	(298)	(86)

Gamma = –.10, chi-square = 7.2, df = 4, p <.13

	Leftist Journalists	Centrist Journalists	Rightist Journalists
(b) To fight for maximizing local autonomy beyond 1997			
Agree	86	90	95
Uncertain	9	4	2
Disagree	5	6	2
(N)	(80)	(298)	(88)

Gamma = –.29, chi-square = 5.98, df = 4, p <.02

[a]Numbers are percentage of respondents

Hypothesis 5

Further analysis from a different perspective (Table 13.5) shows that journalists' ideology does cause them to take different positions when conflicts of interest between China and Hong Kong arise (gamma=.26, chi-square=20.09, df=4, p < .001). A majority of centrists (65%) prefer media neutrality in such situations. Almost six out of ten leftists (58%) also choose a "neutral" position, presumably not on professional grounds, but out of the wish not to offend or embarrass Beijing. In contrast, six out of ten rightists (58%) prefer a pro-Hong Kong stance, while four out of ten (42%) advocate professional neutrality. In general, they strongly oppose China's infringement on Hong Kong's local interests.

There is no empirical support for the hypothesis that non-partisan journalists tend to value media professionalism more than partisan journalists. This is because most journalists express such strong support for pro-

TABLE 13.5   Journalists' Ideologies and Their Stance on Sino–Hong Kong Conflicts

	Leftist Journalists	Centrist Journalists	Rightist Journalists
Pro-China	3[a]	1	0
Neutral	58	65	42
Pro–Hong Kong	39	34	58
(N)	(62)	(248)	(77)

Gamma = .26, chi-square = 20.09, df = 4, p <.001

[a]Numbers are percentage of respondents

fessional norms (if only at face value) that partisan differences are minimized. They specifically endorse objective reporting (91%), in-depth analysis and interpretation of complex problems (90%), the role of the media as government watchdog (85%), the media's role in speaking for the public (77%), and balanced reporting (69%). They value accuracy over timeliness in reporting (87%) and do not condone breaching the confidentiality of their sources (91%).

Despite their endorsement of professional values, ideology is by no means irrelevant. Journalists seem to mix professional values with partisan commitment. The relative importance of these competing norms depends partly on the nature of the issues being covered. Ideology tends to prevail in the judgment of political issues, whereas professional norms are more likely to guide the coverage of social issues.

Finally, media professionalism is a double-edged sword for China. On the one hand, it presupposes the authorities as a prime point of reference for newsmaking, and may thus bestow upon them the visibility and legitimacy they badly need in Hong Kong.[41] On the other hand, the premium put on news objectivity, balanced reporting, and the media's watchdog function may prevent the media from swiftly complying with the dictates of the Chinese authorities.

DISCUSSION

Since the conclusion of the Sino-British Joint Declaration in 1984, Hong Kong has been thrown into a state of flux. Significant social and political forces, including mass media, have realigned themselves in favor of China vis-à-vis the lameduck colonial regime. This stampede to woo the new ruler's favor has been somewhat checked by an embryonic democratic movement in Hong Kong, the urgency of which was notably stirred by China's Tiananmen Square crackdown. But the structural forces China has set into motion to incorporate Hong Kong have irreversibly set in and will strengthen as 1997 approaches.

Besieged Hong Kong journalists doubt the feasibility of China's "one country, two systems" policy and are overwhelmingly pessimistic about the future of press freedom in Hong Kong. At least one-fourth of the journalists admit feeling apprehensive when criticizing the Chinese government, and many more (54%) say that their colleagues at large feel so. Nevertheless, ties to local interests seem important in deterring them from bending hastily with the political winds.

This survey reveals that journalists' ideology follows that of their organizations. Although leftist journalists tend to find the direction of political transition less objectionable, they express more apprehension about criticizing China than do their colleagues. While centrists are more ardent subscribers to professional norms, journalists across the ideological spectrum urge the media to speak on behalf of local interests against Beijing's intrusion.

Besides partisanship, Hong Kong media are also subject to market constraints in ways similar to what is observed in other systems.[42] But a plurality of journalistic perspectives is being preserved within structural limits. Journalists fear that China may institute stronger regulative censorship in the long run, but at present they must contend with the more immediate tendency of self-censorship. Many journalists have called for more candid criticism of self-censorship. As an integral part of the international political economy, it seems that Hong Kong's vibrant market conditions help to maintain its liberal news order.

A cataclysmic prognostication is therefore unwarranted, despite an atmosphere in which distrust prevails. China's reforms in the 1980s, despite setbacks, have advanced too far to be reversed. China, moreover, must make its "one country, two systems" policy work in Hong Kong before it can lure Taiwan into unifying with the mainland. As part of this policy, press freedom in Hong Kong will be closely watched by Taiwan. In sum, we view press freedom in Hong Kong over the long term with tempered optimism, but are wary of the difficult times Hong Kong journalists may face in the near future.

NOTES

Reprinted by permission of Kluwer Academic Publishers.

1. Joseph Man Chan and Chin-Chuan Lee, "Shifting Journalistic Paradigms: Editorial Stance and Political Transition in Hong Kong," *China Quarterly*, no. 117 (Mar. 1989), pp. 98–118; Joseph Man Chan and Chin-Chuan Lee, *Mass Media and Political Transition: The Hong Kong Press in China's Orbit* (New York: Guilford Press, 1991).

2. Chin-Chuan Lee and Joseph Man Chan, "Thunder of Tiananmen: The Hong Kong Press in China's Orbit," in Chin-Chuan Lee (ed.), *Voices of China: The Interplay of Politics and Journalism* (New York: Guilford Press, 1990).

3. Max Weber, *Economy and Society*, Günther Roth and Claus Wittich (eds.) (Berkeley: University of California Press, 1969), pp. 33–38.

4. Chan and Lee, *Mass Media and Political Transition*; Joseph Man Chan and Chin-Chuan Lee, "Power Change, Cooptation, Accommodation: Xinhua and the Press in Transitional Hong Kong," *China Quarterly* (1991), pp. 290–312.

5. Gaye Tuchman, *Making News* (New York: Free Press, 1978); David Paletz and Robert Entman, *Media, Power, Politics* (New York: Free Press, 1981); Robert Manoff and Michael Schudson (eds.), *Reading the News* (New York: Pantheon, 1986).

6. Chan and Lee, *Mass Media and Political Transition*; Youngchul Yoon, "Political Transition and Press Ideology in South Korea 1980–1988" (Ph.D. diss., University of Minnesota-Minneapolis, 1989); Daniel Hallin, *The "Uncensored" War* (New York: Oxford University Press, 1986).

7. Howard Aldrich, *Organizations and Environments* (Eaglewood, NJ: Prentice-Hall, 1979); J.M. Pennings, "Strategically Interdependent Organizations," in P. Nystrom and W. H. Starbuck (eds.), *Handbook of Organizational Design*, vol. 1 (London: Oxford University Press, 1981).

8. Joseph Galaskiewicz, "Interorganizatinal Relations," *Annual Review of Sociology* 11 (1985): 281–304.

9. James Ettema and Charles Whitney (eds.), *Individuals in Mass Media Organizations* (Beverly Hills, CA: Sage, 1981).

10. Chan and Lee, *Mass Media and Political Transition*; Chan and Lee, "Power Change, Cooptation, Accommodation."

11. James Shen, "The Law and Mass Media in Hong Kong," *Chung Chi Journal* 2, no. 1 (1972): 60–125.

12. Chin-Chuan Lee, "Partisan Press Coverage of Government News in Hong Kong," *Journalism Quarterly* 62 (1985): 770–76; Chin-Chuan Lee and Joseph Man Chan, "Government Management of the Press in Hong Kong," *Gazette* 46 (1990): 125–39.

13. John Plamenatz, *Ideology* (London: Pall Mall Press, 1970), p. 150.

14. Philip Converse, "The Nature of Belief Systems in Mass Publics," in D. E. Apter (ed.), *Ideology and Discontent* (NY: Free Press, 1964).

15. Michael Schudson, *Discovering the News* (New York: Basic, 1978).

16. Herbert Gans, *Deciding What's News* (New York: Pantheon, 1979); Gaye Tuchman, *Making News*; Lance Bennett, Lynn Gressett and William Haltom, "Repairing the News: A Case Study of the News Paradigm," *Journal of Communication* 35, no. 2 (1985): 50–68.

17. Gans, *Deciding What's News*.

18. Todd Gitlin, *The Whole World is Watching* (Berkeley: University of California Press, 1980); Pat Lauderdale and Rhoda Estep, "The Bicentennial Protest: An Examination of Hegemony in Definition of Deviant Political Activity," in Pat Lauderale (ed.), *A Political Analysis of Deviance* (Minneapolis, MN: University of Minnesota Press, 1980); Pamela Shoemaker, "Media Treatment of Deviant Political Groups," *Journalism Quarterly* 61 (1984): 66–75, 82.

19. Edward Said, *Covering Islam* (New York: Pantheon, 1981); Edward Herman and Noam Chomsky, *Manufacturing Consent* (New York: Pantheon, 1987).

20. Andrew Arno, "News as Storylines," in Andrew Arno and Wimal

Dissanayake (eds.), *The News Media in National and International Conflict* (Boulder, CO: Westview Press, 1984).

21. Collin Syemour-Ure, *The Political Impact of Mass Media* (Beverly Hills, CA: Sage, 1974).

22. For instance, J.W. Frieberg, *The French Press: Class, State, and Ideology* (New York: Praeger, 1981).

23. David Weaver and Cleveland Wilhoit, *The American Journalist* (Bloomington, IN: Indiana University Press, 1986), p. 137.

24. Jack McLeod and Ramona Rush, "Professionalization of Latin American and U.S. Journalists," *Journalism Quarterly* 46 (1969): 784–89.

25. Weaver and Wilhoit, *The American Journalist*.

26. Wolfgang Donsbach, "Journalists' Conception of Their Audience," *Gazette* 32 (1983): 19–36.

27. Weaver and Wilhoit, *The American Journalist*.

28. Joseph Man Chan and Chin-Chuan Lee, "Journalistic Paradigms on Civil Protests: A Case Study in Hong Kong," in Andrew Arno and Wimal Dissanayake (eds.), *The News Media in National and International Conflict* (Boulder, CO: Westview Press, 1984); Chan and Lee, *Mass Media and Political Transition*.

29. Chan and Lee, *Mass Media and Political Transition*.

30. Lee Siegleman, "Repairing the News: An Organizational Analysis," *American Journal of Sociology* 79 (1973): 132–51.

31. Joseph Man Chan and Chin-Chuan Lee, "Press Ideology and Organizational Control in Hong Kong," *Communication Research* 15, no. 2 (1988): 185–97.

32. Chan and Lee, *Mass Media and Political Transition*; Chan and Lee, "Power Change, Cooptation and Accommodation."

33. While the first question is an enduring issue, the latter two represent new controversies. Some have argued for a swifter pace of democratization as a preemptive measure against Beijing's encroachment, while others believe that this would antagonize Beijing and thus not be in Hong Kong's best interest. Similarly, some industrialists argue that Hong Kong should continue to give investors' interests top priority in order to sustain its economic prosperity, while critics maintain that the interests of the lower class should outweigh those of the upper class.

34. Journalists' identification with the Beijing regime correlates negatively and significantly with their choice for capitalism (gamma=$-.50$, chi-square=31.97, df=4, p<.001) and their pro-democracy attitude (gamma=<.19, chi-square=13.34, df=4, p<.01); journalists' choice of capitalism correlates positively and significantly with their pro-democracy attitude (gamma=.44, chi-square=56.58, df=4, p<.001) and their favor for upper-class interests (gamma=.25, chi-square=32.06, df=4, p<.001); journalists' pro-democracy attitude is negatively and significantly related to their stance on class interests (gamma=$-.20$, chi-square=32.99, df=4, p<.001). Journalists' regime identification also correlates significantly with their stance on class interest.

35. This "objective" categorization was based on Lee, "Partisan Press Coverage of Government News in Hong Kong." To cross-validate it, we also developed subjective measures that asked journalists to identify on a 11-point Likert scale their *media organizations'* (a) affinity toward Taiwan or Beijing; (b) preference for social-

ism or capitalism as a way of life; (c) preference for slowing down or speeding up Hong Kong's democratization at present; and (d) opinion that the government should give priority to the interests of the upper class or those of the lower class. Hypothesis 1 is confirmed when each dimension of the *journalists'* political ideology is used to correlate with the corresponding dimension of the *media's* ideology. Again, for the sake of brevity, only the objective measure of the media's regime identification is reported in the following. The subjective and objective measures of the media's regime identification highly correlate with one another (gamma=.88, chi-square=141.70, df=4, p<.001).

36. Chan and Lee, "Journalistic Paradigms on Civil Protests."

37. China promises to let capitalism and the present socioeconomic system in Hong Kong remain unchanged for 50 years after 1997, thus creating a "capitalist Hong Kong" and a "socialist mainland" within China's jurisdiction.

38. Chan and Lee, *Mass Media and Political Transition*; Chan and Lee, "Power Change, Cooptation, Accommodation."

39. Chan and Lee, *Mass Media and Political Transition*.

40. Two explanations are plausible. First, some journalists working in pro-Beijing media may have been alienated by the Tiananmen crackdown, the ripple effect of which remained strong when this survey was conducted one year later. Second, as some commercial media have turned increasingly leftward, their staff may lag behind ideologically.

41. Tuchman, *Making News*.

42. Sue Currey Jansen, *Censorship* (New York: Oxford University Press, 1991); Frieberg, *The French Press: Class, State, and Ideology*.

14

FROST ON THE MIRROR: AN AMERICAN UNDERSTANDING OF CHINA IN THE COLD WAR ERA

Edward Farmer

My task is to consider how the Cold War affected scholarly understanding of China. I will try to do this by commenting on my own experience as a student of China and, where relevant, how that understanding was shaped by the media. The Cold War corresponded closely in time to my own consciousness of the political realm and shaped and colored my academic career. The story will walk on two legs, an academic narrative and a personal narrative. It will probe subjective categories of understanding rather than attempt a comprehensive or systematic account of scholarship on China.

American scholarship on China has always been beset by ambiguities and contradictions. But the chill of the Cold War further clouded our indistinct vision of China and perhaps distorted our sense of ourselves. One noteworthy aspect of the Cold War era is an asymmetry that further complicated an already tangled picture. The Cold War was defined primarily in terms of the Sino-Soviet rivalry of the postwar era. Implicit in that rivalry was a sense of comparability, parity, and competition. The United States and the Soviet Union were both revolutionary, land-based empires of recent historical evolution, European and yet outside of Europe. Looking at the other was a bit like looking in a mirror. The same could not be said of the relationship between Chinese and Americans. China and America shared little in historical experience or social character.

Let us note, too, that the Cold War affected Sino-American relations unevenly. China was one of a handful of nations divided by the Cold War. Chinese were entangled in the East-West rivalry without dominating either pole of the relationship. Initially, the People's Republic was part of the Soviet bloc while the Republic of China on Taiwan was allied with the

United States. Furthermore, the Chinese were able to extricate themselves from the superpower rivalry years before the principals declared an end to the Cold War.

UNDERSTANDING CHINA

At the heart of our effort to understand China lie basic problems of knowledge. What do we know and how do we know it? Some of what we know we learn from experience but most of what we take to be true about the world we derive in an indirect manner. The bulk of what we think we know about China is derived from reading newspapers and books, watching television and films, or listening to lectures and conversation. We may be able to selectively confirm bits of our worldview through direct observation but our ability to do so is severely constrained. Even direct experience is unreliable. It is affected by our age, our state of mind, our emotions, and environmental influences of all kinds. And in the case of something as vast and amorphous as China we can only hope for a glimpse here and there. A scholar who studies China also has to contend with theories about the nature of Chinese society and culture. Reconciling academic theory, personal experience, and the flow of information from the media sets up a three way tug-of-war in our minds.

I raise this point not as a cry of despair but simply to suggest that what we think of as China is really a mishmash of theoretical assumptions, received information, impressions, and opinion. We are constantly in the process of trying to sort these things out. If we want to evaluate how the Cold War has influenced our understanding of China we need to be aware of a range of levels on which influence has been felt.

News reporting on China—especially newspaper reporting—is undoubtedly the best it has been in my lifetime. Ironically, this has come to pass at a time when China is not very important to most Americans. In the present climate of opinion it is hard to appreciate how politically sensitive feelings about China were at the beginning of the Cold War. Early in the twentieth century many Americans felt a special concern for the Chinese. China was an important target of American missionary activities: thousands of young Americans went to China to carry on religious, medical, and educational work. Some have seen American gestures toward China as the logical extension of America's westward expansion. Americans assumed that progress for China meant doing things in the American way. During World War II we were allied with the Chinese in the war against Japan. American policymakers had hopes that China would emerge at the end of the war as a friendly power able to stabilize the western Pacific. China's status as a great power was confirmed by the assignment of a permanent membership on the Security Council of the United Nations. When

the Chinese Communist Party (CCP) came to power in 1949 and established a Marxist dictatorship, Americans felt both betrayed and imperiled.
The Chinese who had been allies now explicitly rejected and denounced
many of the most treasured elements of American life such as democracy,
individualism, Christianity, and free enterprise. The "loss of China" cast
doubt on the validity and universality of our core values.

At this juncture I am moved to reflect on how the Cold War shaped my
own experience and understanding of China. I was born in 1935. My historical memory reaches back before the Cold War to the era of World War
II when I was just beginning school. I might claim consciousness of the
1940 presidential election although the only evidence for that is my mother's report that I was heard singing in the bathtub: "Wee Wendell Willkie
ran through the town, upstairs and downstairs in his nightgown." More
direct is my memory of Pearl Harbor. I can recall the size of the headline
announcing that war was declared and just where my brother threw the
newspaper down on the dining room floor.

My first grasp of what a popular song was came while listening to
"Coming in on a Wing and a Prayer" over an old wood-encased radio in
the living room. The framework of my understanding of world affairs was
formed in the uncomplicated good-against-bad war to defeat the evil Axis
powers. The Russians and Chinese were our allies in those days. A Russian engineer and his family moved in next door. My mother and their
grandmother attempted communication in rusty, school-girl French
across the hedge separating our yards. Mostly, I remember the *piroshki*
and meat pies and their preschooler, Nicki, roasting in a new snowsuit
when the California temperature hit ninety degrees on New Year's Day.
Uncle Joe was our friend and the Russian soldiers were heroic. Although I
could not read the stories, I still remember *Time* covers with
Artzybasheff's airbrush caricatures of German, Italian, and Japanese leaders being ground up by anthropomorphic allied war machines. Japanese
were the enemy we feared most. "Cops and Robbers" or "Cowboys and
Indians"—the inexhaustible frontier war that surged through our neighborhood—often turned its weapons on the treacherous "Japs."

As I think back on it, the manipulation of imagery must have been considerable. A passionate gardener as a child, I first came to know the Japanese Tea Garden in San Francisco's Golden Gate Park as the "Chinese Tea
Garden," a wartime subterfuge intended to dissuade misguided patriots
from defacing a valuable civic facility. I was not immune from the ideological pressures of the war effort. In elementary school I won an award in a
poster contest for a picture of a Japanese fighter plane descending in
flames, one wing torn off. In my experience, anti-Japanese sentiment, so
frighteningly portrayed in movies of Japanese soldiers creeping through
jungles that I long thought Japan must be a tropical country, did not attach

to Japanese-Americans. No doubt my parents and teachers deserve some credit here given the level of popular sentiment prevailing in California at the time. I was in the sixth grade when the Japanese-American students returned from the camps and immediately formed friendships with several classmates. Where they had been and what had happened to them was never discussed. Only later in the army did I observe a pattern of obsessive overachievement that must have been derived from the stigma which wartime incarceration unjustly imposed on Japanese-Americans. I have no particular early memories of China during the war. Liberation and the "loss of China" occurred when I was in junior high school, but I have no recollection of my impressions of those events.

THE COLD WAR AS A CULTURAL CONSTRUCT

The Cold War had its uses. During the Nixon administration Secretary of State Henry Kissinger was fond of the concept of "linkage." Any aspect of foreign relations, it seemed, could be linked to the East-West conflict of the Cold War. Simply by dividing the world into camps the Cold War infused clarity and purpose where otherwise there might be only confusion. More was at stake than the justification of military expenditures. The concept of the socialist world as a rival and a threat provided the basis for political, cultural, and scholarly programs of action. From both sides of the iron curtain or, as Owen Lattimore put it, the "dollar curtain," people looked across to an alternative order against which their own ideals could be measured. Chinese looked at each other across the Taiwan Strait.

The Cold War turned the formation of a sense of national identity into an essentially negative process. This is well illustrated in the case of Americanism. In the hysteria of the 1950s Americans sought an alternative to the smug certainty of Communist dogma. But the United States was not guided by an orderly and articulated ideology that could be defended as an alternative to Marxism-Leninism. Beyond patriotism, flag-waving, and simplistic cultural stereotypes, the concept of Americanism lacked both specificity and force. It was easier to say what was "un-American" than to say what was American. Witch-hunting of the sort engaged in by the House Un-American Activities Committee told one what to avoid or disavow but not what to believe in. Newspapers, news magazines, and the infant television were the vehicles of this new ideological construct that fostered popular hysteria about hidden enemies in our midst. Senator Joseph McCarthy was a pioneer in the political use of television to enthrall audiences with committee hearings that were more for manipulating feelings than finding facts. Ironically, many beliefs and practices central to the life of a pluralistic democracy could be viewed as un-American. Due process of law, religious freedom, and tolerance for unpopular opinions were all endangered values in the great struggle against Communist subversion.

But what of China? On the other side of the Pacific Ocean the revolutionary program called for the creation of socialism with Chinese characteristics. There, too, the emphasis was often on the negative. Thought reform and mass campaigns were orchestrated to change values and behavior. Class labels were used to divide the population and muster majorities for the attack on designated targets. After domestic enemies such as landlords had been neutralized, special attention was directed at Western-trained intellectuals who harbored the germs of bourgeois infection. To a much greater extent than was the case with Americanism in the United States, effort was devoted in China to defining socialism in positive terms. But the most powerful political movements demonized antisocialist or counterrevolutionary individuals and groups, hunted people down, and castigated and punished them for errant thought and action. As in the American case, but with a much higher human toll, the Chinese revolution displayed a penchant for turning on its brightest and most idealistic supporters, giving license to unscrupulous opportunists in the process.

Whatever one thinks of the practicality of socialism, there can be no doubt that many Chinese sincerely aspired to create a just and modern society in the People's Republic. In 1949 the need to believe in the revolution was very strong and hopes were high. Even in the face of policy disasters, injustice, and personal suffering, individuals clung to their faith in Chairman Mao, or Marxism-Leninism, or the CCP. But as time went by the task became more difficult. The attacks of the Anti-Rightist Movement and the Great Proletarian Cultural Revolution taught people the danger of honest expression of views. The sending of intellectuals to the countryside, initially a way of building links between urban and rural populations, became simply a means of control and punishment. Propaganda and ideological instruction became the tools of warring political factions.

During the Cold War the politically ambitious in both the United States and China used the climate of confrontation to enhance their own power through intimidation. Scholarship suffered in both countries as a result. In China the dictatorship exercised comprehensive control over journalism, scholarship, and many other aspects of life. In the United States political influences were far looser and less systematic. A pall was nevertheless cast over China scholarship. In the wake of the "loss of China" charges were made about subversion in the Department of State. Passage of the McCarran Act and the institution of "loyalty boards" quickly deprived the foreign service of officers capable of informed and objective reporting on China.[1] Suspicion soon spread to the realm of scholarship. Senator McCarthy's persecution of Owen Lattimore and governmental pressure on the Institute of Pacific Relations sent a loud message to the leadership of the Association for Asian Studies that they had better keep their distance from scholarly examination of U.S. foreign policy in Asia. Academic bodies that should have been studying, evaluating, and debating U.S. policy toward China were prevented from doing so by a climate of fear.

I Discover the Cold War

My family did not own a television set in the 1950s but I was not unaware of its political power. One day when two of my friends and I had a Saturday job doing yard work for a wealthy family, we looked in the windows and saw snatches of Senator McCarthy on the tube. We knew that something important was going on. In high school *Time* magazine provided me with a window on the wider world. *Time*, of course, was notorious for the pro-Chiang Kai-shek stand of its publisher, Henry Luce. I recall sitting on the steps of my high school auditorium in 1953, reading about Stalin's death. The dictator and the great composer Prokofiev lay in state at the same time. I was sure that Stalin's death was an historic event of great significance.

I was spared the obligation to fight against Asians. I was still in high school when the Korean Conflict took place and was overage by the time of the Vietnam War. And yet the Cold War hit very close to home. Mandatory loyalty oaths struck terror throughout the public institutions in California. At Berkeley several professors resigned their posts rather than certify their political allegiances to the state. My father, a professor at Stanford, was not affected, but my mother, a high school teacher, had to sign. (One summer while working in a logging town in northern California I had to provide a notarized loyalty oath before I could be paid for digging a hole and installing a piece of playground equipment outside a deserted one-room school house.) Artists and liberals, my parents had many associates whose lives were affected by the witch hunts of the 1950s. An uncle who worked in the motion picture industry lost his job.

One had to be careful about what one said and what one did. This all came home to me when I was in high school. My first brush with Cold War orthodoxy came in geometry class. The teacher, Miss Younkin, was something of a character. A grey-haired spinster, she took pride in her physical prowess which she attributed to Indian ancestry. She ran to school every morning and for years held out the reward of a can of tennis balls to any student, boy or girl, who could beat her in a set of tennis. One of the annual events in Miss Younkin's class was a contest to draw a figure on graph paper, describing each point in the figure in terms of values on x and y axes. Members of the class voted on the figure they liked best, which was then framed and hung above the blackboards alongside winners from previous years. My entry, calculated to be provocative, was a hammer and sickle. Classmates appreciated the daring quality of the design and selected it over a more conventional silhouette of Mt. Fuji. The principal of the school, however, appreciated his job more than the humor of my design. Miss Younkin was advised that a hammer and sickle could not be displayed in a classroom. The solution to the problem was that I was allowed to draw an alternative design, an Islamic crescent and star as I recall, which was placed in the frame on top of the illicit hammer and sickle. Miss Younkin promised that whenever it became acceptable to display the Communist symbol she would unmask my original design. So far as I know she retired before that day came.

I Discover China

The origins of the Cold War are to be found in the early twentieth century, but the roots of the matter go further back in the advent of the modern age. If we think of the Cold War as a struggle between systems or ideologies, the problem was implicit in the emergence of modern society. The industrial revolution and nationalism were twin products of the eighteenth century. The American and French revolutions introduced normative concepts of individualism, self-determination, and equality which continue to claim universal applicability. By the nineteenth century industrialization provided the material base for urban bourgeois society and the mass media which made nationalistic politics the dominant force in world affairs.

The dangers of industrialized economies mobilized for national rivalry were fully realized in World War I. One can think of the historical agenda of the twentieth century as a working out of the "ambiguities and contradictions" implicit in the coexistence of industrialization and nationalism. In the simplest terms the interwar years saw a contest among expansive and colonialistic regimes organized along democratic, fascist, and socialist lines. Essentially, World War II discredited both the fascist models and colonialism. The postwar period, the era of the Cold War, can thus be understood as a continuing contest between the surviving democratic and socialist models. While colonialism was generally phased out, there were important survivals of imperialist domination. World War II ended the modern maritime empires but not, in all cases, the holdovers of the great early modern land-based empires. The Soviet Union, India, and the People's Republic of China—the three largest polities on earth—were the most obvious descendants of that earlier era.

The failure of the socialist system has been celebrated in this country as a victory for market capitalism and political democracy. A flurry of press speculation was set off by Francis Fukuyama's article, "The End of History?," that characterized the conclusion of the Cold War as the triumph of Western liberalism.[2] The relaxation of Soviet hegemony in Eastern Europe and now the disintegration of the Soviet Union itself requires us to adjust our understanding. Nationalism, it appears, is still a force to be reckoned with. In the wake of the Soviet breakup the prognosis for the survival of India and China has worsened and fault lines are clearly visible. Tibet appears to be headed toward independence. The people of Tibet do not identify with China and world opinion will make it increasingly difficult for Chinese to retain control of that country by military force. Inner Asian portions of the People's Republic, such as Xinjiang and Inner Mongolia, are less clear-cut cases. These regions have been more susceptible than Tibet to the infiltration of Han Chinese. Non-Han populations are small and, the Mongols excepted, poorly situated to rally world opinion. Still, the breakup of the Soviet Union promises to unleash powerful nationalistic forces throughout Inner Asia before the end of the century. It is quite conceivable that these forces will prove strong enough to tear off pieces of "Chinese" territory. On the east coast, Taiwan presents another story entirely. There, advocates for independence are already pointing to the Baltic states as models for a course of action Taiwan should follow.

I think the breakup of the last empires should be viewed as the consummation of an older set of processes, the end of colonialism, and not as something new. The current dominant trend, I believe, is the growth of transnational linkages. The question in the wake of the Cold War is what form these linkages will take. I raise the subject of alternatives to nationalism here because I believe that China cannot adequately be understood in terms of nationalism alone. It is true that patriotic sentiment, forged in the humiliations of the nineteenth century and the Japanese intrusions in the twentieth century, has played a central role in modern Chinese politics. But nationalism and the concept of the nation have not sufficed to provide China with a viable identity and sense of direction. The People's Republic of China has always been portrayed as a multinational state guided by the universal truth of Marxism-Leninism as adapted to Chinese conditions by Mao Zedong Thought.

It was questions such as these that initially attracted me to the study of China. My undergraduate objective, after an unhappy brush with biochemistry, was to make a comprehensive overview of world history. I first took a course on China out of a desire to learn about a society as remote as possible from my own, a "radical other" by which to measure the range of human possibility. The first course I took on China proved so interesting that I went on for more, eventually making Chinese history and philosophy my undergraduate majors. In college my study of China was directed primarily at prerevolutionary history and thought. The issue that interested me most was the problem of China's cultural identity in the modern world, framed in terms of how China had responded to the West. The question was most clearly posed in a collection of documents compiled by Ssu-yü Teng and John K. Fairbank.[3] Joseph Levenson was exploring the Chinese options in a brilliant series of speculative essays on the "modern fate" of Confucian China.[4] (Fairbank's influence on academia and the media alike was unrivalled. His book, *The United States and China*, was given out to members of the press corps who accompanied Richard Nixon to China in 1972.)

In general I had the sense that the Communist revolution was probably a good thing and that the Kuomintang (KMT) richly deserved to lose the Mandate of Heaven, but in the mid-1950's I still knew very little about the People's Republic of China. My desire to study China was based in part on its very remoteness. Inaccessibility and hostility were factors that made China important. The classmate whom I eventually married shared similar views about the Soviet Union and spent four years studying Russian and Russian history. We were liberal Democrats with a bias toward public service and teaching. We assumed that knowledge of the Cold War enemy would be valuable in making a better world.

My sophomore project to catalogue world cultures was a personal agenda born of the undergraduate's desire to impose on human affairs a classification scheme with the elegance and explanatory power of the periodic table. When I eventually got to graduate school the demands of specialization quickly drove such thoughts from my mind. It was only when I began teaching at the University of Minnesota that I returned to my projected overview of human history. There I joined with a group of colleagues to write a comparative history of Asian civilizations.[5] Participation in that effort drastically transformed my perspective on both Chinese history and the Cold War.

My Career as a Cold Warrior

I have the Cold War to thank for my training in Chinese studies. After college I enlisted in the army with the intention of studying Chinese at the U.S. Army Language School in Monterey, California. In order to get to Monterey I had to go through basic training and advanced individual training in an intelligence agency that had a quota for the Language School. Only then could I apply for what turned out to be a single opening in Mandarin Chinese. Luck was with me and upon agreeing to extend my term of service I spent a happy year and a half learning Chinese on a pine covered hilltop above Monterey Bay. The chill of the Cold War was keenly felt in the Monterey fog. I was told by teachers that, at the height of McCarthyite hysteria, the military authorities of the language school supervised the burning of Chinese Communist documents that had been used to teach students current Chinese usage. We were allowed to see nothing more controversial than the agreements signed to end the fighting in Korea. Lin Biao's florid signature made an indelible impression, but I was left to imagine what People's Liberation Army documents would look like.

Upon completion of the Chinese language course in 1959, I was sent to South Korea. My counterintelligence duties had nothing to do with China, but provided a rich education in the politics of the Cold War. In the line of duty I worked with Korean government agencies on security matters. During my free time I sought out members of the Chinese community who had their own schools and were bound by close ties to the Nationalist government on Taiwan. The Chinese newspaper I subscribed to, the *Han Hua Ilbo* (*Korean Chinese Daily*) told me little about the mammoth home country that lay across the Yellow Sea. I learned more by listening at night to Chinese broadcasts on a portable radio that consisted mostly of ecstatic claims about production figures exceeding targets, vivid testimony to the madness of the Great Leap Forward, and the formation of communes. Occasionally there would be a snatch of *xiangsheng*, the droll cross-talk between interlocutors squeezing laughter out of topics like water conservancy and steel production. The excited tone of those broadcasts helped form a picture in my mind of a dynamic country building socialism at full throttle. Later, when I first visited China in 1975, I was shocked by the slow-motion pace of a population riding sedately on one-speed bicycles. It was not at all what I had pictured.

During a two-week leave, riding free on military air transports, I made my first visits to Taiwan and Hong Kong. In Hong Kong I looked across the border to the silent green hills of the mysterious country I could not enter. At the consulate I talked to a military official engaged in press monitoring. On the street outside the Chinese press office I inspected photographs of the latest public relations coup: the return to the mainland of Li Zongren, a former president of the Nationalist regime long resident in the United States, going home to die on native soil.

Military service enabled me to study the Chinese language and to get close to China, but it inhibited my access to the Chinese media. Simply subscribing to a mainland Chinese publication would have precipitated a "complaint type investigation" by counterintelligence authorities, a serious matter for any one with a security clearance. Fear of accusation was a powerful inhibitor. I was even nervous about contacts with family acquaintances who had associated with Communists in the 1930s and 1940s. Subscribing to a skeptical publication like I.F. Stone's Washington newsletter was out of the question.

THE BAMBOO CURTAIN

The Cold War isolated Chinese and Americans from each other in ways that made mutual understanding very difficult. In the absence of personal experience of events in China, scholars were dependent upon secondary sources of information, mostly documents. The science—or craft—of China-watching was born very shortly after Liberation, with Hong Kong as the main base of operations. There one could have access to various printed materials from the mainland and occasionally the accounts of persons who had visited China or fled the country as refugees. China watchers came in four principal categories: government agents, scholars, journalists, and missionaries. The missionaries probably knew the most; the scholars and journalists the least. What the government agents learned, and what they understood, will not be known until classified files are opened and future researchers piece together the inner history of Cold War espionage.

In technique China watching was much like historical study of the past. Since the real China was not accessible, not visible, one was obliged to fabricate a picture of it using the best information available. China was like a black box that emitted bits of evidence. One had to figure out from the pattern of the bits what was going on inside the box. This task was made harder by two aspects of the Cold War. One was the fact that governments were in a position to influence the flow of information. The Chinese severely restricted the amount of information outsiders received and drastically modified, colored, or distorted much of what was let out. The U.S. Government operated one of its largest consulates in Hong Kong precisely for the purpose of collecting information about China. Vast quantities of translated documents and transcriptions of broadcasts were routinely made available to interested persons. But the kinds of information collected were determined by government intelligence priorities and many kinds of information were overlooked or denied to scholars and journalists.

A second way the Cold War made China watching difficult was by casting doubt on the judgment of precisely the people who should have known the most. After 1949 any one who had extensive experience in China was suspect in some way. The "old China hands" in the Department of State came under a cloud of suspicion in the late 1940s and were soon all driven out of positions from which they could contribute to an understanding of what was happening in China. Missionaries, who in many cases had excellent language skills and long experience of residence in China, were suspect because of their hostility to Communism. Their interest in religious belief and in the fate of Christians in the People's Republic, a small and unrepresentative group who were singled out for particularly harsh treatment, were grounds for believing that their view of the revolution was unduly negative. Even Chinese émigrés, many from bad class backgrounds, found it difficult to judge what was happening in China. If they had left China because it was undergoing a revolution, how could they be sure that the nature of the society had not changed?

In addition to a climate of intimidation which discouraged or colored
China studies, there was also obstruction of access to China and to information about China. Travel to China was virtually impossible. Governments on both sides were anxious to keep their citizens from seeing what
the other country was like. China denied entry to most foreigners and
some Americans were unable to obtain passports to go abroad. The flow
of publications and documents was also restricted. Copies of Chinese
publications sent to the United States had to be filed with the Justice Department and subscribers were made aware that the federal government
was keeping a record of their receipt of magazines or journals. When William Hinton returned from China with the notes for *Fanshen*, his classic account of land reform, the authorities seized his papers and held them for
years.[6] Even historical records were not left unmolested. The documents
Mary C. Wright collected in Yanan in the late 1940s were impounded by
the U.S. Government for years before they were released to the Hoover Library.

Beyond intimidation and the obstruction of information flow lay more
subtle means employed by the government to influence journalism and
scholarship. How far such action could reach in the academic world is illustrated by the case of the *China Quarterly*.[7] In the 1950s an organization
with a title something like the Congress of Intellectual Freedom started
the journal *Encounter*. Published in England, it provided a forum for views
that might not have found easy expression in the Cold War atmosphere of
the United States. Around 1960 the same organization launched the *China
Quarterly* as a vehicle for U.S. and European scholarly publication on
modern and contemporary China. Instantly, a new field was born. China
scholars in the United States had an outlet for scholarship free of the prevailing taboos. Years later it was revealed that the funding to start the
China Quarterly had come ultimately from the Central Intelligence
Agency. What influence, if any, government support might have had on
scholarship was not clear.

One of the first things the Communist leadership did when it came to
power was seal the mainland off from foreign contact. The hostility of the
Cold War, the American project of military containment, diplomatic isolation, and a trade embargo helped maintain the isolation, but the impetus
to close the country clearly came from within. The regime was not anxious
for foreigners to roam about the landscape or for Chinese to travel freely
abroad. Watching and reporting through the keyhole of the British Crown
Colony of Hong Kong could not possibly give us an adequate picture of
the fifth of humanity that resided in China. How wrong things could go
was suggested to me by a Chinese dinner party I attended in Hong Kong
early in 1967. I had been studying Ming history in Taiwan on a fellowship,
well-insulated from news of the Cultural Revolution then unfolding on

the mainland. In the midst of a lively banquet (including several bottles of scotch taken straight in small glasses) at the home of a Chinese professor, I was astounded to hear the head of a leading China watching institute declare flatly that Mao Zedong was dead and was being impersonated by a stand-in at public events in Beijing. This incident tempered the credence I gave to the reports of China watchers.

China scholars were quick to point out that the twentieth century was not the first time China had closed its borders. In recent centuries China was more often closed than open to outside influences. Under the Ming Dynasty Chinese were not supposed to go abroad and outsiders were allowed to enter only for specific purposes. The greatest concern was always with the northern border, the direction from which Inner Asian peoples had invaded the Middle Kingdom. Such peoples had repeatedly succeeded in seizing Chinese territory and establishing non-Han states. The Manchu Qing was the last and most successful of all the conquest states. Before the nineteenth century the seacoast was a secondary source of trouble from piracy on a modest scale. Traditionally, trade by sea was to be restricted to selected southern ports, to Canton in particular. In the People's Republic the annual Canton Trade Fair bore a striking resemblance to the controlled access trading arrangements established by the Qing in the eighteenth century.

If we take the view that China had been a closed society for centuries, then its closure during the Cold War can be seen as a return to a "normal" condition. It can be characterized as a restoration of an element of the traditional order. It does not have to be seen as something entirely new created by the conditions of the Cold War. The same could be said of the highly centralized bureaucratic state, the semi-deified leader, the imposition of a state sanctioned orthodoxy, and the penchant for employing didactic devices in the exercise of state power. Like the traditional Confucian imperial order, the Marxist-Leninist dictatorship needed isolation, unchallenged control of education and communications, and constant promotion to retain its legitimacy.

CHANGING SIDES

In the summer of 1961 I was granted an early release from the army so that I could start classes in graduate school the following fall. I missed the mandatory extension of my term of service and a transfer to Germany for the Berlin crisis by a matter of days. A German language classification appended to my military occupation specialty made me a logical candidate, and many of my office mates in Seattle found themselves on aircraft headed for Berlin as I set out for Massachusetts. Had I gone to Germany, I might never have had the chance to continue in Chinese studies.

Discharge from the service changed, but did not end, my long relationship with the federal government. My enrollment at Harvard was made possible by a National Defense Education Act fellowship for the study of Chinese. The name of the scholarship is indicative of how the Cold War was used to justify expenditures for basic education. (A notarized loyalty oath, disavowing membership in organizations on the Attorney General's list, was a routine requirement for receiving the funds.) Dissertation research in Taiwan was supported by a Fulbright fellowship, another product of Cold War rivalry.

Distress over the war in Vietnam was just beginning to mount when I left for Taiwan in 1965. The first antiwar teach-ins were taking place in Washington as the Fulbrighters gathered at the State Department for a predeparture briefing. My age, sensitivity to the pressures of anti-Communism, and indebtedness to the U.S. Government all inclined me initially to be supportive of the war. Doubts about the war and about American foreign policy grew rapidly. From Taiwan, a number of graduate students wrote to our professors in the United States questioning the failure of the Association for Asian Studies to act as a forum on China policy. Some of my fellow students went on to play an active role in founding the Committee of Concerned Asian Scholars (CCAS). By the time I came back from Taiwan in 1967, however, the climate of opinion had changed dramatically and my own views on the war shifted to opposition.

When I got to Minnesota in 1968 I helped sponsor a local CCAS chapter. This led to many enlightening experiences, from participation in the campus strike to peace marches and heated debates with hawkish types in the suburbs. Particularly instructive was a meeting in the Richfield House of Prayer at which a colleague and I were solemnly denounced as Communists by a total stranger. The accusation was particularly poignant because my companion was an émigré from East Germany, where he had narrowly escaped arrest by Communist authorities for starting a democratic forum in his high school.

As disillusion with the war in Vietnam mounted, so did enthusiasm for Mao's China. We can now see that admiration for the new China was not always deserved. But then, in the absence of intimate contact with Chinese life, it was possible to project an image of China that was really a negation of what was distressing about the United States. Even the brief exposures to China which became possible in the 1970s did not suffice to dampen romantic enthusiasm for the unknown other. As Paul Hollander has documented in his book, *Political Pilgrims*, the pattern of utopian wishful thinking that began with visitors to the Soviet Union during the Depression was repeated by those who made trips to Cuba and China during the Cold War.[8] The impact of such enthusiasm on our understanding of China was considerable. Members of the CCAS were among the first serious students of China allowed to visit the mecca of proletarian culture, and their initial reports were ecstatic.

My own views were ambivalent. After my return from Taiwan in 1967 I compared the information in Chinese propaganda publications such as *Peking Review* to the *New York Times*, which occasionally carried accounts by Canadian reporters stationed in Beijing. I carefully clipped newspaper articles about China on a daily basis. My mother-in-law, a retired research librarian, was recruited to paste them on sheets of paper which gradually filled a row of binders that stretched around my office on top of the bookshelves. What I got from those articles, more than a feel for Chinese reality, was a sense of the struggle to report on China and Beijing's effort to control its image in the Western press.

A 1975 trip to Hong Kong gave me a few insights into the kinds of opinion manipulation going on. I visited the *New York Times* representative, Joseph Lelyveld, who was the brother of one of my colleagues in Minnesota. I found him a frustrated man. He had learned Chinese in hopes of being among the first American reporters posted to Beijing but found himself trapped in Hong Kong because the United States and China had not yet established diplomatic relations. I declined his invitation to go on a boat ride.

A Communist newspaper published in Hong Kong carried a story which reasoned that the Americans were about to surrender in Vietnam because U.S. soldiers were given phrase books that told them how to say "surrender" and "throw down your arms" in Vietnamese. I attended a meeting of the Marco Polo Club devoted to mobilizing friends of China in the British colony. It was presided over by Percy Chen, the son of Eugene Chen, a Caribbean-born overseas Chinese who had worked with Borodin at the time of the Northern Expedition. I shared a table with staffers from the New China News Agency (Xinhua) who seemed to know a great deal more about politics than about news. I was introduced by Chinese friends to the publisher of an English-language magazine, *Eastern Horizon*, which I understood to be aimed at sympathetic British and commonwealth opinion much as *China Reconstructs* was aimed at Americans. The comprehensive and systematic outreach through united front techniques was quite apparent.

My first visit to the People's Republic came in 1975 as a member of the U.S.-China People's Friendship Association (USCPFA), an open membership organization born of the need to conduct people-to-people exchange in the period prior to formal diplomatic relations. A few years later I was purged from the steering committee of the local chapter for nominating a member of the Revolutionary Union faction for an office in opposition to the leadership's slate. It was my proudest moment as an ultraleftist.

CHINA IN THE WORLD SYSTEM

If the closure of the "bamboo curtain" was a return to the norm, was the century from the opening of China in the 1840s to the closing of the borders in the 1940s nothing more than an historical aberration? I think not. The opening of China to external influence should be regarded as the long-term trend and the closure of the Cold War as a "restoration" of limited duration. If this is so, we need to ask what forces brought about that opening and how they can be expected to influence China's future development. It may be helpful to think about the intrusion of the external world into the Chinese cultural realm in terms of three modes or processes. War was one mode of intrusion. The imperialist powers in the nineteenth and twentieth centuries invaded with the result that China lost political sovereignty and was unable to control its own territory. The unification by the People's Republic succeeded most clearly in the restoration of sovereignty. With the important exceptions of Hong Kong and Taiwan, all of Chinese territory was brought under a strong central rule capable of effective defense. The threat of invasion continued in the Cold War period but never came to pass. The possibility of a serious attack on China now seems remote.

Trade was another mode of intrusion. It attacked the system at the social and economic level, moving people around and changing their occupations. China long resisted or tried to control pressures for trade along both the inland frontiers and the coast. Economic and social forces of the world trading system, however, proved irresistible. Goods, money, and people moved in and out of China, tying the Chinese economy to the global system and scattering Chinese emigrants throughout the world. During the Cold War Taiwan developed a booming export trade while China became part of a socialist bloc separated from the market economies of the West. A disastrous period of independent development in China followed the Sino-Soviet break. Zhou Enlai's opening to the West in the early 1970s and Deng Xiaoping's four modernizations at the end of the decade were concessions to the power of the world trade system. Even in the wake of the massacre on 4 June 1989 China's foreign trade links have continued to develop. Deng's hope that socialism can continue to exist in China as trade develops appears naive indeed. It reminds one of Zhang Zhidong's prescription of Chinese learning for the essence and Western learning for the practical application (*zhong xue wei ti, xi xue wei yong*).[9] A nice idea, but not a realistic account of how things work.

Communication is the third mode of intrusion. Its consequence is subversion. It attacks the system at the cultural and ideological level. Voices of subversion have come in many forms, from the early Jesuits to the later Protestant missionaries, all urging a different world view on susceptible

Chinese. The missionaries were joined in the twentieth century by agents of the Comintern whose teachings yielded spectacular results. The current regime's hostility to human rights advocates and those who call for democratic reform testifies to the continuing danger of "spiritual pollution." The question is whether a modernizing economy, ever more closely linked to the world trade network, can be insulated from the subversive influence of foreign ideas and values. It is my assumption that it cannot and that a corrosive process of value change is underway which will eat away the value system upon which the regime is based.

China Up Close

As a child of the 1940s and 1950s, I grew up with the assumption that the United States was on the side of justice in the world and that history was naturally progressive. My experience confirmed this. The allies won World War II, founded the United Nations, and brought stability to the world. A growing consumer economy constantly improved our lives. The changes from an icebox to a refrigerator and from a wringer to a dryer were particularly dramatic. Health, education, and welfare were all improving. I was relatively insulated from the postwar repression of women and the harsher realities of racial prejudice. By the time I was in high school I was a regular reader of *Time* magazine, squirming at the tortured prose but drinking in the picture of a world that was getting better with each passing day.

The darker side of the Cold War struggle between Communism and democracy did not seriously cloud my belief in progress. When the army sent me to serve in Korea for a year in 1959, I had to confront the fact that I might be asked to risk my life defending the Republic of Korea. In that exercise I persuaded myself that Korea was indeed worth fighting for. Part of my reasoning was that if Western Europe was worth defending then allies in Asia were no less worthy of support. (I must note that this kind of thinking led me initially to support the Vietnam War.) I did not have an idealized picture of Korean democracy. Indeed, I had a close-up view of the scurrilous corruption of the Syngman Rhee regime and had the pleasure of reporting on its downfall. I left Korea more hopeful about the prospects for its political evolution than for its chance of economic development. Corruption, I believed, posed an insurmountable obstacle to economic takeoff. I have since had to revise my thinking on this matter.

My first exposure to China, i.e., Taiwan, came during a short leave from Korea in 1960. I later lived there for two years from 1965 to 1967 as a graduate student on a Fulbright fellowship. Taiwan was very much a garrison state in those days. The military and police apparatus sat heavily on the people and voices of dissent were dealt with harshly. Foreign news magazines received by mail were delayed while functionaries in some office tore out pages, stamped "Communist bandit" (*fei*) on photos, or used magic markers to carefully ink out any pictures or news of the mainland. The journal *Free China* (*Ziyou Zhongguo*) was suspended about the time I got there.[10] Dozens of other publications were silenced and many whose views were suspect were taken into custody or simply disappeared. All of this fed my conviction that both Chinas were authoritarian dictatorships. The political change that was to come was not yet apparent.

Despite the repressive character of the political system Taiwan was clearly on the path of economic development. In the 1960s living conditions were still primitive by U.S. standards. Bicycles and pedicabs were common means of conveyance and soft coal was still used for cooking in Taipei. Labor was so cheap that people made a living repairing umbrellas or picking through garbage. Despite these conditions one could see the groundwork being laid for economic takeoff. The first export processing zone was opened in Kaohsiung, an aggressive family planning campaign was under way, and heavy investment was being made in the infrastructure. A planner bragged that rice cookers in Taipei at noon drew more power than the entire generating capacity of the island when the KMT took it over.

It was a visit in 1975, after an eight-year absence, that drove home to me that Taiwan was headed for full economic development. In 1965 academic families had electric fans and were getting refrigerators. By 1975 a handful of people had private cars. I had a lively conversation over a matter of shared interest with the uneducated, older wife of a scholar during lunch at his residence at the Academia Sinica. The new refrigerator was self-defrosting! Progress was underway in Taiwan.

Changing China

The problem of how to view China long preceded the Cold War and will continue long after its conclusion. When I took up the study of China in the 1950s, modernization and development theory enjoyed currency in American academic circles. In those approaches the pattern of Western industrialization was taken to be normative. Any society progressing along the path of modernization would have to pass through certain stages until it reached economic takeoff into sustained growth. The economic model had corollaries that applied to political, social and cultural development as well: it was assumed that convergence would make all societies become more like the advanced industrial nations. Convergence theories passed out of vogue in the 1960s and 1970s partly because the Cold War division held out the possibility that there were multiple paths to development. Since Mao's death in 1976 and the collapse of Commu-

nism in Eastern Europe, the viability of socialist models has been thrown
into doubt. Under Deng Xiaoping's second open door policy the People's
Republic has been subjected to massive doses of Western cultural influence. How deeply this influence has been felt and how far it will go in
changing the China is anyone's guess.

In my heart I shrink from the implications of convergence theory. It
seems to promise the death of the great civilizations which are the repositories of humanity's most precious heritage. I was hopeful that the Chinese revolutionary experiment would prove successful. I am still not sure
that it was impossible but I am now convinced that it failed and failed decisively.

The political liberalization of Taiwan and the emergence of a democracy movement on the mainland support the view that Chinese society is
not impervious to the convergent forces of Western liberalism. Taiwan
succeeded by pursuing a textbook course of economic development followed by liberalization of the political system. Chiang Kai-shek in his later
years used to talk about Taiwan becoming an example to people on the
mainland, talk easily dismissed as wishful thinking by one who had been
decisively defeated in the civil war. Ironically, his wish has now come
true. Not only does Taiwan stand as the best model for China's future, it is
clear that Chinese from Hong Kong and Taiwan will play essential roles in
the economic development of the mainland.

Over the years I have been the recipient of many publications from Taiwan, most of them free and unsolicited. Tract literature from something
called the World Anti-Communist Crusade is utterly worthless and finds
the wastebasket unopened. But the *Free China Review* is quite another matter. It uses a soft sell to tell the Taiwan story with a lot of features on cultural and economic topics. Its lush photography makes it a rich source for
classroom slides. Its language and story topics are pitched to an American
reader's ear and interests, thanks in part, I imagine, to the input of Westerners whose names appear on the masthead. The upbeat, sensual, and
culturally astute image projected by this magazine captures perfectly the
spirit of a society modernizing while seeking to harmonize elements from
Chinese and Western traditions.

Convergence is more than an abstract theory. It is experienced on the
personal level as the world appears to become smaller and societies closer
together. In visits to Taiwan in 1980 and 1983 I was impressed with the
progress of economic development and by an increasingly robust cultural
cosmopolitanism, but perplexed by what appeared to be political stalemate. I got a strong signal that political change was underway from the return to Minnesota of Rita Yeh, a graduate student in sociology who had
been imprisoned in Taiwan for subversive activities. She simply appeared
on campus and arranged to complete the "Plan B" papers required for her

M.A. degree. The existence of rapid political liberalization in Taiwan was confirmed for me when I attended a conference there in December 1986. The transformation of the once illegal opposition into a legal political party was the crucial watershed.

The conference itself was symptomatic of the trend in a remote way. Gone were the political speeches and group pictures of an earlier era. While the hospitality was faultless, it was less deferential and more relaxed than I remembered from earlier decades. It became clear in the scholarly give-and-take of the sessions that the linguistic, methodological, and conceptual distance between scholarly work in Taiwan and the United States had shrunk to insignificance. Many of the scholars in Taiwan had studied in the United States or Europe and most of the Americans had studied in Taiwan. Included in their numbers were old classmates from graduate school, friends from student days in Taiwan, and former students.

Repeated trips to the People's Republic since 1975 have allowed me to observe change there. The decline of Mao Zedong Thought was symbolized for me in 1986 by peanut vendors on the street selling their products in paper cones made from pages of the late chairman's *Selected Works*. In over a decade of cooperation with Nankai University in conducting an annual summer language program, many friendships have grown up. In Minneapolis an influx of visiting scholars and graduate students has created an extensive network of personal and professional relationships. The Cold War is over, but access to China and friendships with Chinese individuals have not necessarily made understanding China easier. The Chinese I know tend to be intellectuals—university teachers and students—who share many of my values. They are apt to come to my lectures and to ask *me* what *I* think is going on in China. Where once there were barriers and clear differences, there is now a hazy and confusing tangle of connections and interactions.

Americans and Chinese were drawn much closer together in 1989 during the student demonstrations in Tiananmen Square in Beijing. The cosmopolitan character of those events, which were witnessed on television by viewers around the world, was graphically represented by the erection of the figure of the Goddess of Democracy shortly before the demonstrations were brought brutally to an end. That Chinese students called for democracy and human rights, employed Gandhian techniques of nonviolence, and chose as their symbol a cousin of the Statue of Liberty all suggest the degree to which Chinese political culture has been influenced by international trends beyond the open door.

Within a matter of weeks I was present at the erection of a local avatar of the Goddess on the mall in the center of our campus. One hundred days after the 4 June massacre a memorial service was held at Macalester College in Saint Paul. For that event a smaller version of the Goddess of Democracy was constructed by a group of art students, some of whom were from Africa. To my delight, I saw at once that the figure they produced, although in white papier-mâché, had decidedly African features and wore an African style robe. This was cultural convergence at its best.

CONCLUSION

At the height of the Cold War, when China was a remote and hostile Communist monolith—"Mao's China"—it was easier to theorize and generalize about. It was unlike America; the product of different forces, different values, and headed in a different direction. Now that China is more open and less remote it defies easy generalization. China today is a project under construction. How it will turn out is still an open question. It is my impression that, given the opportunity to choose and to express themselves, Chinese will demand many of the things that people in Eastern Europe and the states that made up the Soviet Union are demanding and many of the things that Americans enjoy or desire. China's size and relative isolation means that merger with the industrialized world may take a long time, but the process is already under way. The prognosis for Chinese culture is drastic change. While I am sympathetic to those who want to preserve elements of the Chinese tradition, I do not think that the tradition can be preserved. Rather, I think that selected aspects of it will be revived as constituent elements in the construction of new Chinese identities. I am also hopeful that contributions from the Chinese tradition can help to temper some of the ambiguities and contradictions, including the rampant individualism and excessive concern with rights, that the West has loosed upon the world.

NOTES

1. A good account of this sorry tale is E. J. Kahn, Jr., *The China Hands* (New York: Random House, 1975).

2. For critical press coverage see Richard Bernstein, "Judging 'Post-History,' The Theory to End All Theories," *New York Times*, 27 Aug. 1989 and "Awaiting the Great Boredom," a *New York Times* editorial, 11 Sept. 1989. A thoughtful reflection on the state of the world after the end of the Cold War is Francis Fukuyama, *The End of History and the Last Man* (New York: Free Press, 1992). This book goes well beyond Fukuyama's article, "The End of History?," *The National Interest* 18 (Winter 1989), pp. 3–18, which is more celebratory in tone.

3. Ssu-yü Teng and John K. Fairbank, *China's Response to the West: A Documentary Survey, 1839–1923* (Cambridge, MA: Harvard University Press, 1963).

4. Joseph R. Levenson, *Confucian China and Its Modern Fate*, 3 vols. (Berkeley: University of California Press, 1958–1965).

5. Edward L. Farmer, Gavin R. G. Hambly, David Kopf, Byron K. Marshall and Romeyn Taylor, *Comparative History of Civilizations in Asia*, 2 vols. (Reading, MA: Addison-Wesley, 1977).

6. William Hinton, *Fanshen: A Documentary of Revolution in a Chinese Village* (New York: Monthly Review Press, 1956).

7. *China Quarterly* received support from the International Association for Cultural Freedom. In 1968 it began a transition to the Contemporary China Institute, established at the School of Oriental and African Studies at the University of London with a grant from the Ford Foundation.

8. Paul Hollander, *Political Pilgrims: Travels of Western Intellectuals to the Soviet Union, China and Cuba, 1928–1978* (New York: Oxford University Press, 1981).

9. See Wm. Theodore de Bary, Wing-tsit Chan and Chester Tan, comp., *Sources of the Chinese Tradition* (New York: Columbia University Press, 1960), vol. 2, pp. 81–87.

10. See John Israel, "Politics on Formosa," *China Quarterly* 15 (1963): 3–11.

15

PUSH AND PULL: A CHINESE-AMERICAN JOURNALIST'S "HOME JOURNEYS"

Wendy S. Tai

There is a symbiosis between the insider's and the outsider's views of China. Norman Fu maintains that an understanding of China hinges on the possession of a "Chinese mind."[1] Chin-Chuan Lee argues, however, that the balance sheet of insider observers resembles that of outsider observers: both have their distinctive assets and liabilities. Furthermore, we are all "plural persons" who must manage the tension between the roles of "insider" and "outsider."[2] As a Chinese-American journalist,[3] I address in this chapter some of the seemingly contradictory challenges I faced reporting on China: putting aside the ethnocentrism that underlay my Chinese upbringing, injecting fresh perspectives into my reports about China, seeing China as Chinese did, and interpreting the relevance of China, the Chinese way of life, and events in China to an American audience.

In 1985 and 1989 I went to China as a reporter for the Minneapolis-based *Star Tribune*. In 1985 my relatives offered an intimate glimpse of Chinese life for American readers; after the June 1989 Tiananmen crackdown I roamed about China to confirm stories from an abundance of rumors and lend them a personal voice. I promoted both trips to my editors by emphasizing that I could reflect the voices of Chinese individuals, rather than institutions, and thereby humanize issues which could strike an emotional chord among readers. It seemed that most of the stories about China from American reporters had focused on the Chinese leadership, political campaigns, institutions, and other issues that tended to portray the complexities of life in the upper echelons of society. The more recent stories about discos doing a booming business, the peasant-turned-millionaire, and the return of prostitution offered an unduly narrow view of China. I wanted to trace how official policies played out in villages and in everyday life. I preferred to portray the complexities of Chinese life and problems, rather than present an impersonal voice of generalities.

I told my editors about my advantages in pursuing stories without reliance on Chinese officials, interpreters, or the Chinese press, thus escaping official scrutiny and safeguarding my sources. Not only would living with relatives expose me to everyday life in China, but I would be able to talk to ordinary Chinese who were underrepresented in dispatches from China. The advantages of being an insider were especially valuable in a restrictive, closed, and homogeneous society such as China, which strictly segregates "us" from "them." I further ensured my anonymity by not filing any stories in China.

Like any journalist I bring to my job a mixture of preconceptions and biases shaped by environment, education, and experiences. But as a Chinese immigrant, my baggage became harder to shed in covering China: I was often a relative or a fellow Chinese first while my journalist status lingered in the background. I felt emotional attachment to sources—some of whom were relatives—and places, including my family's ancestral village. The Chinese perception of me as one of them came with a set of assumptions regarding my understanding of China. My familiarity with the Chinese language meant I overlooked interesting and telling translations that a non-native speaker could spot more readily. At times I failed to grasp what was news until after I left China.

CHINESE FAMILY, AMERICAN EDUCATION

I am an insider to both Chinese and American cultures, yet an outsider to both. I have a foot in each, yet am not firmly planted in either. In nearly all my assignments, this has hardly mattered. But the China assignments brought to surface all the meshing, adopting, and discarding of elements from each culture that had been occurring in my mind over the years in some inexplicable, subconscious way. This process began after my family moved to the United States from Taiwan in 1965.

As children we always spoke Chinese at home. It was a practical way to maintain our language skills and, more importantly, a link to staying Chinese. Our home was the citadel from which I viewed the outside world of school, work, and friends. The view I developed at home, strongly influenced by my parents and their friends, was what Robert K. Merton calls an extreme "insider's view," which presupposes that only members of a certain group can understand that group.[4] Americans were not expected to really understand China no matter how long they had studied Chinese language, history, and culture. This view seemed particularly acceptable at a time when China was closed to the outside, and only those who had fled China could speak about it with the validity granted to firsthand reports. Their view of their homeland, however, was deeply shaped by their bitter experiences and often frozen in the past, in the years before 1949.

Anti-Communist views were drummed into me during my early school years in Taiwan when the Communists were "bandits" in elementary texts—outlaws who took away our homeland. My father's father and his brother were killed by Communist guerrillas, and my parents fled the mainland in 1949. Thus, my parents reinforced my early anti-Communist view by repeatedly bemoaning American naiveté regarding the "tricks of the Communists."

Because my family did not consider itself "American," we looked at Americans and the largely white community of Santa Barbara as "outside." Despite outward appearances of assimilation, deep down we separated ourselves from Americans and watched their behavior with simultaneous detachment and fascination. But through the years, the detachment lessened and the distance I perceived between our respective views of the world narrowed.

I was first exposed to new perspectives on Chinese Communism and its history at the University of California at Berkeley. My professors were mostly Westerners who had studied in Taiwan, Hong Kong, and other places outside mainland China. Books were often long on political structure and theories and short on the role of communism in real lives. The few that provided real flesh, such as Edgar Snow's *Red Star Over China*, painted a picture of a poor country stitched together by a shared sense of struggle and common good.[5] One class taught the Cultural Revolution as Mao's attempt at maintaining ideological purity, a move that promoted egalitarianism and preserved the common good.

I remember vividly one film shown in class that exalted the diligence and sacrifice of "barefoot doctors" who served the peasants. It was a China-produced propaganda film. But liberal viewpoints, especially sympathy toward Third World nations, remained prevalent in Berkeley in the 1970s. My leanings then, in many ways, were greatly influenced by the romantic notion of America's China scholars who studied China from afar and whose views were affected by disillusion at home.[6] Those inclinations were a counterpoint to the staunch anti-Communist views of my youth. As a Chinese I wanted to believe China was utopian, strong, and righteous. But rationally, I figured the truth lay somewhere between my parents' China and my American professors' China.

JOURNEYS HOME

In September 1985 I went to China for the first time with a *Star Tribune* photographer and my mother, who was visiting after being away for 36 years. The photographer, Stormi Greener, and I spent four weeks in China: one week in Beijing; one week in Shanghai; four days in my ancestral home, Dai Village, located about 110 miles northwest of Shanghai; and several days each in Xian and Changzhou, my mother's hometown about an hour's drive from Dai Village. Our three-day series, entitled "A Journey Home," provided readers with an intimate look at China through the experiences and everyday lives of relatives living in cities and the countryside.

With the exception of Xian, we concentrated on visiting relatives and lived with some of them, including a cousin who lived in the same house in the bustling city of Shanghai that my mother lived in as a youngster. In the countryside we lived with my uncle in his single-story house with no running water, television, or radio, and only sporadic electricity. There were no public phones—not to mention private phones—nearby. He tilled the same land in Dai Village that his oldest brother—my father—did 50 years earlier. A huge basket of grain took over half of the main room, and he supplemented his farming with towing goods for others on a collectively-owned tractor.

In Beijing we stayed in a hotel and visited my cousins, a relatively high-level cadre family marked by the material trappings of that rank, including a housekeeper-cook-babysitter and private violin lessons for their only daughter. Chinese custom and the convenient location of our hotel—across the street from a cousin's home—meant that we would be with these relatives from dawn to dusk everyday we were in Beijing. Everyone agreed to be photographed and identified by name.

In 1985 China seemed bathed in optimism, its people looking forward to a better life. My relatives, too, were upbeat. They talked about their suffering during the Cultural Revolution, but regarded it as yet another political upheaval whose time had passed. It did not seem likely that Deng Xiaoping, mastermind of the economic reforms, would sacrifice prosperity for political dogma, they said. The people were behind him, they assured me. While I had read newspaper accounts of a rising standard of living, I was still surprised at China's economic progress and the openness of the people.

I found talk of money and ways to make more. There was a rush for consumer goods and major appliances, despite rapidly rising prices. But tension was just beneath the surface, and I saw the value of personal connections, or the "backdoor," in getting things done. I got tickets for a sleeping car immediately because one of my uncles worked for the railway bureau, whereas my cousin's neighbor had to camp overnight at the train station. I heard some grumbling about people who were getting rich too fast, China opening too quickly to the outside world, and Chinese improperly idolizing the West. These complaints, and others, fermented before exploding in 1989.

By the time I returned to China in the fall of 1989, impassioned expressions of political opinion were reserved for family and close friends. At a time when Chinese were too frightened to speak to foreign reporters, I was particularly interested in exploring the concept of "democracy" in the Chinese context. Again, I stayed about four weeks: one week each in Beijing and Shanghai; three days in Dai Village; and the rest of the time in Xian, Nanchang and an adjacent village, and Guangzhou. My relatives in Dai Village were the only ones with whom I stayed and used again as sources. In other places I lived in hotels and interviewed people who were friends and relatives of contacts I had made earlier in the United States. Nearly everyone requested anonymity. Doing the 1989 stories as a non-Chinese is difficult to imagine.

By the time I arrived, cynicism had replaced what some observers considered romantic notions of political reform. Nearly everyone I met grumbled, some about the Communist government, but more commonly about inflation, spoiled only children (the consequence of the government's attempt to reduce the birthrate), and the clampdown on private enterprise. Some of the people I had met four years earlier obviously had gained more material wealth, but they complained about the lack of personal freedom, widespread corruption and graft, and the breakdown of social order. My three-day series, entitled "China Stories," was a collage of ordinary Chinese voices. For nearly everyone interviewed, the concept of democracy that Western media portrayed as the rallying point for hundreds of thousands in Tiananmen Square that spring really meant freedom: freedom to choose a job, to divorce, to make more money. Overall, the series showed people coping in a society fraying at the edges and a nation that was clamping down politically and economically.

My interviews were often a mixture of a friendly visit and talk, many times over long meals at the person's home, beginning with chats about each other's family life and my impressions of China before steering toward the real topic. While I usually had my tape recorder going and took notes, the distinction between guest and journalist was much less clear than in the United States. Sometimes I used a direct approach which included asking pointed questions: What is democracy? What were the protesting students after? Why can't Chinese band together and rebel, as protesters and voters in the United States often do over controversial issues? The responses usually carried a patient tone, implying naiveté on my part. To the last question, I always got laughter and an answer that conveyed powerlessness. Once after hearing such a question, a man said, "You've been in America too long." People forgot that I was a Western-educated outsider who had never lived in China.

In contrast to my visit in 1985, I made sure my relationship with sources was as professional as possible in 1989. Nevertheless, the nature of the relationships often embodied personal aspects. There were several occasions when being introduced by a trusted intermediary was enough for the speaker to cook dinner and answer questions, all the while never asking why I was taking notes or why I asked such questions. Because I focused more on politics in 1989, I identified myself as a reporter before full-length interviews and only interviewed relatives in Dai Village. As in 1985 I found that other sources regarded my Chinese background as an unspoken bond.

STRENGTHS AND WEAKNESSES

Surveillance, Deception, and Access

Many veteran China reporters have experienced the difficulties of being a *waiguoren* (foreigner or, literally, an "outside country person") in closely controlled China. John Fraser of the *Toronto Globe and Mail* (1977–1979) described himself as an "observer" who "forced" himself on Chinese by taking bike rides around Beijing city streets.[7] Similarly, when Frank Ching reported from Beijing for the *Wall Street Journal* in the early 1980s, access to official information was severely restricted, and journalists had to seek out people exempt from government control measures or willing to risk punishment—primarily political dissidents, foreign teachers, and students.[8] Jay and Linda Mathews have reflected at length on Chinese's sensitivity toward foreigners and how that got in the way of honest reporting.[9] As foreign correspondents, they found themselves isolated, treated with distant respect, and subjected to staged events where Chinese attempted to put their best face forward. In some cases, they were put under surveillance or, even worse, became the news themselves.

The Chinese government assigned foreign journalists assistants who functioned as drivers, translators, housekeepers, and even spies.[10] The difficulty of developing ordinary Chinese sources followed the political winds, but it was generally a frustrating experience. Amanda Bennett, who was stationed in Beijing from 1983–1985, remarked that keeping in touch with ordinary people consumed far more time in China than in other foreign posts, and that the Chinese press thus became a resource for otherwise unobtainable anecdotes.[11] Protecting the safety of sources, moreover, was always a paramount concern. Wang Dan, one of the most-wanted student activists in 1989, was arrested after he spoke with a reporter from Taiwan. Former *Washington Post* correspondent Dan Southerland stated that surveillance of foreign journalists was so oppressive after the Tiananmen crackdown that his colleagues wanted to leave

Beijing. For Southerland, the search for truth became so frustrating that he lowered his expectations and settled for finding one Chinese a week who "would go beyond the official lies."[12]

The barriers that foreign correspondents discovered in China stood in the area of my strengths. I never thought any central official in Beijing knew I was there in 1985 and 1989, and this anonymity was critical to my reporting. Beyond the dangers of surveillance, looking Chinese and speaking Chinese translated into greater freedom and easier access to genuine opinions often withheld from foreigners on the basis of politeness or "saving face." Most Chinese with whom I spoke felt that we shared a set of cultural assumptions limited to people with the same history and orientation. This assumption was voiced in comments such as "You're Chinese. You know how it is." Sometimes I found myself not pressing the speaker to elaborate as I would for stories in the United States, because I understood what was not said, but implied. In American journalism, we tend to reply to what is said, while in China I watched more for what was left unsaid and not visible. Thus, I sometimes found myself short of quotes when I sat down to write and was faced with the task of trying to convey what I knew but was not said.

Chinese exhibit a cultural and social orientation that treats non-Chinese with courtesy, but such cordiality does not generally exist in a Chinese family. In 1985 my relatives in China were amazed at my excessive politeness and remarked that I was not a *wairen* (outsider). In contrast, Stormi Greener's mere presence often caused such a commotion that it became impossible to observe and record our surroundings. On the streets, I had to smooth the way for her before or after she took a picture, telling people do whatever they were doing. Invariably, people wanted to pose and objected to anything that might be considered a negative reflection on themselves or, worse yet, on China. Garbage piles or a child sitting on a toilet bucket by the roadside or urinating in the street were scenes that many Chinese did not want Stormi to photograph. When a bystander did not want her to see a couple arguing on the street in Shanghai, he said, "Don't argue anymore. There's a foreigner taking pictures." This notion of presenting the best side to outsiders was carried to an extreme on one occasion when shoppers urged a chicken vendor to pick a better looking chicken to hang on a scale for Stormi to photograph.

We always lost a day or two at the beginning of visits to each family while relatives got used to having Stormi around. She got the most intense scrutiny in Dai Village, where she was the first foreigner that residents had seen in the flesh. They not only stared, some women lifted up her sweater to see if she was a woman. Children outside pushed open a bedroom window to get another look at her after she retreated there from hours of stares. Just when we were considering Stormi a liability, the com-

motion died down enough for us to work. But it took time, and she was always considered an odd guest, raising snickers and chatter wherever she
went. Stormi became the news so much that I ended up writing a piece in
the series about the villagers' reaction to her.

Bringing my mother back to China, in contrast, dissolved the invisible
line separating family from outsiders. Living with relatives also hastened
the demise of pretense. Relatives were instant sources, ordinary Chinese
whose lives reflected certain generalities about urban and rural life in
China. In cities they represented crowded living, curiosity about the West,
a keen awareness of politics and such new appliances as television sets
and VCRs. In the countryside they told stories through their backbreaking
agricultural labor, meals, laundry, and methods of earning extra income,
such as raising pigs and silkworms. The general attitude I found in the village was one of intense interest in politics only as it directly affected daily
living. More often, peasants adopted a powerless and fatalistic stance toward life.

Observing and living the intimate details of everyday life took the
place of reliance on official sources. Stormi and I rode the buses, went gro-
cery shopping at daybreak, gathered for a family meal on National Day
and, later, rode in an old sedan reserved for retired military cadres to take
in the festivities around Tiananmen Square. We took turns feeding the
kitchen fire with dried rice stalks while my aunt cooked. A cousin talked
to me about her abortion while we strolled through Beijing streets; another cousin pumped me for details about living in America late at night.
A third cousin washed clothes by hand despite owning what was still seldom seen in homes, a washing machine. Yet another related her dreamy
future of a husband, a kind mother-in-law, and a roomful of new furni-
ture.

Emotional Attachments

Being a Chinese-American meant that my status as a journalist was only
one of several roles I filled while in China. In fact, my relatives tended to
let my professional role linger in the background. They saw me as one of
them, and talked freely. In the United States I always worked on the premise that everything said to me after I identified myself as a reporter was
usable and quotable. But that would have been impossible and unfair to
my Chinese relatives. As an adopted family member I was privy to certain
information, but also implicitly responsible for the future well-being of
sources and knowing what could not go on the record.

Aside from gingerly treating their tales of suffering and unfavorable
opinions that could be politically sensitive, I also had to consider the loss
of face caused by revealing their naiveté. A cousin in the countryside

asked, as we stared into a starry sky and listened to the chirping of the cicadas, if I saw the same moon and stars as she did. It was a telling anecdote that illustrated the simplicity of country life and the sheltered existence of this teenager whose only plan for the future was to marry a tractor driver from the adjacent village. Would recalling this make my cousin look unreasonably stupid to an American audience? I used the anecdote because it both revealed something interesting about her life and provided a glimpse of peasant life in general.

Naturally, I was emotionally attached to my relatives, all of whom I met for the first time. I also felt an unexpected bond with places I visited. When I realized that my father and generations of other ancestors probably saw the same horizon in Dai Village, noticed how much a cousin and I looked alike, and saw my 85 year-old grandmother with bound feet, I felt grounded. Although I did not write about these experiences and the emotions they provoked, I later wished that I had let them become a natural, powerful force in my stories. Instead, I worked at staying as detached as a foreign journalist could be, although I was not always successful.

Different Lenses

It was difficult for me to evaluate how my "Chineseness" colored specific perceptions and my news judgment. But it did play a role. Stormi's presence provided me with a different lens for viewing China. She was sometimes preoccupied with a China that I took for granted, or at least did not see fit to emphasize.

By U.S. standards, China was poor, dirty, crowded, and backward, and life was harsh. People cleared their throats and spit on city streets, and apartment stairways were often slick and shiny with mucous. Most homes did not have flush toilets; nearly all lacked running hot water. Littering was rampant and environmental consciousness virtually nonexistent. All this was news and presented a life dramatically different from ours in the United States. It made compelling photos and copy. It also fit an American definition of news: conflicts and negative or unusual events or people. But to Chinese, many of the conditions were accepted daily inconveniences. Emphasizing them would represent the imposition of a Western judgment, while ignoring the contrasts would result in an incomplete portrayal of Chinese life. In the end, I tried to express aspects of China as they occurred in the natural course of events—such as when my cousin pointed out the fine for spitting or realizing the absurdity of having electricity come on in the village at 10 p.m. when we were already in bed—rather than concentrating on them out of context.

At times I was simply blind to some elements that a non-Chinese might find newsworthy. My closeness to the language made me somewhat insensitive to linguistic curiosities and comparative insights that would appeal to a U.S. audience. I originally treated the attention that Stormi received as a nuisance and recurring hurdle every place we went. Only after returning and pouring out my experience to colleagues and editors did I discover the story. The same was true about my relatives' perceptions of the West, snippets from different conversations that I later assembled into a story. Because of my non-religious upbringing, I neglected to pay attention to the influence of religion in China. In hindsight, given the large number of churchgoers in Minnesota, I should have anticipated the questions about religion that several readers raised after my series ran.

AFTER THE TIANANMEN CRACKDOWN

In 1989 I took the very Western concept of democracy as my framework to talk about life and how it had changed in four years, especially after the Tiananmen massacre on 4 June. I set out to determine what was meant by democracy and freedom, two words loaded with American appeal but lacking in Chinese contexts. Because so many stories had already been written about how China was becoming more like America, my series had a natural peg to show how that process was taking place, or failing to take place. Again, what restricted foreign correspondents in Beijing heightened the value of my strengths.

Four months after Chinese troops opened fire on Chinese citizens, fear was pervasive in Beijing. When I mentioned Tiananmen Square in Beijing, people lowered their voices or rolled up the cab window and did not want to be identified by their real name. They talked, though, about changes and unsettling times: abused women who wanted to divorce their husbands; a college-educated architect who wanted job satisfaction; an industrious bar manager who used incentives, such as field trips and birthday parties, to keep workers happy; and a CCP member who lamented that Party membership was no longer the key to climbing the political ladder.

Less casual and more private sources, however, could be seen with me without fearing repercussions. My strongest endorsement came from Zhang Yalai, whom I contacted through a mutual acquaintance upon arrival in Beijing. I had not seen any direct interviews of victims until that time. Zhang, who held a graduate degree from the University of Minnesota, pedaled out on his bike on the night of 3 June and was shot by the marching troops, and could thus verify that shooting was heaviest outside the Square, something widely believed by Chinese but little known in the West. He described the kindness of a stranger, a skinny youth who later left the hospital wearing clothes soaked in Zhang's blood and was being investigated at the time of our interview. He told me later that he agreed to my interview because I was Chinese and my presence would not arouse the suspicion of elderly ladies who kept watch at his apartment's entrance. I protected Zhang's identity by not revealing the full details of his background until after he arrived in Minneapolis in 1992.

CONCLUSION

I sought to portray life in China as ordinary Chinese saw and experienced it. At the same time, my "lens" was colored by my immersion in Western culture and an acceptance of its journalistic principles. In 1985 and 1989 I wrote for a U.S. audience; more specifically, a Midwest audience. It was not always clear to me which values I discarded, kept, or blended together. More common in the reporting process were feelings of ambivalence and sometimes contradiction—intensified all the more by the emotional ties I felt toward my relatives and my people.

I never implied, however, that the relatives I wrote about in 1985 exemplified *all* Chinese families, or that the voices in 1989 typified all peasants, workers, and children. Journalism can never achieve so panoramic a view of life. Nor can it portray subjects of stories as the only true images of the groups to which they belong. By the same token, no journalist brings the "right" set of values or perspectives to stories. While certain standards mark the craft, the objective yardstick for measuring the assumptions that we all bring to bear on stories is more elusive.

During both trips I experienced my roles as an insider and an outsider in flux. While I found it increasingly difficult to maintain a professional detachment, my awareness of differences between me and local Chinese grew. This constant push and pull relationship is one that I suspect I will always carry with me in reporting about China.

NOTES

1. Norman Fu, "Reporting on China from Washington: Some Observations and Reflections," in Chin-Chuan Lee (ed.), *Voices of China: The Interplay of Politics and Journalism* (New York: Guilford Press, 1990).

2. Chin-Chuan Lee, "Mass Media: Of China, About China," Ibid., pp. 27–29.

3. I was born in Taiwan and emigrated to the United States when I was nine years old. Growing up in Santa Barbara, I spoke and read Chinese at home. At the University of California-Berkeley, I majored in political science and Asian studies, concentrating on modern Chinese history. I later received a master's degree from the School of Journalism at the University of Missouri-Columbia.

4. Robert K. Merton, "Insiders and Outsiders: A Chapter in the Sociology of Knowledge," *American Journal of Sociology* 77 (1972): 9–47.

5. Edgar Snow, *Red Star Over China* (New York: Random House, 1938).

6. Edward L. Farmer, "Sifting Truth From Facts: The Reporter as Interpreter of China," in Lee, *Voices of China*, p. 250.

7. John Fraser, *The Chinese—Portrait of a People* (New York: Simon and Schuster, 1980), p. 38.

8. Frank Ching, "China's Second Opening to the West," in Lee, *Voices of China*, pp. 277–87.

9. Jay and Linda Mathews, *One Billion—A China Chronicle* (New York: Harper and Row, 1983).

10. Ibid., pp. 26–27.

11. Amanda Bennett, "American Reporters in China: Romantics and Cynics," in Lee, *Voices of China*, pp. 270, 273.

12. Dan Southerland, "Dealing With Sources" (Paper presented at conference, Voices of China: Ambiguities and Contradictions in China Reporting and Scholarship, Minneapolis, Minnesota, 4–6 October, 1991). During earlier times when the Chinese government restricted the movement of foreign journalists more severely, Fox Butterfield, a former *New York Times* reporter in China, hired Jan Wong, a Chinese-Canadian who dressed and talked like a native Chinese, to interview political dissidents and broaden his contacts among ordinary Chinese. Fox Butterfield, *China: Alive in the Bitter Sea* (New York: Bantam, 1983), pp. 33–34. This arrangement achieved some success: Once Wong was able to mingle with disgruntled students and workers during a demonstration and even made friends with the protesters. Ibid., p. 287.

16

THE VOICE OF AMERICA AND CHINA

David Hess

In 1980 one of my friends in Shanghai told me that, as the Cultural Revolution closed in on him and his family, he took his 13-year-old son aside and said, "Son, tomorrow the Red Guards will arrest me and I may never see you again. I will never be able to care for your education as a good father should. Take this shortwave radio, and whatever happens, keep it with you. Listen to the Voice of America and learn English. It is the only education available in China now." The son complied and was accepted to a university on the basis of his command of English when nationwide entrance exams were held in 1977. The father was rehabilitated at the end of the Cultural Revolution and by 1980 held an influential position in the Party. He completed his story with tears in his eyes, "God bless the Voice of America."

The effectiveness of the VOA in China and the working environment at the VOA's Chinese Branch in Washington is somewhat of a contradiction. A colleague once described the Chinese Branch as an organization which combined 3,000 years of Chinese obfuscation with the lethargy of the U.S. Civil Service system to produce a totally unmanageable institution. Like the legendary junkyard dog, it could be neither cajoled nor kicked into submission. The only sure thing was that it would bite you when your back was turned. Traditionally, a Foreign Service Officer from the U.S. State Department was the Branch Chief, but the Chinese Branch's reputation seemed to deter career-minded officers.

My background was unusual in that I had worked as a professional broadcaster for ten years before joining the Foreign Service, and six of those years were spent in Taiwan. While in Washington for Junior Foreign Service Officer training, I paid several calls on the Chinese Branch, because I actually looked forward to sometime serving as Branch Chief. With that in mind, I was a constant listener while I served in Hong Kong, Kuala Lumpur, Beijing, Shanghai, and Taipei. While living in Beijing and

Shanghai (1980–1984) I asked just about everyone I met if they listened to the VOA (most did), and if so I inquired about their favorite program (news) and least favorite program (book reviews, since they could not buy the books). I had decided to retire by 1990, so my final assignment (1988–1990) was to be Washington, D.C. I asked to be chief of the Chinese Branch and worked in that capacity from September 1988 until I retired in 1990. This chapter represents my personal view of events during that time, not those of the U.S. Government. In attempting to understand the response of the VOA's Chinese Branch to the Tiananmen crisis, we must consider questions of organizational structure, staffing, programming, policy, and intelligence analysis.

ORGANIZATION

The VOA's Programming Division includes all of the language services as well as central news and feature sections. According to VOA guidelines, all news used by the language services must originate in the central news section and is only translated by the services. There are supposed to be enough stories on the wire at any time to give the language services the latitude to select news relevant to its audience. Thus, in the Chinese Branch we would carry almost all the regional news from Asia at the expense of less important stories from Africa, Latin America, and other regions. Some feature material, such as science and education stories, was easily translated into Chinese, but material on political processes, customs, and culture required much additional information to make it understandable to our Chinese audience.

In September 1988 the VOA broadcast eight and a half hours a day in Mandarin and 30 minutes a day in Cantonese. Mandarin was broadcast from 6 a.m. to 10 a.m. and from 8 p.m to 12:30 a.m. Beijing time. Cantonese ran from 12:30 a.m. to 1 a.m. Our staff of around 40 full time professional broadcasters was divided into four sections. One section consisted of Mandarin announcers, news writers, and editors in the news section. Another section wrote regular features. Producers, who worked with both news and features, and Cantonese were the third and fourth sections, respectively.

In earlier years the staff had numbered 60, but government-wide cuts had reduced that number, increasing the work required from each staffer and reducing the total possible output. One result was that news personnel came in well before broadcast time to translate and edit the news, but had little energy left to update it during the broadcast block. If you heard the first newscast of a broadcast, it was pointless to continue listening for new developments.

The time difference between China and the United States required the news writers and editors working on the evening program (Beijing time) to start work at about 3 a.m. Washington time. Only one employee liked this shift. Most of the rest tried to avoid it, citing concerns such as transportation and the deleterious effect of such a schedule on their health and family life. The most effective way to get out of the hated night shift was to be transferred to the feature section, since feature writers worked normal five-day weeks. Night shift allergy combined with earlier staff cuts created a patchwork staffing pattern which might have someone writing news on the night shift one day and writing a feature the next two, followed by two days writing news on the day shift. Editors on both the day and night shifts not only had insufficient staff, they rarely had the same staff two days in a row.

The Chinese Branch had installed a computerized system for writing and editing. The romanized Chinese word would be typed in and the computer would generate the Chinese character. While it had been mandated that all staff would learn to use the new system, a number of the full-time feature writers claimed they could not and continued to write in longhand. Since all of the news was done on the computer and all of the news people had learned how to use it, one might be justified in suspecting that this learning disability was just another shield against the hated night shift.

In October 1988 I reorganized the news section into three teams. Each team had a supervisor and a fixed staff, and worked three months on days, three months on nights, and three months on a split shift. At the same time I introduced translation rate standards. For the first time it became possible to estimate how much news could be translated during a shift and compare that with how much was actually done. While it did not address the quality of translation, it was fine for volume, and we were at last able to identify slowpokes and invent incentives to increase their speed. Unsurprisingly, most staffers did not enjoy being held to such a standard.

PROGRAMMING

In September 1988 the Chinese Branch was heavy with features including: space; science; medicine; Asian politics; world politics; Hollywood; sightseeing in Washington D.C.; pop music; culture; literature; American drama; personalities in the news; world economics; and U.S.-China relations. Given adequate staff, most would have been worth doing, but since good features require four to eight times the staff effort of a similar volume of news, I decided to cut features and assign the "freed" personnel to news teams. "Freed" is in quotes because those affected felt just the opposite.

I was disturbed with how we dealt with political subjects. Sometimes a story would be taken from the central feature file, such as "Lincoln Frees the Slaves" or "Iowa and New Hampshire ... Bellwether Primary States." With the exception of specialists in American history and politics, few Chinese had the basic knowledge to fully comprehend the topics. There was (and is) a great need to explain the most basic aspects of U.S. concepts of democracy and human rights such as the role of the individual, rights of the majority and minority, and compromise. The Director of East Asian Broadcasting, Ivan Klecka, and I wrote an extensive proposal for a series that would explain the development of American democracy from a very basic cultural and historical level. The series would have been pitched at the knowledge level of a Chinese high school graduate and would have used common Chinese knowledge of history and human relations to describe American human and political relationships. Because the series would have required considerable research and even focus groups to assure that the message was getting across, we requested additional funds. The upper levels of the VOA and the United States Information Agency (USIA) liked the idea, but the money never materialized. Chinese Branch programming continued to be driven by reduced budgets and personnel ceilings.

As commercial American radio stations know, music is the cheapest way to fill air time. To fill the gaps created when we reduced features and transferred personnel to news teams, we introduced a daily, live pop music show (*Washington Express*). The program was directed at the 14- to 26-year-old audience that had made the Top 40 format the king of radio in the rest of the world. The music was interspersed with features focusing on Americans in the target age group. We made copyright arrangements with diverse magazines such as *Seventeen*, *Boy's Life*, and *Reader's Digest* so we could translate articles on everything from grooming and interpersonal relations to Westinghouse science scholars and young businesspeople. Although our broadcast covered three time zones, we instituted time hacks ("It's 23 minutes past the hour") and weather for about 20 key cities. Nothing on the program lasted longer than three minutes. It sounded like American radio.

English teaching remained a significant part of our programming. Two hours of our eight and a half hour daily schedule were devoted to it. The courses had been taped years ago and there was virtually no staff time involved in repeating them. We assumed that after one or two years of studying with the Chinese Branch's basic and intermediate courses, students would graduate to the VOA's Worldwide English broadcasts. Hundreds of listeners wrote to tell us this was so.

POLITICS AND LANGUAGE

Over the years the Chinese Branch had developed a novel pecking order. Feature writers were at the top because of their independence and normal working hours. They had also, at some point, convinced one or more Branch Chiefs that they were better, more creative writers than the poor souls left pulling news duty. The news editors came next because they could correct others' work. Next were news writers and translators, followed by the announcers. Producers came last. In the U.S. radio industry, the men and women on the air are at the top of the heap and make the most money. Personality is a large part of American broadcasting, even news; but at the Chinese Branch, the Chinese scholar (editor/writer) held sway. My experience in Taiwan and China indicates that this pecking order is traditional in Chinese broadcasting. It has left announcers with little power to edit the material they read and sounding more academic and less conversational. For a parallel, compare the writings of Henry James with those of Ernest Hemingway. Roughly, Chinese broadcasters sound more like James while Americans sound like Hemingway.

Broadcasting is different than written communication in that once the words go by, you cannot re-read them. Simple sentences and common words are the essence of good broadcasting. After discussions about making the Chinese Branch sound more like American radio, I allowed announcers a final edit for style. For some of the editors and writers, it was as though I had invited a large, unbathed hog into their homes. The ensuing war, which revolved around language and status, lasted throughout my tenure. It was not, moreover, the Branch's first language war.

An earlier conflict had been fought as U.S.-China relations warmed and we began to recruit broadcasters from China. Before that, most of our staff had come from Taiwan. Naturally, most from Taiwan chose to follow the Taiwan broadcast stylebook, while many from China followed their own. Both stylebooks were influenced by China's desire to unify language, and as a result were more restrictive than the living Chinese language. Unfortunately, they often chose different options, and this became the battlefield. Charges were extreme. "Not one of China's billion people will understand if you write it that way!" "No educated person would be caught dead with those words in his mouth." "He is a KMT agent!" "Commie spy!" These differences were put to an unquiet rest by relying on Chinese dictionaries compiled in China for usage, and editor/writer (and later announcer) discretion for structure.

Pronunciation was also a bone of contention because the Chinese Branch had held to the Beijing area accent standard so strongly over the years that it was difficult for people from other areas to get on the air. In U.S. broadcasting, standard pronunciation is important, but it takes a back seat to the ability to communicate and project an interesting or credible personality through the voice. As U.S. broadcasters know, the ability to communicate is far rarer than the ability to pronounce—the former tends to be a native talent while the latter may be improved through careful instruction. As we began recruiting air personnel based ability to communicate rather than just pronunciation, some staffers from both China and Taiwan objected on the grounds that Chinese radio placed pronunciation first. This division revealed a deeper issue: whether the Chinese Branch was an American or Chinese radio service. I felt that as an operation designed to inform Chinese about America, it was important to have the sound, news, and features representative of the best of American radio. A few staffers agreed, some disagreed, and others did not know what I was talking about.

PLANNING AHEAD

U.S. intelligence reports and classified documents played practically no role in Chinese Branch planning. I felt that it would be dangerous from both security and public image standpoints to base our programming decisions on a secret literature. In November and December 1988, however, it became apparent that groups of students in China were planning to make strong statements about the need for continuing political liberalization that would coincide with the 1989 anniversary of the May Fourth movement. Our sources for this were the Foreign Broadcast Information Service (FBIS) China extracts, the word of friends and associates returning from China, and the U.S. press. Friends told us that the Democracy Wall era taught the student planners to stress organization and discipline over raw enthusiasm. FBIS reports of regional conferences in China as the Party planned official May Fourth functions, partly designed to blunt the effects of the students' efforts, reflected the seriousness of the threat.

In December 1988 we began preparing special programs for the May Fourth anniversary. It was our intention to focus on both the historical importance and the current relevance of the movement's goals. The reminiscences of survivors from 1919 were mixed with comments from modern historians (Chinese and American) and activists such as Liu Binyan. While Liu's remarks were predictably extreme, the overall tenor of the two-part documentary was historical and evenhanded. We deliberately avoided being inflammatory.

We also began watching Soviet President Gorbachev's plans to visit China, and began a liaison with the VOA's Soviet Division toward arranging joint coverage of the visit. While the VOA's language services generally translate and broadcast reports originally compiled for central news in English, the language services are occasionally allowed to send their own reporters to cover special events. Cost, however, was a major factor in keeping this kind of coverage to a minimum. We proposed to send a reporter each from the Russian and Chinese Branches for the Gorbachev visit, and this was fortunately approved in time for us to apply for the visas well before the occupation of Tiananmen Square.

By February 1989 the great majority of the Chinese Branch's staff was working on news. This increased flexibility made it possible for us to respond to more opportunities for news interviews. For instance, when we found that Qin Benli, managing editor of Shanghai's *World Economic Herald*, would be in town for a few days, we were able to get an extensive interview with him on press freedom and China's economic development. Later that month when President Bush visited Beijing, we managed to send Chinese Branch reporter Chao Kelu along. In addition to getting an interview with Fang Lizhi shortly after he had been prevented from attending the president's dinner party, she spent a day at the *World Economic Herald* learning about the paper and developments in Shanghai. These were only a few of many such interviews done by the news teams that stretched the muscles of the new organization.

TIANANMEN

The VOA had a sister station relationship with Radio Beijing. In 1989 it was our turn to host a delegation from Beijing including the Director and Li Dan, the chief of the English Language Division. The delegation arrived in early April and visited commercial radio stations in New York and Tampa after a week of consultation in Washington. On the morning of the 14th Li Dan and I were guests on a rather wild morning drive show called the Q105 Morning Zoo in Tampa. After the host commented on a telephone exchange with a listener by remarking, "What an asshole!"—on the air—I asked Li if China would ever see such freewheeling radio. He answered that it would get better than it was at present, but he hoped it would never be that wild. We heard of Hu Yaobang's death on the following morning, and the delegation left for Los Angeles and Beijing as I flew back to Washington.

The students first appeared on Tiananmen Square on 17 April. Our central news correspondent, Al Pesson, had been on vacation in Hong Kong and was unable to find transportation back to Beijing. As a result, central news had to rely mostly on wire service reports. Because of the importance of the events, I requested and received permission to clip newspaper reports and editorials for translation and broadcast on our news commentary programs. Previously, each use of non-VOA material required the approval of the East Asia Division. We developed a hot line to get copyright clearance and after a week received it faster than we could translate the articles. This procedure lasted throughout my tenure in the Chinese Branch.

Two events on 26 April led me to believe that there was little likelihood of concessions from the authorities: the front page editorial in the *People's Daily*, "Take a Clear Stand to Oppose the Turmoil," and the firing of Qin Benli as editor of the *World Economic Herald*. The editorial's identification of those behind the occupation of Tiananmen Square as counter-revolutionaries clearly announced the authorities intention to extract a price for the turmoil. Qin's firing was the first salvo of a barrage that would silence the liberalizing press, and although he was optimistic that he would be reinstated, passing days added weight to pessimistic projections.

As the occupation of Tiananmen Square went into May, we used the increased flexibility of the news teams to do interviews reacting to events, plumbing the opinions of visiting Chinese, Chinese students, Chinese-Americans, China specialists, and ordinary Americans.

On 12 May the Chinese Branch's reporter for the Gorbachev visit, Betty Tseu, arrived in Beijing accompanied by a reporter from the Russian Branch. Only about 10% of her stories from then until her departure dealt with the Gorbachev visit. The rest was the turmoil of the democracy movement. She was on Tiananmen Square reporting the beginning of the hunger strike on 13 May. Because her reports were in Chinese, we could broadcast them within 30 minutes of reception in Washington if they came in while we were on the air. Betty recalls a strange feeling of participation as she heard her voice coming out of the loudspeakers set up by the demonstrators on the Square to amplify VOA broadcasts. Just identifying herself as the VOA reporter got her through impassable crowds and into the interview situations she was seeking.

On the evening of 18 May Li Peng met with student representatives in the Great Hall of the People for the famous televised debate. One could sense Li's fury as Wuer Kaixi publicly trashed him. The shambles of the Gorbachev visit and the televised mockery of Li Peng further led us to believe that the Tiananmen incident would end violently.

The regime imposed martial law on 20 May and Betty returned to Beijing the next day, the same day Chinese authorities began jamming VOA Chinese language broadcasts. VOA English broadcasts, however, were not jammed. Taxis disappeared in Beijing with the advent of martial law, so Betty rented a bicycle and continued reporting. Although martial law regulations made any kind of responsible reporting illegal, they were uniformly ignored by the international press and what appeared to be a majority of Beijing's population.

Betty began receiving threats by telephone and from official-looking men in the lobby of her hotel. At one point, she was informed by telephone of an opportunity to interview Wang Dan, one of the student leaders, some distance from the Square. Because of earlier warnings and the chance of a provocation, I advised her to meet Wang only in a public place and not go to the appointed location. Later, she found that he had been on the Square all along and was unaware of any interview offer. With this development, we decided that the danger to Betty dictated that we reduce her visibility. Her reports were still filed by phone, but we transcribed them and used the voice of an announcer in Washington. Betty was not identified. On 26 May I told Betty to leave China because of the worsening situation. She was naturally reluctant, because this was the biggest story she had ever covered. I repeated the order the next day, and she finally made it out on 28 May.

On 29 May the students announced their intention to stay on the Square until the National People's Congress Standing Committee meeting scheduled for 20 June. This added further weight to our pessimistic view of the outcome, and when troops were moved to strategic points around the city on 2 June it appeared the violence would begin that weekend. At the East Asian Division staff meeting on the morning of 2 June, I informed the other language services that the weekend would probably be violent and that extra news staff should be laid on to cover fast-breaking events. The same message was passed to central news. In the Chinese Branch, we made sure that all news teams were fully staffed for the weekend and that the remaining feature writers were available for news duty.

The shooting began late Saturday morning (3 June) (Washington time). Our Mandarin broadcast was scheduled to end at 12:30 p.m. Washington time, which was 12:30 a.m. Beijing time. The Cantonese broadcast was to begin at 12:30 a.m. and run for 30 minutes, but because the Mandarin audience was so much larger, I canceled Cantonese and continued with Mandarin. By 6 p.m. Saturday (6:00 a.m. Beijing time, 4 June) we had so much news that we began cancelling feature programs and extending news and commentary into those time slots.

On 4 June, after consultation with the director of the VOA and the Engineering Division, we increased our Mandarin broadcast hours from 8 and one-half to 11, and by the 6 p.m. broadcast dropped all feature programs and went to an all-news format. Ten minutes of news on the hour and half hour was followed by 20 minutes of correspondent reports and commentary. The commentary was made up of interviews with Chinese and Americans, news analysis, and editorials from the American press. None of this commentary was in the nature of a VOA editorial. All sources were clearly identified.

The Chinese Branch staff, which had fought the increase of news coverage and news teams, had resisted the reduction of features, and had dragged its feet on the institution of a broadcast Chinese language suddenly pulled together in a magnificent demonstration of teamwork and self-sacrifice. Many came in on their days off; some worked up to 24 hours straight. Their increased contribution made it possible to do things that would not have been imaginable under normal circumstances. Every half hour saw newscasts updated on the basis of the fast-paced events rather than how many people were normally scheduled for a shift. We were able to cover almost all of the demonstrations in the Washington area protesting the massacre. We were also able to use the telephone to bring a new dimension to our coverage.

In 1988, before my arrival, the Chinese Branch ran its first experiment with a call-in show. The topic was medical care and the guests were two American doctors who spoke Chinese. Listeners were invited to phone collect to a number we broadcast and ask our guests questions about American medical care and practice. Hundreds called. We ran another call-in show on the morning after the 1988 U.S. elections, with guests representing the press, academe, and the Republican Party (because it had won the presidency the night before). On 4 June we got management permission to open up the collect line again, asking callers to tell us how they were receiving the VOA's signal, now that it was being jammed. We wondered, in light of martial law, if the telephone operators in China would put the calls through. One of the first calls came from Shanghai, where the operator said, "Now don't hang up after this first call. There are three more waiting and they have *so* much to tell you!"

Most of our callers heard our signal clearly, but called primarily to tell us what was happening in their part of China or to bless us as one of the only news sources reporting the China story. When they reported local events, we asked if we could use their taped voices on the air. Most said yes. Because VOA news policy requires two sources for a story, however, we felt that one or more calls from an area could only be counted as a single source. For instance, we had a call reporting that students had blocked the strategic bridge across the Yangtze River at Wuhan. We sat on the story for six hours until a wire service confirmed it. Then we ran the tape.

To support the increase in our broadcast hours from 8 and one-half to 11 hours, VOA management agreed on 5 June that our personnel ceiling could expand from 41 to 50, and we would be allowed to hire 10 to 15 temporary workers to cover the emergency. I pointed out that China would soon close as a news source. It was important for the Chinese Branch to have part-time reporters in other Asian capitals to maintain our emphasis on the news. Management agreed to let us hire stringers in Tokyo, Seoul, Taipei, Hong Kong, Manila, Jakarta, Bangkok, Kuala Lumpur, and Singapore. In addition, it was important to report U.S. reaction to Chinese events, and I requested and received permission for the Chinese Branch to continue unrestricted use of articles from the U.S. press on China.

In the heat of reporting the chaos of Tiananmen, mistakes were inevitable. The number of people reported killed and wounded grew from tens to thousands within 24 hours. The VOA tried to verify the numbers, and as a result was always two to six hours behind CNN and the U.S. TV networks. Still, our reports climbed into the thousands before settling back to around 700, which today remains the most reliable figure. On 5 June, we received a call from Hangzhou reporting that students had lowered the flag over the Provincial Headquarters to half mast and that local labor unions had contributed more than 100,000 *renminbi* to the students' cause. Months later, the young man who had phoned in the report was identified by the Chinese police, arrested, and sentenced to prison. It was my responsibility to assure that all reports for broadcast had two sources. When we heard of the Hangzhou caller's arrest, I reviewed our records from 5 June and could not find the second source. I recalled that there was a second source, but its absence in the record left me with the grinding doubt that my failure may have contributed to the young man's imprisonment.

Other Chinese who spoke to foreign reporters suffered. Via satellite, ABC TV fed the scene of a man telling a crowd that 20,000 had been killed in Beijing. ABC did not air the footage, but the Chinese police taped the feed and subsequently sent the man to jail. Clearly, the Chinese authorities regarded the two incidents as treason: Chinese citizens conspiring with a foreign power to injure the state. For most Americans, it was a case of people exercising their inalienable right of free speech.

Repeating news reported by the VOA was also a crime. Agence France Press reported that the *Liaoning Legal Daily* had disclosed the arrest of Liu Chengwu. On 7 June Liu put a radio tuned to the VOA outside his mother's restaurant in Shenyang. The paper said many people stopped to listen and traffic was seriously disrupted. Liu was accused of openly propagating reactionary words. On 20 November the *Sichuan Daily* reported the cracking of a counter-revolutionary propaganda and incitement case. "For many years, Pu Yong had listened to the VOA, read reactionary publications and worshiped the capitalist social system practiced in Western countries ... On the nights of 29 and 30 October, after listening to the VOA, which spread the rumor that a greater turmoil would break out in China during China's National Day period, Pu Yong secretly wrote more than 400 counter-revolutionary leaflets ..." There were many similar cases.

Emotions in the Chinese Branch ran very high against the Chinese authorities. On 5 and 6 June, when Hong Kong rumors (carried on CNN) reported Deng Xiaoping was dying of cancer and Li Peng had been wounded in an assassination attempt, great cheers went up in the newsroom. Even though several TV networks reported these stories, we did not, because we found no source other than the Hong Kong rumor. Still, these were major rumors in the ears of our audience and could not be ignored. Finally, we phoned Al Pesson, the VOA's correspondent in Beijing, and asked him if he could get an official reaction from the Foreign Ministry. When they denied the rumors, we reported the denials.

Some staff members were unable to contain their emotions. While covering a demonstration outside the Chinese Embassy in Washington, one staffer, voice trembling with rage, asked demonstrators questions like "What do you think of beasts who murder their own children?" To the best of my knowledge, we caught all of these understandable excesses before they aired.

On 14 June the Chinese authorities gave Al Pesson 72 hours to leave. He was accused of illegal news gathering, distorting facts, spreading rumors, and instigating turmoil. He was replaced by Mark Hopkins, who had been our Beijing correspondent until 1988, when he was transferred to Boston. Mark managed to stay in Beijing until 8 July, when he too was thrown out for "distorting facts" and "instigating propaganda." The VOA's central news stringer, Hedi Chay, managed to hold on until 1990, when the authorities allowed us to send in another full time correspondent.

TECHNICAL ISSUES AND TELEVISION

For the past decade or so, all of our Chinese language broadcasts were sent by satellite to VOA transmitters in the Philippines and broadcast from there. Asian language services competed for time and frequencies from the Philippine facility. When jamming began on 21 May, the VOA's Engineering Division tracked its effectiveness and gave us additional frequencies with which to get through. The competition for transmitter time turned Engineering's juggling for additional hours after 4 June into a world class act.

The Engineering Division had developed a wealth of experience overcoming jamming in the Soviet Union which they brought to bear in China. Previously, all of our Chinese language broadcasts were on shortwave. After 4 June we opened up with a million-watt medium wave transmitter that had been used exclusively for Southeast Asia. This was so powerful, one engineer joked, that in some parts of China radios would not be necessary—just the fillings in your teeth would be enough to pick up the signal.

Additional shortwave frequencies were allocated for each broadcast, making it more difficult to block us out completely. Subsequent reports indicated that signal quality had deteriorated on some frequencies because of the jamming, but that we could be understood in almost all of our previous broadcasting region. When we changed from a jammed frequency to a new one, jamming would continue on the old frequency for a week to ten days before moving to the new frequency. One wag commented, "Gee, China has a civil service, too."

Television was another response to jamming. We were aware that China had more than 2,000 satellite dishes capable of taking down TV transmissions. On 6 June we set up television cameras in one of the VOA's big studios and began feeding the sound and picture of our broadcasts via satellite. Promotional messages sent over the radio told operators how to tune us in. Some of our staff worried that sending their picture to China might adversely affect relatives there, so we occasionally just broadcast the picture of a VOA logo in Chinese with sound.

STAFFING

Budget cuts put VOA management in the impossible position of cutting staff while maintaining all its functions. Almost all parts of the VOA had seen staff cuts in the preceding three years. As Chinese Branch numbers had gone from 55 to 41, there had been no perceived need to do any staff recruiting. Bringing on new staff was a laborious process involving advertising, applications, air checks, written exams, security investigations, and interviews. It took six months to a year to hire a candidate.

By October 1988 we expected retirements over the next few years. It is a sad fact of bureaucratic life that when staff ceilings are being cut, vacancies open for longer than a month often lead management to cut the position, regardless of its importance to the mission. It is easier to abolish an unfilled position than to fire someone. Since we were already understaffed, retirements could have devastated us, unless we had already selected candidates to fill the vacancies. That fall we began aggressively recruiting new staff and developed a ranked list of candidates. Before Tiananmen we were able to replace several retirees before their positions were axed.

With Tiananmen, we were inundated with job applications and had to review hundreds of tapes and written exams to maintain a list of candidates. While we could not offer all qualified candidates a permanent position, we had been authorized to bring on temporary help and used the list of candidates for this. We knew that VOA management would have to take personnel slots from other parts of the VOA when they raised our ceiling to 50 as a result of Tiananmen. The pain that such a shift of resources would cause hastened our search for candidates to fill the new positions, and we managed to fill five before VOA management reneged on the deal.

Because the new staff required training, it was usually one to three months before they could pull their weight. So instead of bringing immediate relief during the crisis, the new staff—though enthusiastic—were an additional burden for our veterans.

WINDING DOWN

The intensity with which the staff met the Tiananmen crisis could not be maintained indefinitely. As we approached the end of June, signs of exhaustion were evident. Although we increased our broadcast hours to 12 on 25 June, we reintroduced two hours of English teaching a day, which helped lighten the load. We also began planning how we would sound after the around-the-clock news emphasis of the crisis diminished. We came up with the following ideas for features that reflected the new understanding of our audience gained from the Tiananmen experience:

The Entrepreneur   Catering to the hugely expanded interest in small business, this program was pegged to those who wanted to make money on their own. Material was used from the Small Business Administration and every outside source we could tap. We joined the Soviet Division in appealing to central features to develop programs in this area we both could use.

Labor in America   Noting the unexpected participation of Chinese labor in the democracy movement, we designed this program to introduce the role and history of U.S. labor unions.

Media in America   After 10 June the Chinese authorities mounted a campaign attacking the VOA. This program was designed to describe American practice in news gathering and reporting.

Washington Express   This was the music program we had initiated in late 1988. As a departure, one of the two MCs was a European-American for whom Chinese was a second language.

Our staffing pattern changed during this period. There was no longer a feature section; almost everyone was on a news team. Each team was responsible for one of the above features in addition to its news duties. *Washington Express* was done by three people who worked full time on it, and we had a two person unit working on recruiting, training, and quality control. We eventually brought back other features, such as *Personalities in the News*, but production responsibility remained with the news teams.

In the middle of June the telephone calls from China started to drop off as the authorities gained control of the operators and exchanges. After a flurry of hate calls attacking the role of the VOA, we stopped accepting collect calls.

As news from China was strangled by the authorities, the Chinese Branch increasingly relied on our new stringers in Asia, and on editorials and analysis from the U.S. press. When the Scowcroft mission was revealed, U.S. editorial opinion lined up 80-85% against the president's

China policy. We translated and broadcast everything we could lay our hands on.

Although we broadcast editorials accusing the president of kowtowing to the butchers of Beijing, we only once received any suggestion that we alter our policy of giving our listeners full knowledge of U.S. editorial opinion about China. One middle-level diplomat in our embassy in Beijing cabled to suggest that we "balance" our coverage of editorial opinion to always show that at least some writers approved of the president's policy. We re-read the VOA charter and ignored the suggestion.[1]

On 10 June the media in China, now under the firm control of the authorities, began a concerted attack on the VOA. It started with claims that the VOA was spreading rumors and expanded into charges that these rumors were part of a 40-year-old plot. The *Guangming Daily* put it succinctly in an 8 September article with the catchy title "Unswervingly Train and Bring up Successors to the Cause of Revolution." "From Dulles in the 1950s to Brzezinski in the 1980s, they all dreamed of winning an easy battle, pinning their hopes on the third and fourth generation of Chinese, and encouraging them to set up a capitalist country through internal evolution. During the recent storm, reactionary forces abroad gave counsel to, incited, and supported a very small number of diehard advocates of bourgeois liberalization in openly carrying out counter-revolutionary demagogy and crime to topple the government in a vain attempt to establish a bourgeois republic. The VOA even took the lead in violating basic journalistic ethics, trying its utmost to stir up trouble and spread rumor out of a desire to see China plunged into chaos ..." These attacks continued off and on into the spring of 1990.

POLICY

As stated in its charter, the VOA's mission included the presentation of U.S. policies.[2] Part of this presentation was done in the news, when covering statements of U.S. policymakers. In a similar vein, we carried newsworthy policy statements by leaders from all over the world, including China. Also, in each broadcast block we carried a five-minute editorial, clearly identified front and back as an editorial reflecting the policy of the U.S. Government. I am unaware of any Chinese complaints about VOA editorials during the crisis. It was our news the authorities hated. The "31 Rumors" we were accused of spreading were all news reports.

Lastly, we may ask whether the VOA actively worked to subvert the Communist Party and the Government of the People's Republic of China. The answer is yes and no. No, there was no policy seeking those ends. The only policy discussions I had with VOA management and central news concerned the importance of maintaining objectivity and the news policy mentioned above. While the USIA and the State Department took an interest in what we were broadcasting, they did not instruct us regarding content. We never heard a word from the White House, even during the heat of the editorial comments following the Scowcroft mission when we might have been accused of Bush-bashing.

The problem is that China in its present state is allergic to objective news reporting from any source. One friend describes China as a sixteenth-century culture governed by a nineteenth-century system in the presence of a small, unhappy minority that threatens to drag the whole mess into the twenty-first-century. The resulting contradictions make it almost impossible for a totalitarian system such as China's to govern without controlling and pre-shaping the information available to society. Introduce objective news reporting and a variety of views, and people begin to think and act for themselves. Although subversive, this is not a VOA plot, just human nature.

CONCLUSION

As we entered the winter of 1989 everyone's focus shifted away from China to Eastern Europe. Letters from and contacts with our audience in China showed intense interest in those developments and we covered them in depth, just as the VOA's Eastern European and Soviet language services gave full coverage to Tiananmen. I was heartened by a report from Czechoslovakia that in early negotiations between the government and reformers, Gustav Husak asked that the transition go peacefully and not end up like Tiananmen. It did so, and I have wondered whether the terrible Chinese example did not save thousands of lives in the Soviet Union and Eastern Europe.

As my term at the VOA wound down in 1990 I was again involved with all the issues that I started with: programming, news, language, and staffing. Our Chinese Branch heroes of Tiananmen had returned to their more traditional work style. In a sense, we all looked forward to my retirement. As I cleaned out my desk, one memento stood out as a symbol for those chaotic months. Each of us in the Branch had received the USIA Director's Award for Superior Achievement. It read:

> For extraordinary dedication, teamwork, personal sacrifice and sustained superlative professionalism under the most difficult circumstances in holding the mirror of truth before the Chinese people and their leaders during China's quest for Democracy.

NOTES

1. Throughout my tenure at the Voice, the Chinese Branch was run according to the VOA charter, which states:

a. VOA will serve as a consistently reliable and authoritative source of news. VOA news will be accurate, objective, and comprehensive.

b. VOA will represent America, not any single segment of American Society, and will therefore present a balanced and comprehensive projection of significant American thoughts and institutions.

c. VOA will present the policies of the United States clearly and effectively, and will also present responsible discussion and opinion on these policies.

2. Ibid.

17

U.S. MEDIA COVERAGE OF THE CULTURAL REVOLUTION: A POSTSCRIPT

Hsiao Ching-chang and Yang Mei-rong

The Chinese Communist Party (CCP) officially declared the Cultural Revolution a disaster in June 1981, but today's hardline leaders, many of whom were victims of that experience, have used rhetoric reminiscent of that period in their fight against "peaceful evolution." Moreover, despite the cursory treatment of many Chinese who simply describe the Cultural Revolution as "ten wasted years," the consequences of Mao's radical political and social experiment are still felt. The Cultural Revolution—a period of intense xenophobia in China—did not go unnoticed by the outside world, including the international media.

An outsider's perspective of localized phenomena is often valued merely because her removed position lends "objectivity" to her analysis. The broad purview of an outsider can recognize the dimensions of the forest while insiders get lost among the trees. Our analysis in this chapter, however, shows that journalists allowed into China after the height of the Cultural Revolution did not necessarily render a more reliable portrait of China than those who had to observe China from the outside. Analysis done from a distance—the only analysis possible for most foreign journalists during the height of the Cultural Revolution—dealt with available information in a more balanced manner, and did not as easily succumb to the romantic tendencies which clouded the vision of more recent China-watchers.

This review focuses on two kinds of U.S. publications. The first category encompasses mainstream publications which have a large circulation—an indication of their access to the public both directly and through influence on other media sources. They are represented by the *New York Times* (circulation, 1,200,000) and the three largest newsweeklies: *Time* (4,100,000), *Newsweek* (3,200,000) and *U.S. News and World Report* (2,300,000). The other category is a selective, but not exhaustive, sample of opinion magazines representative of the ideological spectrum in the United States: *The Nation* (92,000), a liberal-left weekly; *The New Republic* (97,000), a moderately liberal weekly; and *National Review* (140,000), a conservative biweekly. The different political perspectives of these publications paint a coherent mosaic in their coverage of China.

Coverage of China is divided into three periods. The first period is marked by the most radical period of the Cultural Revolution (1966–1968) and concludes with the advent of "ping-pong diplomacy" in 1971. At this time, U.S. reporters largely relied on long-distance observation and analysis of China. The second period covers the "China Fever" period which included President Richard Nixon's visit to China in 1972 and represents the beginning of first-hand contact between the U.S. media and Communist China. Finally, the third period covers U.S. media treatment of China following the establishment of diplomatic liaison offices in both countries in 1973.

THE PERIOD OF LONG-DISTANCE OBSERVATION

Before President Nixon's visit in February 1972, China was closed to most foreigners and virtually all U.S. journalists. U.S. journalists had to rely on second-hand information, primarily from research institutes and government intelligence agencies—particularly the U.S. consulate in Hong Kong—that relied on official and unofficial Chinese sources. Even though none of the sinologists—many of whom were Chinese-born children of U.S. missionaries—had been to mainland China since 1949, U.S. journalists considered the quality of their information "as good as, or even a little better, than any that Beijing's leaders have themselves."[1] *Time* claimed that the United States knew more about China than did any other nation "with the possible exception of the Soviet Union," an assessment shared by some U.S. China experts.[2]

Barred from entry into China, the U.S. media also drew upon the work of the few non-U.S. correspondents based in Beijing, including Canadian and Japanese reporters. These colleagues complained of the difficulty of covering China, typified by a Canadian reporter's remark that getting information from Chinese government spokespersons was like "trying to get blood out of stone."[3] Likewise, a Japanese editor groaned that covering Beijing was like being "thrown into a burning city without a police or fire department to give you the facts."[4]

Despite a number of scholarly and intelligence sources available to U.S journalists, one crucial deficiency remained: they could not cover the news directly. As *The Nation* noted:

> Vital dimensions of insight and understanding are lost when direct observation is lacking. A team of scholars pouring over documents in a research in-

stitute, interviewing persons who have visited China, reading transcripts of radio programs and studying pronouncements of the Chinese Communist Party can no doubt piece together a fairly coherent picture of what is happening. But there is no substitute for on-the-spot, continuous, day-to-day observation.[5]

The absence of direct contact meant that U.S. reporters could only speculate about China's leadership, its government organizations, and its policy intentions. Some of these speculations were rather accurate, while others were misleading. The Chinese press, meanwhile, was not allowed to speculate.

The Beginning of the Cultural Revolution

Considering the CCP's longterm obsession with secrecy, including the process of high-level decision making, the long-distance observations of U.S. press coverage of the Cultural Revolution benefited from a dispassionate stance, but inaccessibilty to detail led to some inaccurate conclusions. In mid-February 1966, when the average Chinese was unaware that a unprecedented political movement was on the horizon, the *New York Times* reported that the famous writers Tian Han and Wu Han were being attacked as part of a "rectification drive" within the literary world "personally directed by Mao Zedong." Soon after this, *Time* explained in greater detail that

[a]s China's reputation in the outer world slides, its internal policies are hardening and its struggles to erase revisionist tendencies increasing. The army has been singled out for stepped-up ideological indoctrination, but the campaign is much broader. Mao Zedong recently banished 160,000 artists and writers to the boondocks "to remold their thinking." Vicious attacks have just been launched on two top Chinese communist writers, Playwright Tian Han, 66, who wrote the Red Chinese national anthem, and Historian Wu Han, 56, the former vice mayor of Beijing.[6]

The U.S. press picked up on the emphasis the CCP had traditionally placed on the role of the seizure of power in a revolution, but was unable to shed light on the origins of the present power struggle, identify the actors, or describe the process in more than a general way. As *Newsweek* noted, "Trying to follow the course of a power struggle in a Communist state is like watching half a dozen men wrestle under a rug: it is possible to detect that a fight is going on and even that somebody is having his leg twisted, but until the rug is lifted it is impossible to tell who is on top."[7]

Initially, the U.S. press speculated on Mao's long absence from the political scene as a sign of serious illness and an acute power struggle over his succession. In March the *New York Times* reported that Mao had not been seen in public for four months, and in May said Hong Kong press reports indicated that the Chairman was recuperating from heart troubles.[8] Similarly, *Newsweek* reported that Mao had been out of sight for more than five and a half months and used China's denials about Mao's health to reinforce the magazine's conclusion that he was "indeed seriously incapacitated."[9]

Time soon followed suit. "At 72, Mao is ailing and overweight, smokes two packs of cigarettes a day, and suffers either from Parkinson's disease or the symptomatically similar aftereffects of a cerebral hemorrhage," the magazine said, "He is also believed to have a liver ailment." In a 1965 interview with U.S. journalist Edgar Snow, Mao wryly said he was "getting ready to see God very soon."[10] This speculation continued until 25 July, when Chinese newspapers ran an article with photos of Mao swimming across the Yangtze river on 16 July and looking quite healthy. The Western press was stunned.[11]

The heavy reliance on leaders' public appearances as a cipher for the turbulent and unfathomable political situation is understandable, considering the importance of personal power in China and the highly classified status of Chinese leaders' health. In this context, however, foreign correspondents can fall prey to misperception and deliberate manipulation. Chinese leaders prefer to remain silent in the face of such speculation and wait patiently for the chance to make the Western media look like rumor-mongers. Mao Zedong and Deng Xiaoping have both excelled at taking advantage of such propaganda opportunities.[12] Both were reported to have advocated not appearing in public as a strategic device to "confuse enemies," only surfacing when the appearance of "being led by the nose" was not possible.

From the beginning of China's rancorous power struggle, the U.S. press seemed to misinterpret who was fighting whom. In the early spring of 1966, the U.S. press correctly recognized the purges and criticisms within the intellectual community as the prelude to a major power struggle. When Beijing mayor Peng Zhen, long regarded by Westerners as a potential heir to Mao, was ousted, U.S. journalists noted that the myth of a monolithic Chinese leadership was shattered.[13] But who saw plotting behind the scenes? Who stripped Peng of his post? *Newsweek* postulated that Peng was ousted by then-Party General Secretary Deng Xiaoping, "a hard-nosed dogmatist of consuming ambition, in cahoots with Defense Minister Lin Biao."[14] The magazine claimed that the motives of Deng and Lin were "to eliminate rivals for ultimate succession to Mao's power"[15] and to shape Beijing's "government-party structure to their own uses."[16] While Deng may not have gotten along with Peng Zhen, nothing indicates that Deng collaborated with Lin Biao to purge Peng. Actually, Deng was then also a major purge target.

Although the U.S. media had speculated about the fate of President Liu Shaoqi, an ally of Deng Xiaoping, in August 1966, they did not seem to grasp that the struggle within China's leadership was actually between the Mao/Lin group and Liu until mid-December 1966.[17]

Other articles echoed official Chinese explanations that the Cultural Revolution was not about power struggles, purges, or a succession crisis, but a conflict between two different ideas about how to both prevent revisionism and arouse revolutionary enthusiasm. In this conception, the Cultural Revolution became an inevitable and normal continuation of the Chinese revolution. Typical of this perspective was Keith Buchanan's article in *The Nation*, claiming that after visiting China he had found himself "reaching conclusions drastically different from those offered by much of the Western press":

> The "purges" of intellectuals and of party officials that were making headlines in Hong Kong in late June appear as a normal continuation of the process of establishing a proletarian state that was formally initiated in 1949. In the years after 1949, the masses took over the economic bases of the country; they are now expanding the Socialist revolution into the cultural and ideological fields.[18]

Perhaps the sharpest assessment came several years later from none other than journalist Edgar Snow, the famous chronicler of Mao's civil war days. Snow's unique relationship with the Communist leadership enabled him to get first-hand information from the highest-level officials. Writing for *The New Republic* in 1971, Snow called the Mao-Liu struggle "one of the fundamental differences over means and ends in the fate of the great Chinese revolution itself":

> Liu Shaoqi stubbornly opposed Mao's first and primary point [regarding the Cultural Revolution]: "to overthrow those persons in authority who are taking the capitalist road, to criticize and repudiate the reactionary bourgeois academic authorities and the ideology of the bourgeoisie and all other exploiting classes, and to transform education, literature and art and all other parts of the superstructure not in correspondence with the socialist economic base." ... And thus on January 25, 1965, at a decisive meeting, and not before, Mao decided that Liu had to go. So I was told by a very responsible person. ... Why should the founder and acknowledged leader-genius of a powerful party deliberately set out to wreck it? That was not Mao's original intention; he aimed to remove only a handful from power. ... But by 1964 Mao had lost effective control over much of the Party hierarchy set up by his "successors," and also over the state administrative apparatus.[19]

Mao's Mobs and the Battle over the Red Throne

In addition to the theme of power struggles, some journalists focused on the Cultural Revolution as a way for China to prepare for war with the United States, or as an attempt to recreate "the spirit of Yanan."[20] Even at this early stage, however, many U.S. journalists had already concluded that the Cultural Revolution was a tragedy, contrary to China's official rhetoric. On 26 August 1966 *Time* said that the Cultural Revolution "was a product of desperation and is unlikely to solve Red China's problems of backward industries and a famine-prone agriculture system." A writer echoed this view in *The Nation*: "Mao's tactics are ultra-Left rather than Left; and his radical verbiage and the fireworks of the 'cultural revolution' conceal a policy which is essentially passive and inert."[21] Above all, Dr. L. La Dany wrote in *U.S. News and World Report* that Mao and Lin had erred in toppling the Beijing Party Committee, openly threatening to change the entire Party leadership, and above all, "trying to destroy Chinese culture with their infamous campaign against the 'four olds'—old culture, old thoughts, old customs, old habits."[22] The U.S. press was also immediately sensitive to the meaning of the Red Guards, whom *Time* described as "Mao's mobs" and a new version of the *Hitler Jugend*,[23] reflecting "Mao's desperate intent to rekindle a revolutionary spirit in a country that he fears has gone flabby."[24]

The U.S. press was astute in its characterization of Mao's wife, Jiang Qing, and his heir-apparent, Lin Biao. In early 1967 *Time* commented, "Mrs. Mao, being only 52 in an inner circle of old men, may have considerable say about who will succeed to the Red throne after Mao's last battle is fought, even if she does not herself join the ranks of Chinese empresses."[25] Seven years later, however, Mao would also assert that Jiang Qing herself wanted to take over his position as Party chairperson. As for Defense Minister Lin Biao, *U.S. News and World Report* interviewed Chiang Ching-kuo, Chiang Kai-shek's son and Taiwan's defense minister, who was quick to note that "Outwardly [Lin] appears to support Mao, but in reality he is against him."[26] Five years later, Lin Biao shocked the world by leading a failed coup before meeting his death in a plane crash on 13 September 1971.

Some members of the U.S. press were, however, particularly reluctant to accept the official explanation of Lin Biao's death. Typical were two articles run by *National Review* in 1973 that speculated Marshal Lin was murdered in China and his body loaded onto the plane before it took off. They further speculated that the plane crash was not accidental, but rather was booby-trapped or shot down by a Chinese plane.[27] The *New York Times* called the Lin Biao affair "one of the great unsolved mysteries of the Communist world."[28]

THE CHINA FEVER PERIOD

The high euphoria and romanticism that characterized the attitude among U.S. journalists toward China in the early 1970s can be traced to historical and political roots. China's long bond with U.S. missionaries and its role as a wartime ally helped foster nostalgia for the Chinese within the collective heart of the United States. *Time* noted that "The U.S. has always been fascinated by China, whether it was seen as an ally, a fanatical adversary or, as now, a somewhat remote power that has entered into some limited foreign policy partnership with the U.S."[29] With the resumption of U.S.-China relations, many U.S. reporters seemed to see themselves as modern Marco Polos who would dispel prejudices, erase misconceptions, and bring about a sympathetic understanding of China. Wishful stories about China were soon rising out of correspondents' typewriters.

But this unique, partially subconscious feeling for China in the minds of Americans was also embedded in the special circumstances of U.S. politics. In what he describes as a "political pilgrims" syndrome, Edward Farmer points out that idealistic Western observers did not see the oppressiveness of Communist dictatorships because they were not really seeing the country they were visiting.[30] They just saw what they wanted to see—"the opposite of what they saw at home."[31] The clean, orderly streets and unlocked doors of urban Shanghai and the anti-establishment-qua-egalitarianism presented irresistible signs of utopia for Americans undergoing the civil rights upheavals, racial turmoil, and anti-war demonstrations. In contrast to their doubts about equality and justice in their own society, reporters found Chinese youth seemingly dedicated to improving their country in a peaceful manner.[32]

The "ping-pong diplomacy" that broke the ice in 1971 and President Nixon's subsequent visit to China in 1972 signalled that China, after 20 years of isolation, finally could be visited—and observed—by U.S. journalists. According to one *Newsweek* report, more than 30,000 Americans sought visas to visit China from Beijing in 1972.[33] The Chinese government specifically culled the most influential and sympathetic reporters out of the vast pool of foreign journalists applying to visit China to improve its image abroad.

U.S. journalists were classified according to their political stance—left, centrist, or right. Decisions regarding where they could travel, what they could see, whom they could visit, and how Chinese officials should respond to their questions and impromptu demands were made in advance. Foreign guests received the best hotel accommodations and food that China could offer. In short, the CCP did all it could to ensure that U.S. journalists only saw China's best side.

The stream of U.S. visitors to China began with veteran Associated Press correspondent John Roderick, who covered the table tennis visit. Next came Tillman Durdin of the *New York Times*, who had previous experience reporting on China and received a one-month exclusive visa. Durdin was soon followed by his assistant editor-in-chief, Seymour Topping, and his colleague, James Reston, the most influential U.S. political reporter of that era.

These reporters described their privileged treatment as evidence of China's confidence. They did stories on their cordial welcome and also on China's remarkable cleanliness, which the *New York Times* described as "the most visible change in China since the Communist take-over in 1949." Even Durdin, who knew he was visiting showcase factories, villages, stores, and schools, could not check his euphoria.[34] Topping's reportage was even more utopian than Durdin's:

> Among the Chinese today there seems to be more of a feeling of kinship than in the old society. ... Crime does not seem to be a major problem. ... A foreigner can leave his hotel room or parked car open with the certainty that his valuables will not be stolen. ... Illiteracy has been wiped out among the new generations.[35]

At that time, phrases such as "no misery," "no hunger," "no drunkards," and "no shoving or pushing (in lines)" prevailed in press coverage of China in the United States.

It was James Reston, however, who added the brightest colors to this romantic painting of China. Granted an exclusive interview and dinner with Premier Zhou Enlai even before Nixon's visit to China, Reston reported in July 1971 that "One is constantly reminded here of what American life must have been like on the frontier a century ago. ... The emphasis is on self-reliance and hard work, innovation and the spirit of cooperation in building something better and larger than anything they have known before."[36] After his visit, Reston described China to a CBS reporter as "one vast school of moral philosophy."[37] As Reston was wildly praiseworthy, most Chinese were in fact displaying qualities that were antithetical to the "frontier spirit": weariness, passivity, and apathy.

Some reporters such as Robert Martin of U.S. News and World Report—who had covered China in the 1940s and could speak Chinese—were not as dazzled by their visits. Although Martin praised China's cleanliness and improved standard of living, his assessment was different from that of most other U.S. reporters:

> The Chinese, as an individual, seems to me to have paid a rather heavy price for these economic gains. His life is regimented. ... He has access only to what the government wants him to know.[38]
>
> A continuing and pervasive propaganda campaign that relentlessly strikes at everyone, day after day, has turned a normally turbulent people into an obedient, well-disciplined mass quite unlike Chinese of the past.[39]

He then made a prescient observation which remains relevant to more recent events, including the Tiananmen Incident, when he said, "Mao has made a number of blunders over the years—and when controls were occasionally relaxed, deep fissures in Chinese society were revealed."

THE FEVER RECEDES

The gradual improvement of U.S.-China relations and establishment of liaison offices in both capitals in early 1973 broadened opportunities for U.S. journalists in China. As journalists looked more closely at China, China appeared less of a utopia, although their euphoric tone did not entirely disappear. Even columnist Joseph Alsop, considered a staunch Taiwan supporter, found praise for "Red China," while others predicted that revolutionary China would soon have a global impact similar to that of the French Revolution.[40] But, as *Los Angeles Times* Hong Kong correspondent Robert Elegant wrote in *National Review*, "Certainly, the first fine careless euphoria that half intoxicated the American people has declined."[41]

Return to Reality

The latter stages of the Cultural Revolution saw the reinstatement of Deng Xiaoping to vice-premier, the "anti-Lin Biao, anti-Confucius" campaign (late 1973-early 1974), the downfall of the Gang of Four and the promotion of Hua Guofeng to Premier in 1976. All of these stories received timely and sober coverage by the U.S. press, stripped of the sentimentality of the previous period. For example, while most Chinese felt a sense of engrossing commotion during the "anti-Lin Biao, anti-Confucius" campaign, while unaware of its significance, *Time* reported the China-watchers' conviction that Zhou Enlai was "on shaky footing" vis-à-vis the Shanghai clique (later called the Gang of Four).[42] In December *Newsweek* accurately reported that the anti-Confucius campaign was actually targeting Premier Zhou—allegedly a supporter of "the old system"—with Mao's approval.[43]

Later, *Newsweek* reported that Hua Guofeng, as a successor to Premier Zhou, was only a "caretaker" whose significance would disappear following the power struggle between Party radicals and Deng Xiaoping.[44] *Time* also noted that Hua's hold on power was tenuous and did not indicate the downfall of "the wily little bureaucrat" Deng and his allies. "There were strong indications that the promotion of Hua left Beijing's moderates still holding the balance of power," *Time* reported.[45] These analyses proved altogether pertinent.

The Purges

The persecution of Chinese intellectuals and others by the ultra-leftists was largely overlooked because the victims were inaccessible and reluctant to openly reveal the truth for fear of reprisal. Chinese intellectuals, moreover, tend to "let bygones be bygones" and agonize over making their shame public; they yearn to look forward, to forget and forgive the regime's atrocities insofar as there is relief in sight. Incomplete statistics disclose that during the Cultural Revolution tens of millions of people were jailed or confined to "cow-sheds," while even more people suffered personal degradation and upheaval. These unprecedented excesses received scant attention in the U.S. press, which only made random remarks about intellectuals, cadres, or students sent to factories or villages which resembled Siberian labor camps. In the context of previous excesses, the downfall of Lin Biao seemed to provide them with a ray of hope, however temporary, and a supplemental argument to keep quiet and avoid political instability.

CONCLUSION

During the Cultural Revolution, those who approached China with a dose of skepticism produced coverage superior to those who were misled by euphoria and sentimentality and lent an uncritical eye to China's socio-political circumstances. The reportage of the first period of coverage analyzed here, though reliant on distant observation and expert analysis, seemed to provide a more accurate portrait of China than much of what was later produced when journalists were selectively allowed to visit China. The deception organized by the CCP seems to have partially circumvented the validity of the U.S. canon of journalistic objectivity that was founded on "raw empiricism" with the presumption that somehow "seeing is believing." A 1973 article in National Review recognized this problem:

> We Americans have a tendency to believe that only we can find out the truth about things, and this tendency reaches formidable proportions in the case of China. Obviously we were not going to understand what was occurring in Mao land until we could get some good red-blooded American in there to see for themselves.[46]

Direct observation undoubtedly enriches vital dimensions of insight and understanding. But journalists may fall victim to official manipulation when treated to carefully scripted performances they would like to believe. In the early 1970s the havoc wrought by the Cultural Revolution was simply dismissed or glossed over, as enthusiasm filled pages and pages of newsprint with Mao's "cuddly" Communism vis-à-vis rigid and bleak Soviet Communism.

Seeing, therefore, should not have been believing—at least not in Mao's regimented China. The U.S. news convention that demands cross-confirmation of a story by multiple sources, however, may not have been foolproof either. During the Cultural Revolution, sources interviewed in different work units could simply regurgitate the official line. Now the situation has undergone vast changes due to reform policies, and U.S. press coverage of China has become much more sophisticated. An important lesson, however, remains for the student of China: only by remaining vigilant against official and cultural barriers to perception can seeing be believing.

NOTES

1. *Time*, 27 Jan. 1967.

2. *Time*, 20 May 1966. For example, George E. Taylor, director of the Far Eastern and Russian Institute at the University of Washington, echoed this assessment in a hearing of the Senate Foreign Relations Committee when he said, "The United States is better informed about Communist China today than is any other country in the Free World." *National Review*, 31 May 1966.

3. *Newsweek*, 23 Jan. 1967. This is a quote of Charles Taylor, the *Globe and Mail* editorial writer who was then stationed in Beijing.

4. Ibid.

5. *The Nation*, 3 Oct. 1966.

6. *Time*, 25 Feb. 1966.

7. *Newsweek*, 29 Aug. 1966.

8. *New York Times*, 10 Mar. 1966, 17 May 1966.

9. *Newsweek*, 16 May 1966.

10. *Time*, 24 June 1966.

11. Some media reports of Mao's famous swim were rather defensive. For example, on 8 August 1966, *Newsweek* called it "a not-really-so-epic swim." The *Daily Mirror* suggested that he was held afloat "by inscrutable Chinese frogmen."

12. For example, *Newsweek* commented on 16 May 1966 that Mao's absence during the arrival of the Albanian Premier in Beijing seemed convincing evidence that Mao was ill. Actually, when Premier Shehu arrived in China for the May First Festival, Mao was in Shanghai, where he met Shehu on 5 May, although Xinhua News Agency waited until the 10 May to run a photo. The next day, the *New York Times* ran Xinhua's wire story, followed by a commentary on 15 May about Mao reentering public view.

13. *Newsweek*, 20 June 1966.

14. Ibid.

15. Ibid., 27 June 1966.

16. Ibid., 25 July 1966.

17. See, for example, *Time*, 16 Dec. 1966; *New York Times*, 15–18 Dec. 1966.

18. *The Nation*, 3 Oct. 1966. Buchanan was then a geography professor at Victoria University in Wellington, New Zealand. *The Nation* described him as a "sympathizer" who had recently visited China to study its rural areas.

19. Edgar Snow, "Aftermath of the Cultural Revolution," *The New Republic*, 10 Apr. 1971.

20. Articles reflecting the war view appeared mainly in *The Nation* and *The New Republic*. See Ross Terrill, "China and Vietnam," *The New Republic*, 29 Oct. 1966.

21. Isaac Deutscher, "Mao at Bay," *The Nation*, 31 Oct. 1966.

22. L. La Dany, "Downfall of Red China: Answers by Top Authority," *U.S. News and World Report*, 27 Feb. 1967. La Dany also published the newsletter *China News Analysis*.

23. *Time*, 13 Jan. 1967.

24. *Time*, 2 Sept. 1966.

25. *Time*, 10 Feb. 1967.

26. *U.S. News & World Report*, 10 Oct. 1966.

27. Charles Murphy, "Who Killed Lin Biao," *National Review*, 8 June 1973; David Nelson Rowe, "The End of Lin Biao, Another Version," *National Review*, 3 Aug. 1973.

28. *New York Times*, 19 Apr. 1990.

29. *Time*, 19 Jan. 1976.

30. Edward Farmer, "Sifting Truth from Facts: The Reporter as Interpreter of China," in Chin-Chuan Lee (ed.), *Voices of China: The Interplay of Politics and Journalism* (New York: Guilford Press, 1990).

31. Ibid.

32. Harry Harding, "To China, With Disdain: New Trends in the Study of China," *Asian Survey* 22 (1982): 934–58.

33. *Newsweek*, 21 Feb. 1972.

34. The *New York Times*, 18 May 1971.

35. Ibid., 20 and 26 June 1971.

36. Ibid., 27 July 1971.

37. Ibid., 31 Aug. 1971. A critical assessment of Reston's optimism about China during this period is conspicuously absent from his memoir *Deadline* (New York: Random House, 1991).

38. Robert Martin, "China Revisited," *U.S. News & World Report*, 13 Mar. 1972.

39. Robert Martin, "Where is China Really Headed Under Mao?" 20 Mar. 1972.

40. See *Time*, 26 Feb. 1973; Harding, "To China, With Disdain."

41. Robert Elegant, "The Honeymoon That Wasn't," *National Review*, 11 Oct. 1974.

42. "Silence in the Hall," *Time*, 3 Sept. 1973; "Revisionist Music," *Time*, 18 Mar. 1974. The latter article reported that "Many observers believe that a group of radicals in the Politburo, headed by No. 3 Man Wang [Hongwen], a leader of the radical cadres in Shanghai, and Mao's wife Jiang Qing, have been trying to use the Confucius-Lin campaign to gain leverage against Zhou—possibly with the goal of determining who will eventually succeed the aging Mao."

43. "Cultural Revolution II?" *Newsweek*, 17 Dec. 1973.

44. Ibid., "A New Chinese Puzzle," 16 Feb. 1976.

45. *Time*, "Protest, Purge, Promotion," 19 Apr. 1976.

46. Richard Walker, "Hot and Cold China-Watchers," *National Review*, 5 Jan. 1973. Walker was director of the University of South Carolina's Institute of International Studies at that time.

ABOUT THE BOOK

In this richly textured volume, leading scholars and journalists engage in a unique dialogue in their exploration of the rapidly evolving conditions of political communication in China. The contributors begin by considering the bureaucratization of media control within the context of economic reform, addressing such questions as: How were the media used and abused to uphold, undermine, and save the regime's legitimacy? How were they decoded in popular resistance, especially in the age of new technology? How does Communist control compare to Nationalist control—both on the mainland prior to 1949 and on Taiwan afterward? What is the relevance of the Taiwan experience to understanding changes in China's media?

The contributors go on to examine how ideology, the available body of knowledge, and professional roles affect both scholarly and journalistic understanding of China. They strive to answer a second set of questions: How has the cold war shaped the picture Westerners have constructed of China? What impact do the U.S. media have on Chinese politics, and what sort of new challenges does the U.S. journalist face in China? In light of the checkered history of "objective" reporting in China, how do Hong Kong journalists attempt to protect press freedom during the political transition?

Bringing together a wide-ranging group of experts, including media scholars, historians, political scientists, journalists, and policymakers, this book is both path-breaking and thought-provoking. Offering fresh insights into Chinese journalism and Sino-American relations, this volume will be important reading for students, scholars, and the general reader.

ABOUT THE EDITOR
AND CONTRIBUTORS

Joseph Man Chan, senior lecturer in journalism and communication at the Chinese University of Hong Kong, is coauthor of *Mass Media and Political Transition: The Hong Kong Press in China's Orbit* (1991).

Lowell Dittmer is professor of political science at the University of California–Berkeley. Among his recent publications are *China's Continuous Revolution* (1987), *Sino-Soviet Normalization and Its International Implications* (1992), *China's Quest for National Identity* (coeditor, 1993), and *China Under Reform* (Boulder, CO: Westview, 1994).

Edward Farmer is professor of history and East Asian studies at the University of Minnesota. His publications include *Early Ming Government* (1976), *Comparative History of Civilizations in Asia* (coauthor, 1977), and *A World History: Links Across Times and Place* (coauthor, 1987).

Edward Friedman is professor of political science at the University of Wisconsin–Madison. *Chinese Village, Socialist State* (coauthor, 1991) is one of his recent publications.

Merle Goldman is professor of Chinese history at Boston University and a research associate at the John Fairbank Center for East Asian Studies, Harvard University. Her publications include *Chinese Intellectuals: Advise and Dissent* (1981), *China's Intellectuals and the State: In Search of a New Relationship* (editor, 1987), and *Ideas Across Cultures: Essays on Chinese Thought in Honor of Benjamin I. Schwartz* (coeditor, 1990).

Carol Lee Hamrin is a research specialist for China at the U.S. State Department and a faculty member at Johns Hopkins University's School of Advanced International Studies. *China and the Challenge of the Future* (1990) is one of her recent publications.

David Hess was head of the Voice of America's China branch from 1988 to 1990.

Marlowe Hood, a free-lance writer, was Beijing bureau chief for the *South China Morning Post.* He is coeditor of *The Cambodian Agony* (1990, second edition).

Hsiao Ching-chang, former senior reporter for the *World Economic Herald* in Shanghai, is a visiting fellow at the China Times Center for Media and Social Studies, University of Minnesota.

Chin-Chuan Lee, editor of this volume, is professor of journalism and mass communication at the University of Minnesota, where he directs the China Times Center for Media and Social Studies. Among his English publications are *Media Imperialism Reconsidered: The Homogenizing of Television Culture* (1980), *Voices of China: The Interplay of Politics and Journalism* (editor, 1990), and *Mass Media and Political Transition: The Hong Kong Press in China's Orbit* (coauthor, 1991).

Paul Siu-nam Lee is a senior lecturer in journalism and mass communication at the Chinese University of Hong Kong.

Li Liangrong is professor and associate dean of journalism at Fudan University in Shanghai.

Lu Keng is publisher of the Hong Kong-based *Pai Shing* newsweekly. His Chinese publications include *Deng Xiaoping's Last Chance* (1992), *The Era of Deng Xiaoping* (1990), and *An Interview with Hu Yaobang* (1985).

Michel Oksenberg is president of the East-West Center in Honolulu, Hawaii. He has served as director of the Center for Chinese Studies at the University of Michigan and as a member of the National Security Council during the Carter Administration. His recent publications include *Policy Making in China: Leaders, Structures, and Processes* (coauthor, 1988), *Science and Technology in Post-Mao China* (coeditor, 1989), *China's Participation in the IMF, the World Bank, and GATT* (coauthor, 1990), and *Beijing Spring, 1989: Confrontation and Conflict* (coeditor, 1990).

Judy Polumbaum is assistant professor of journalism and mass communication at the University of Iowa. A prolific writer, she has previously taught journalism at the Chinese Academy of Social Sciences.

Su Shaozhi, author of *Marxism Reconsidered* (in Chinese, 1992), was director of the Institute of Marxism, Leninism, and Mao Zedong Thought under the Chinese Academy of Social Sciences. He was a Hill Visiting Professor at the University of Minnesota from 1992–1993.

Wendy S. Tai is a staff reporter for the Minneapolis-based *Star Tribune*.

Yang Mei-rong, former senior reporter for the *World Economic Herald* in Shanghai, is a visiting fellow at the China Times Center for Media and Social Studies, University of Minnesota.

INDEX